Stan
VanDerBeek
The
Culture
Intercom

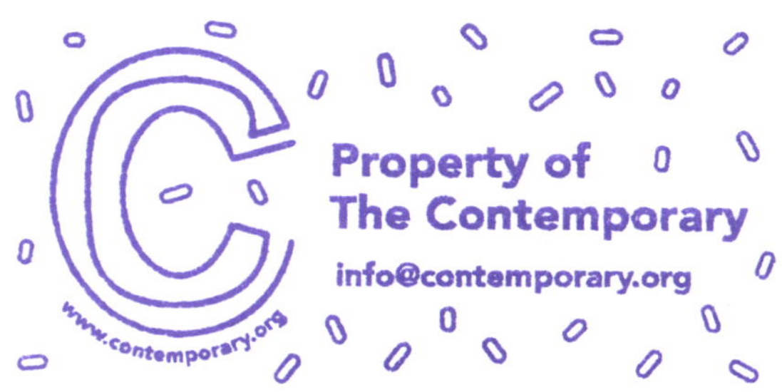

MIT LVAC
CAMH

Untitled, ca. 1955–57. Paint on
wood, 11 x 7 1/4 in.

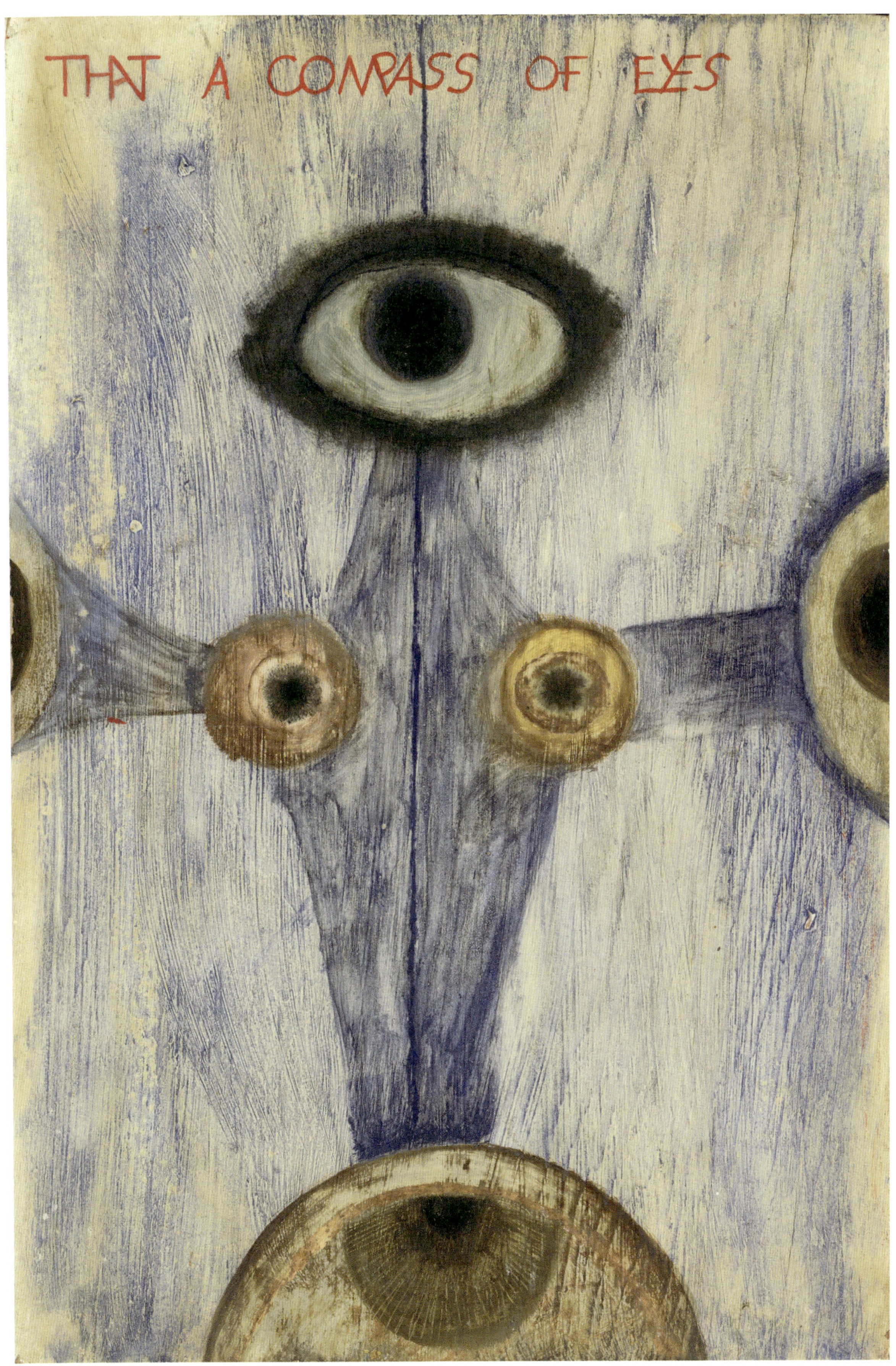
THAT A COMPASS OF EYES
THAT A COMPASS OF EYES

All: *Untitled,* ca. 1955–57. All: Paint on
wood, 5 3/4 x 5 3/4 in.

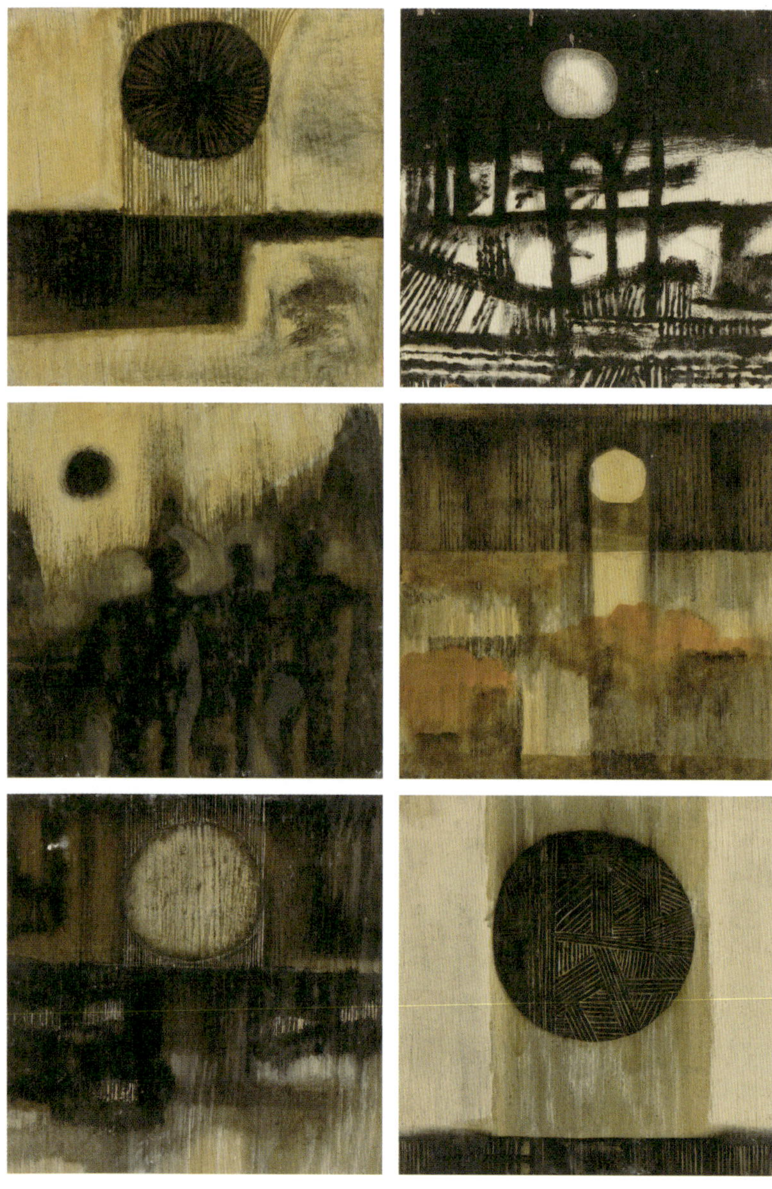

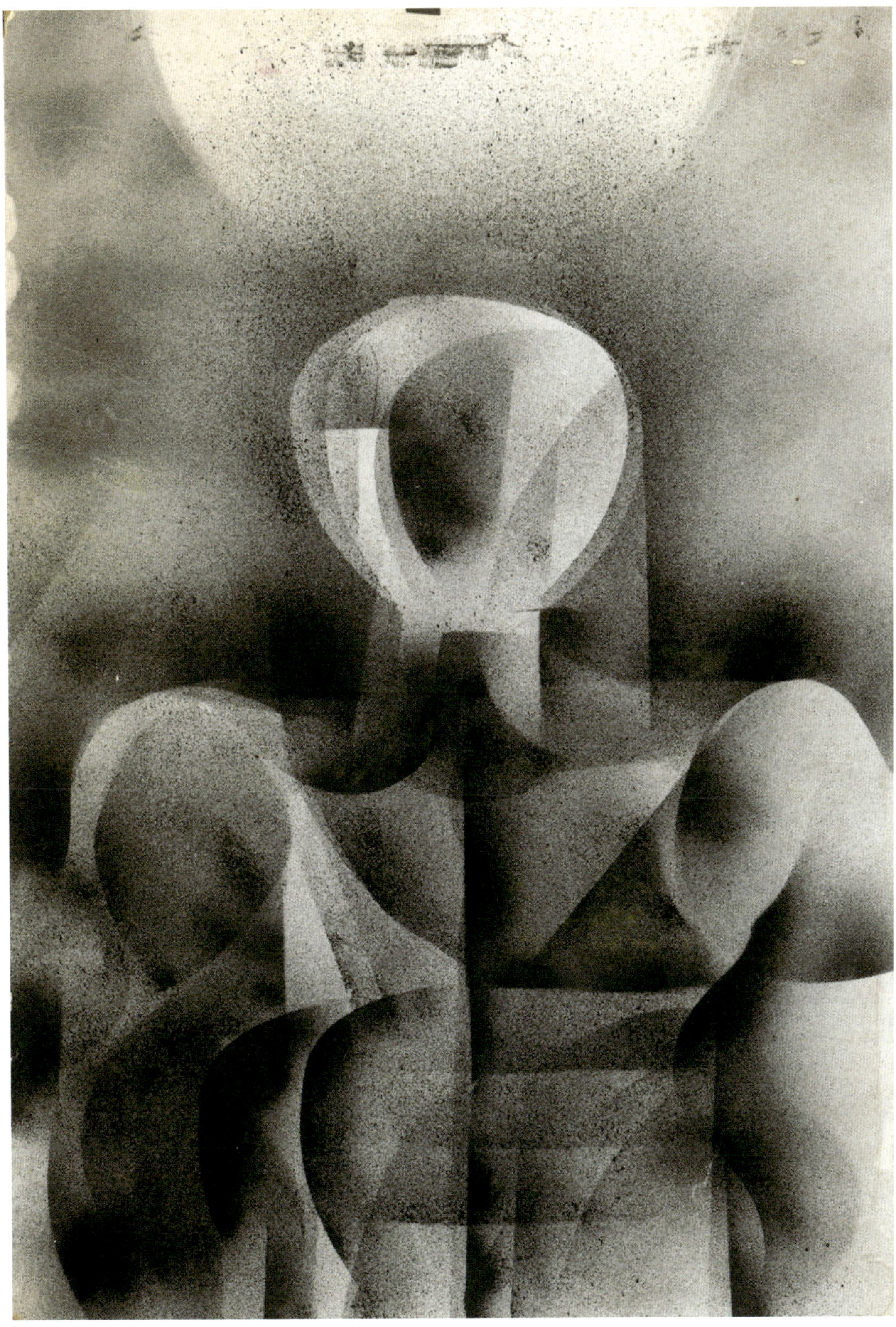

Untitled, ca. 1955–57. Paint on paper,
28 x 20 in.

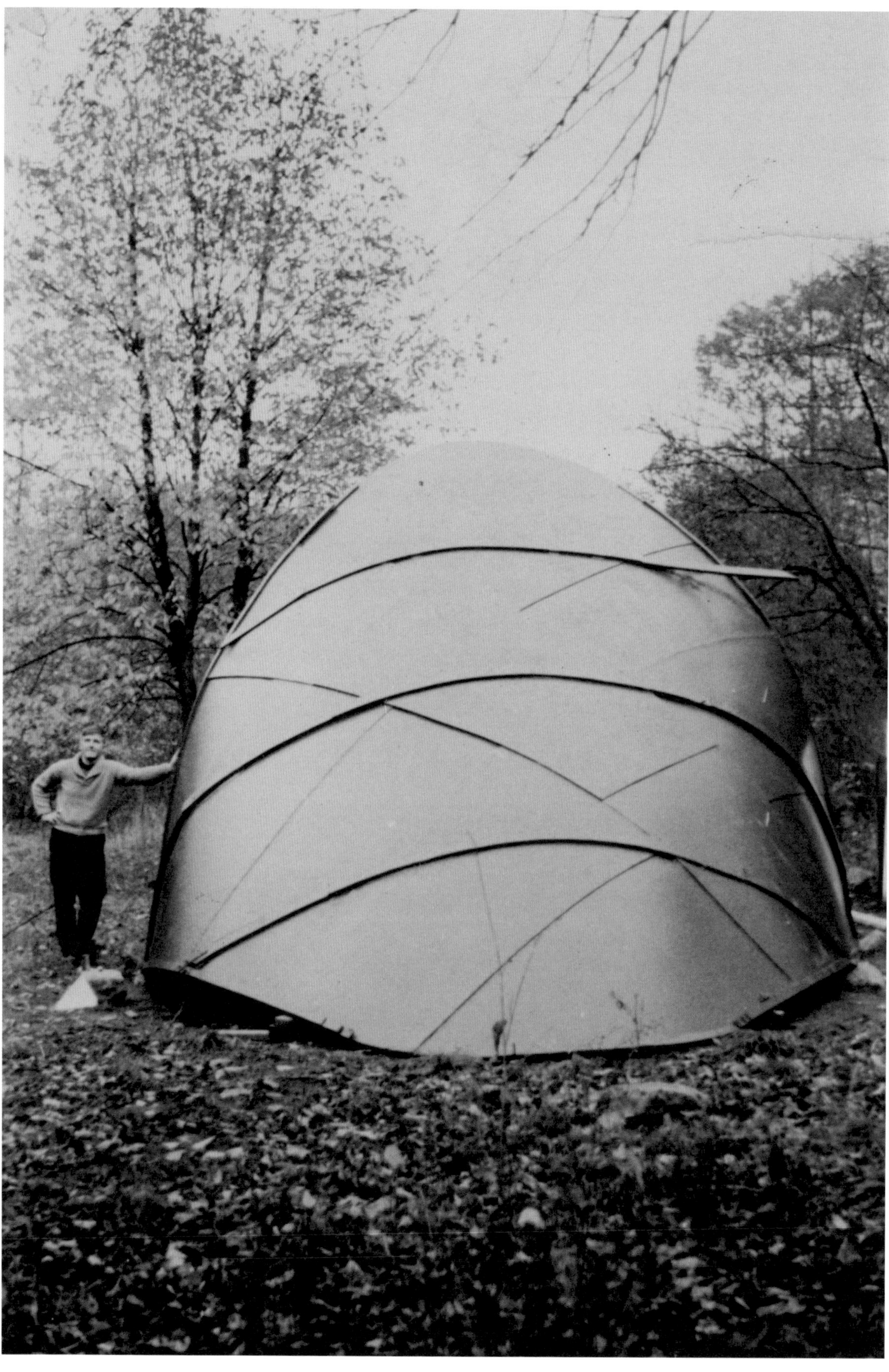

Early Works

Stan VanDerBeek's exploration of the moving
image began while a student at Black Mountain
College from 1949–1951. There, VanDerBeek
began a series of paintings and calligraphic
studies that would become the foundation
for future explorations in visual communication. In their attention to language and form,
VanDerBeek's early works foretell the development of a distinct visual style that would
become present throughout his entire body of
work. Relationships begun at Black Mountain
College also led to several collaborative projects
that furthered his continued investigation of
different media through the 1960s.

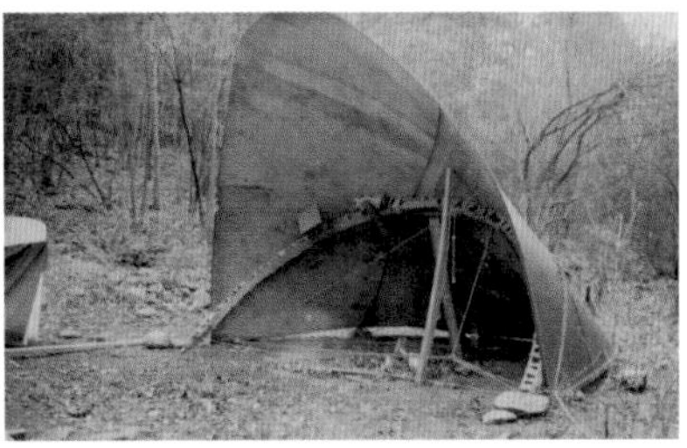

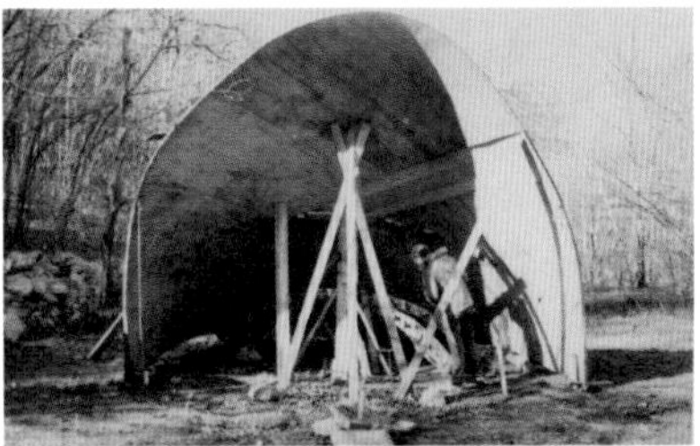

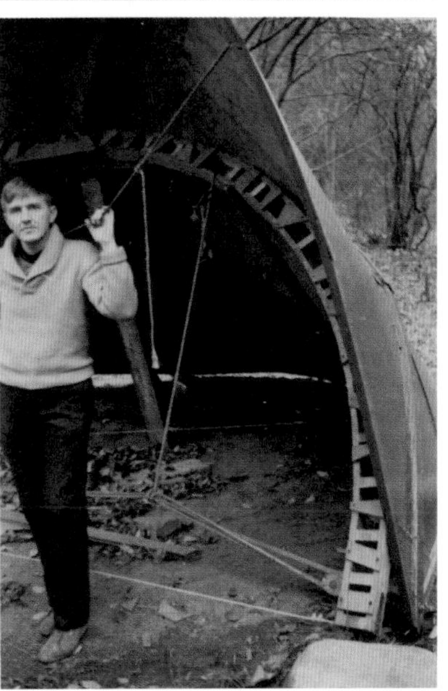

All: Bent plywood architectural experiment,
New England, 1956.

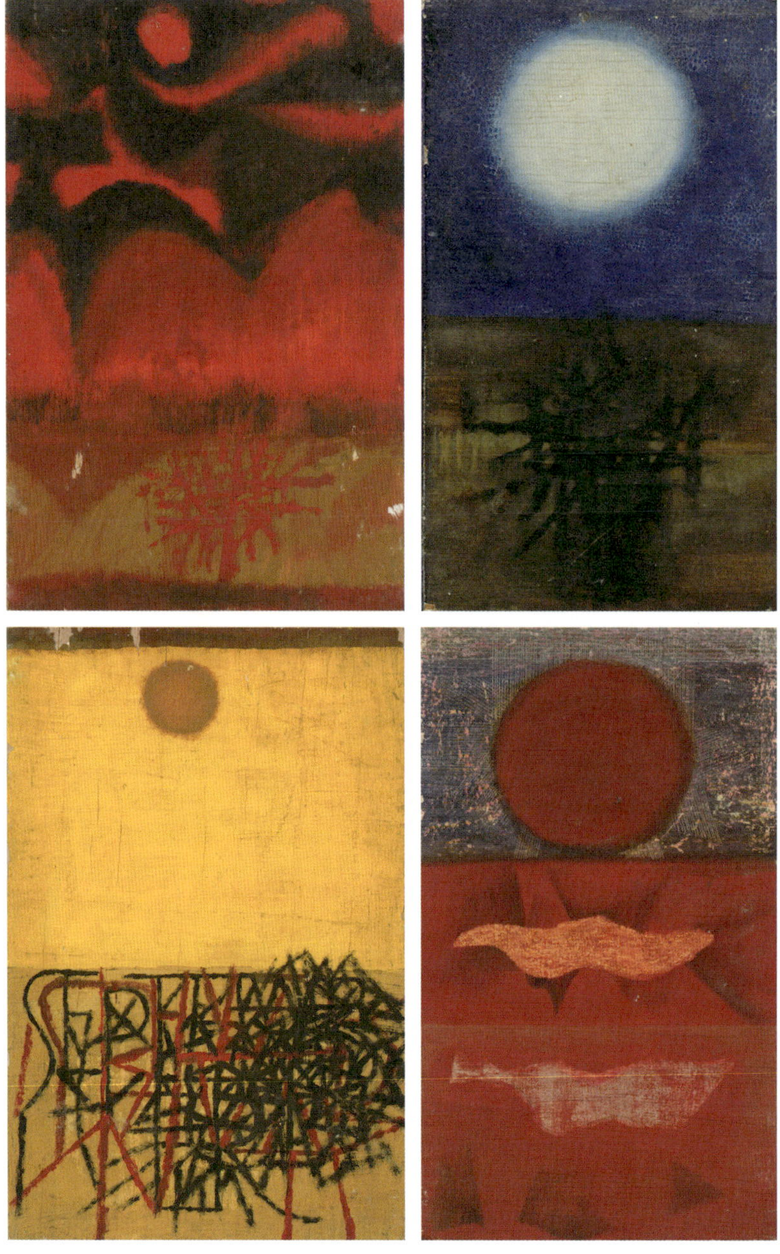

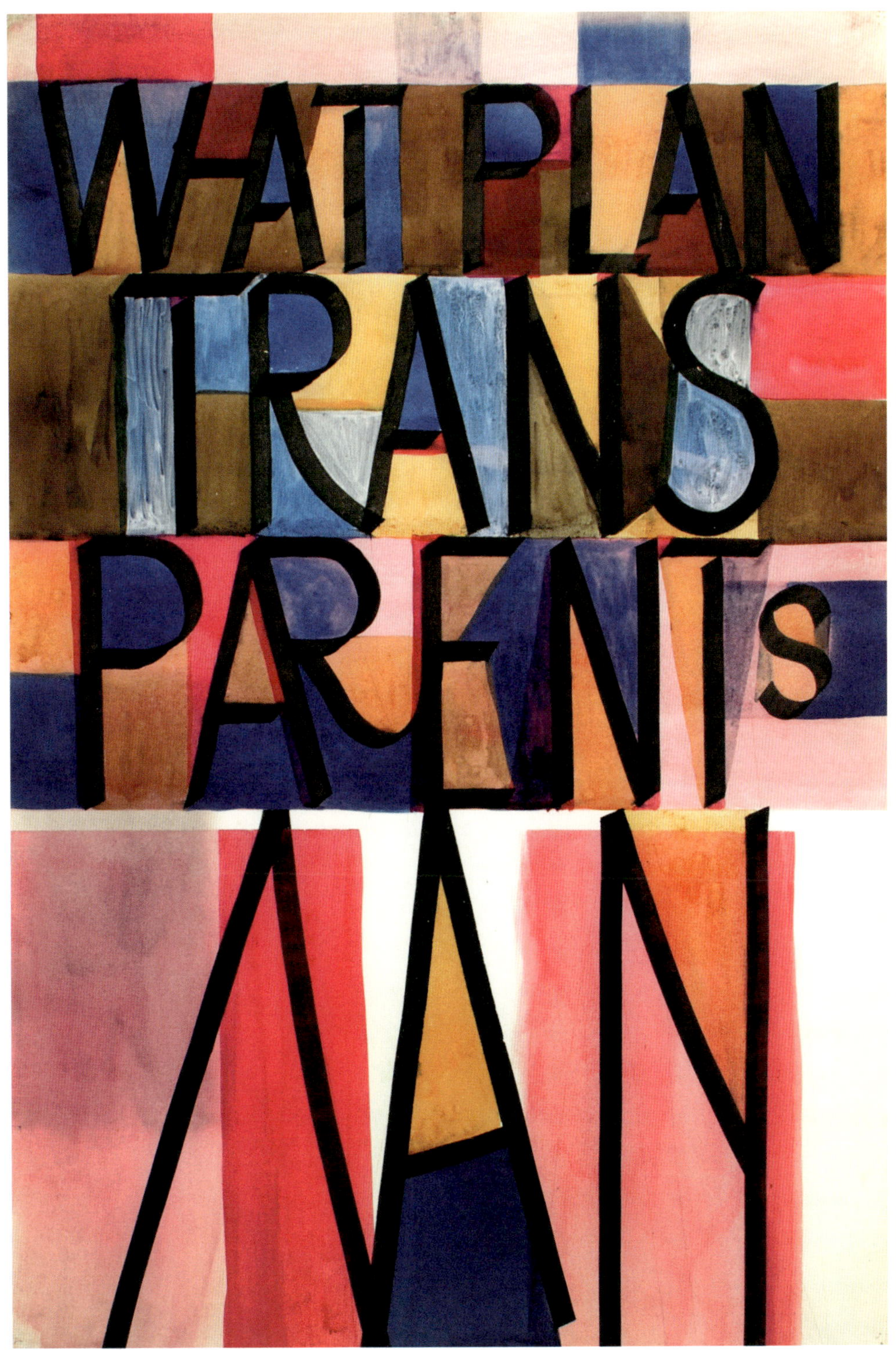

Untitled, 1955. Watercolor on paper,
36 x 23 in.

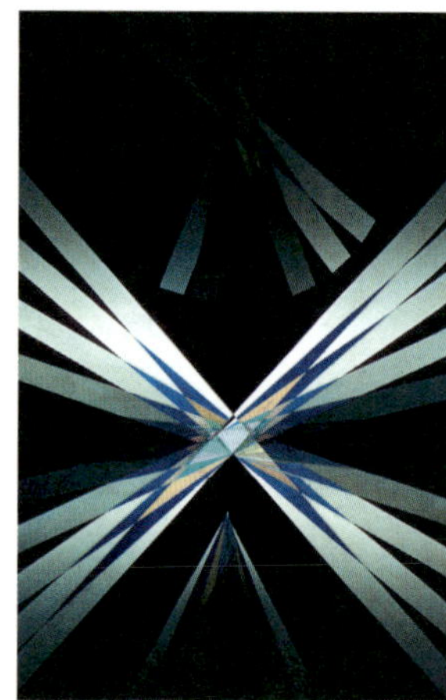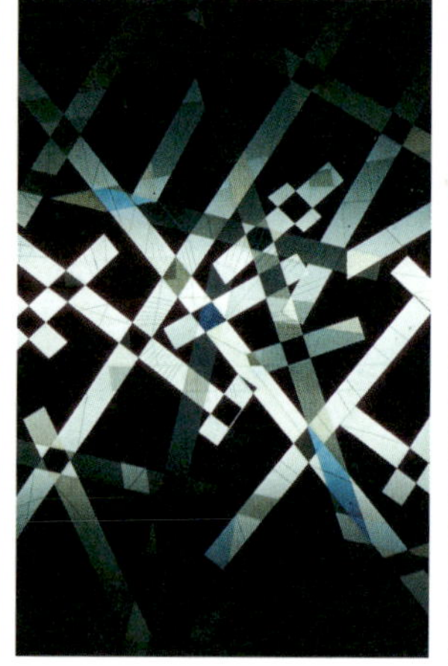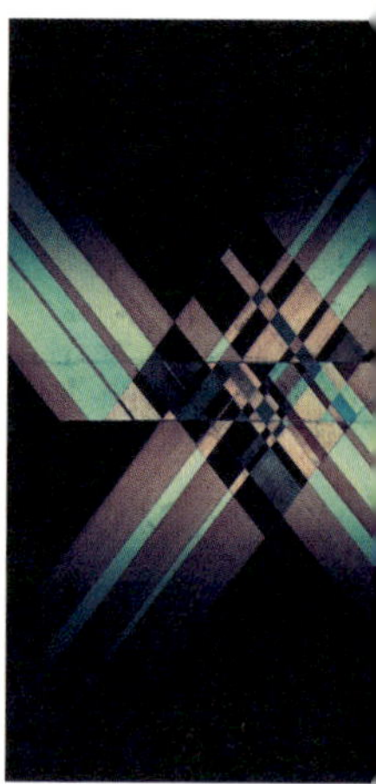

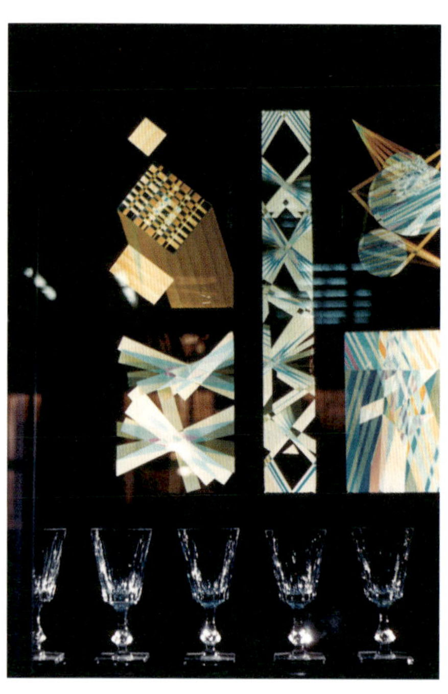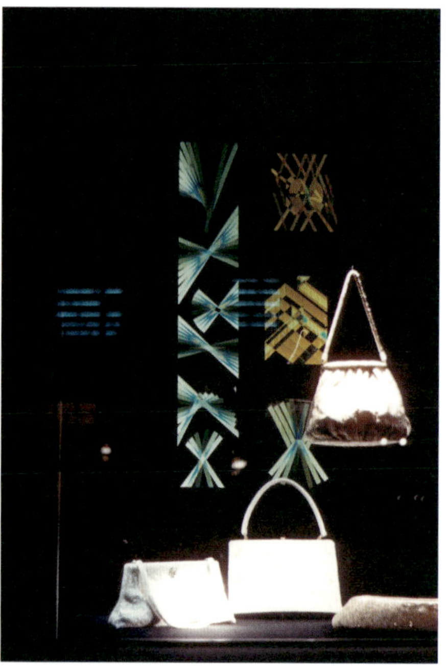

[Above] Tiffany & Co. window display using
polarized film, details, New York, 1956.

[Right] Bonwit Teller window display
design and installation in conjunction
with Robert Rauschenberg, sculpture by
Stan VanDerBeek, New York, spring 1961.

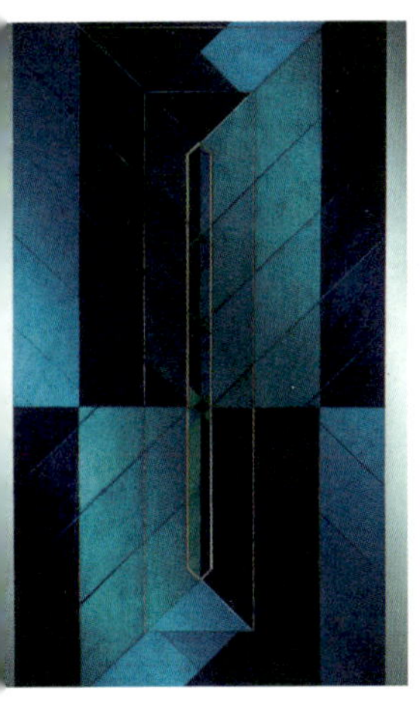
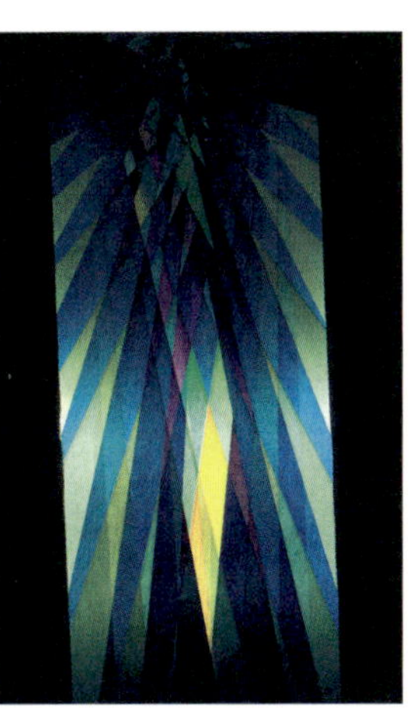
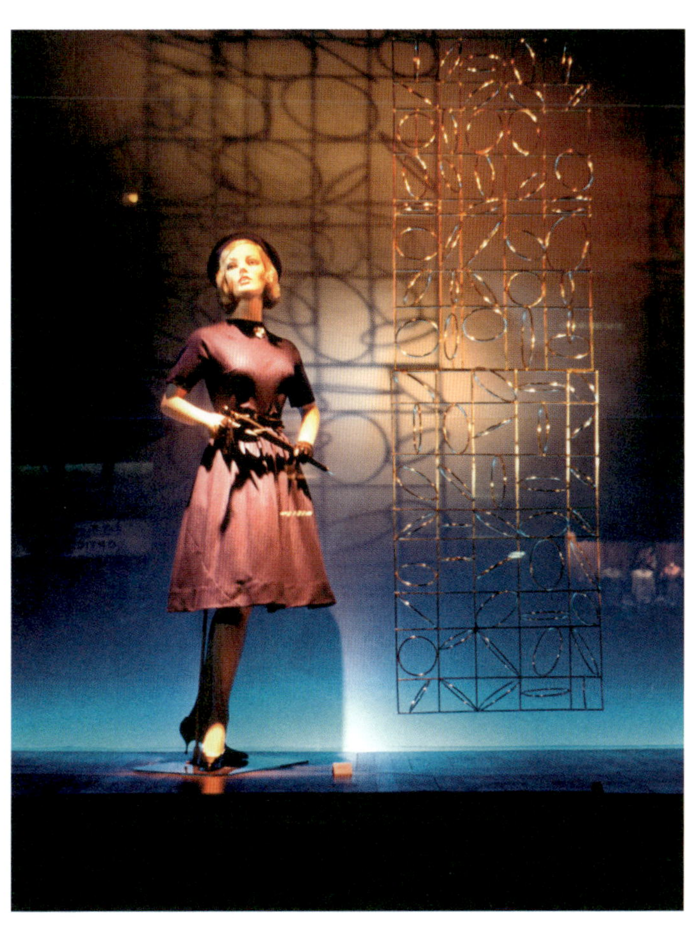

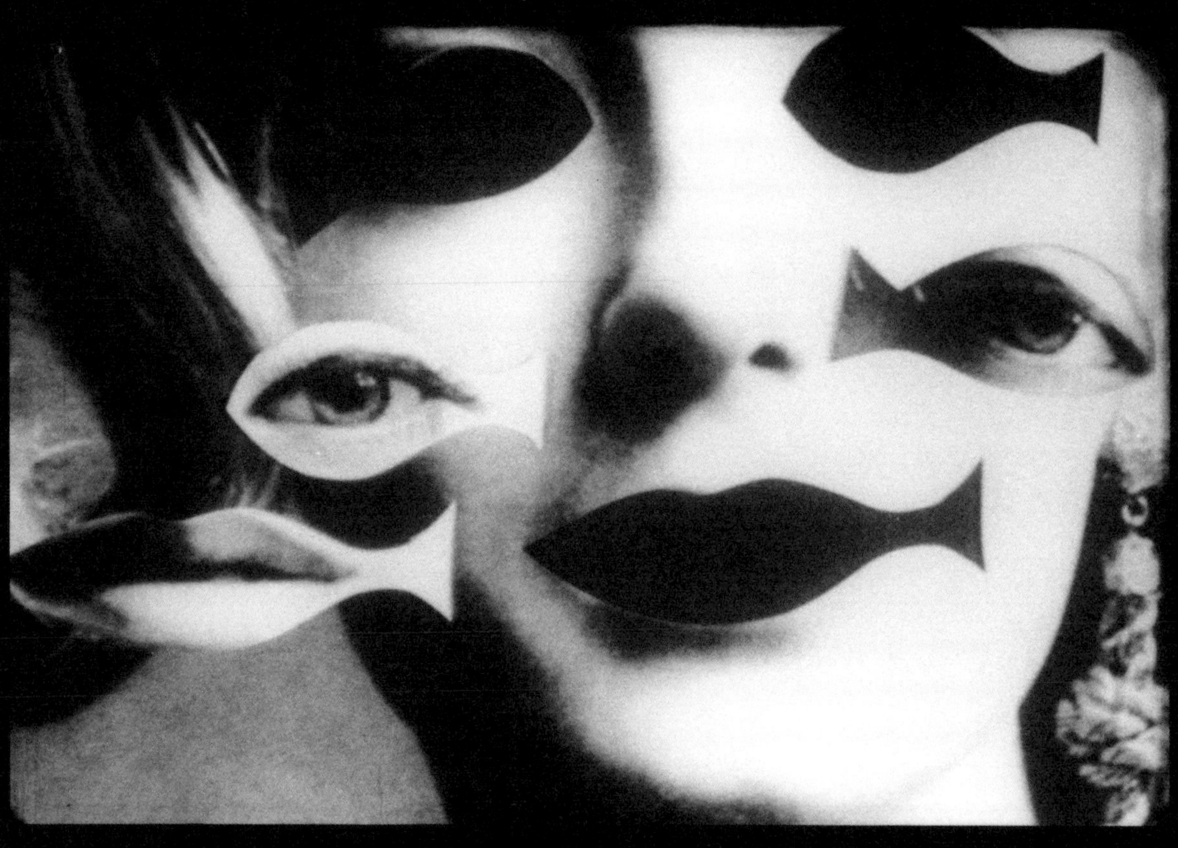

Film still from *What Who How*, 1957. 16mm, black and white, sound, 8 min.

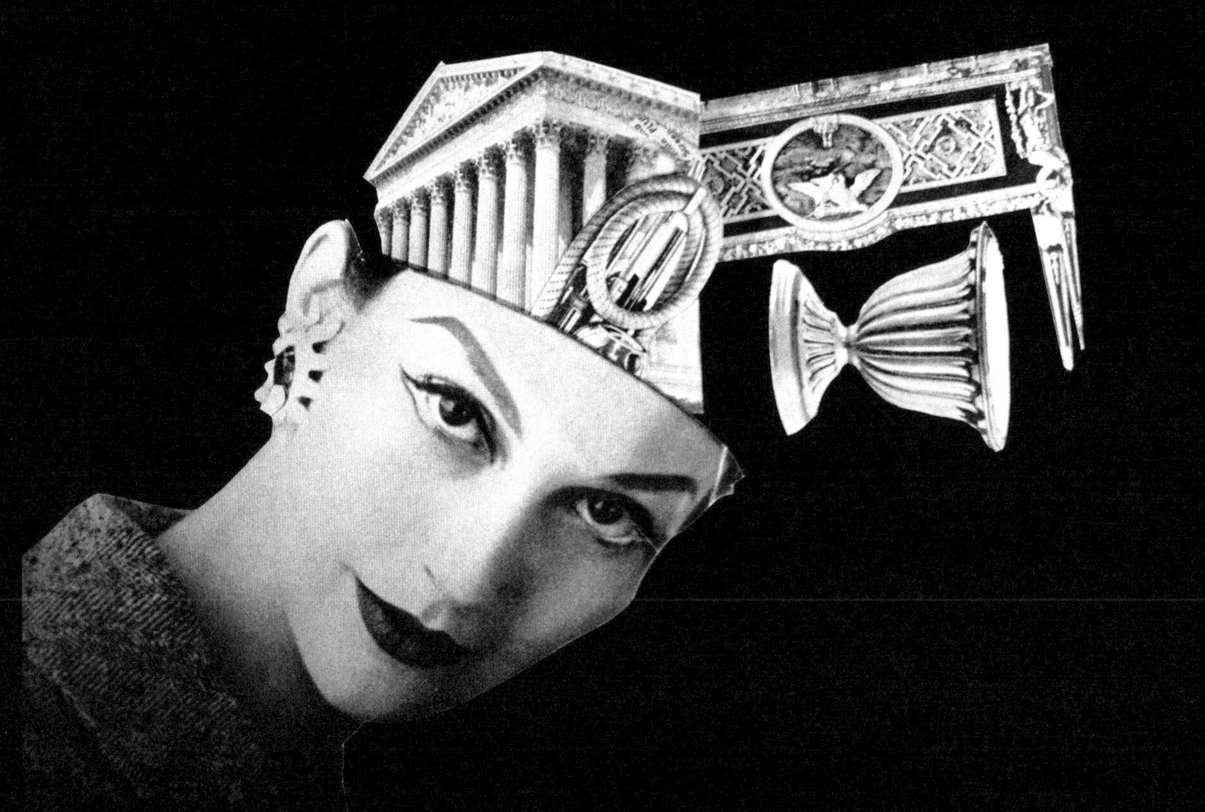

Film stills from *A La Mode*, 1958. 16mm, black and white, sound. 10 min.

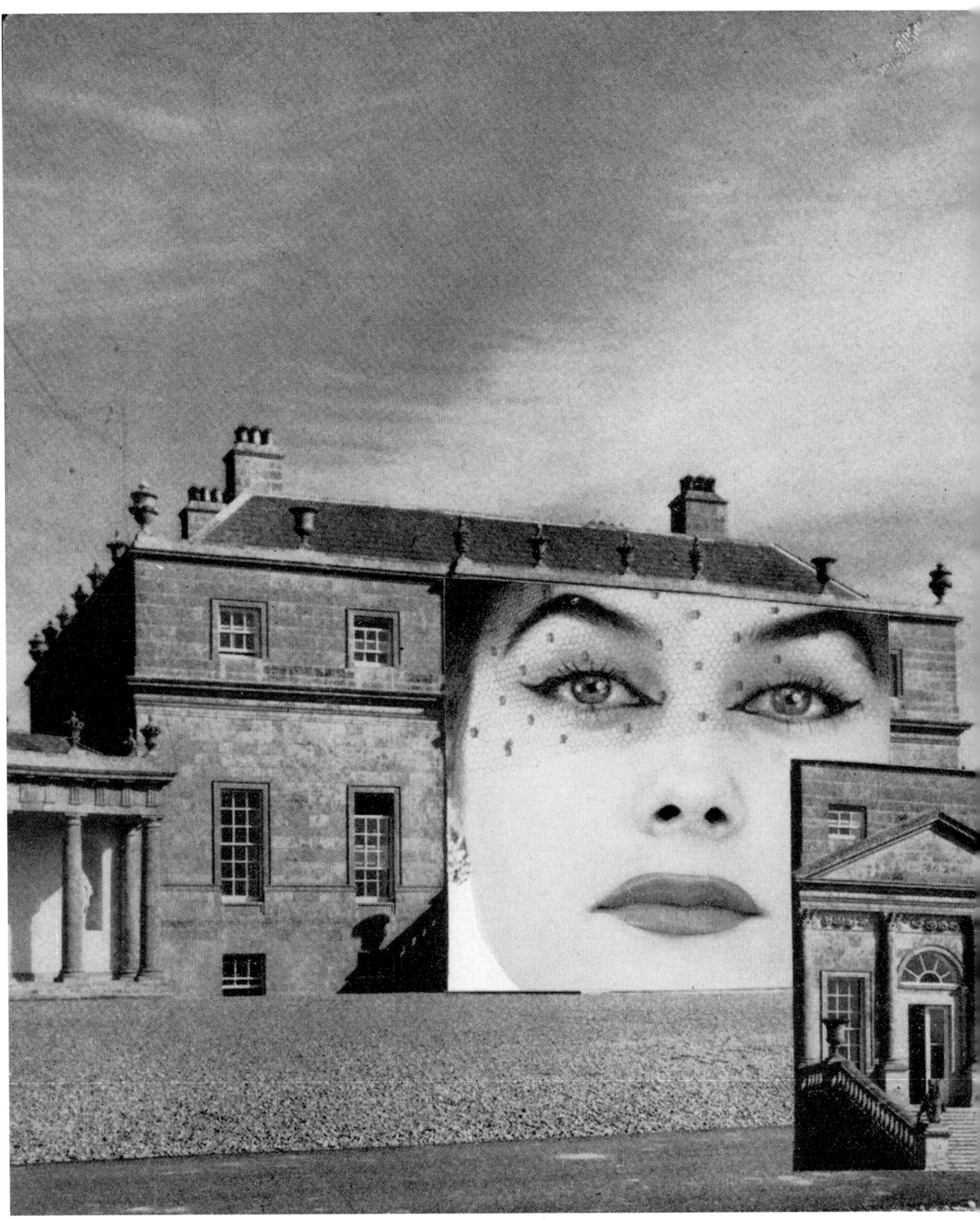

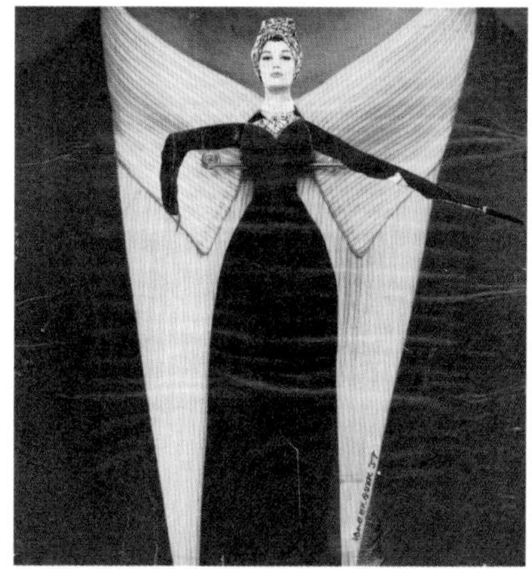

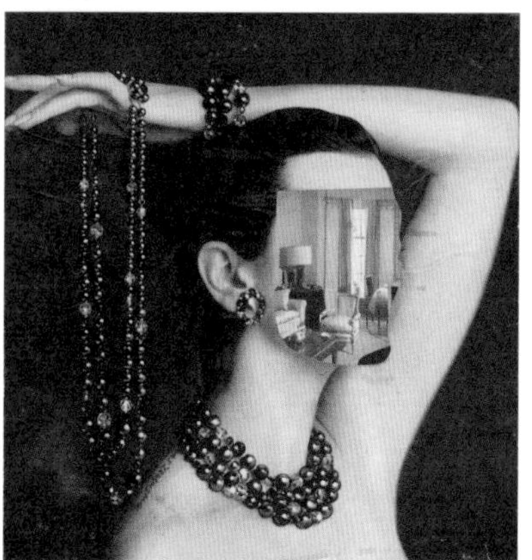

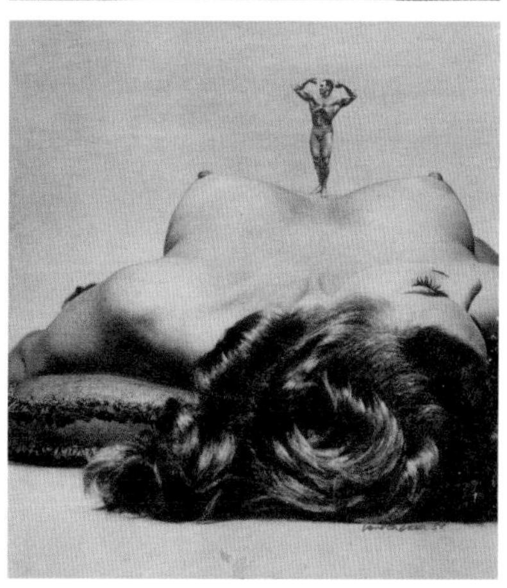

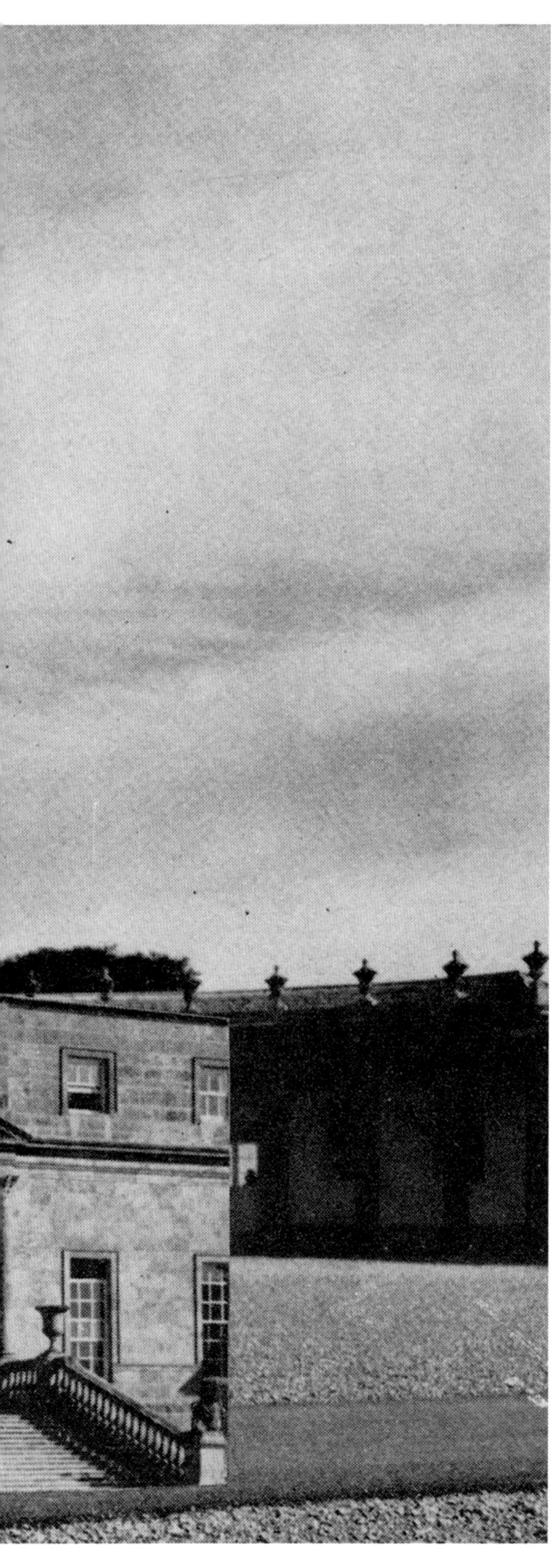

All: *Untitled (A La Mode)*, ca. 1958. Collage, paint, and ink, dimensions variable.

Films

Stan VanDerBeek turned to filmmaking in the
1950s, producing a body of work now regarded
as one of the most significant contributions to
American underground film. His first forays
into film were the result of Black Mountain
College acquiring a Bolex camera during his
time as a student there between 1949 and 1951.[1]
Influenced by Surrealism, Dada, and the expressionism of the Beat Generation, VanDerBeek's
earliest films utilized stop-motion animation skills he developed while working on the
CBS children's television program *Winky Dink
and You*.[2] Combining innovative animation
techniques with filmed sequences and found
footage, award-winning films such as
A La Mode (1958), *Science Friction* (1959), and
Breathdeath (1963) fused experimental film
with social critique. VanDerBeek used animated
collages, live action, found footage, and stop-
motion in his films throughout the 1960s. He
also documented Happenings and performance
pieces by Claes Oldenburg, Allan Kaprow, and
Robert Morris in the late 1950s and early '60s.
The use of computer and image processing
systems at Bell Labs, MIT, and public television stations through the 1970s led VanDerBeek
to produce complex video-based works such as
Symmetricks (1972) and *Microcosmos* (1983),
reflecting his ongoing interest in new forms of
collaboration and moving image media.

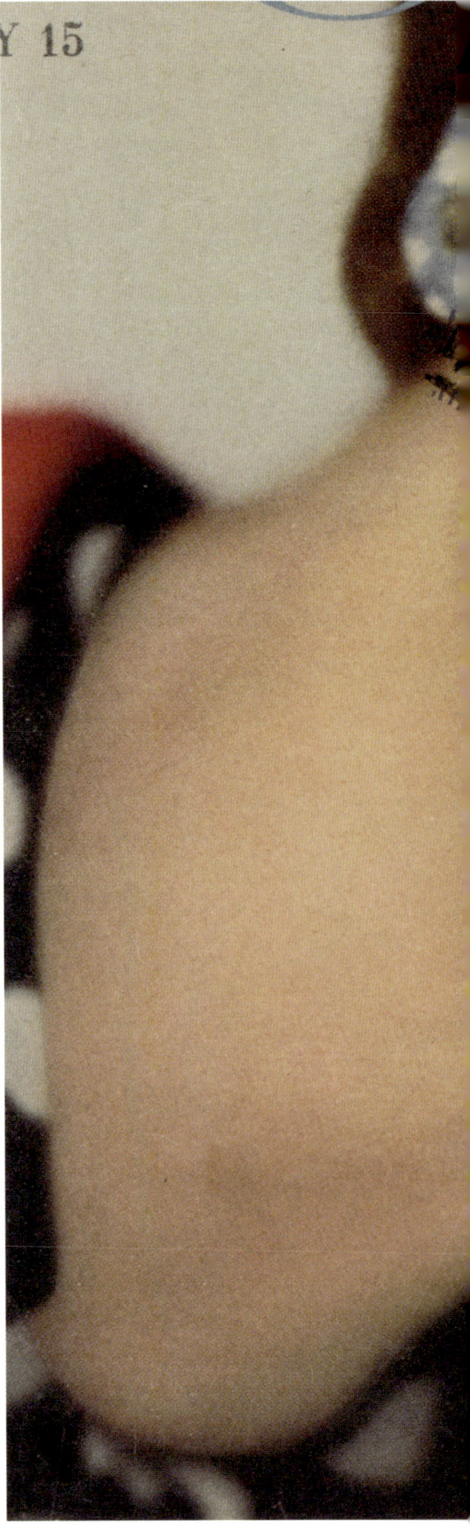

Untitled (A La Mode), 1958. Collage, paint,
and ink, 7 x 8 1/2 in.

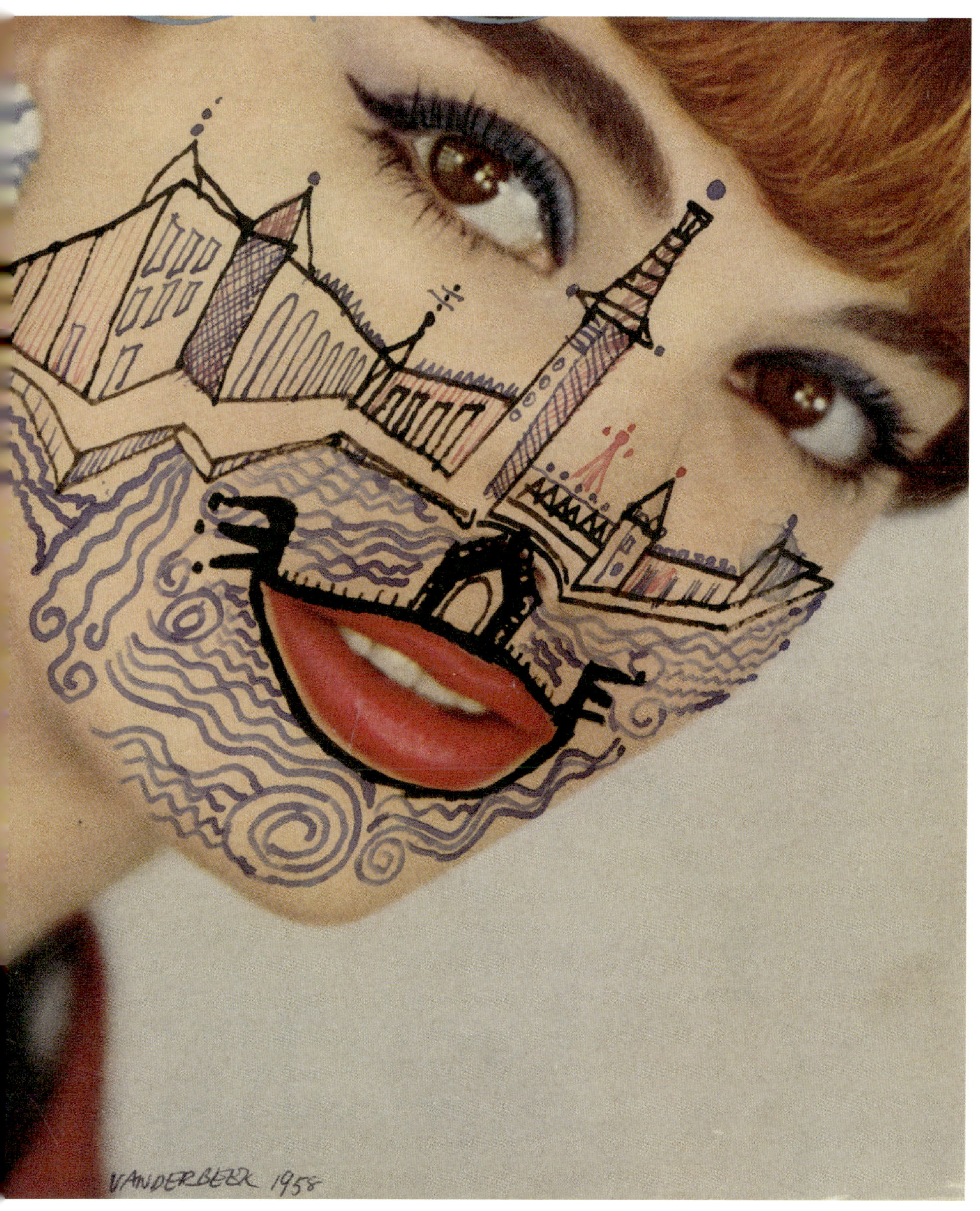

VANDERBEEK 1958

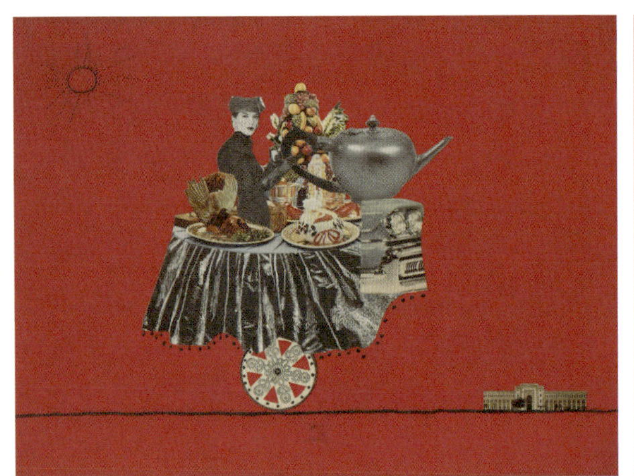 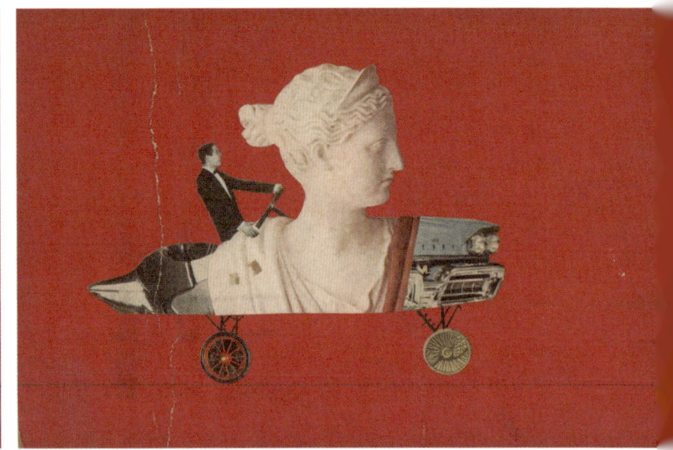

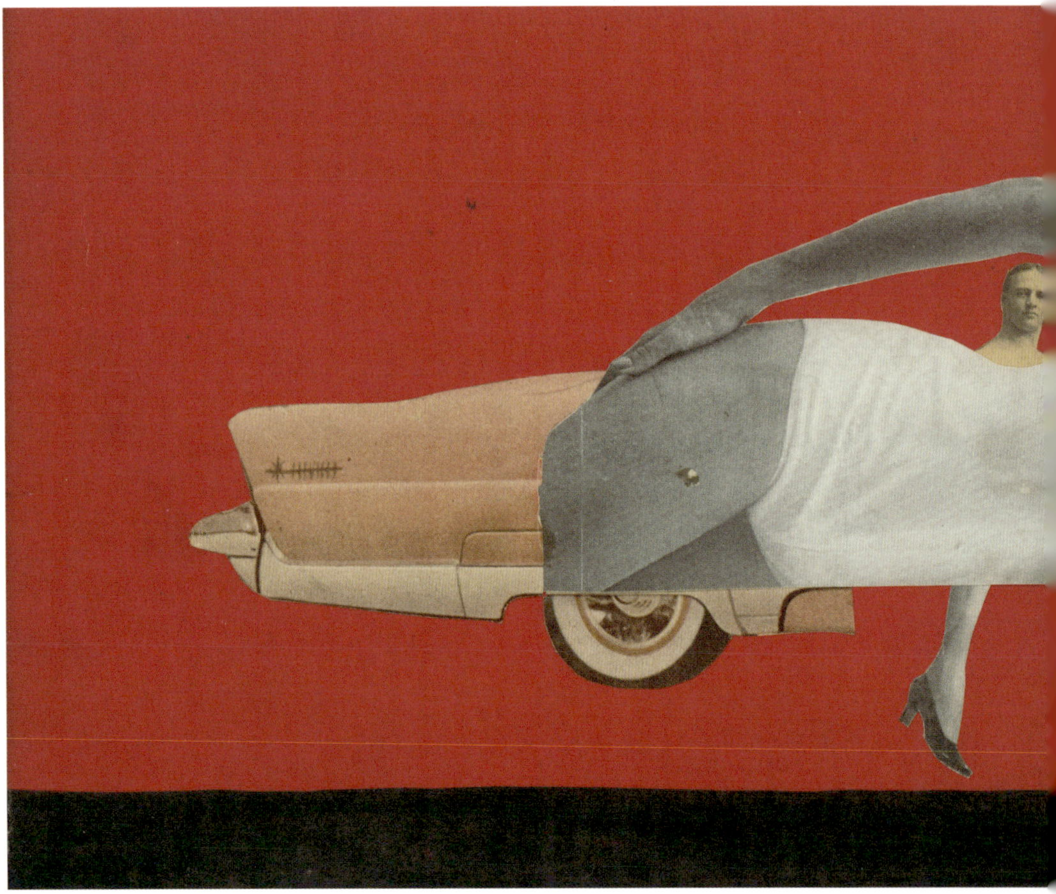

[Top: Left] *Untitled (Wheeeeels No. 2)*, 1959.
Collage, paint, and ink, 12 x 15 in.

[Top: Right] *Untitled (Wheeeeels No. 2)*, 1959.
Collage and pen, 10 x 19 in.

[Bottom] *Untitled (Wheeeeels No. 2)*, 1959.
Collage and pen, 10 x 19 in.

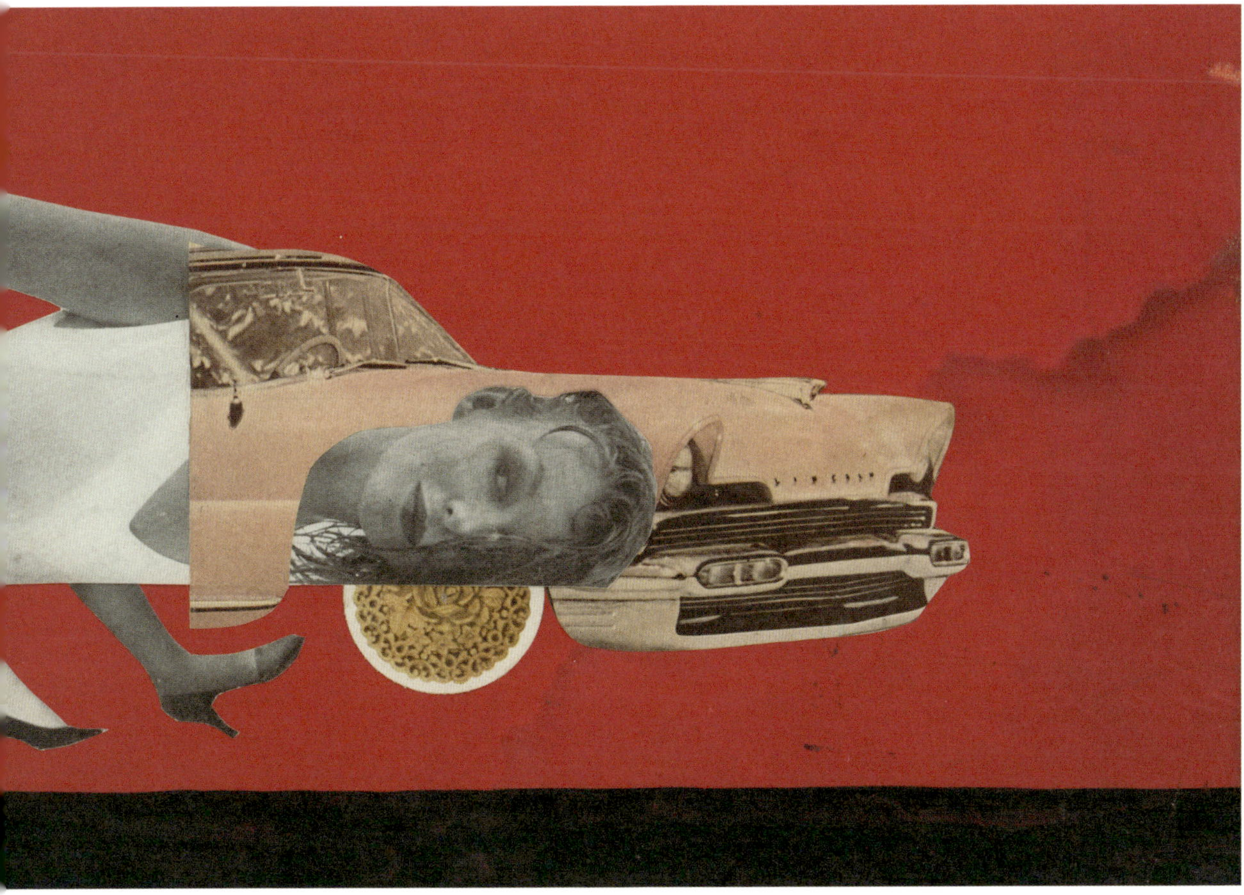

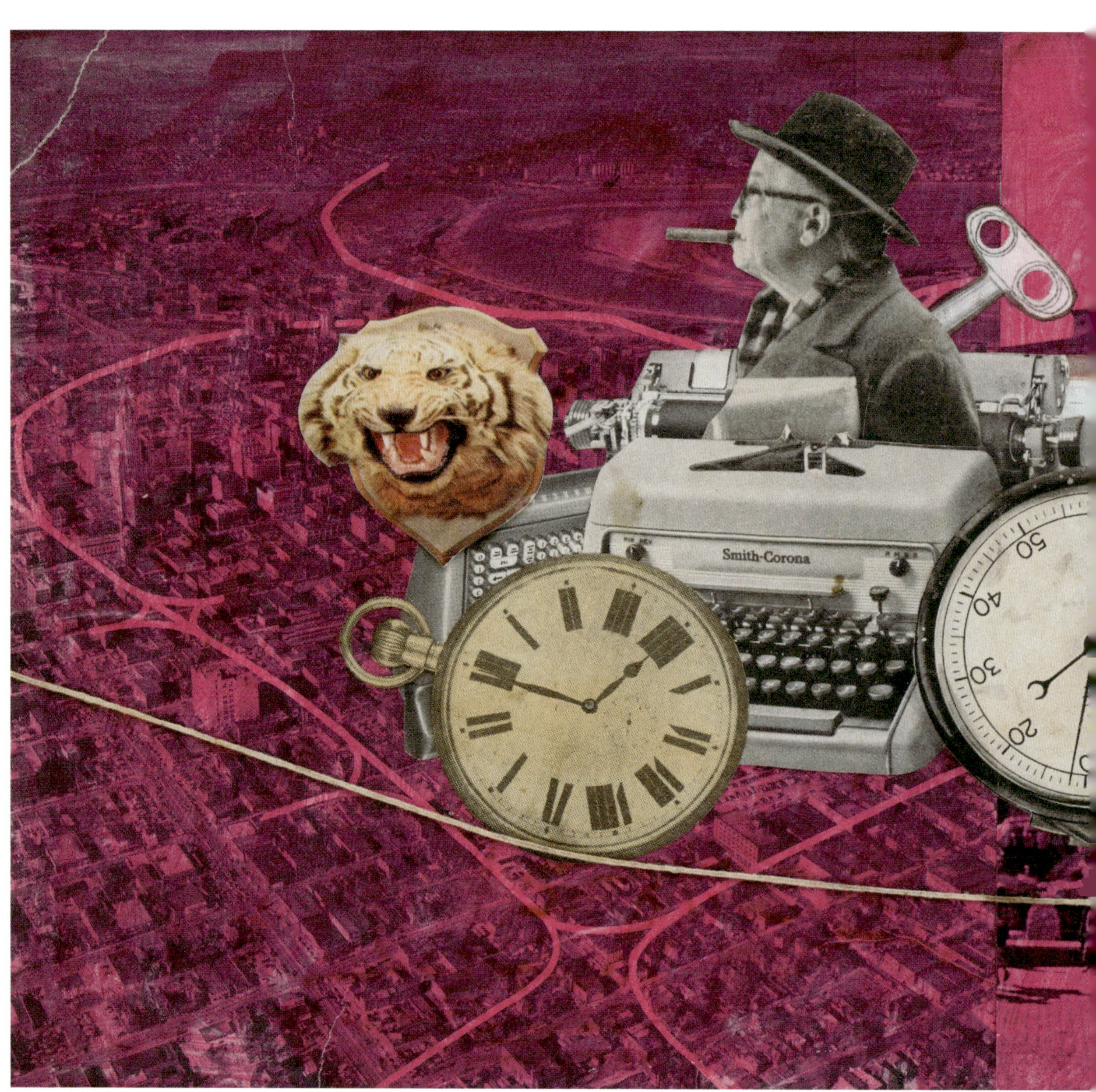

Smith-Corona

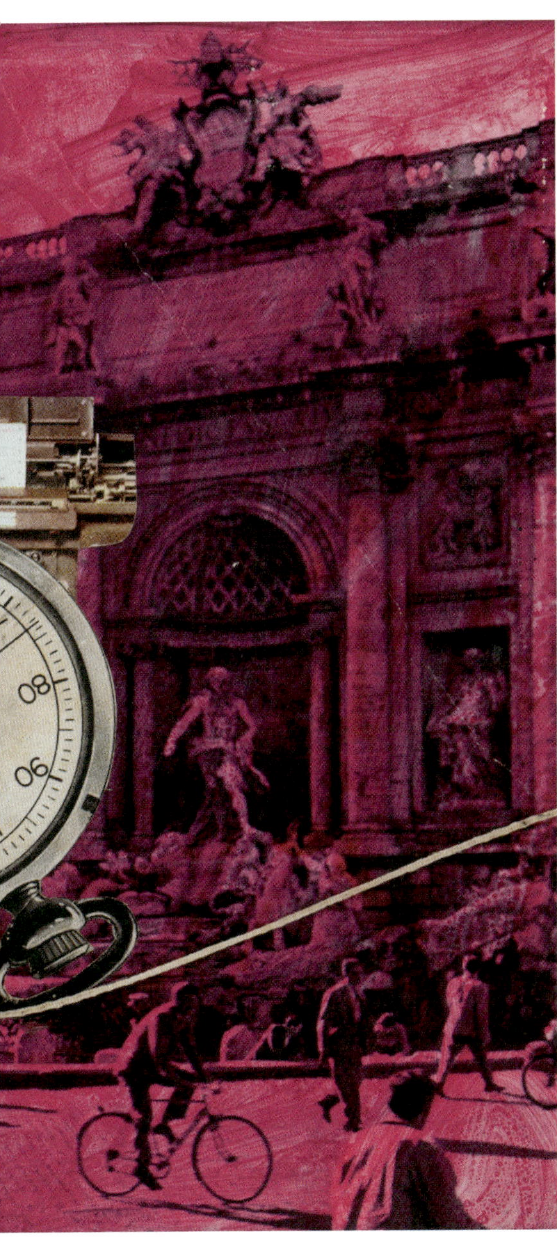

[Left] *Untitled (Science Friction)*, 1959.
Collage, ink, and string on board, 11 x 14 in.

[Below: Top] *Untitled (Science Friction)*,
1959. Collage on board, 11 x 15 in.

[Below: Bottom] *Untitled (Science Friction)*,
1959. Collage and graphite, 9 x 15 in.

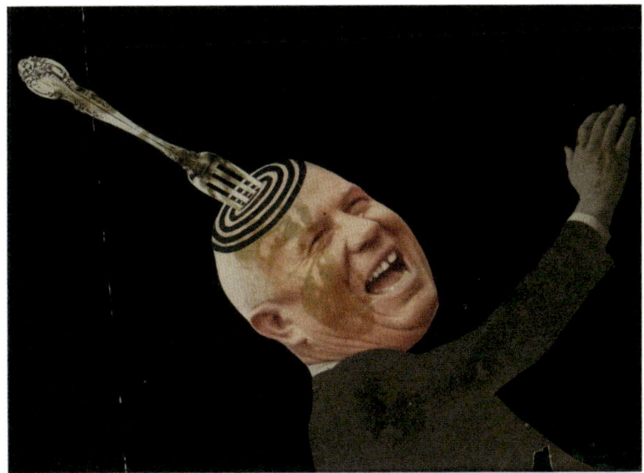

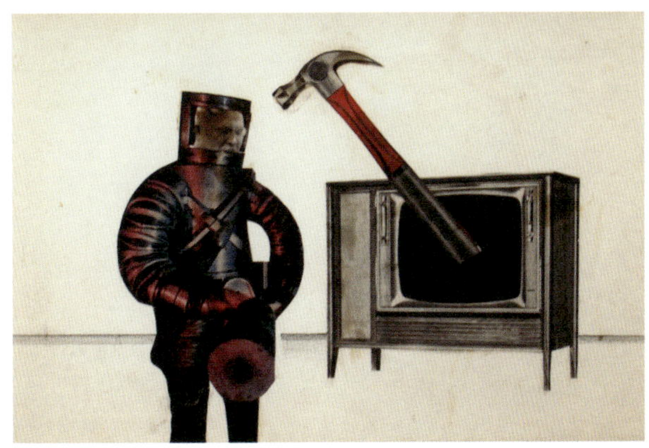

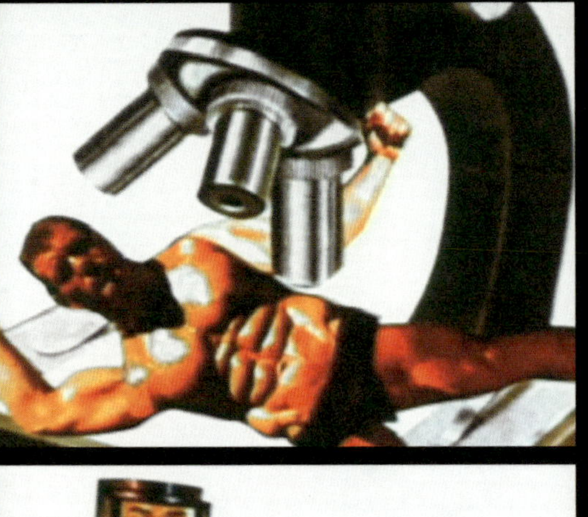
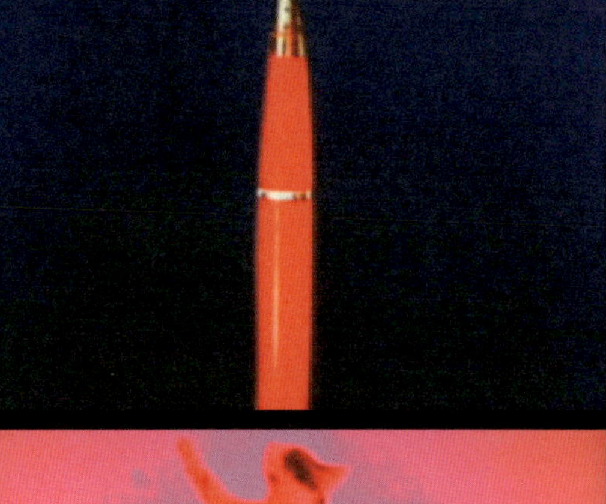
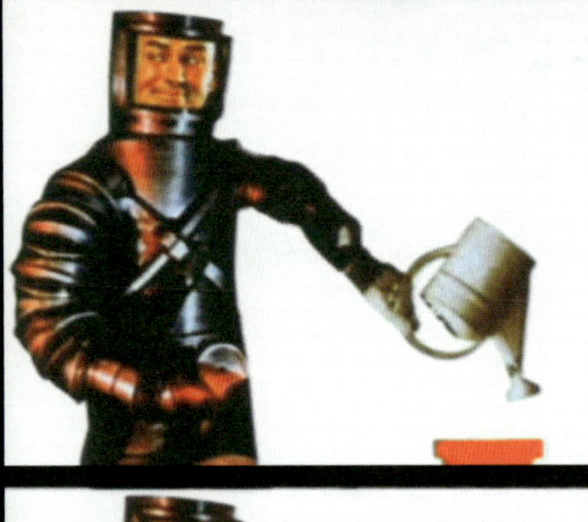
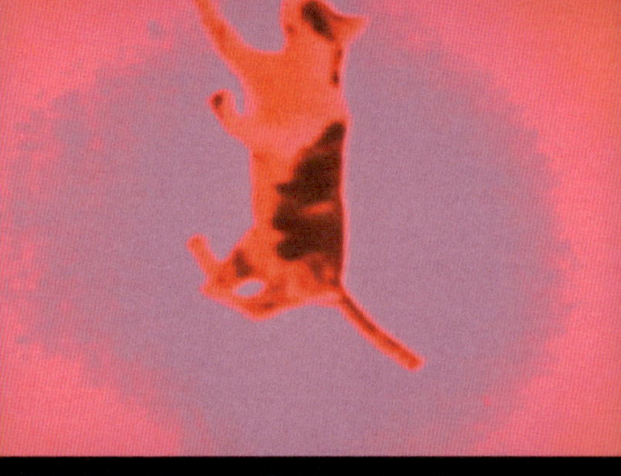
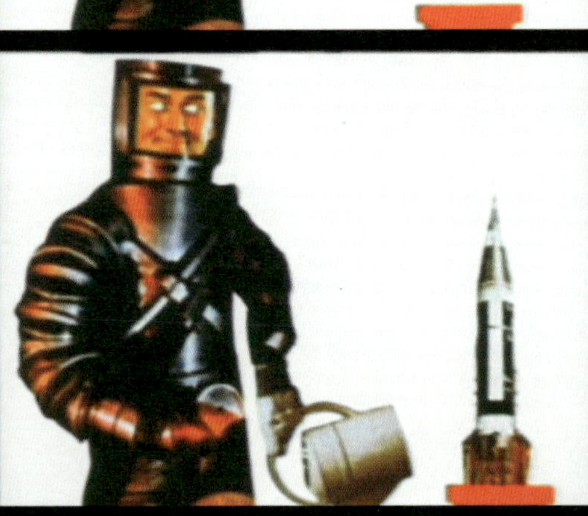
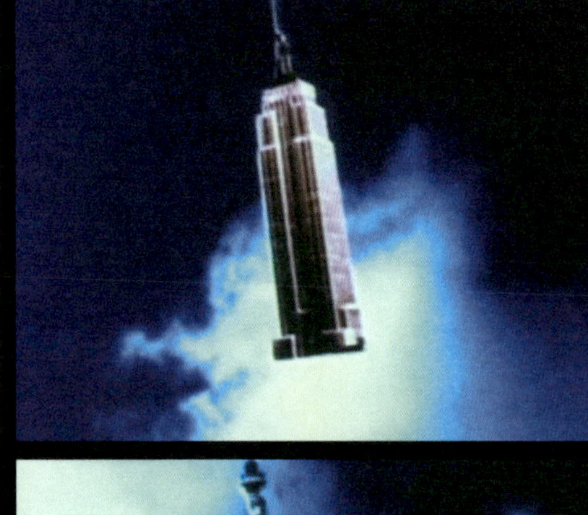
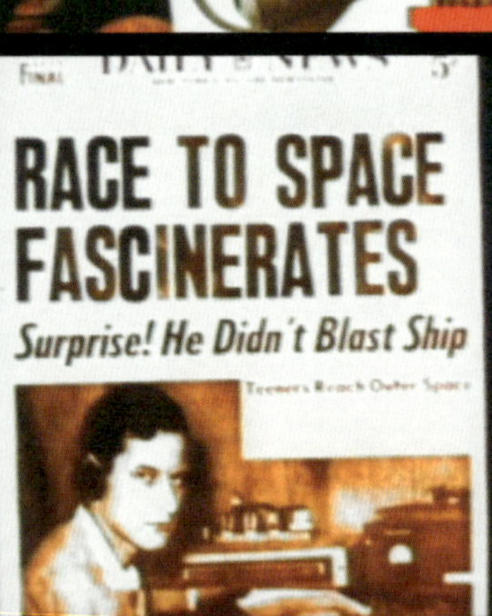
FINAL
DAILY NEWS
RACE TO SPACE
FASCINERATES
Surprise! He Didn't Blast Ship
Teeners Reach Outer Space
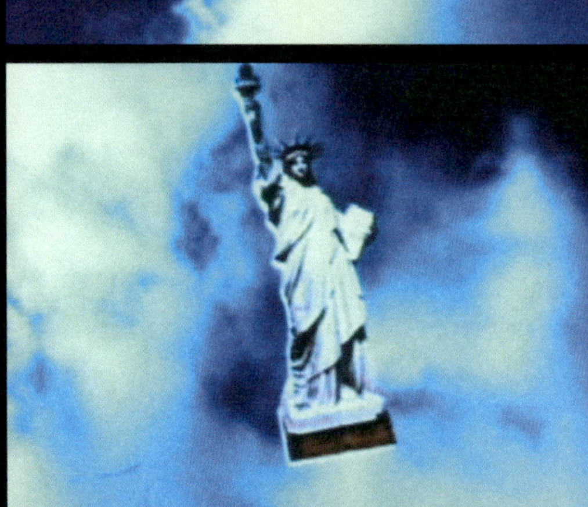

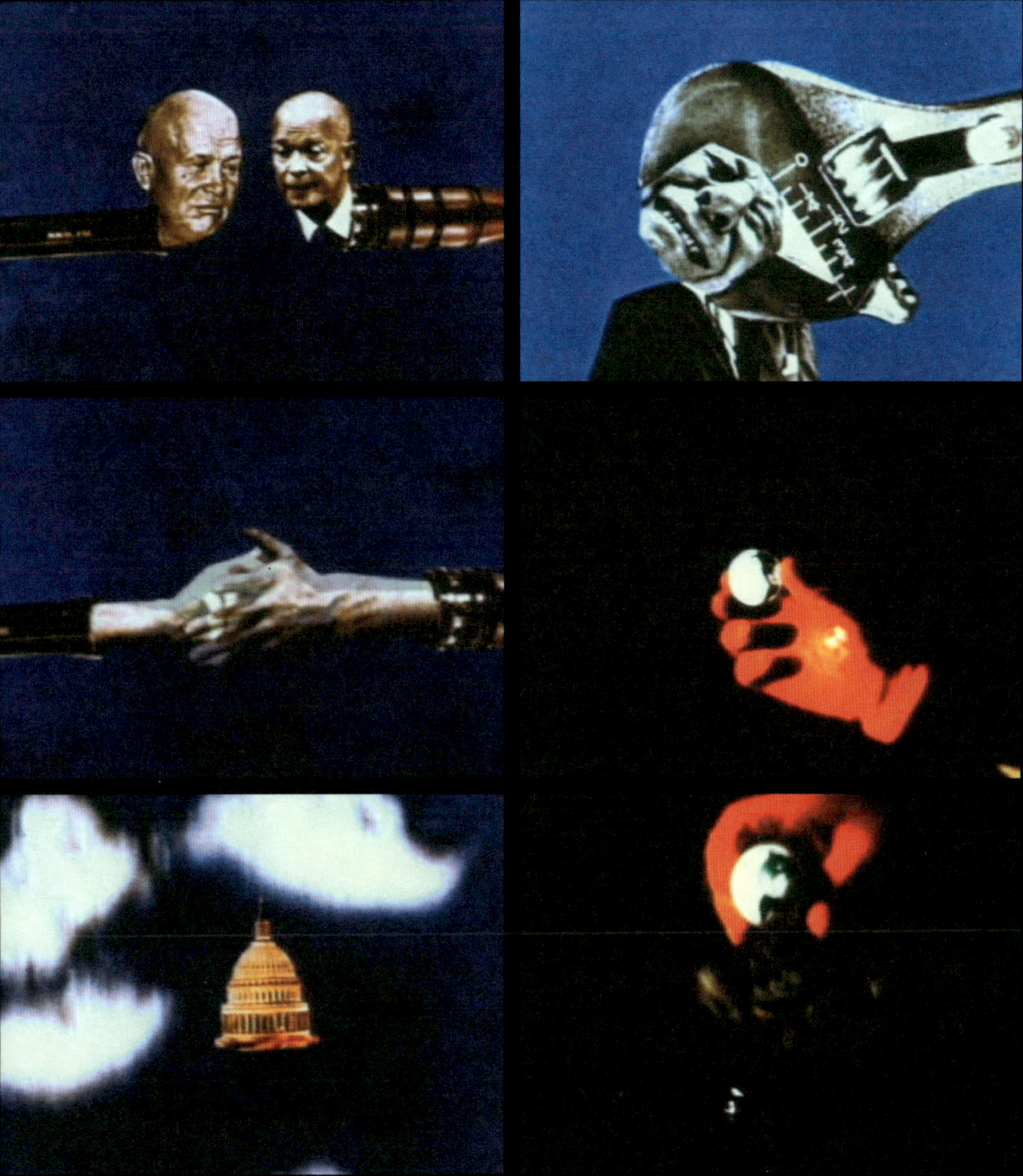

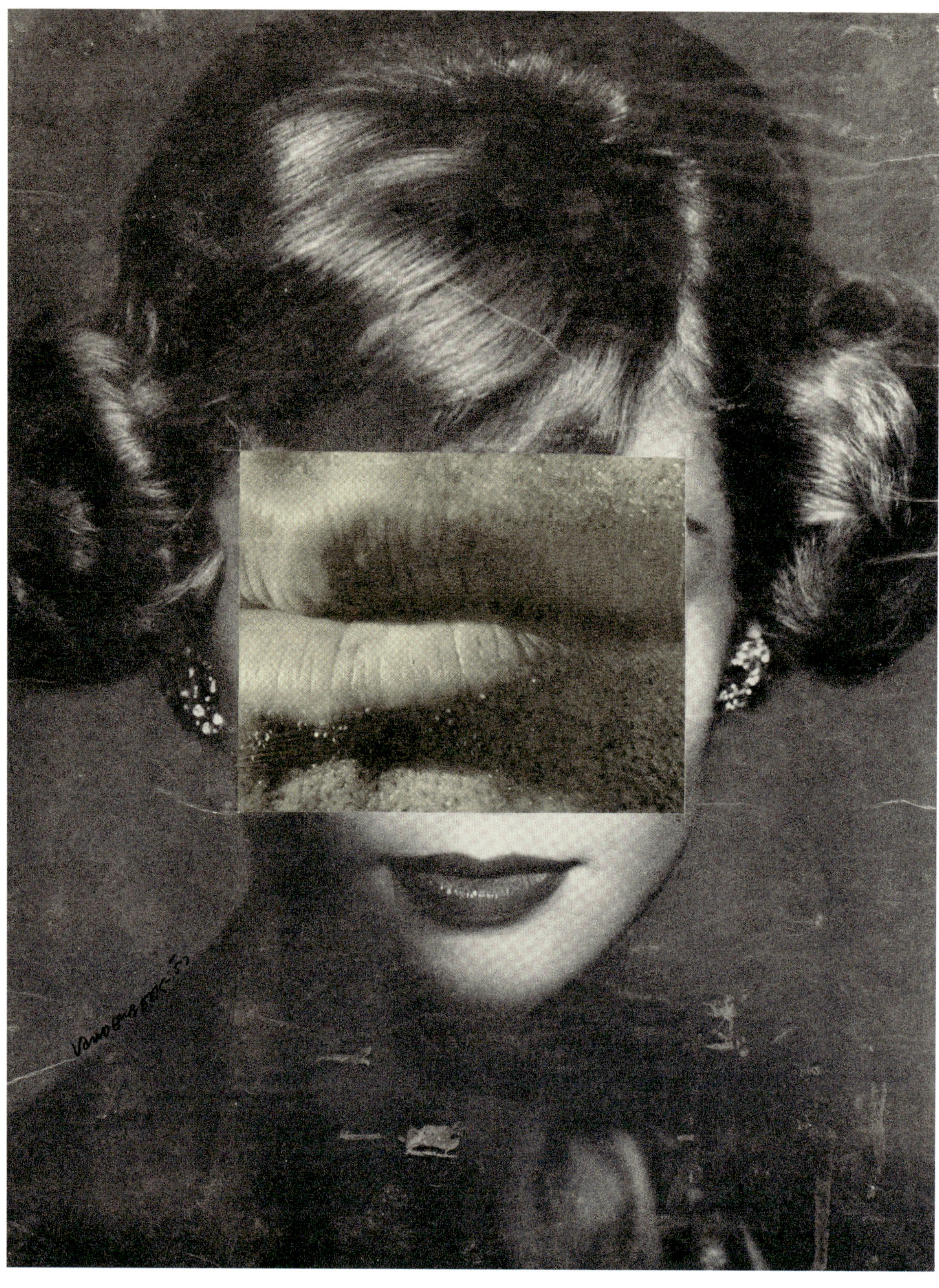

Untitled (Breathdeath), 1963. Collage
and ink, 10 x 7 in.

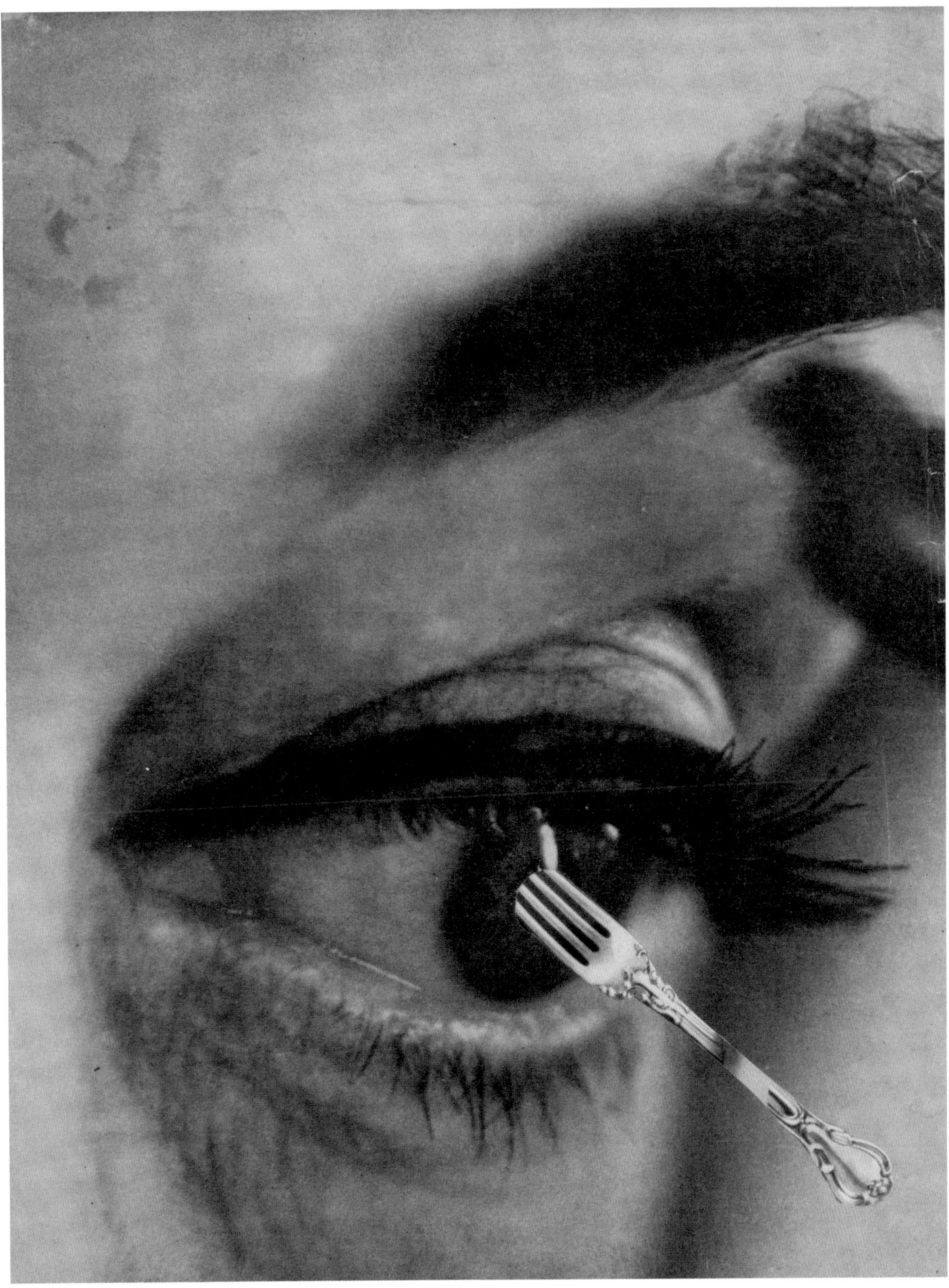

Untitled (Breathdeath), 1963.
Collage, 14 x 10 in.

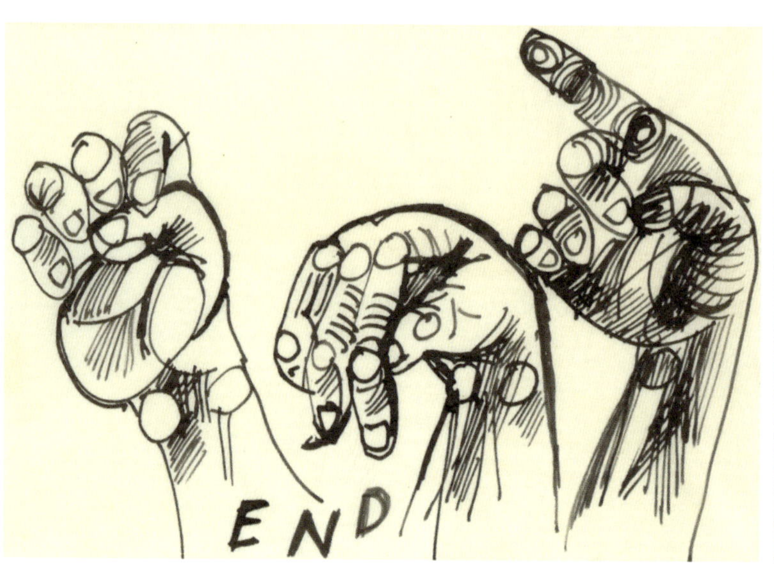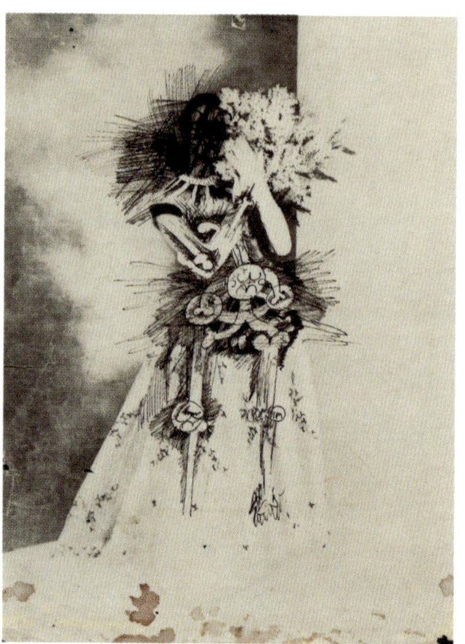

All: *Untitled*, ca. 1963–65. Ink on paper,
dimensions variable.

Untitled (drawing), n.d.
Ink on paper, 11 x 8 in.

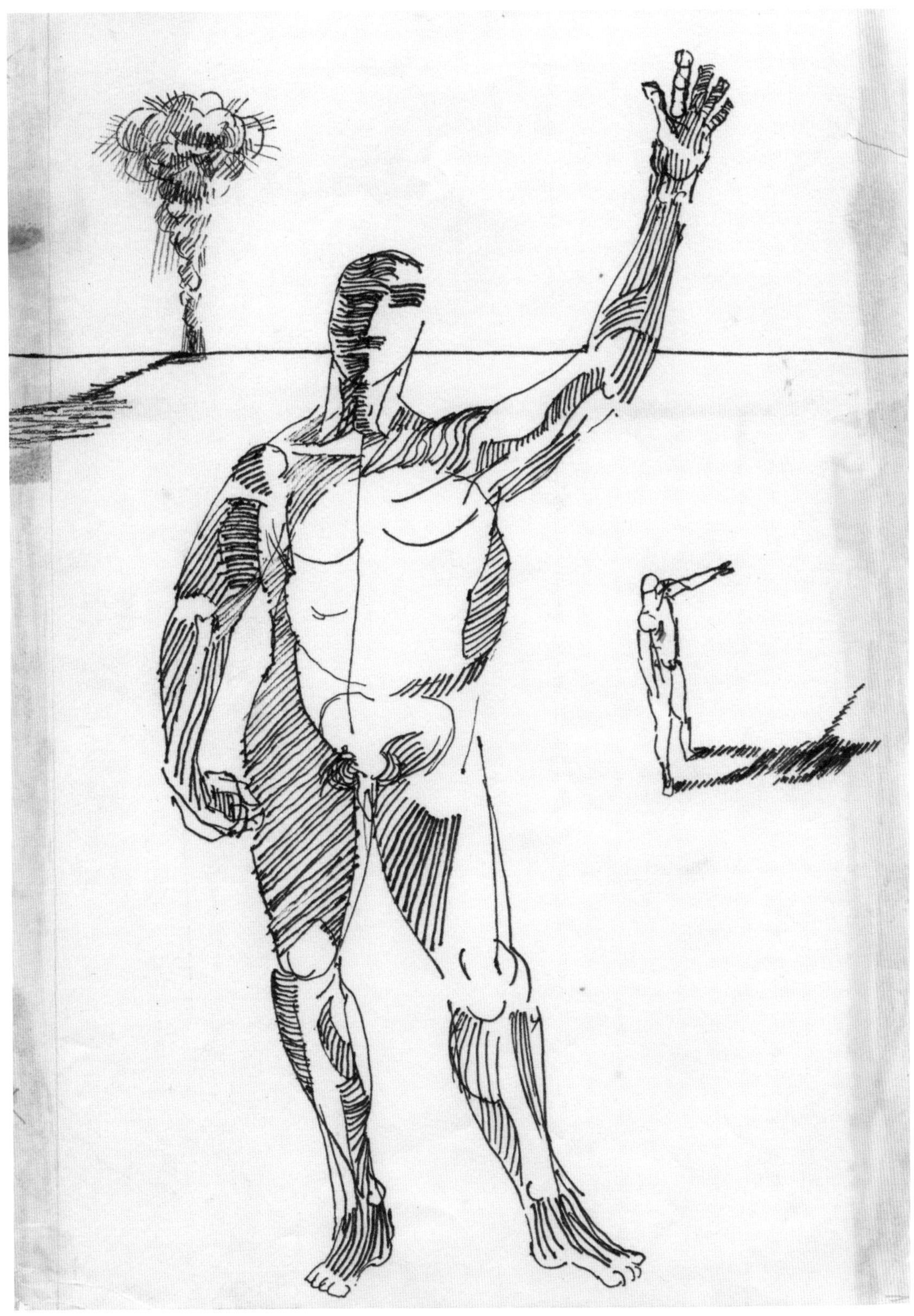

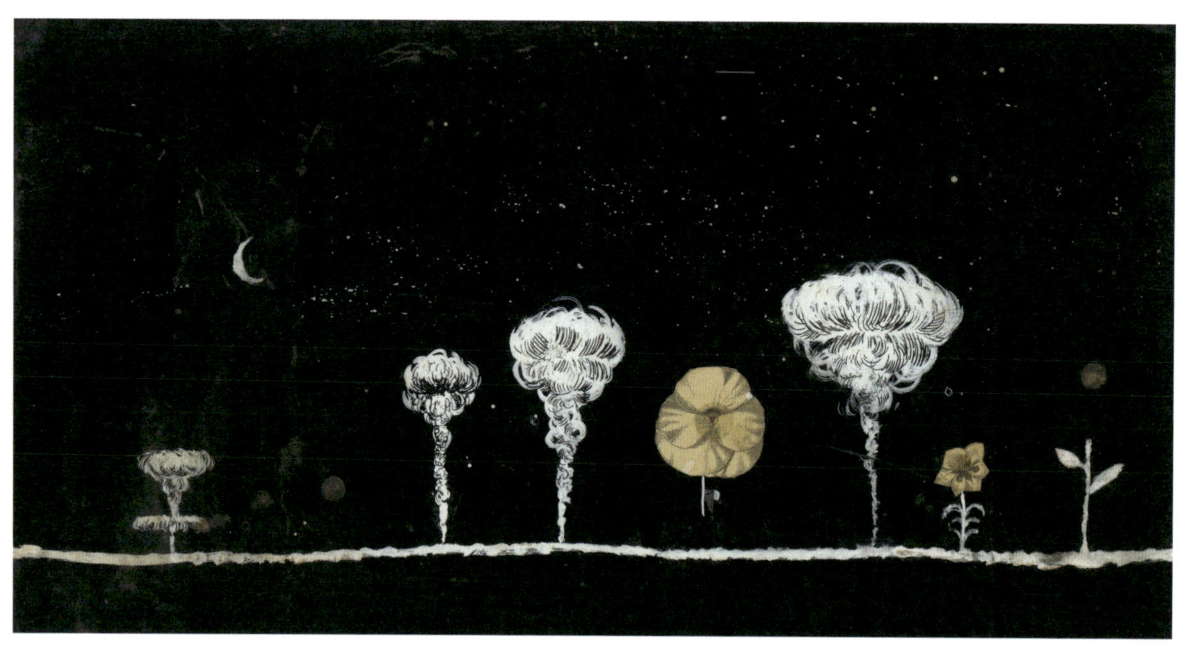

Untitled (Breathdeath), 1963.
Collage and paint on paper, dimensions
variable.

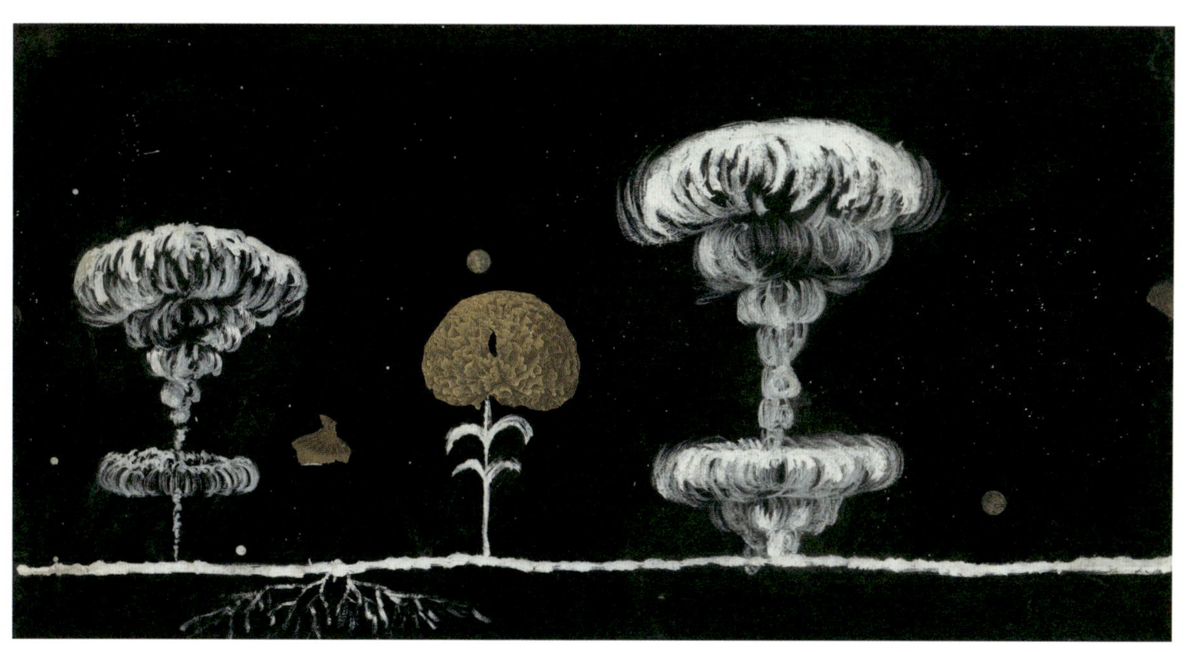

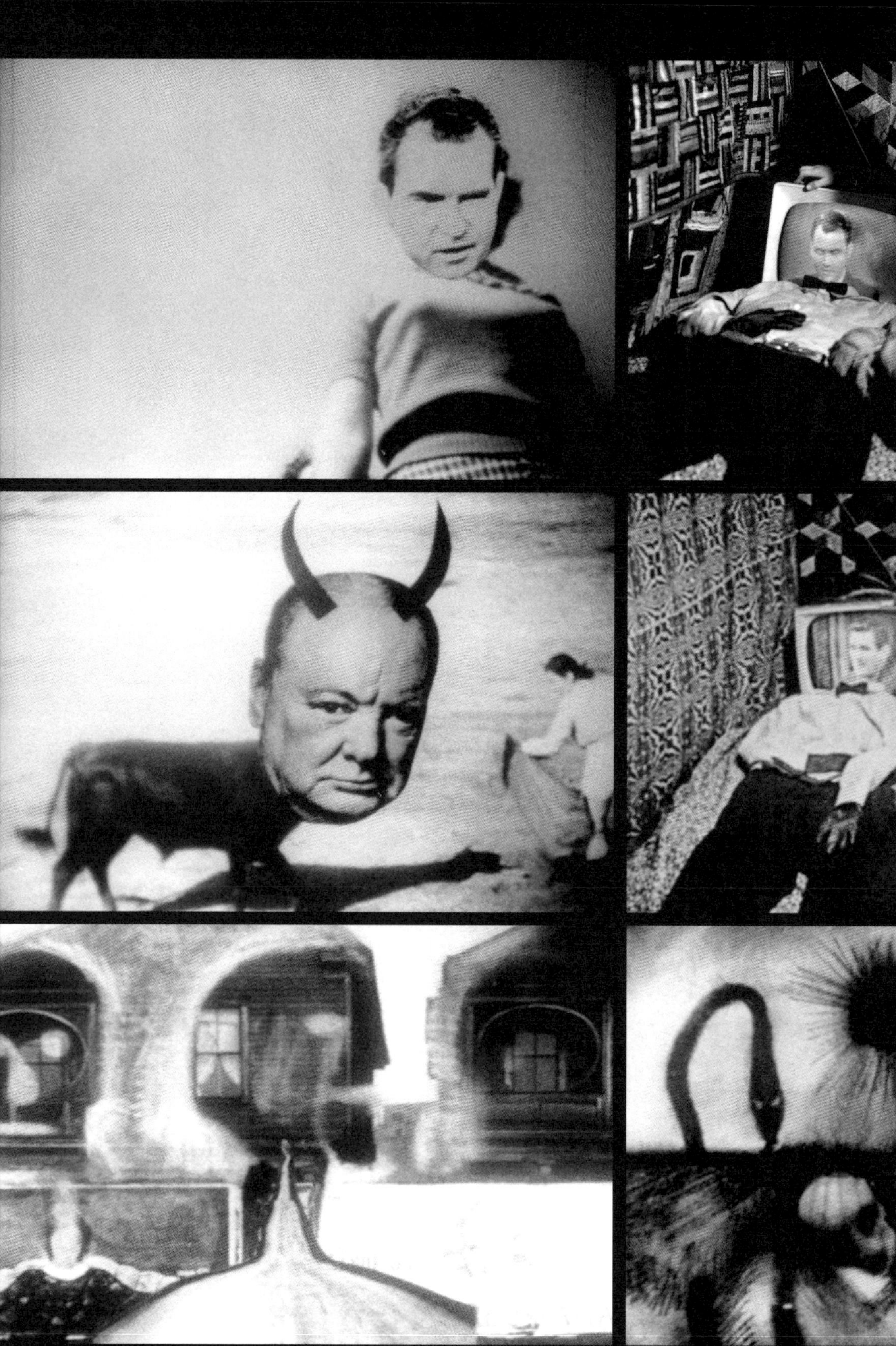

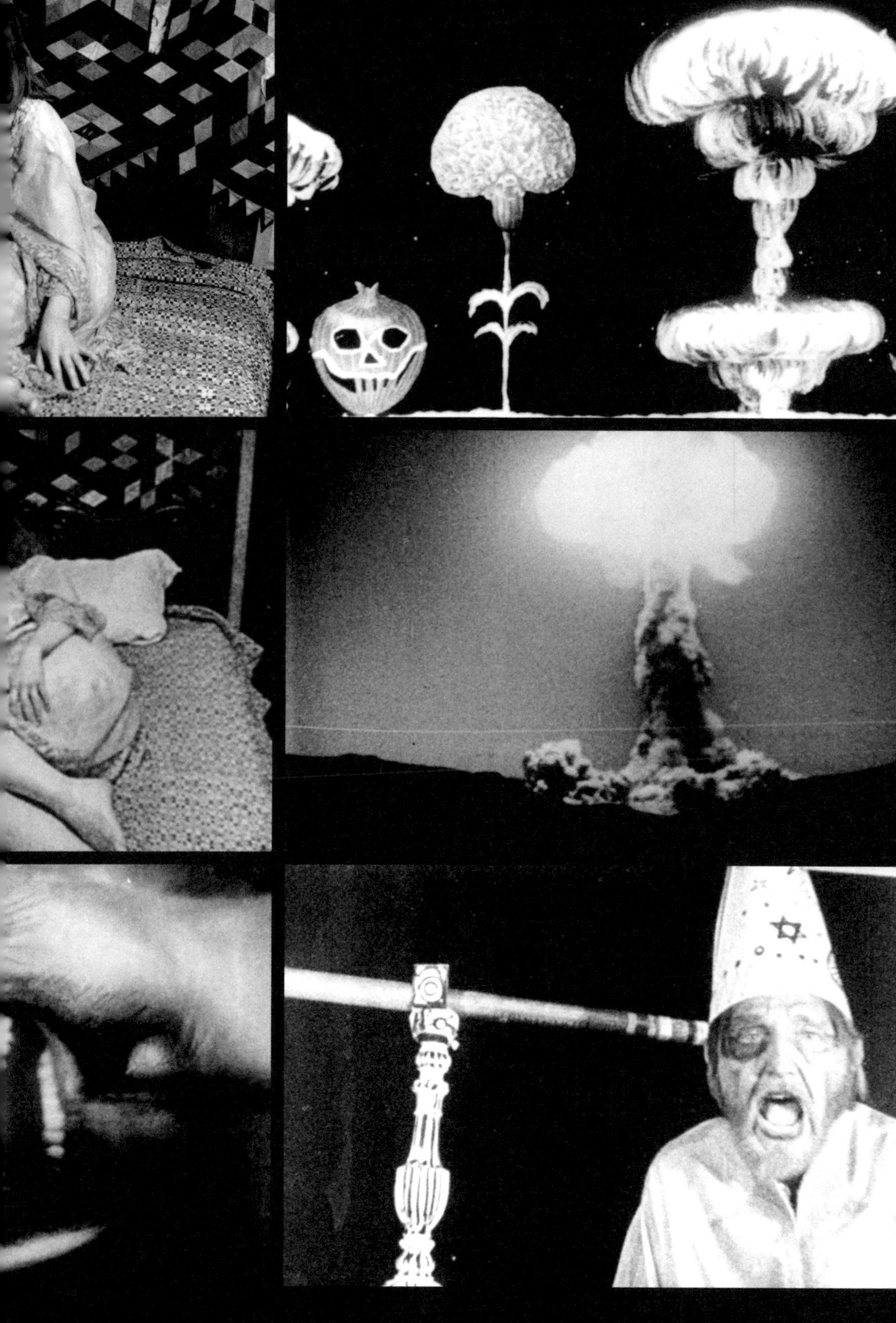

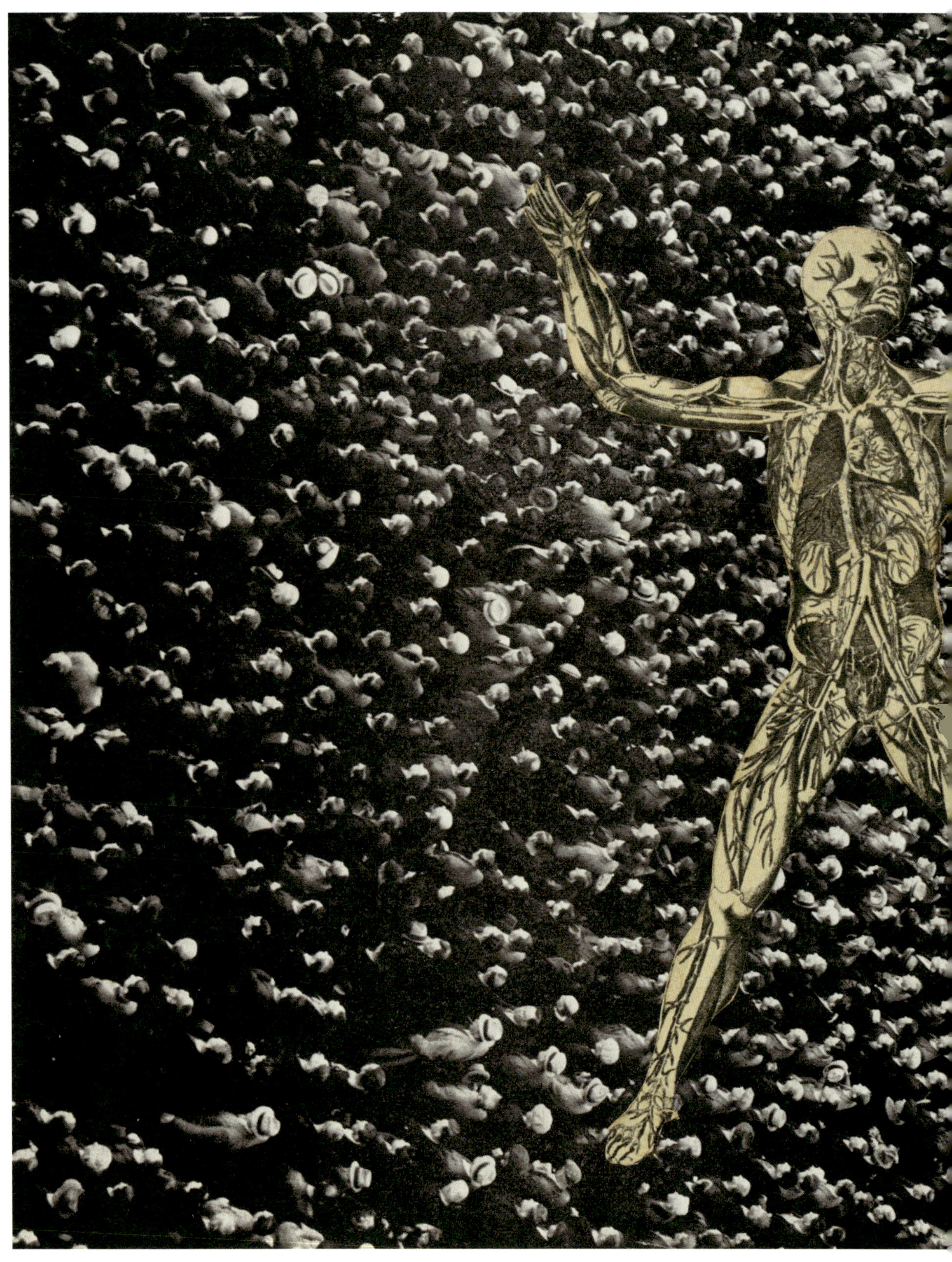

Untitled (See, Saw, Seams), ca. 1965.
Collage, 8 x 11 in.

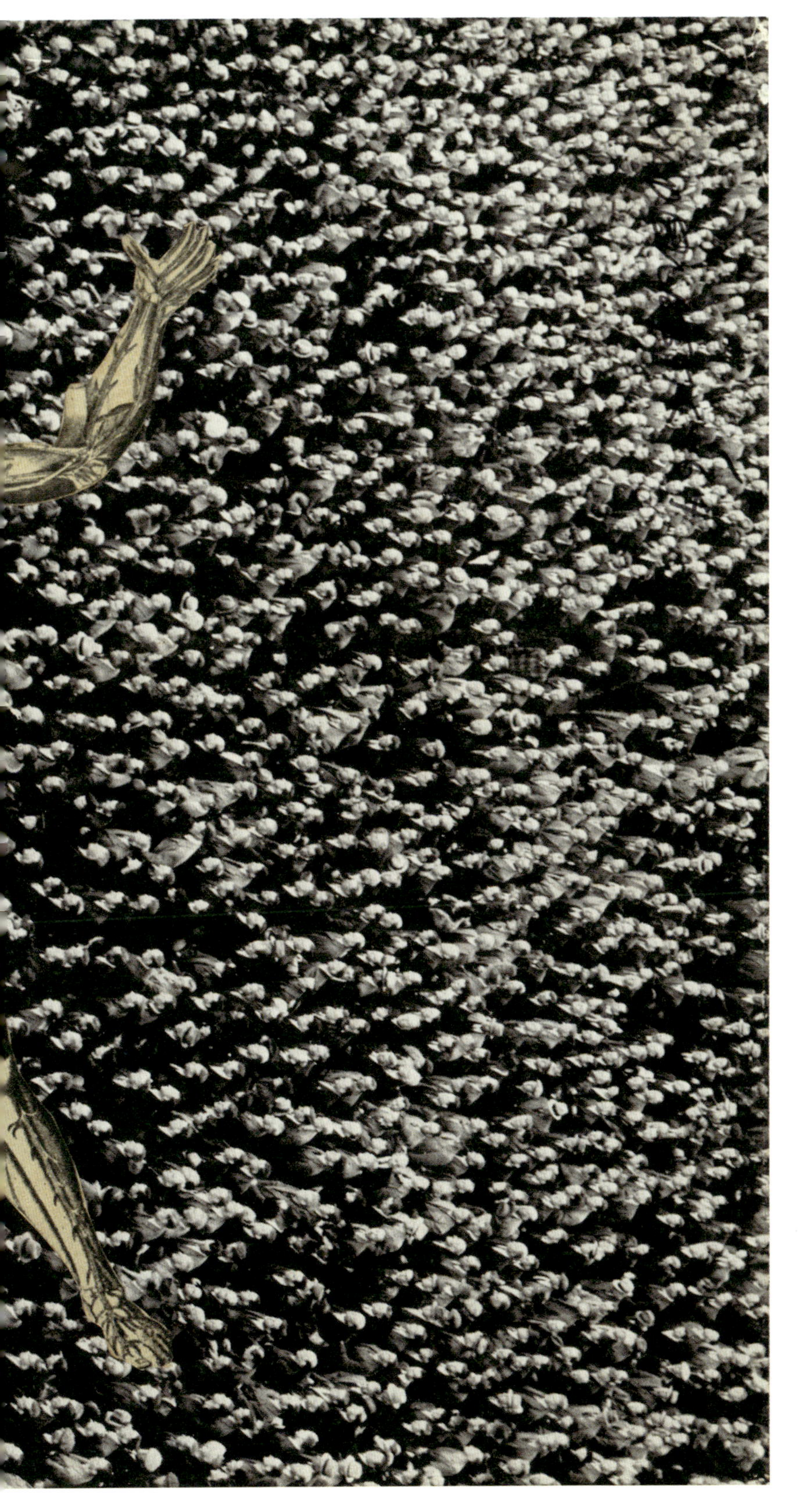

Untitled (See, Saw, Seams), ca. 1965.
Collage, paint. 16 x 12 in.

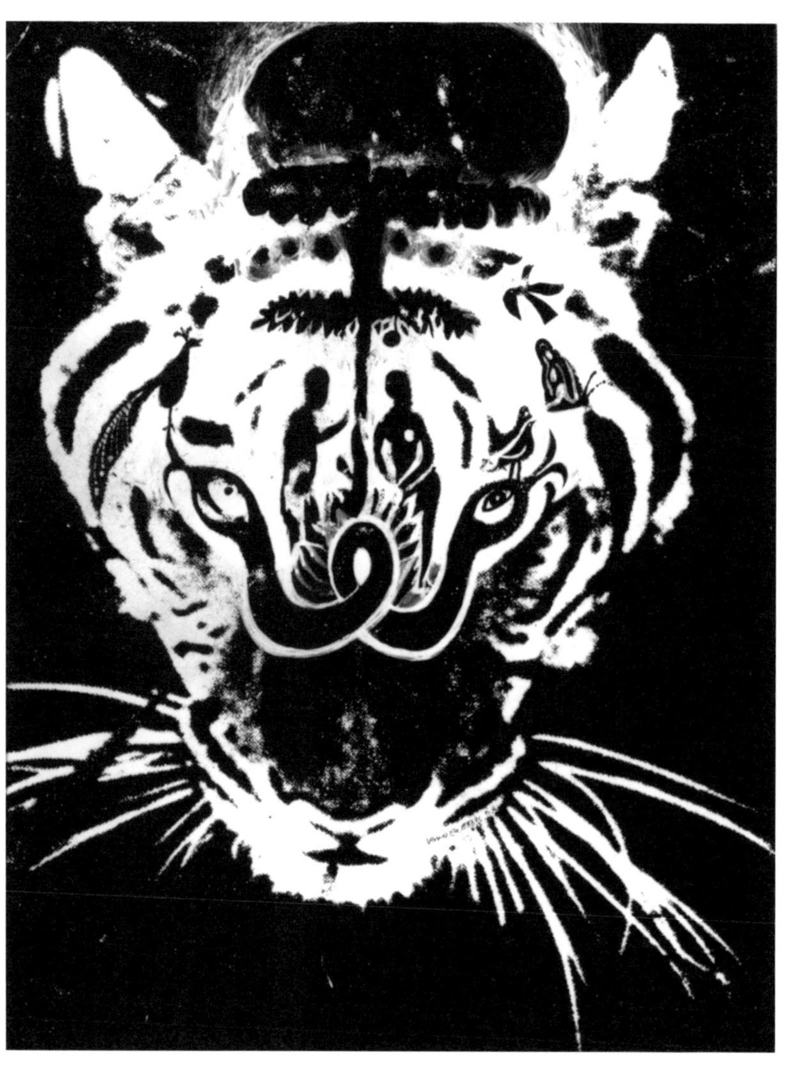

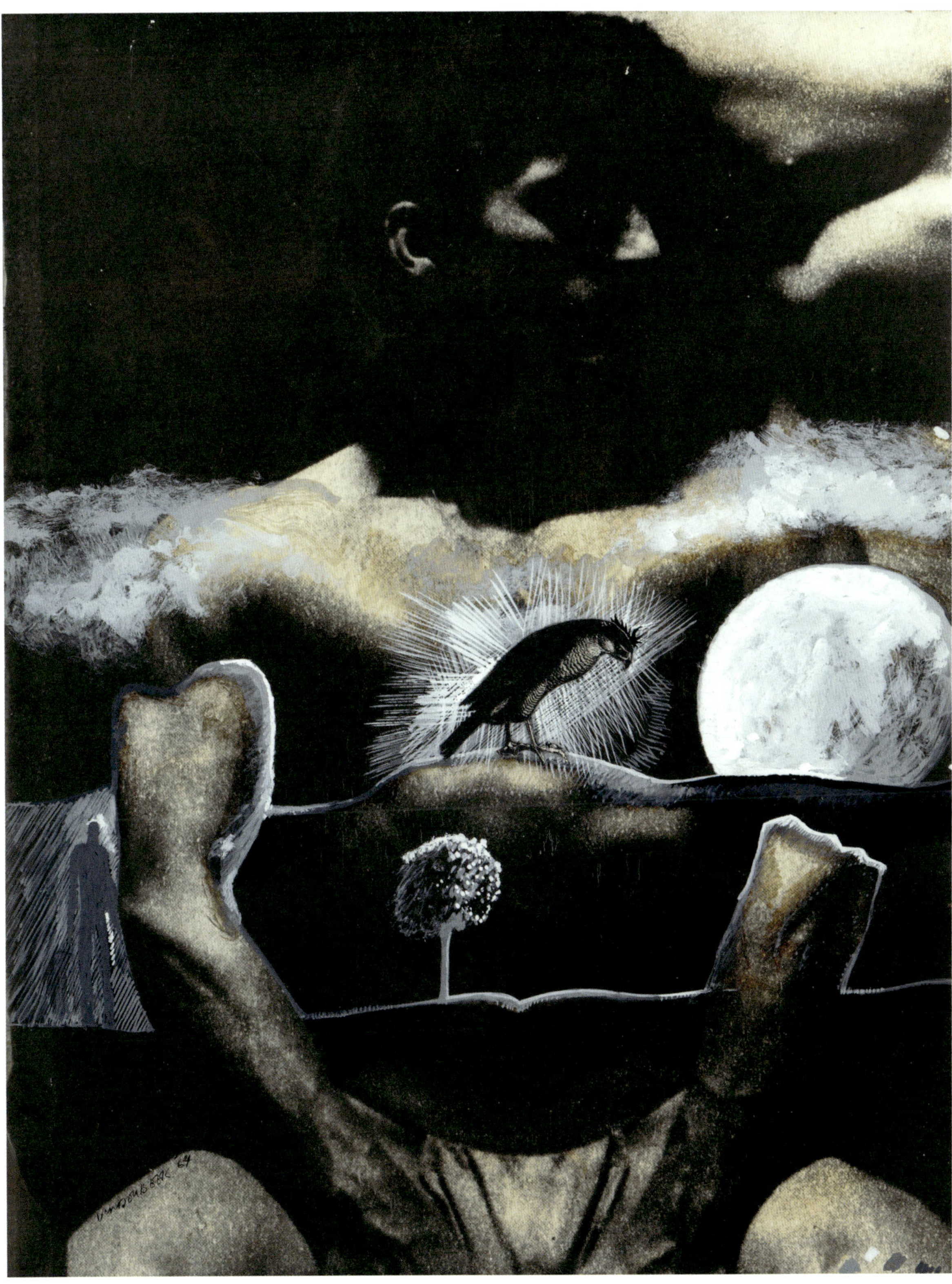

Untitled (See, Saw, Seams), 1964.
Collage, paint, and ink, 14 x 10 1/4 in.

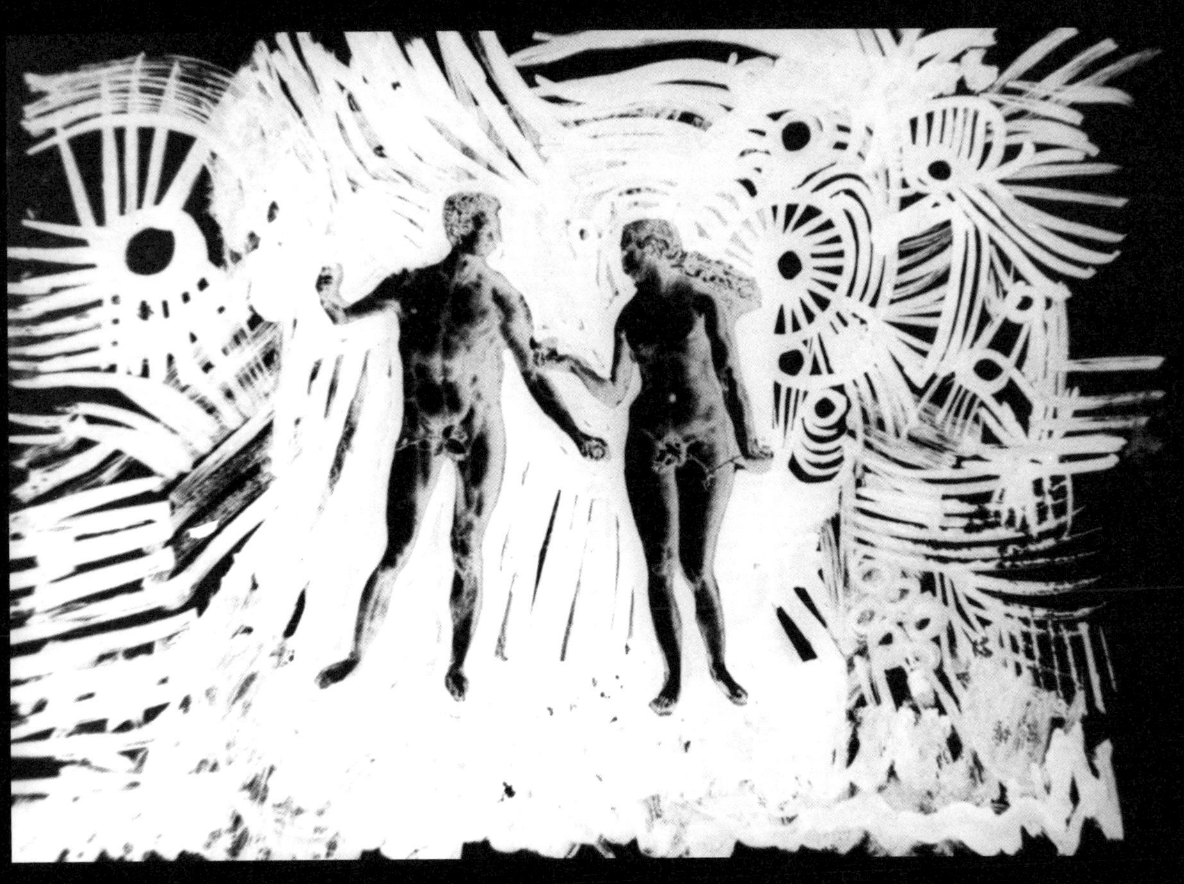

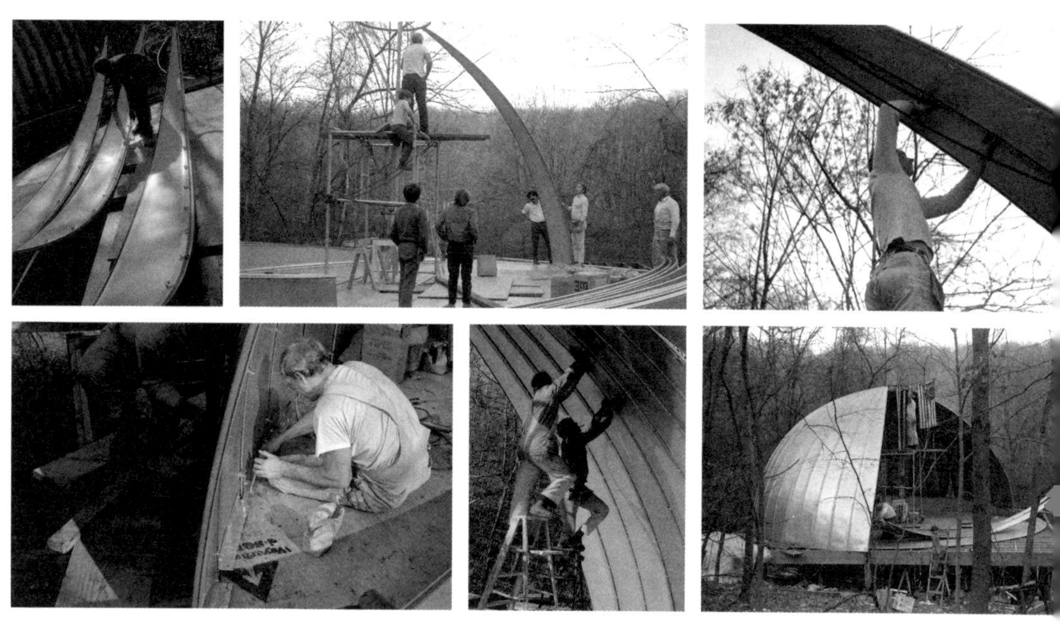

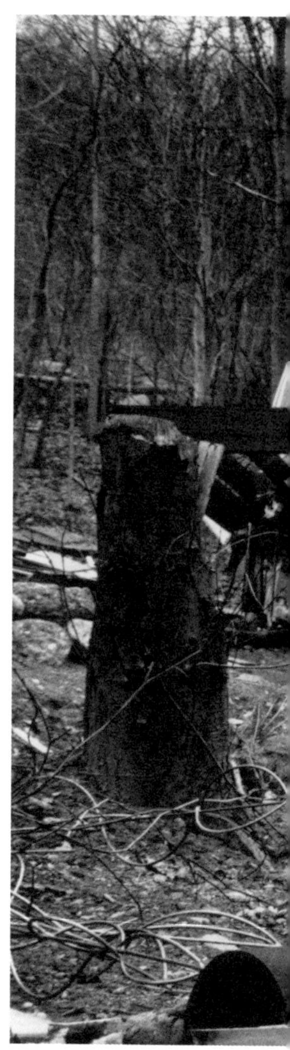

[Above] Stan VanDerBeek and friends
constructing the *Movie-Drome*,
Stony Point, NY, 1963–65.

[Right] Stan VanDerBeek outside
the *Movie-Drome*, Stony Point, NY,
1963–65.

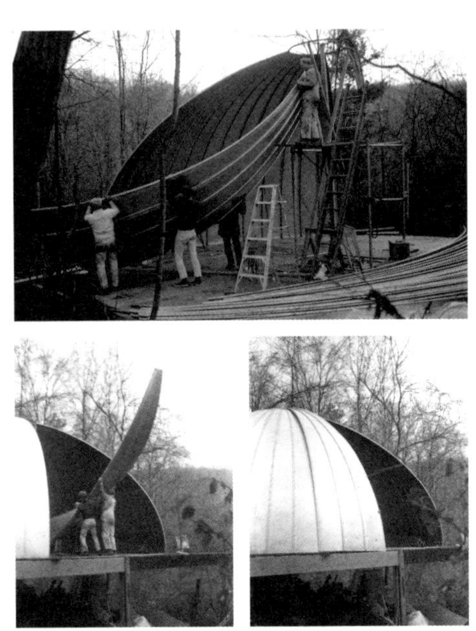

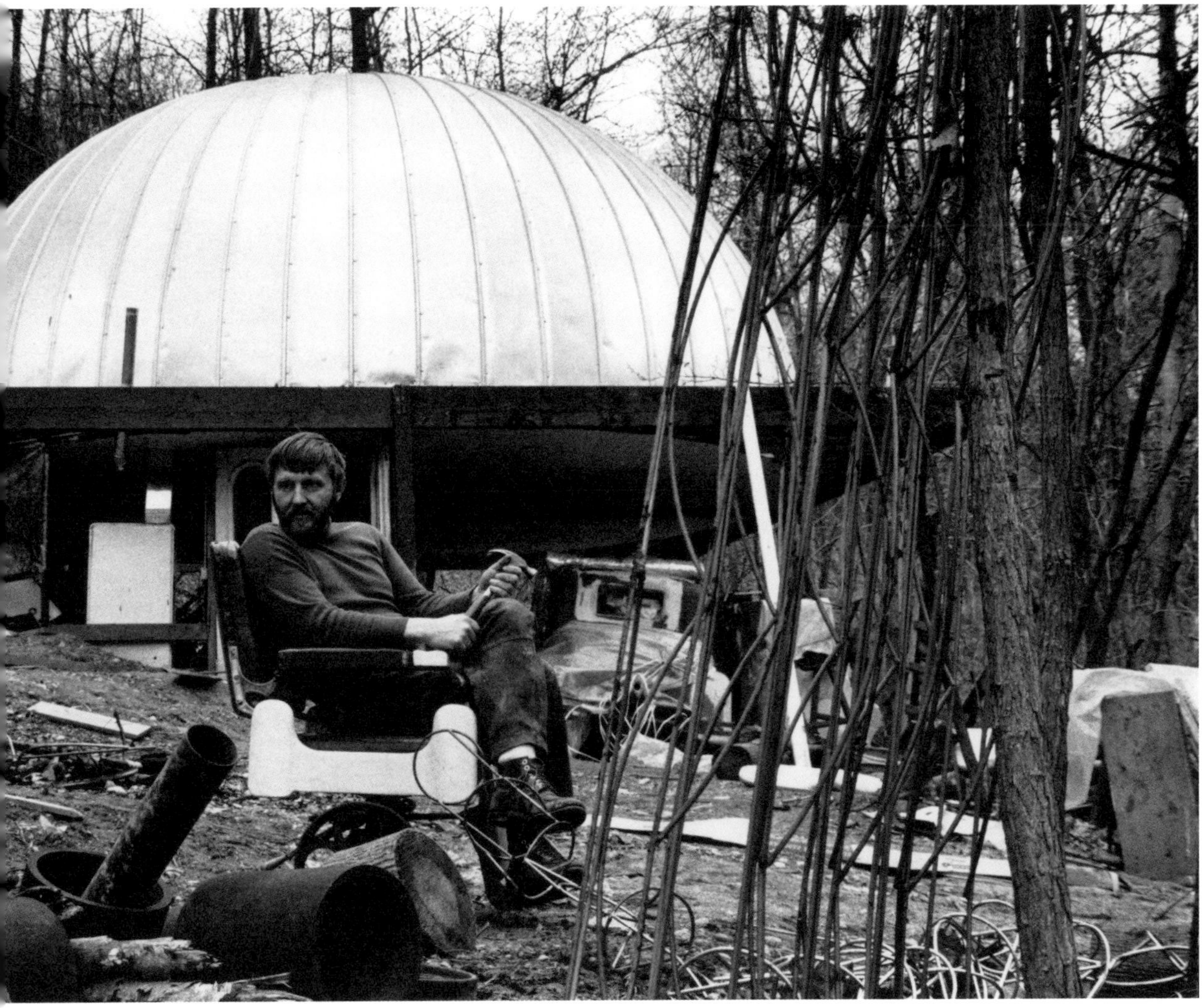

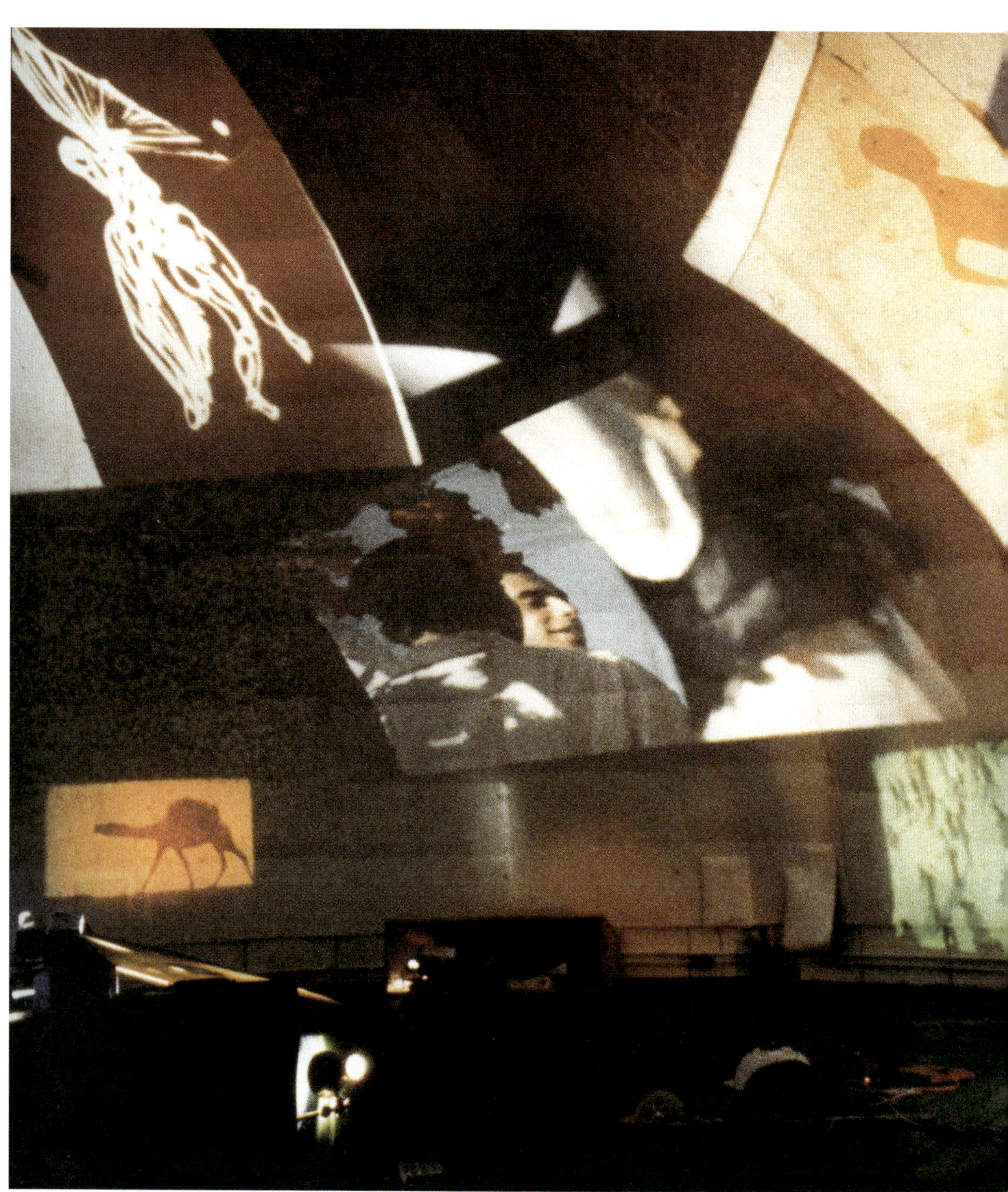

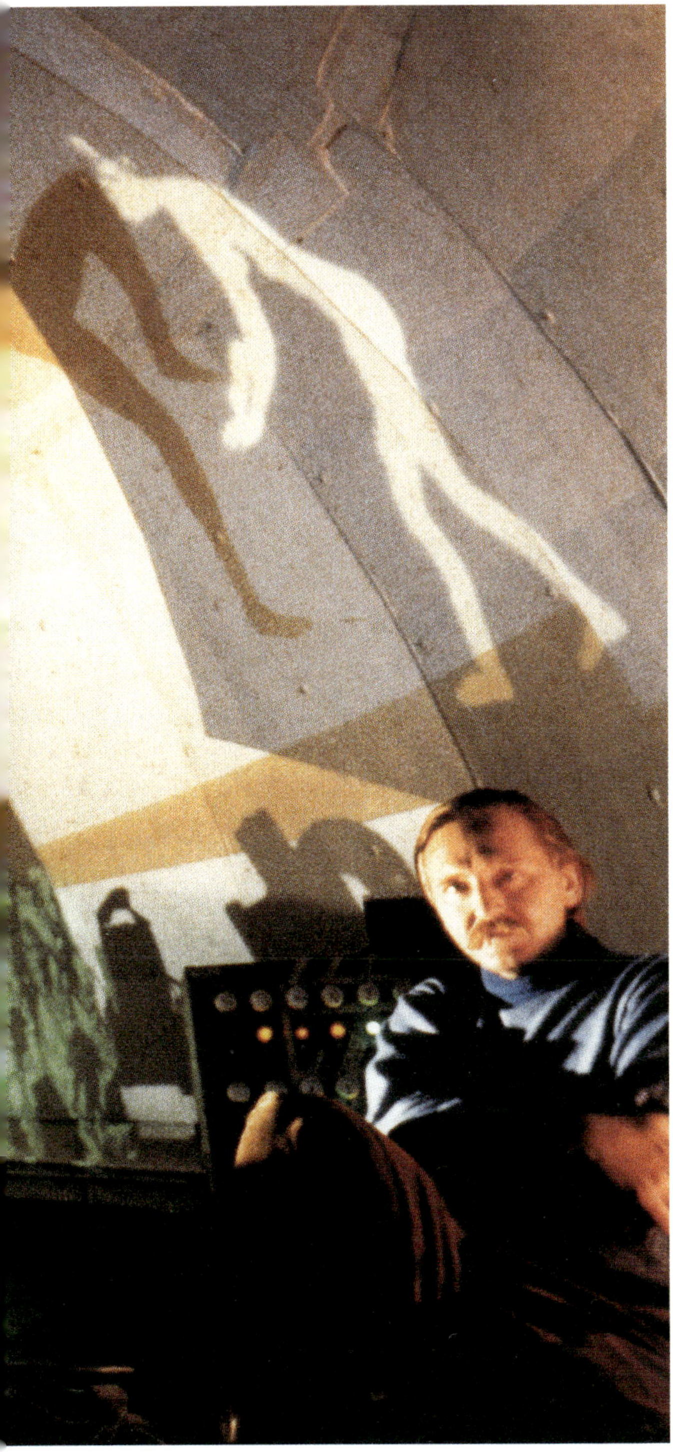

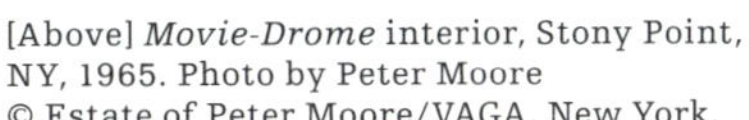

[Above] *Movie-Drome* interior, Stony Point,
NY, 1965. Photo by Peter Moore
© Estate of Peter Moore/VAGA, New York.

[Right] All: Stan VanDerBeek in his studio,
Stony Point, NY, 1965.

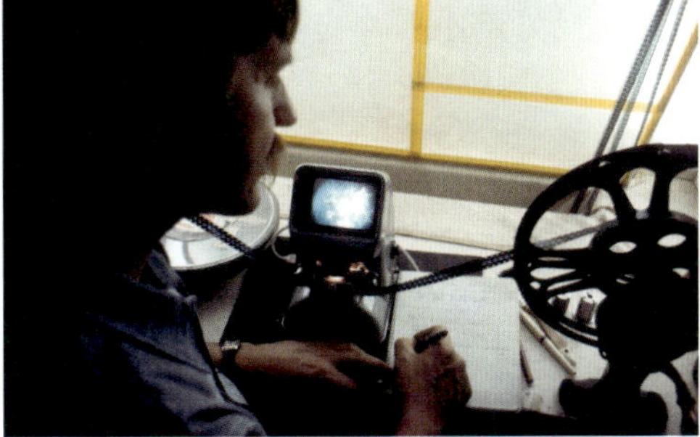

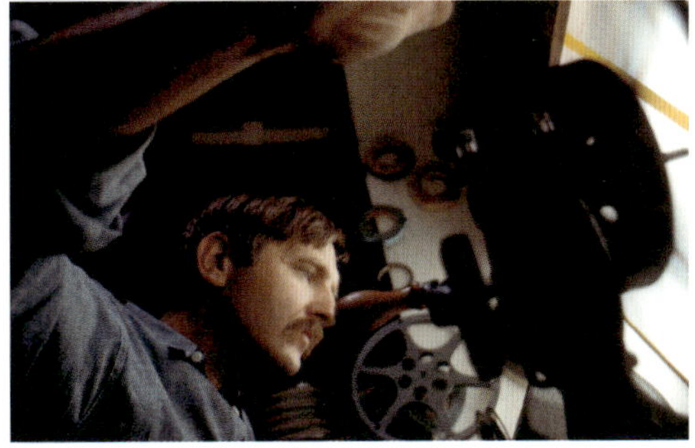

Movie-Drome, 1963–65

From 1963 to 1965, Stan VanDerBeek
constructed a "dome-studio-laboratory-
theatre" in Stony Point, New York, to present
multiple film projection environments. The
31-foot-high structure, called the *Movie-
Drome*, was assembled from a variety of
materials. The site on which the dome was
built was known as the Gate Hill Co-op, or
"The Land," whose residents included David
Tudor, John Cage, M.C. Richards, and Merce
Cunningham, among other Black Mountain
alumni.[3] Projected on the curved walls were
a variety of juxtaposed images culled from
disparate source material, including "old,
new, [and] junk film...slides, film strips or
clips...old magazines, (with pictures) books,
engravings, old photographs, photostats,
[and] negatives." This material was used to
create mosaics utilizing various kinds of
optical and sound equipment, including film
and slide projections. The result was an ever-
changing multimedia array of images and
sounds. VanDerBeek conceived of combining
such audiovisual environments into a
"culture-intercom"; further domes scattered
about the world would receive transmissions
by satellite.

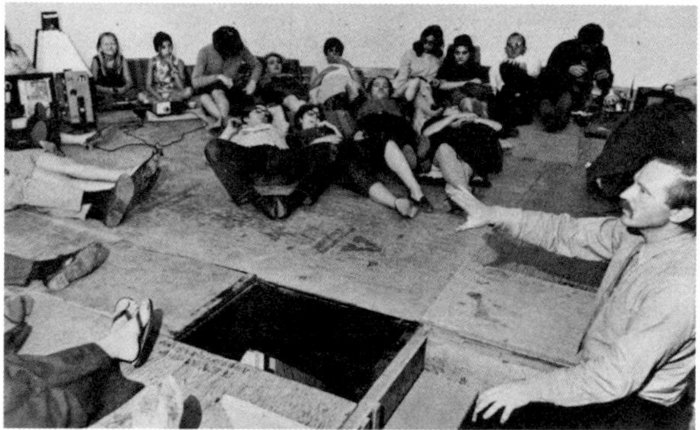

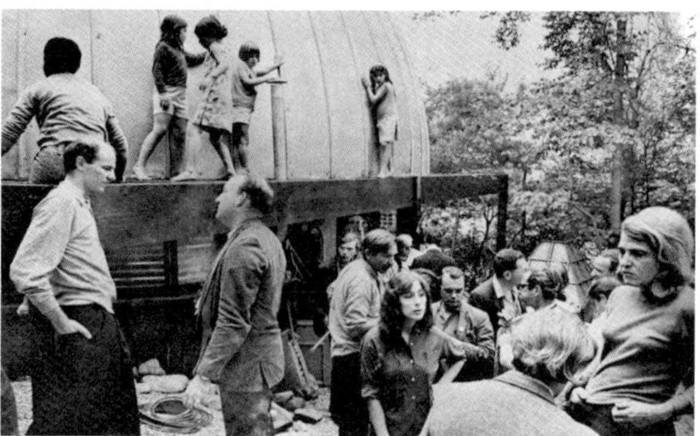

[Above] *Movie-Drome* performance
documentation, Stony Point, New York,
from *Film Culture* 40, (Spring 1966).

[Right] *Untitled (drawing)*, ca. 1963–67.
Ink on paper, 11 x 8 in.

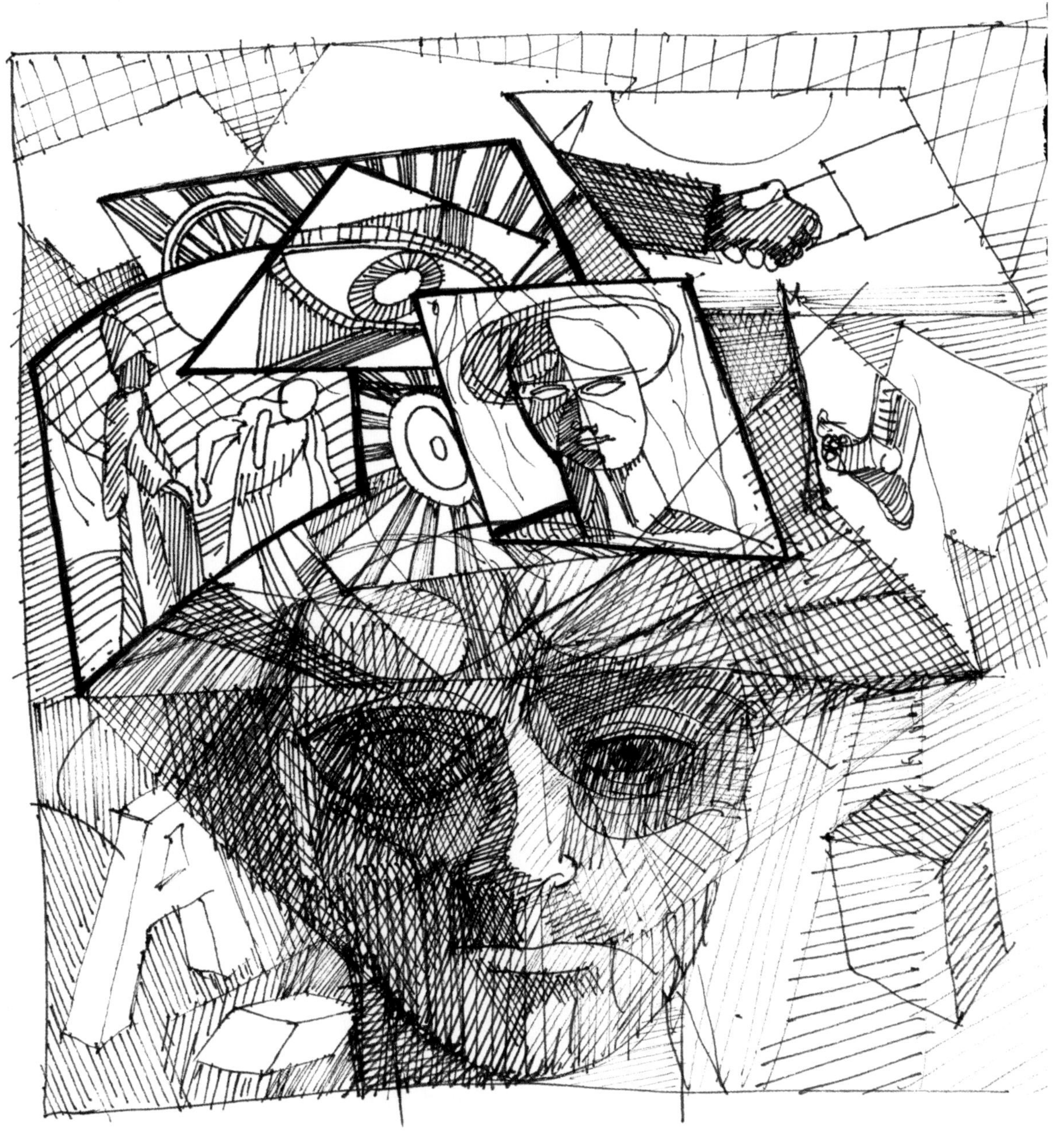

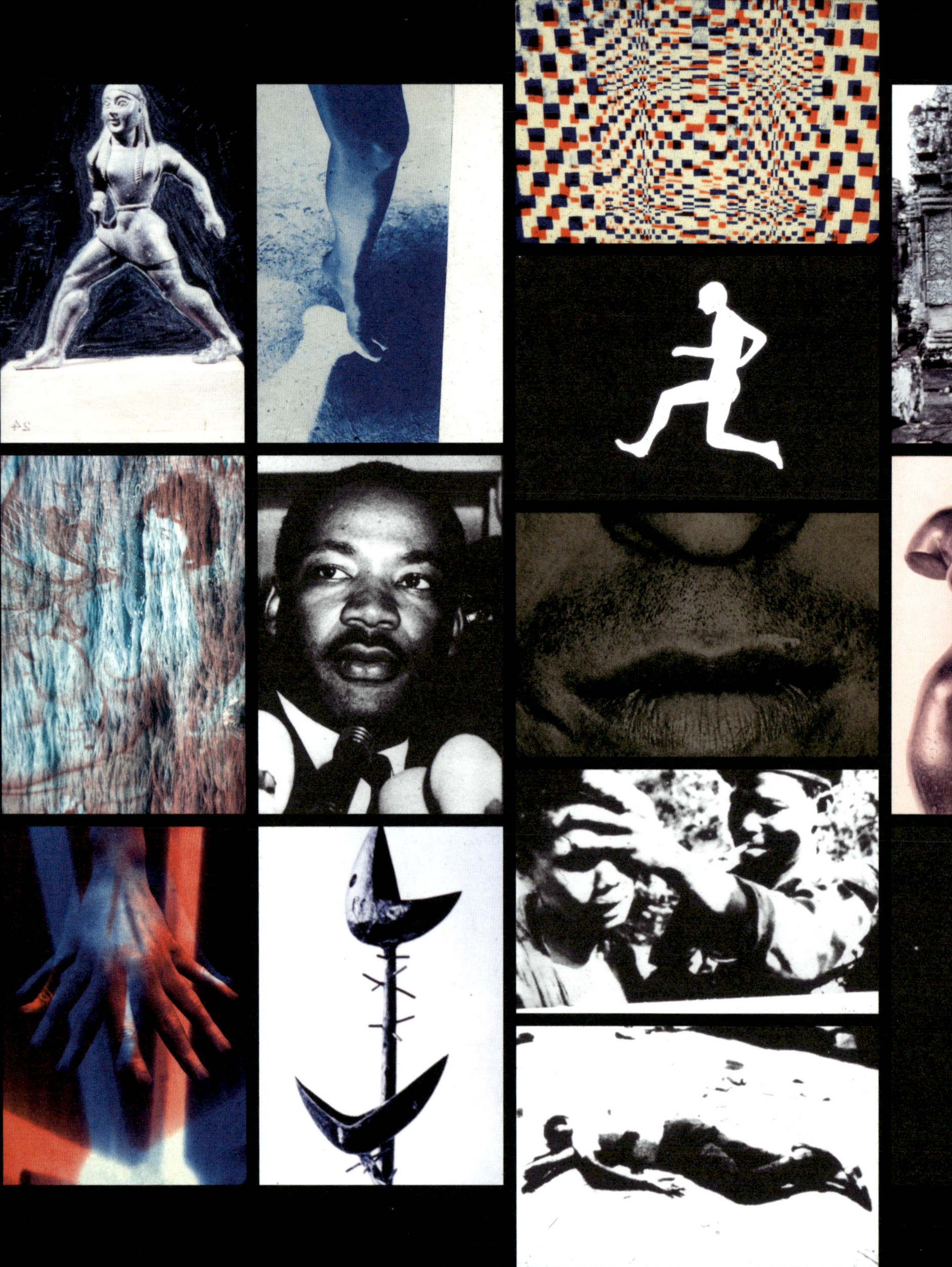

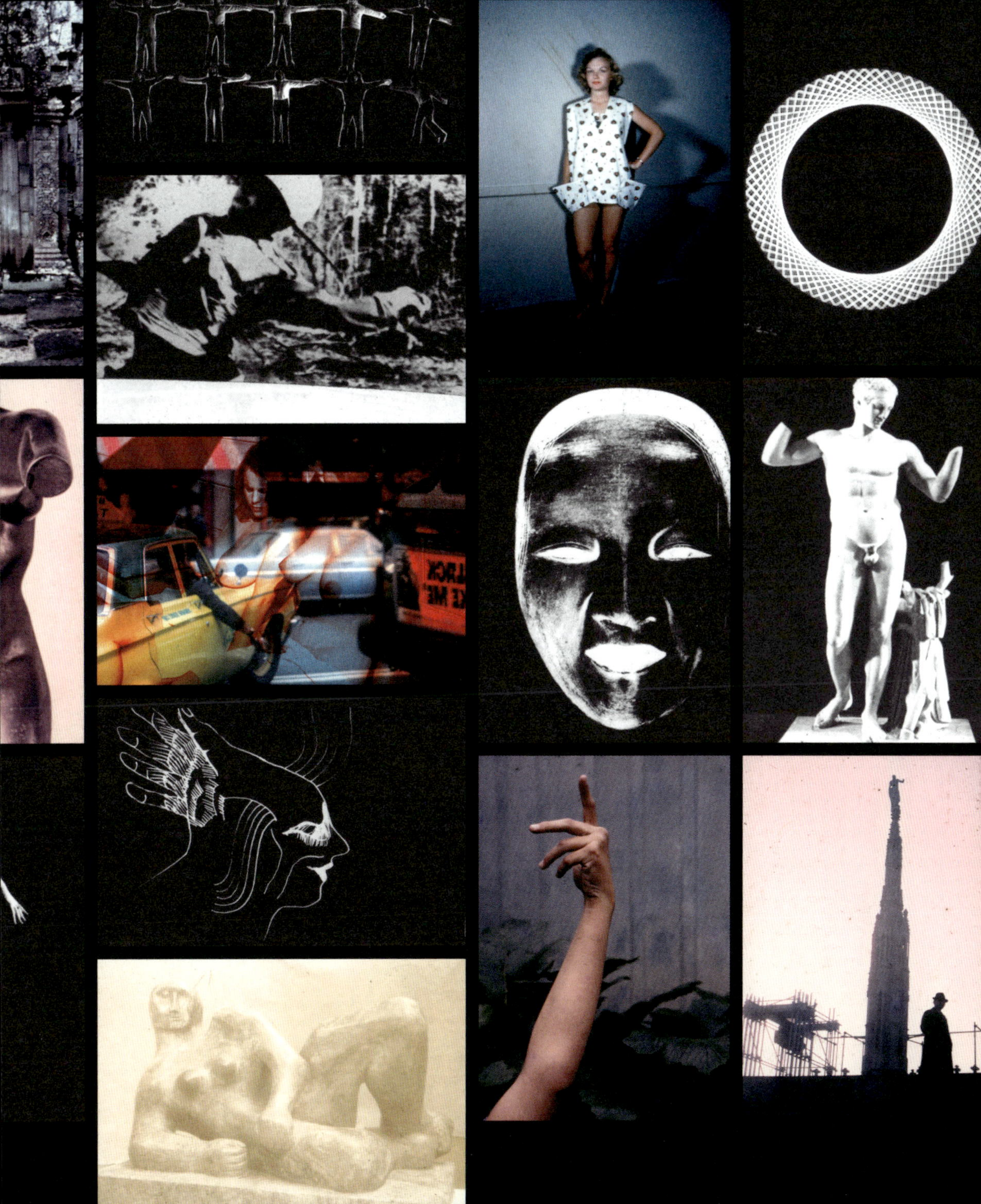

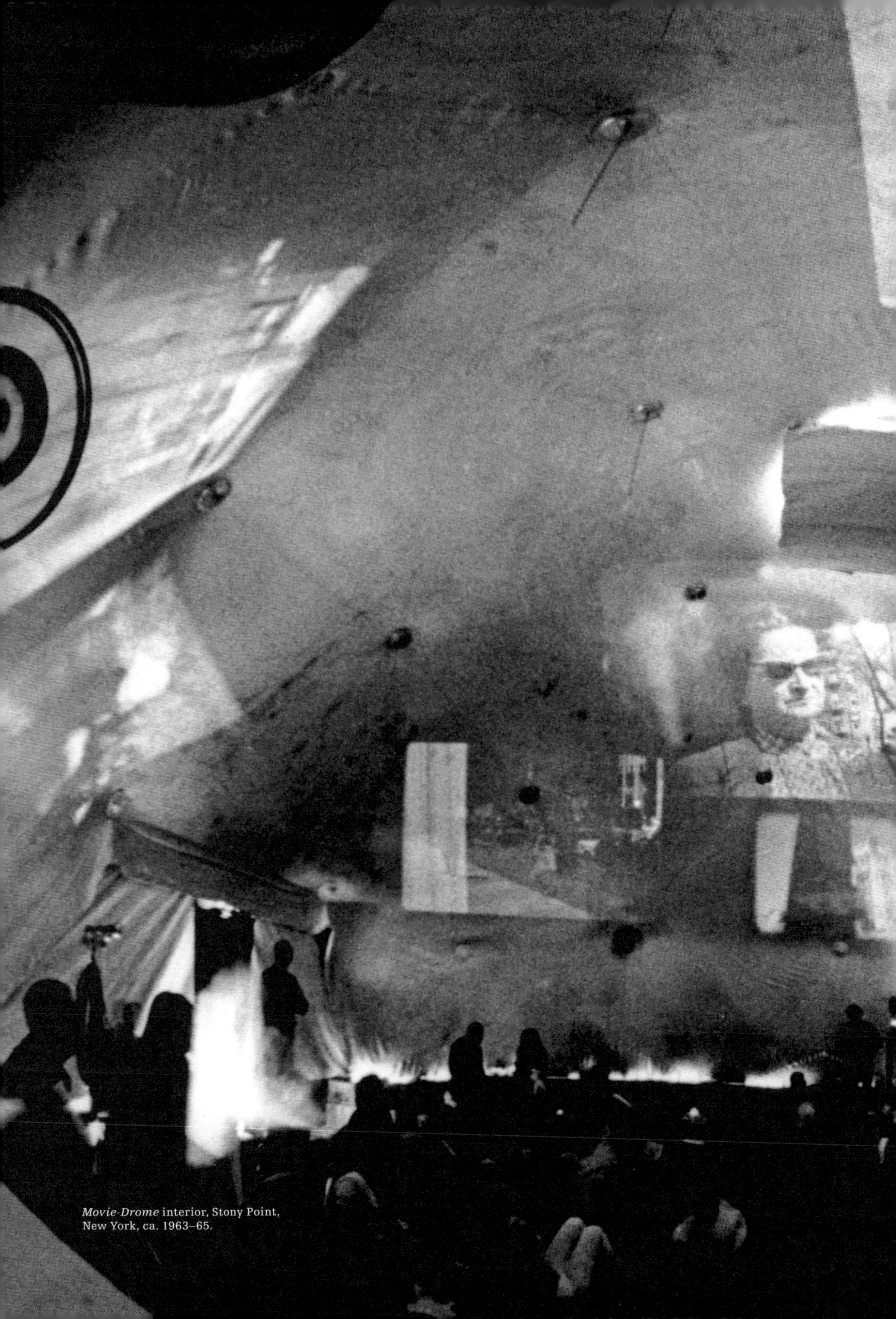

Movie-Drome interior, Stony Point,
New York, ca. 1963–65.

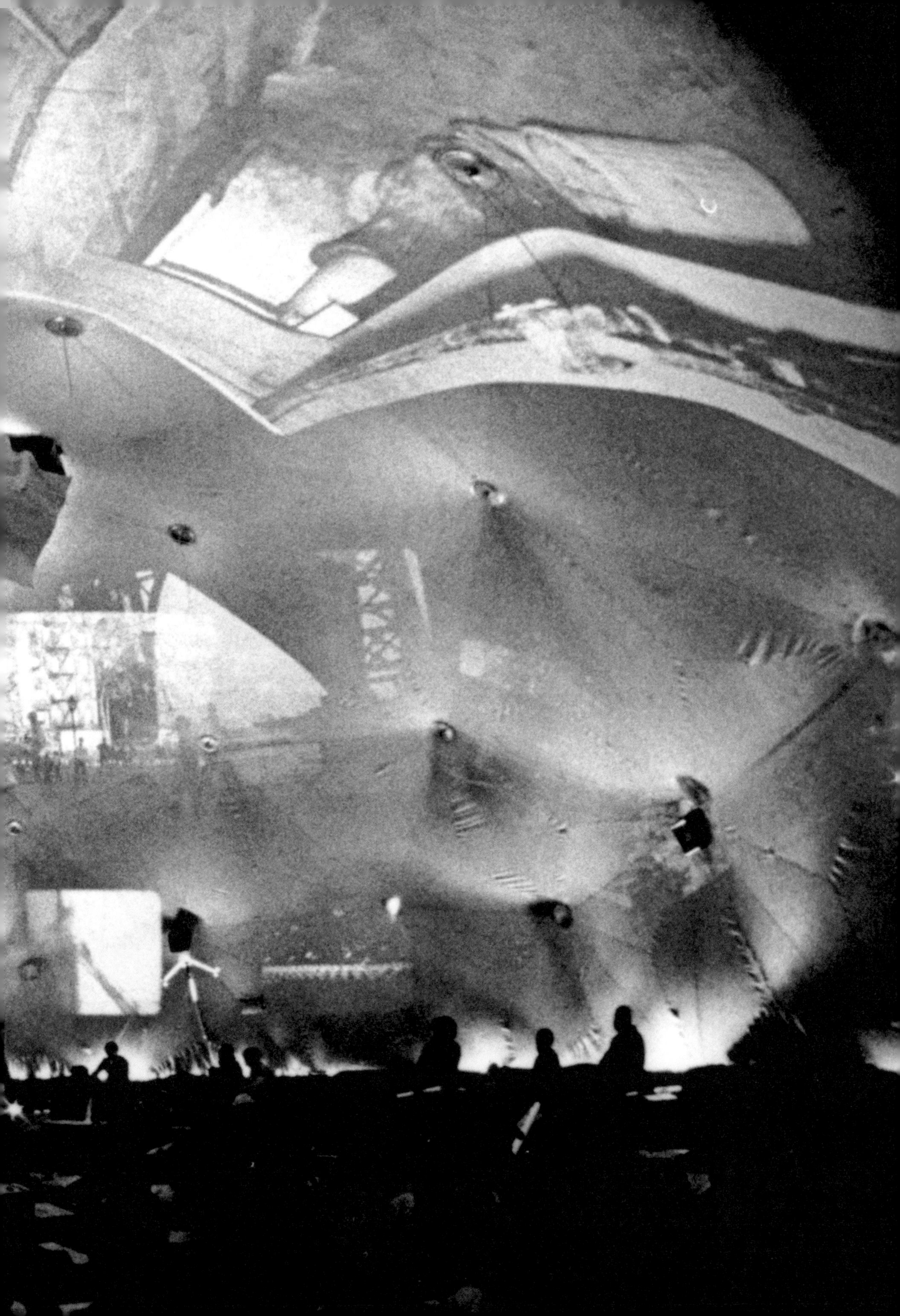

Variations V, 1965

Composer John Cage conceived of *Variations V* for the Merce Cunningham Dance Company in 1965. Part of his composition called for a system allowing sounds to be brought about by movement. A series of 10 directional photo-cells, designed by composer and pianist David Tudor and engineer Billy Klüver, were wired to tape-recorders and short-wave radios, activated as the dancers crossed their path, with Cage, Tudor, and Gordon Mumma operating equipment to modify the sounds.[4] Films by VanDerBeek were projected on a series of screens. VanDerBeek's selections were a characteristic mix of archival newsreel footage and popular film and television programs. The piece was first performed at Philharmonic Hall in New York City on July 23, 1965.[5] In 1966, the collaborators produced a 50-minute film version directed by Arne Arnborn at Norddeutscher Rundfunk in Hamburg, Germany, which included television manipulations by Nam June Paik.

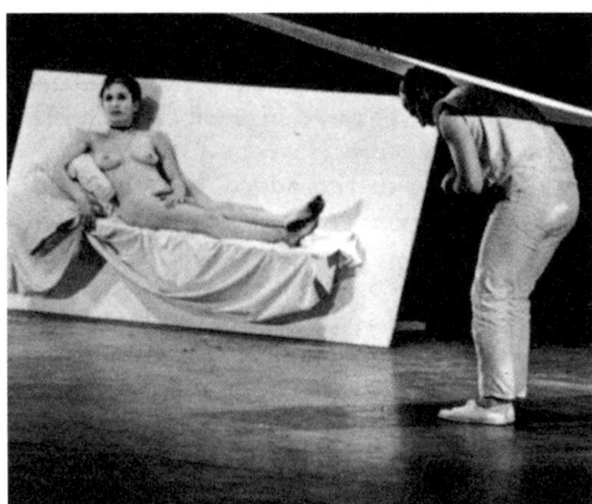

[Left] All: *Site*, 1964. 16mm, black and white, silent, 10 min. Robert Morris, Carolee Schneeman, and Stan VanDerBeek.

[Right] All: *Variations V*, 1964–66.

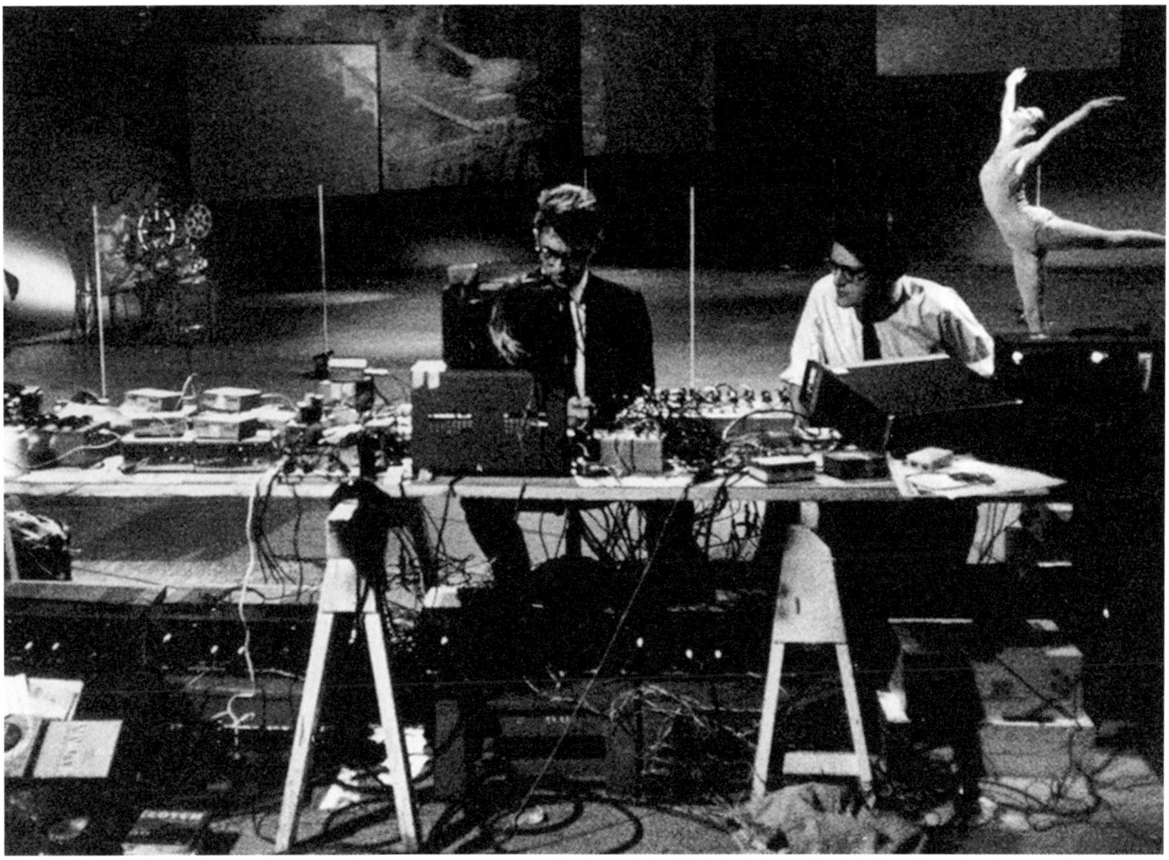

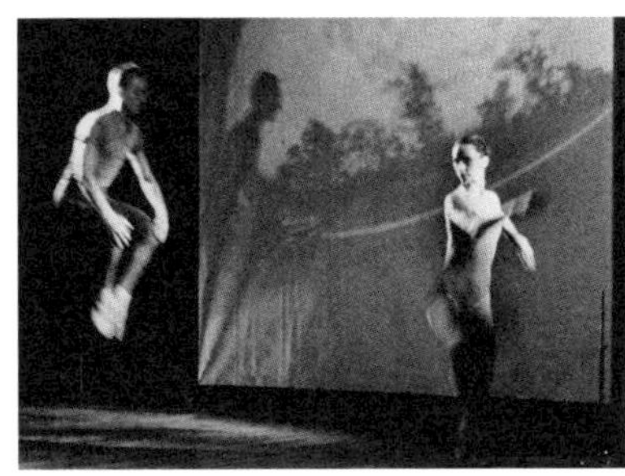
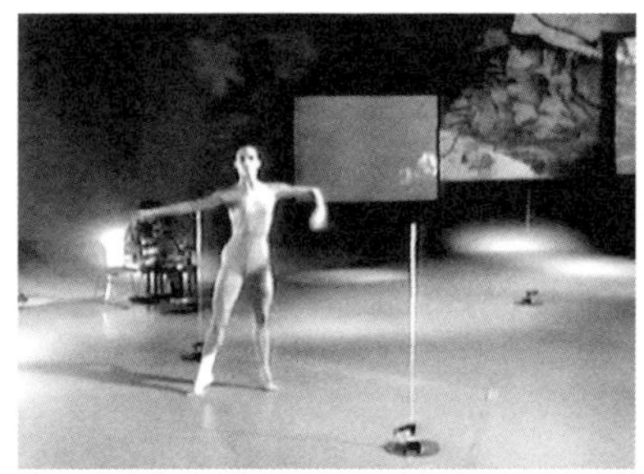
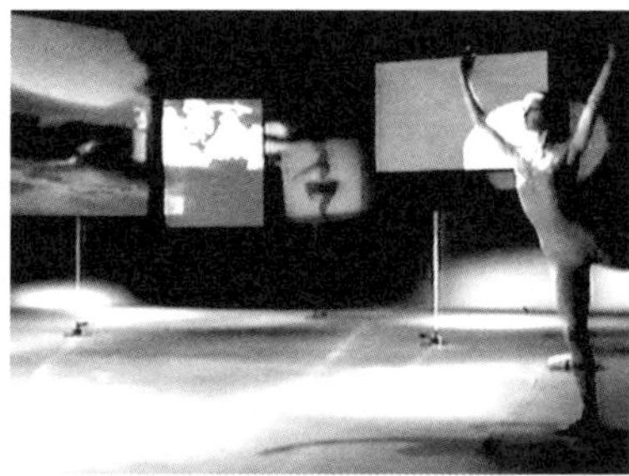

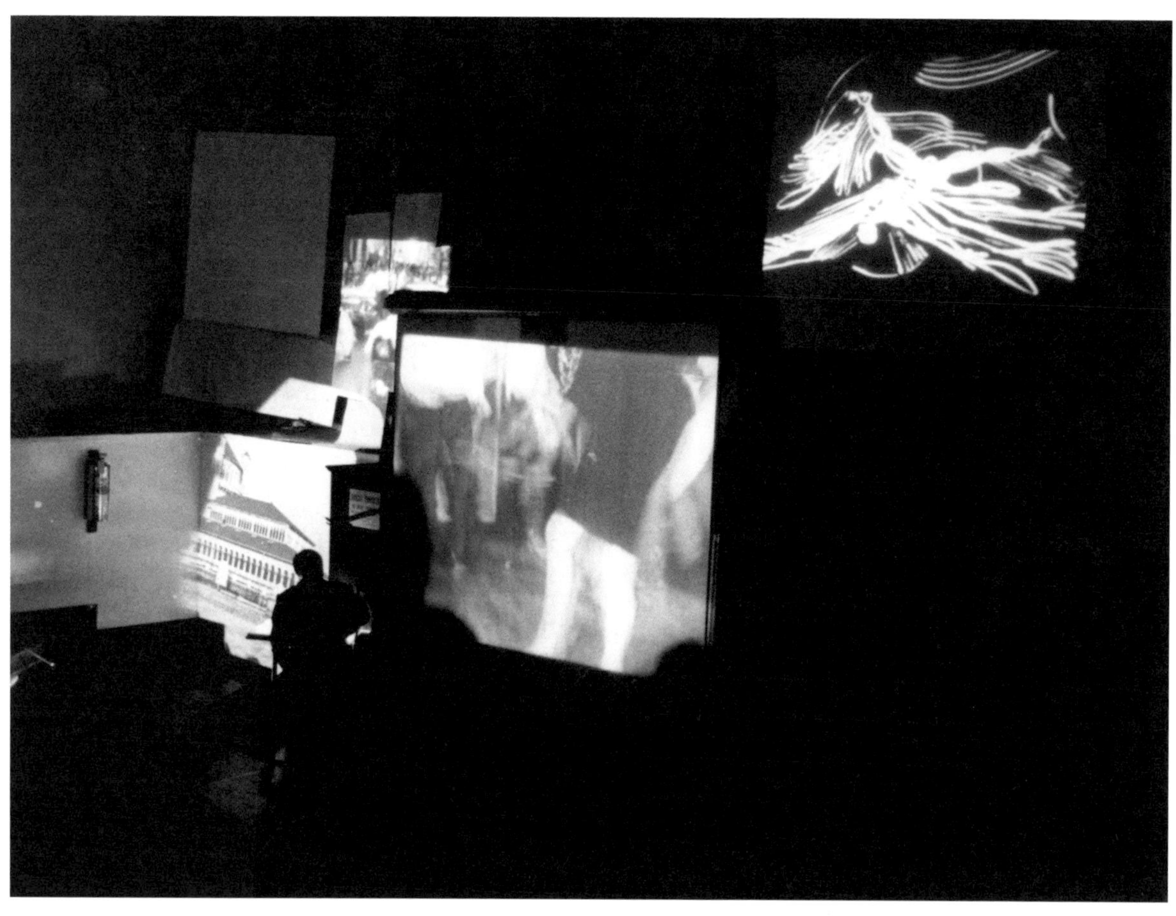

[Above] *Panels for the Walls of the World.*
Installation view, The School of Visual Arts,
New York, ca. 1965.

[Right: Top] *Untitled (Mankinda),* 1957.
Painted animation frame, 12 1/2 x 20 in.

[Right: Center] *Untitled (Mankinda),* 1957.
Painted animation frame, 13 1/2 x 21 in.

[Right: Bottom] Stan VanDerBeek performing as part of *Panels for the Walls of the
World.* The School of Visual Arts, New York,
ca. 1965.

Movie Mural, 1968
Found Forms, 1969

In the early 1960s, Stan VanDerBeek began to
experiment with multiple projection environments of image and sound. These multi-image
arrays, or "movie murals," were comprised
of material drawn from a variety of sources,
including VanDerBeek's own films. Part of the
artist's research into a "non-verbal, international picture language" that could transform
cinema into "a tool for world communication,"
these immersive projection environments—
"collages of media," as one contemporary film
critic called them—would allow for the transmission of vast amounts of information via
optical communication.

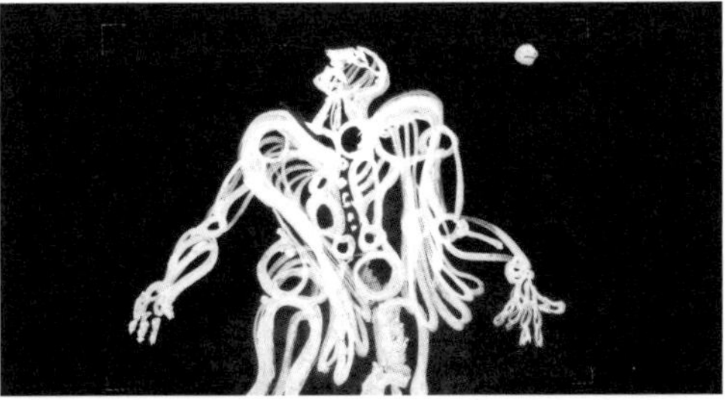

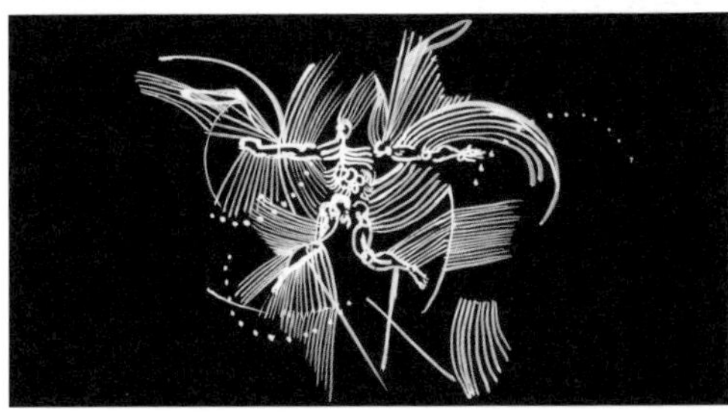

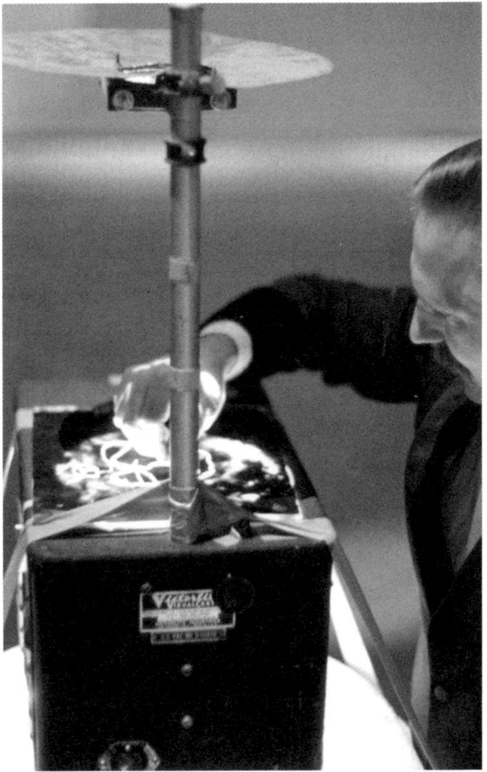

[Below] *Panels for the Walls of the World*.
Installation view, The School of Visual Arts,
New York, ca. 1965.

[Right] Stan VanDerBeek in front of *Movie
Mural*. Installation view, Institute of
Contemporary Art, Boston, MA, ca. 1968.

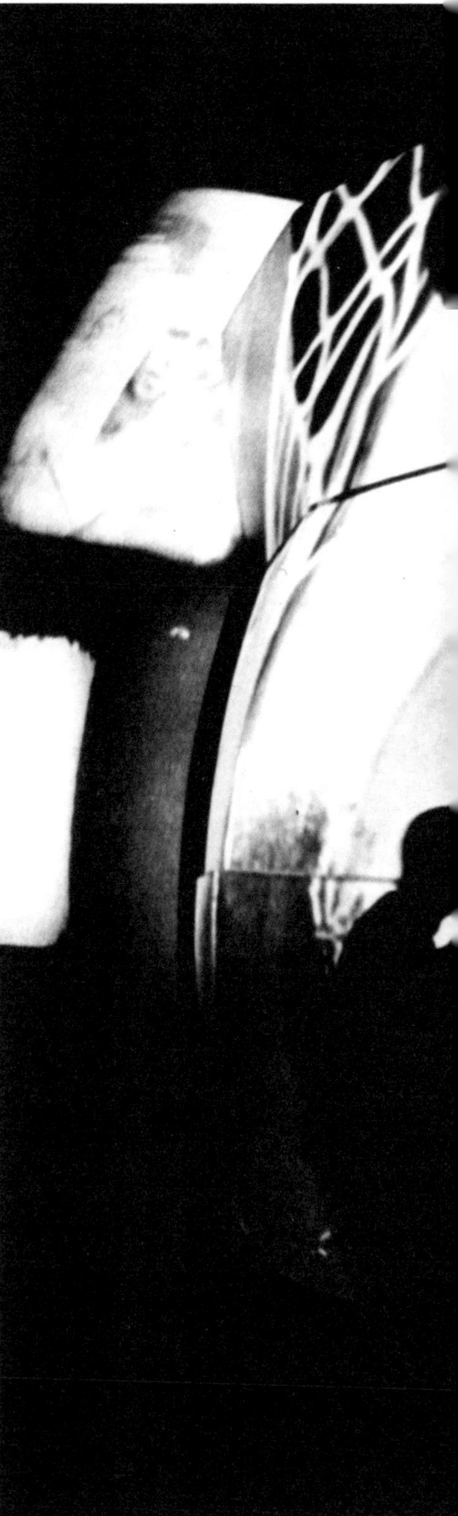

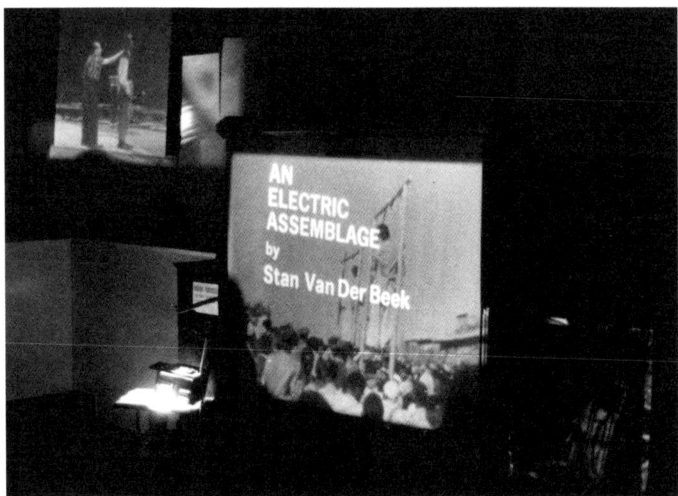

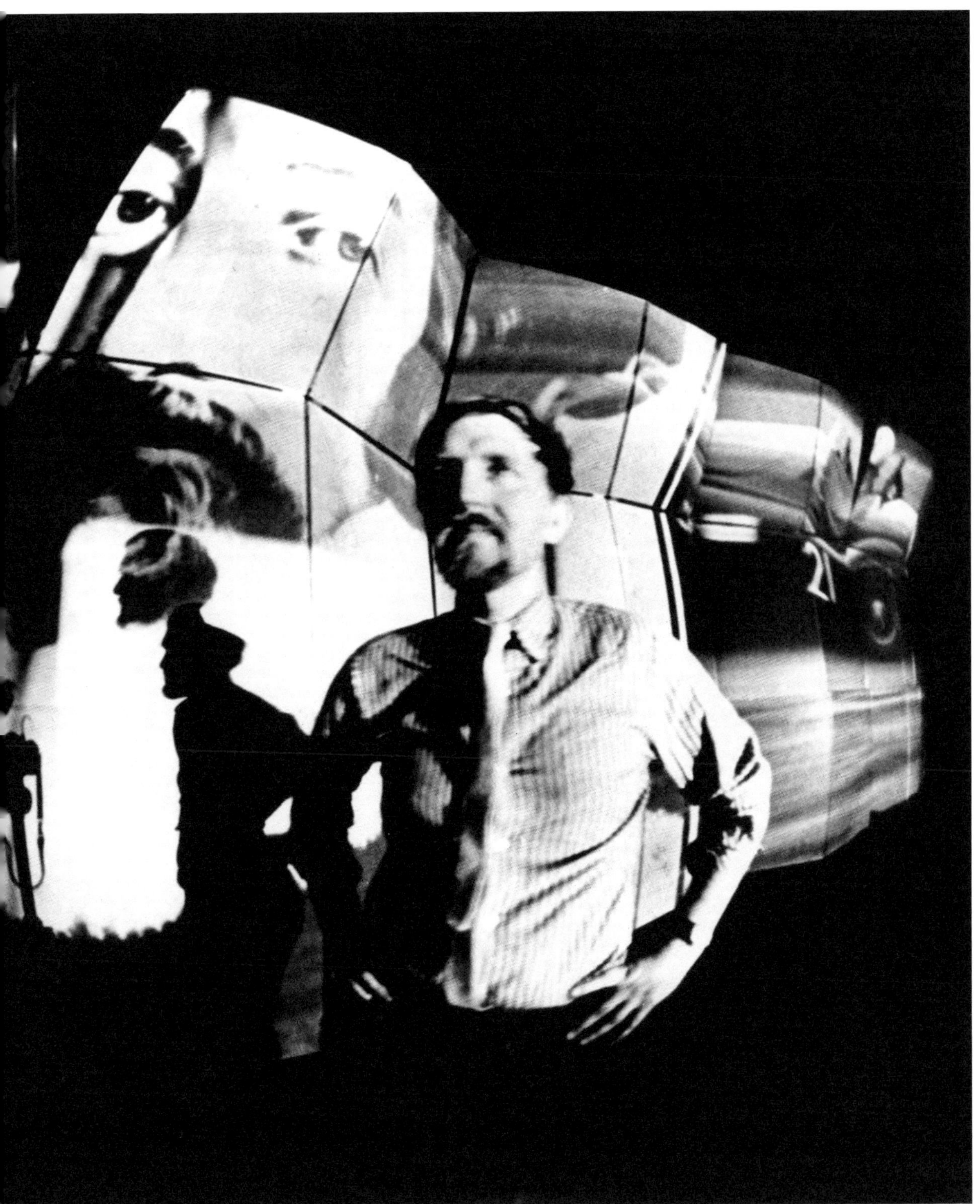

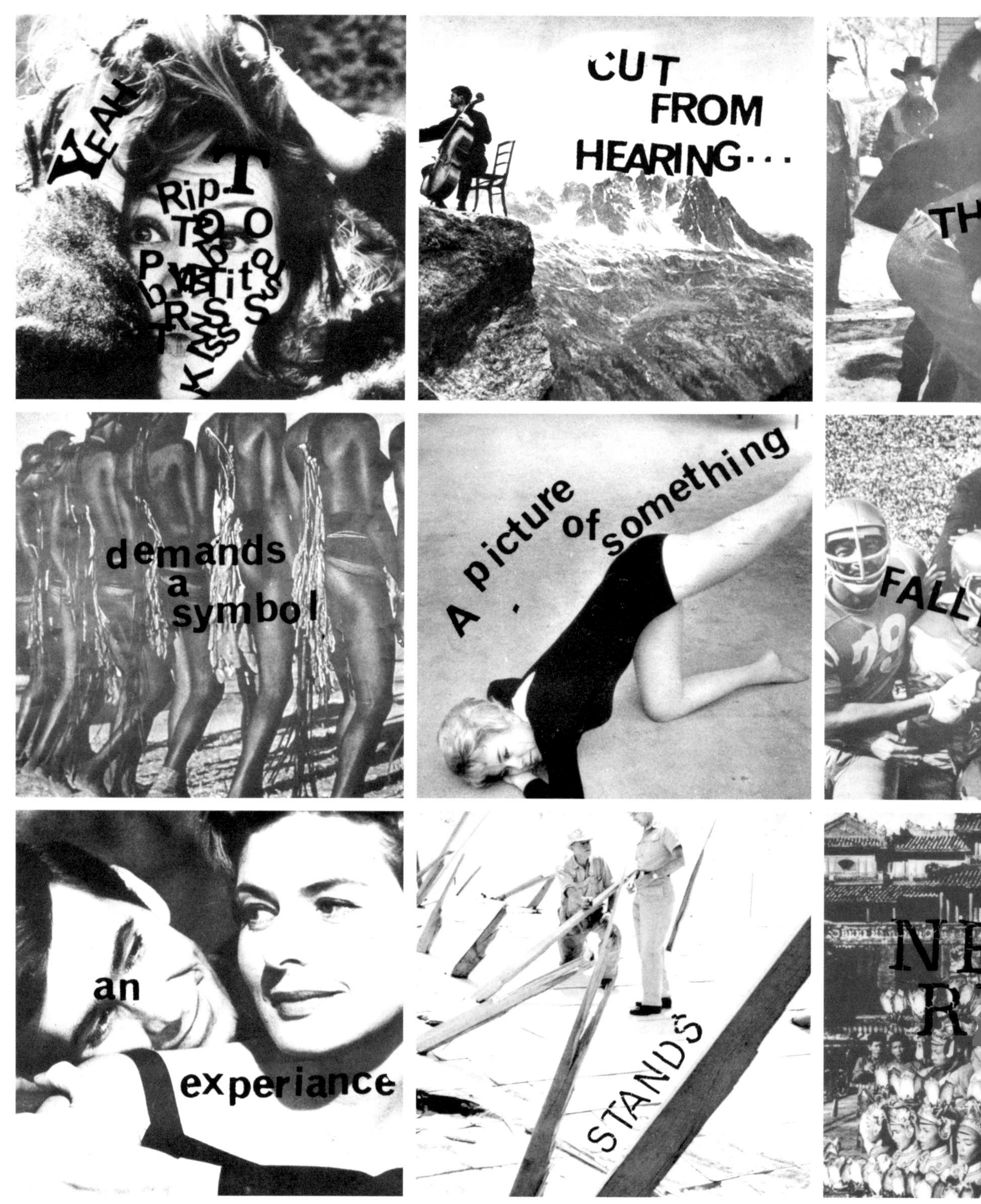

All: *Untitled*, Collage on handmade slides,
used in multi-media installations, n.d.

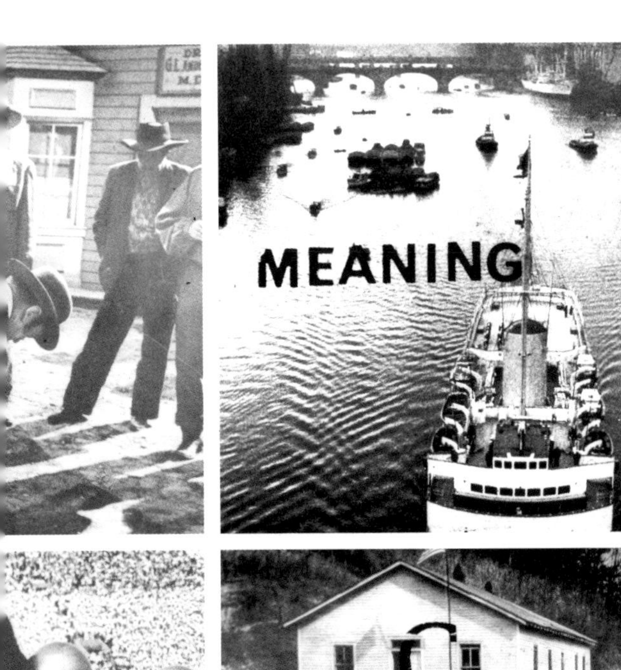
MEANING

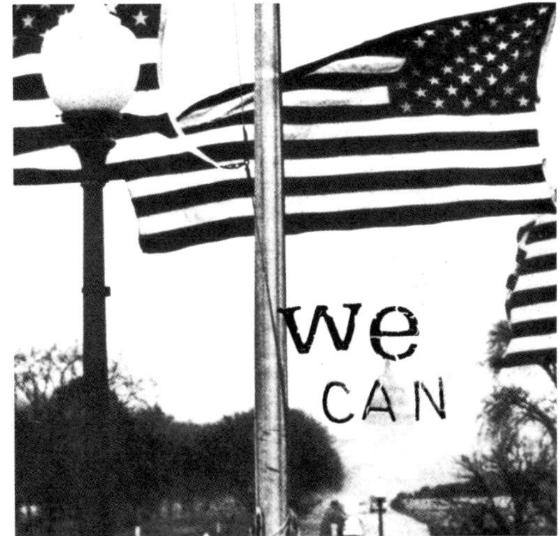
we
CAN

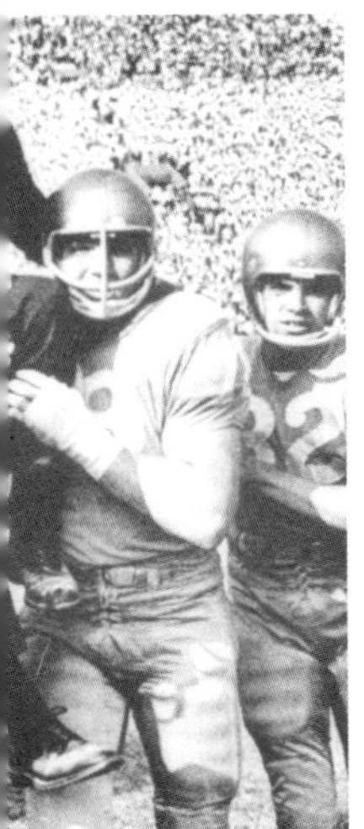

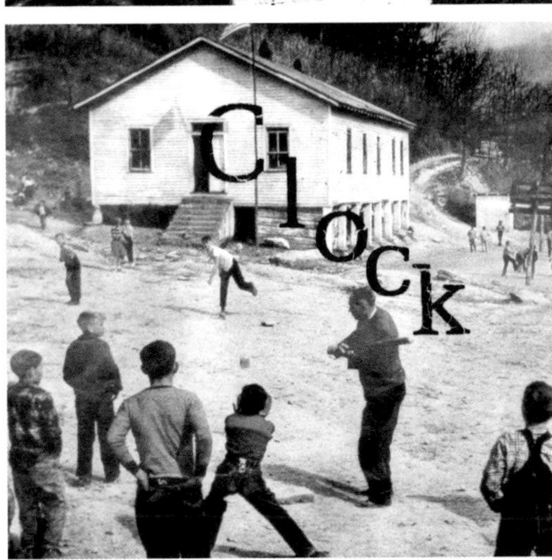
ClOCk

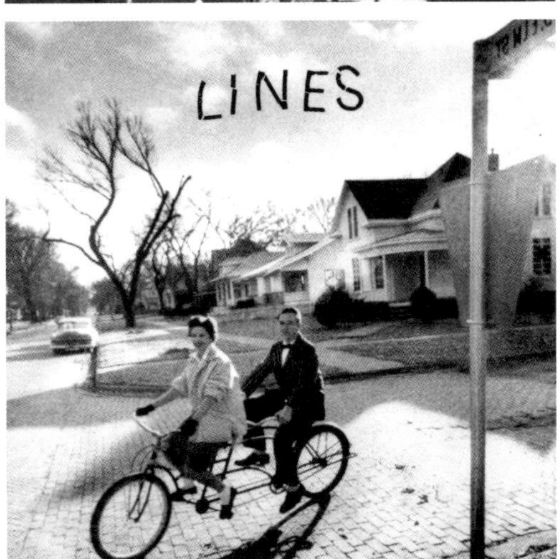
LINES

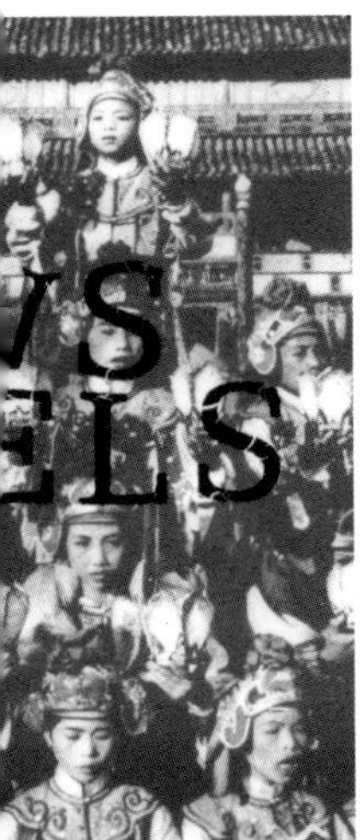

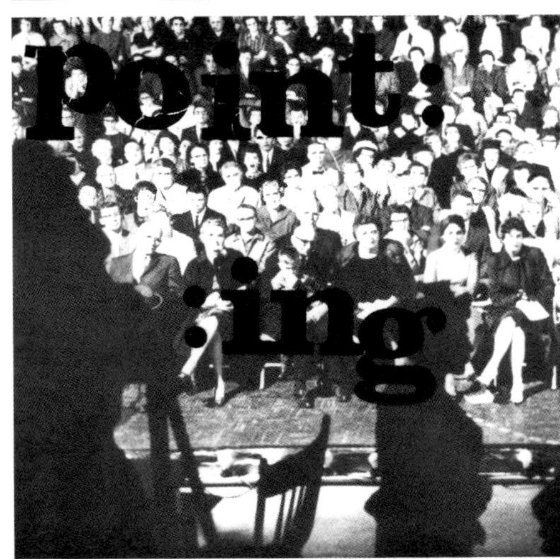
point:
:ing

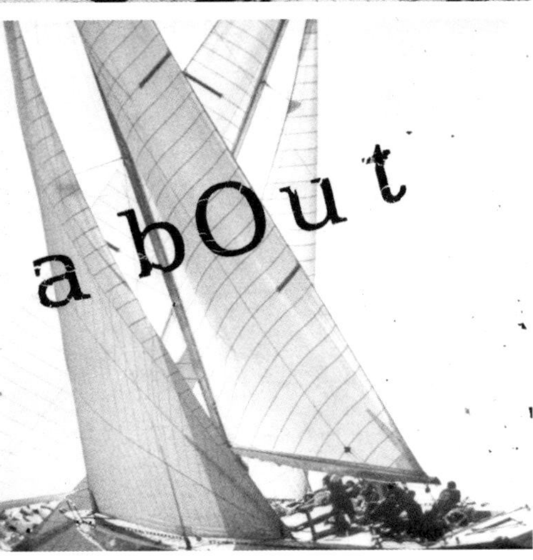
a bOut

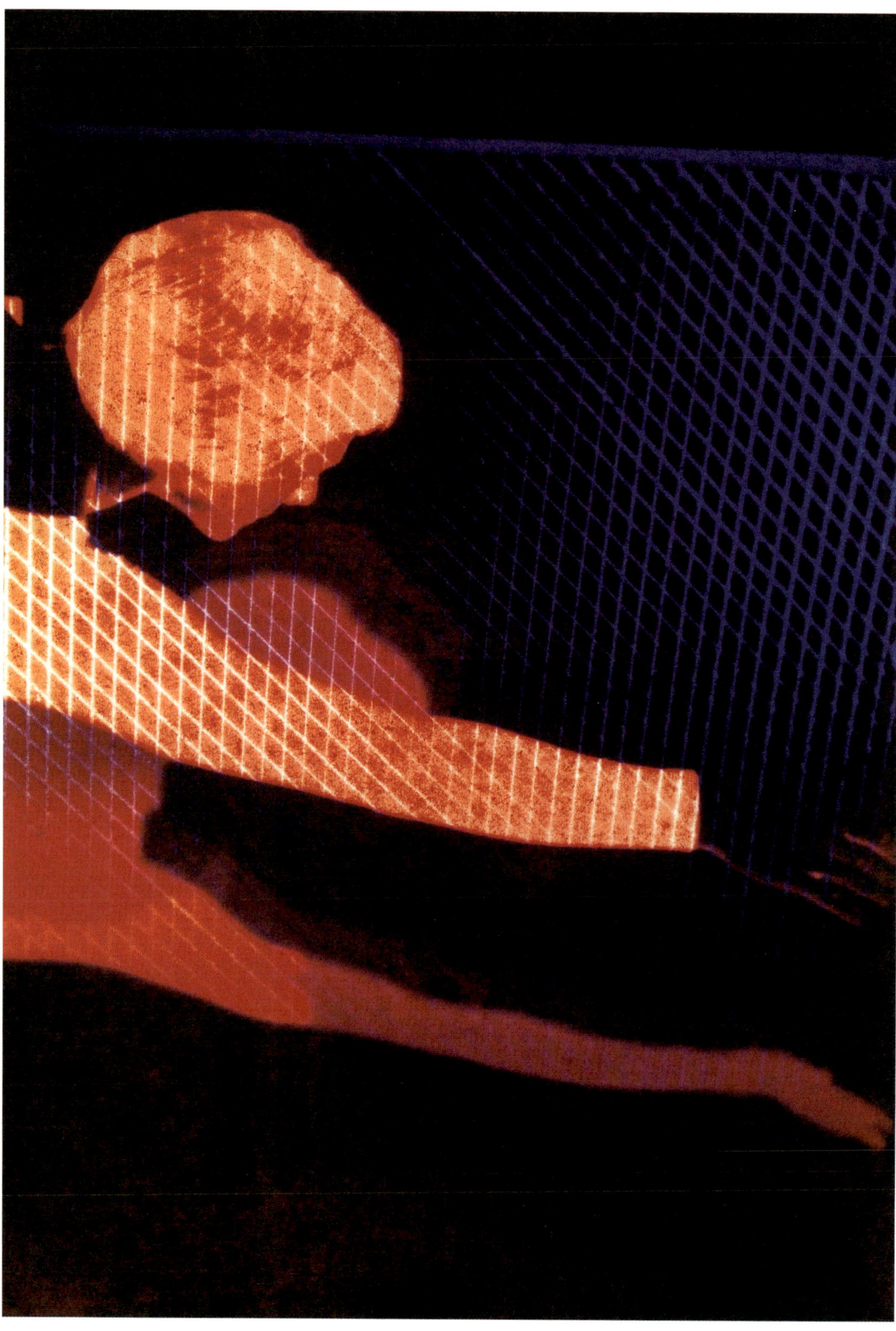

Feedback, 35mm slide projection image, 1967.

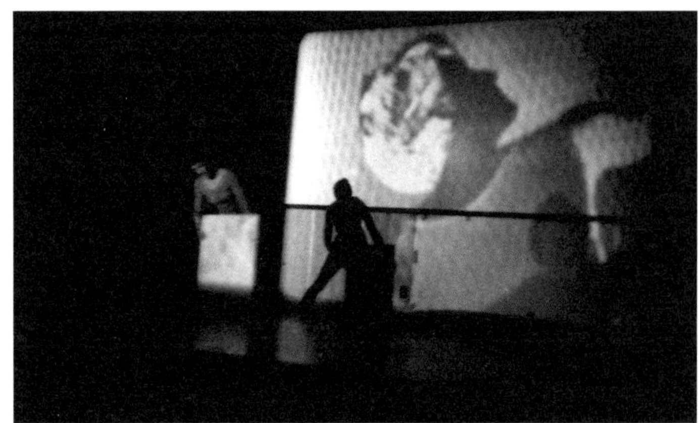

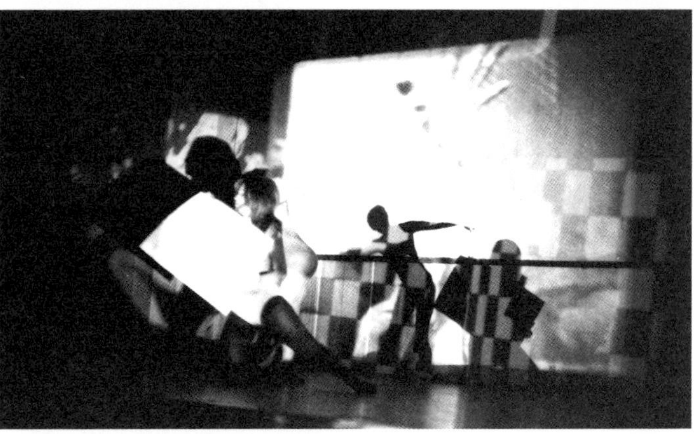

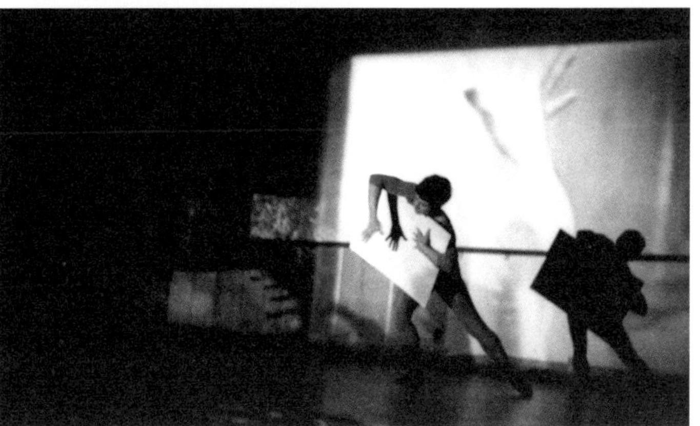

All: *Feedback*. Installation view and
performance, University of Southern
California, Los Angeles, CA, 1967.

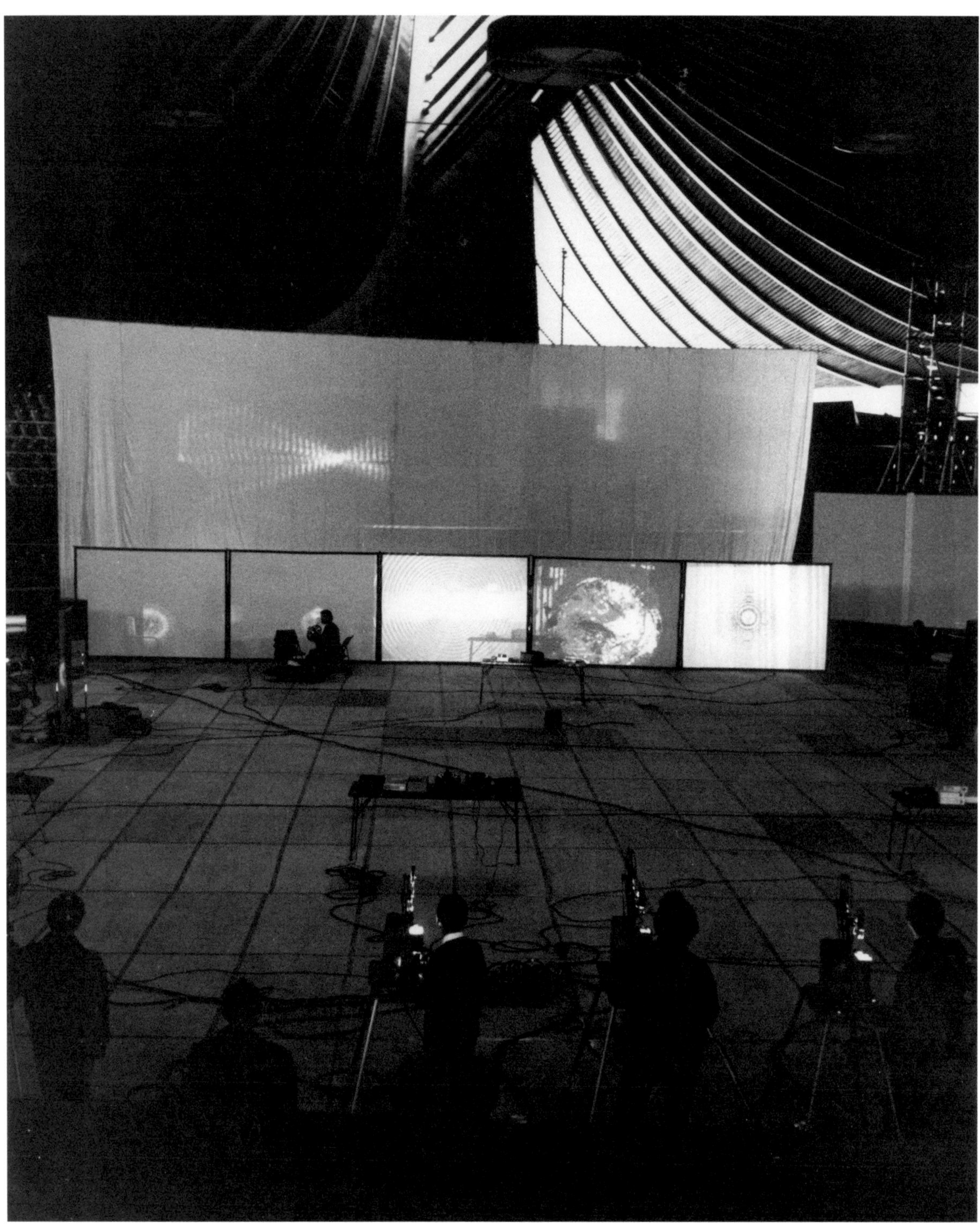
Found Forms. Installation view,
Cross Talk Intermedia, Japan, 1969.

Stan VanDerBeek
The Culture Intercom

Stan VanDerBeek: The Culture Intercom

MIT List Visual Arts Center
Contemporary Arts Museum Houston

Curators
Bill Arning
João Ribas

Essayists
Bill Arning
Mark Bartlett
Jacob Proctor
João Ribas
Gloria Sutton
Michael Zryd

Table of Contents

Foreword

As directors of relatively small-scale contemporary arts museums, we take great pleasure in having a collaborative relationship with another museum that brings out the best in both institutions. This is the second partnership of the MIT List Visual Arts Center and the Contemporary Arts Museum Houston, two venues with modest staffs and budgets, which are nonetheless internationally known for the strength of their exhibitions.

The two shows we have realized together could not be more different. *Matthew Day Jackson: The Immeasurable Distance* was the exhibition of a then-emerging artist who was making new work until the opening day of the show. In fact, he added new works between venues; such is the nature of his fecund creativity.

On the other hand, *Stan VanDerBeek: The Culture Intercom* is the retrospective of a new media pioneer who died in 1984, and whose important and powerful works have been progressively harder to experience since that time. In anticipation of the 150th anniversary of MIT's founding, the List Center began considering the many important artists who had made strides in their work while working at the Institute. Stan VanDerBeek was a significant example of an artist who came and—upon discovering what he could do with the available resources—stayed; and in fact returned as often as he could until months before his untimely death. Houston also appeared as a frequent stop in his professional wanderings. To have the exhibition follow the artist's footsteps 40 years later is sweetly poetic.

Sara and Johannes VanDerBeek have spent untold hours working to ensure their father's legacy, combing through storage spaces and painstakingly archiving materials, to which they generously granted us access. While their dedication to their father's memory is profoundly touching, and we hope we have done justice to the familial love manifested in their labors, it is their significant service to art history—restoring this crucial figure to his rightful place—that will be most remembered. It has been a privilege to be a part of that process.

Roger Conover, Executive Editor at the MIT Press, played a crucial roll in bringing the pieces of this puzzle together by introducing us to Mark Bartlett, theorist of techno-culture and VanDerBeek scholar. We are very grateful for Mark Bartlett's early, important contributions to this project and for his insightful essay and editorial contributions to this publication. It was also a wonderful stroke of luck when João Ribas joined the List team, as he had also been researching VanDerBeek for his critically-lauded exhibition *FAX*, organized with Independent Curators International. His way of considering VanDerBeek's work has added much fresh perspective to the project. This volume's texts are the work of many minds. The essayists Jacob Proctor, Gloria Sutton, and Michael Zryd have all brought their deep knowledge and unique and sometimes contradictory interpretations of VanDerBeek's work, and for that we are very grateful. Together, the texts make for a compelling and complex discussion of an artist who will attract more critical discussion as the effects of this publication and exhibition reverberate through the field.

Support for this exhibition has been provided by the Art Mentor Foundation, Lucerne, and the National Endowment for the Arts, a Federal agency. In addition, the List Visual Arts Center is grateful for the support of Martin E. Zimmerman, the Council for the Arts at MIT, the Massachusetts Cultural Council, and the Phoenix Media/Communications Group.

On behalf of the MIT team, we would like to thank Philip Khoury, MIT's Associate Provost and Ford International Professor of History; Leila Kinney, Director of Arts Initiatives; and the List Center Advisory Committee for their continuing support of the LVAC and its programs. We are grateful to Curator João Ribas for his hard work in organizing this exhibition and for his insightful catalogue essay. We also appreciate the unstinting efforts of Exhibition Designer Tim Lloyd, Assistant Director David Freilach, Registrars John Rexine and Diane Karlik, Educator/Public Relations Officer Mark Linga, Administrative Assistant Barbra Pine, Public Art Curator Alise Upitis, Preparator John Osorio-Buck, Web Wizard Danielle LaFountaine, and Gallery Attendants Sue Bright, Karen Fegley, Kristin Johnson, Bryce Kauffman, and Suara Welitoff. We especially thank LVAC intern Alex Jacobson for his contributions to this exhibition; and we also thank interns Anum Awan, Noelle DeMers, Krysten Keches, Angelika Li, Catherine McMahon, Jennifer Nichols, Zsuzsanna Szegedi, Annebel Yu, and Madeline Zappala for their willing and capable help with the catalogue and the exhibition.

On behalf of the Contemporary Arts Museum Houston, we would like to express gratitude to The Brown Foundation, Inc., which has continued its generous support of our publications program. CAMH is also particularly appreciative of the support we have received from our donors to the Museum's Major Exhibition Fund, which allows us to mount shows that would be too difficult at many museums. CAMH is also very thankful to David Young for the support the Union Pacific Corporation has given towards the Houston presentation of this exhibition.

CAMH's staff has enthusiastically involved themselves with this visionary's work. Senior Curator Valerie Cassel Oliver and Curatorial Manager Justine Waitkus have both been unflagging in their devotion to this project. Special thanks are due to Paula Newton and Peter Lucas for shepherding the live public programs that will bring VanDerBeek's work vividly back to life. We are also grateful to our colleagues at the Houston Museum of Natural Science, especially Nancy Lauletta-Bowen, for inviting audiences to their planetarium to experience an evening of projected media under a dome in homage to VanDerBeek's *Cine Dreams* events. This would not have happened without CAMH's colleagues at The Aurora Picture Show, and we send our profound thanks to Mary Magsamen and Delicia Harvey for their enthusiasm.

This catalogue was designed by AHL&CO and we thank Peter and Joanna Ahlberg very much for their work on this project and in particular, the time they take to learn about and fully involve themselves in an artist's work. We also thank Esme Watanabe for her many contributions to the project.

It is a blessing when directors have teams like this with which to collaborate, with broad scopes of knowledge and passion. We look forward to many future collaborations.

—Jane Farver, *Director*,
MIT List Visual Arts Center

—Bill Arning, *Director*,
Contemporary Arts Museum Houston

Stan VanDerBeek's Currency

Bill Arning

It would be absurd to say Stan VanDerBeek invented, or even foresaw, the Internet and other manifestations of today's cyber reality, but it is impossible to read the essays in this volume or attend the exhibition *Stan VanDerBeek: The Culture Intercom* without being stunned by just how much he predicted in his works and writings. It is also astonishing to discover that VanDerBeek nearly disappeared from art history after his untimely death in 1984.

Despite his significant presence and influence during his lifetime, VanDerBeek's work failed to posthumously maintain the attention of those museum curators and art historians whose job it is to shed light on the sources of our contemporary postwar visual arts culture. His legacy was threatened with becoming just a tantalizing footnote in the development of media art, underground cinema, and expanded cinema (to use the three limited but known buzz-terms most often used to describe his oeuvre), when in fact he was a profoundly foundational artist in the development of those three now-ubiquitous art forms. *Stan VanDerBeek: The Culture Intercom* is a project of reclamation that endeavors not only to restore VanDerBeek's place in the pantheon of innovative artists, but also to make his achievements as available to future generations as they were to the artists who came to maturity in the 1970s.

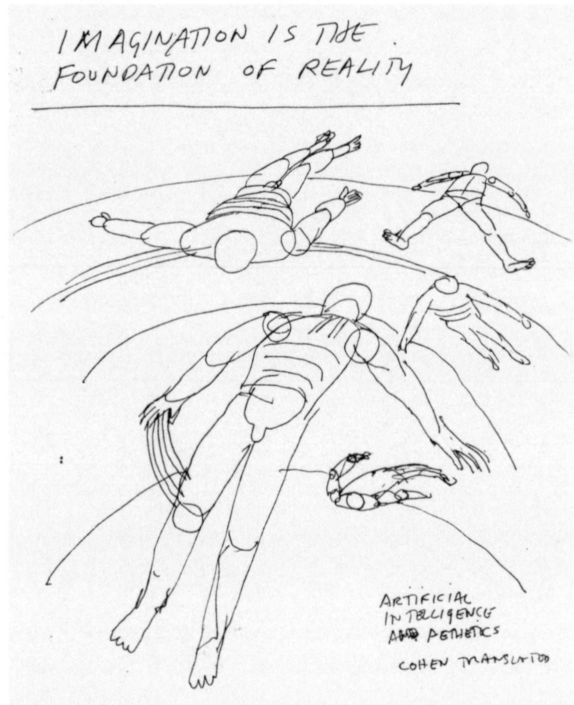

Untitled, n.d. Ink on paper, 11 x 8 1/2 in.

As the essays in this volume make clear, Van-
DerBeek rarely fits neatly in any single discourse.
Even when his work might formally have sat
comfortably under one rubric, such as the art-
and-technology initiatives of the late 1960s, his
manifesto-like writings show that he was always
seeking ways to counter simplistic utopian ideologies. In the same context, he can appear to be
the epitome of the zeitgeist—reveling in the new
connectedness possible on planet earth—or a
lone wolf who sees the dark cloud behind techno-
utopian thinking. One must admit it's a neat
trick for one mere artist.

VanDerBeek's 30-year trajectory began as a
visual artist, along with many of the great
artists of his period, at Black Mountain College
in North Carolina in the 1950s. There, he
made collages, drawings, and paintings, some
highlights of which we have included in this
exhibition and publication to make clear that
his work was grounded in the avant-garde of
his time. These works are charming and poetic,
and although some of his later motifs do first
appear in them, this is not the body of work
we claim as worthy of study today. Though he
was at the preeminent genius loci of the period,
working with the artists and teachers who are
the quintessential examples of a twentieth-
century avant-garde, he felt compelled to push
his work in even more radical directions. Stan
VanDerBeek was, by nature, unable to stay
within institutional or media boundaries.

VanDerBeek achieved his greatest fame in the
field of personal cinema (that made outside of
the commercial system) as an animator of some
of the most wildly eccentric films of the late
1950s and '60s, when underground film and its
support systems were being invented. While
he was not the only practitioner who began
as a visual artist and later—chafing at the
limits of static artworks—found space to work
in film, he is among the most accomplished
of the underground filmmakers. To today's
viewers, his films like *Wheeeeels No. 1* (1958)
and *Breathdeath* (1963) appear as classic animations: absurdist, chaotic, laugh-out-loud funny

emblems of a 1960s sensibility. Their influence is vast enough to make them feel familiar,
but in the context of the period, VanDerBeek
was following a unique personal vision into
uncharted territory. It is these works for which
he is best known today, and which have had the
most consistent presence in the general cultural
imagination. The systems for seeing these works
(cinemas, film societies, museum film programs)
are well established, if fragile given the imper-
iled economies that support them, and are
rapidly being augmented for curious viewers by
crucial resources like UbuWeb Film.

But for VanDerBeek, the vastly expanded possibilities for film (over painting and collage)
were but a starting point, a gateway into the
new expressive mediums he invented. His
work continues to define the playing field of
expanded cinema, and studies of his work are
central when scholars convene symposia on
the ontology of the form. Expanded cinema
commands critical attention today because
contemporary visual artists routinely take
advantage of the proliferation of spectacular
projection technologies. The darkened room
with multiple moving images is the quintessential museum experience of our time.
VanDerBeek's projects such as *Movie Mural*
(1968) or *Found Forms* (1969) look so clearly
of our time that viewers will likely assume a
much more recent vintage. Art historians enjoy
the hunt for the moments of origin; and in that
quest many have found VanDerBeek's works.

It is tempting to award him the trendsetter
prize and be done, but one of the ambitions of
this project is to clarify both his achievements
as the salient inventor of new art forms and the
often contradictory nature of his relationship
to those forms, as well as to the technological
and political cultures that produced them. This
is a social, technological, and artistic history.
The following essays make it clear that simpli-
fying his practice to that of expanded-cinema
maker is unwise. The VanDerBeek scholars
assembled here start the ongoing project of
allowing his achievements to be seen in the

context of their time, as well as for what they offer to today's visual culture.

Working with film, VanDerBeek started experimenting with then brand-new computer innovations as part of a quest to use the latest technologies to make artwork. Thus began his restless pursit of supportive environments for his experiments using multiscreen, immersive environments; live events; telecopiers; broadcast television; underwater concerts; and all-night three-dimensional screenings of films. The venues were most often schools of higher learning, but early public television stations, planetariums, and NASA were also receptive hosts.

This exhibition is co-organized by the Massachusetts Institute of Technology List Visual Arts Center and the Contemporary Arts Museum Houston, as both Cambridge and Houston were sponsor cities for VanDerBeek: MIT through its unique Center For Advanced Visual Studies; and Houston via St. Thomas University, a Catholic school in the Museum District that was briefly the recipient of famed-philanthropists John and Dominique de Menil's largess to start a "new media center" well before the term "new media" had any universally understood meaning.

It is somewhat ironic that the works of a life-long trailblazer like VanDerBeek can look, to modern eyes, simultaneously of the moment and somewhat quaint. The *Poemfield* films (1965–66), made with computer pioneer Ken Knowlton, used the then very new type-generating technology to create floating fields of words: short phrases in some crude typeface that looks today like strange folk art imagined for a 1950s sci-fi film. Glowing cross-stitch samplers, their pixels are the size of softballs when enlarged. Ten years after their making they would have appeared unwanted reminders of the ungainly birth of computer visuals. Now, with a distance of 45 years, we can see in them a primitive beauty and the flowering of a new, technologically-grounded aesthetic.

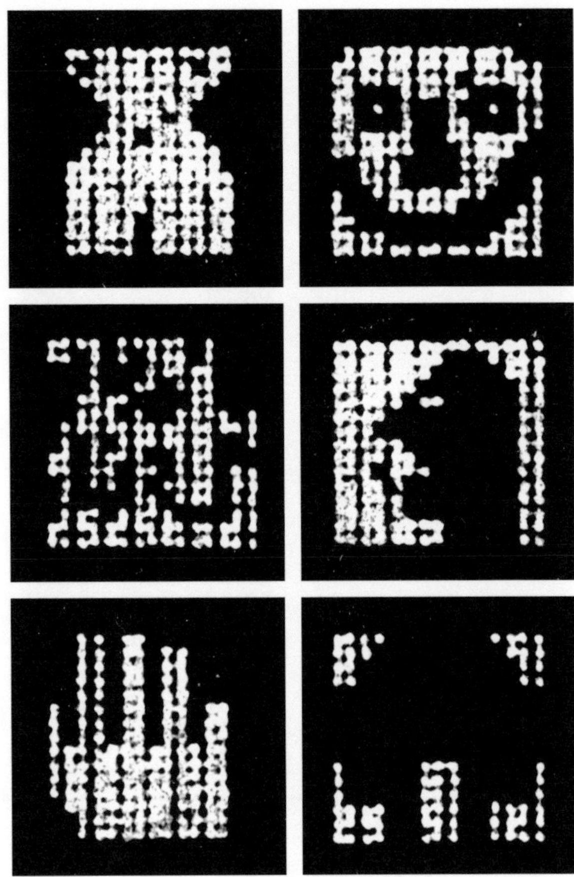

Patterns generated using BEFLIX on a 16 x 16 in. grid, ca. 1970.

The projectors VanDerBeek used for his
CineDreams events are dim and ghostly
compared to today's high intensity beamers
but, at the time, they must have appeared as
revolutionary magic. Televisions then were
small grainy affairs and the only grander
moving images most people saw were sani-
tized Hollywood productions.

The *Telephone Murals* (1970–72) were large
museum exhibitions capable of arriving simultaneously at multiple sites around the world.
They were based on a democratizing impulse
that critiqued the notion of any one site being
the sole location of VanDerBeek's art. He used
the precursor of the fax machine, with its slow
transmission time and grayish printouts that
faded or discolored quickly (these works seem
all the more poignant now as the fax is likely to
disappear in this age of e-mailable pdfs). The
reliquary nature of his art is perhaps clearest
in his use of this technology. Seeing the fragile
original carbon papers held in the VanDerBeek
archive at the Museum of Modern Art, in New
York, is reminiscent of the experience of seeing
the first nearly-invisible photograph by Joseph
Nicéphore Niépce enshrined at the Harry
Ransom Center at the University of Texas in
Austin. How did this mere ghost announce
itself as an agent of a revolutionary change
that would rewrite visual reality? Yet all of the
technologies VanDerBeek explored were indeed
filled with that same potential. These fragile
technological ghosts speak of all the image
processing that has gone on since, and a brief
moment when a visual poet held the reins.

VanDerBeek's frequent collaborations make him
even more irresistible as the archetypal 1960s
media artist. He avoided the solitary genius
model, and his works gained strength through
these collaborations. He made works that functioned as uniquely "VanDerBeekian" platforms
for joint experimentations that enabled his
community of artists to join together—both in
his backyard (literally) and around the world.
The introduction of every new communication
medium brings hope that it will somehow bring

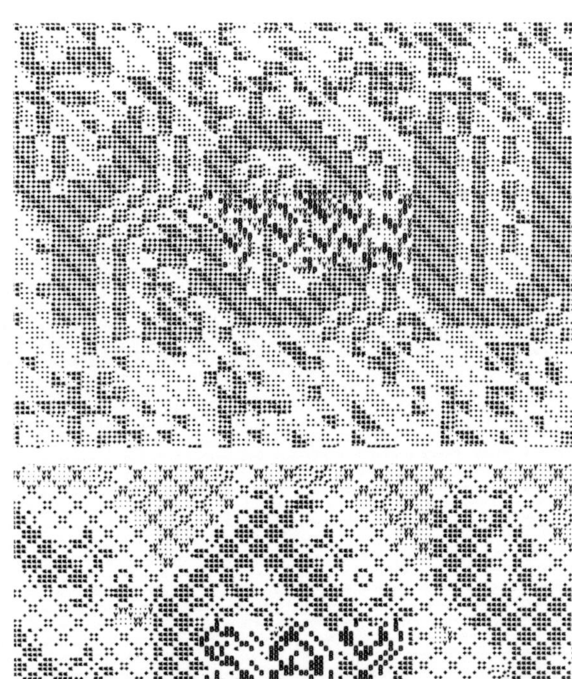

Film stills from *Poemfield No. 2*, 1966. 16mm, color, sound, 5:40 min.

   Stan VanDerBeek's Currency

people together, as recent debates about social networking and political effectiveness among the previously disenfranchised remind us. But while VanDerBeek was no techno-utopian (his writings are as full of doubts, fears, and worries about the future as they are celebrations), it is impossible to think about him and his all-night projection events and not hope for some sort of communal contact high.

Several thorny questions arise when trying to reclaim Stan VanDerBeek. The first is: Why not let these early experiments fade into the obscurity of other long-ago developments in technology; what is gained by preserving them? Furthermore: how should they be presented to an audience today; is it better to update them to today's technological standards, or better to keep them as artifacts, making the new audiences' experience as close as possible to that of the first audiences? And can one, through wall texts alone, contextualize the works for viewers in such a way that they can possibly return themselves to a time when computers and faxes were rare forms of magic available only to the few?

If the revival of interest in VanDerBeek had coalesced a decade or more ago, the answers to these questions might have been very different. A slightly behind-the-times work looks far more dated to a contemporary audience than one that springs from a much older technological aesthetic. It has only recently become clear that even tech-based works can accrue the aura and imprimatur of history.

There is also the question of balancing what the artist himself might have done given the many new, improved technological tools we have available in 2011 with the ethical demands of the art historically-minded curator. Can the original look, topical content, and presentation modes of the event pieces be maintained while providing an audience with something seductive enough to make them linger and learn about who Stan VanDerBeek was?

One must admit that many examples of early "computer art" (to use another soon-to-be-lost categorical term) should be allowed to flow into that vast graveyard of unloved data, unmourned by even their makers. Why are the computer films and fax works of VanDerBeek so different? And with the nearly constant "upping of the ante" when it comes to stunningly bright, high-definition, multiscreen museum installations featuring Hollywood special effects and three-dimensional, hallucinatory images, how can we hope to appreciate the accumulated slide projectors and film pieces VanDerBeek made? It is never uninteresting to see any original moment of a major art category, such as the first photograph, the first monochrome painting, the first readymade, the first appropriation work. Yet the reasons to look at VanDerBeek in this century are more complex.

In VanDerBeek's works and writings we see the exemplary contemporary man who received nothing from the culture without feeling compelled to bat it around, recontextualize it, deconstruct it, and decipher its meaning in the moment, as well as its potential meaning in the future. When new forms of culture emerge, made possible by new technologies such as mash-ups in music or the endless chains of linked visual images via photo-blogging applications such as Tumblr, there are thousands of willing adopters to field-test them and determine if they are indeed an art form with potential for profound expression, or merely a shiny distraction (the stillborn nature of the hologram as an art medium is still fresh enough to give all artistic early-adopters pause). Throughout the 1960s, '70s, and early '80s, VanDerBeek was an inspiring one-man research-and-development department for using untried forms and forcing them to reveal their interior poetics.

VanDerBeek is a massively contradictory figure: in single manifesto-like essay, he goes from celebrating a development to detailing its associated risks. His iconographic choices in works like the *Telephone Murals* and many of his films recall the times of their manufacture. They speak of what in the 1960s seemed to be an overwhelming number of unavoidable

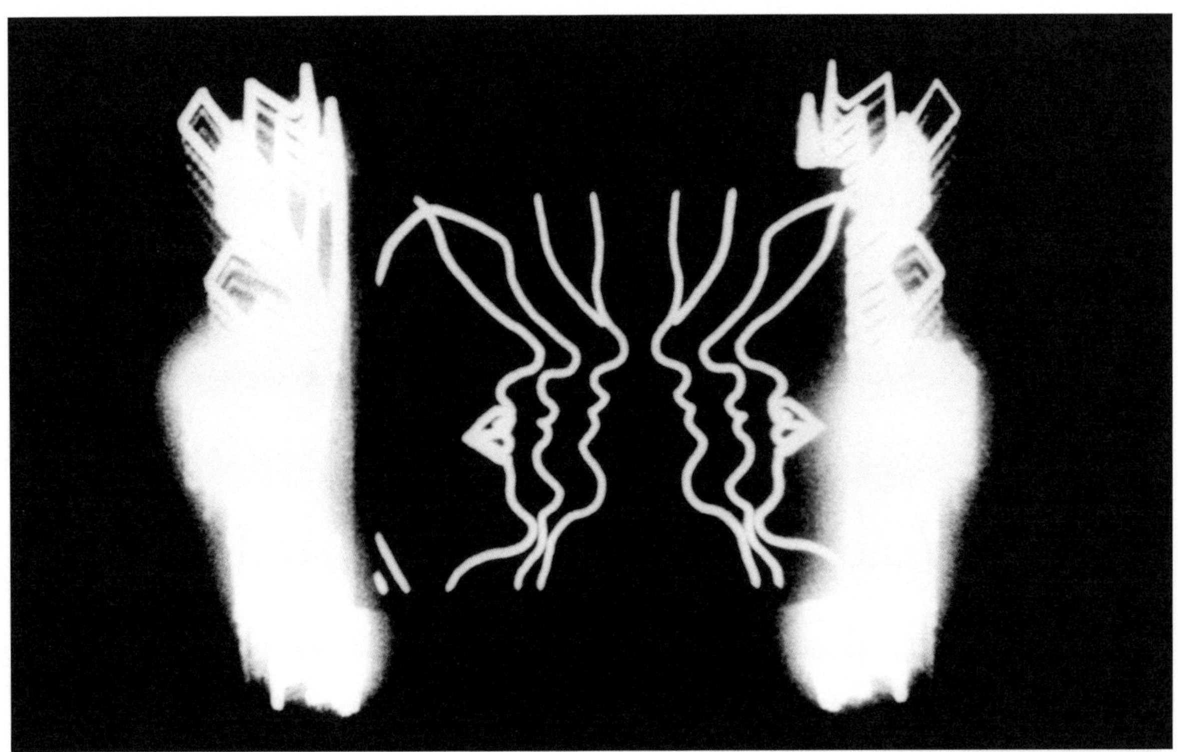

Film still from *Symmetricks*, 1972. 16mm, black and white, sound, 6:12 min.

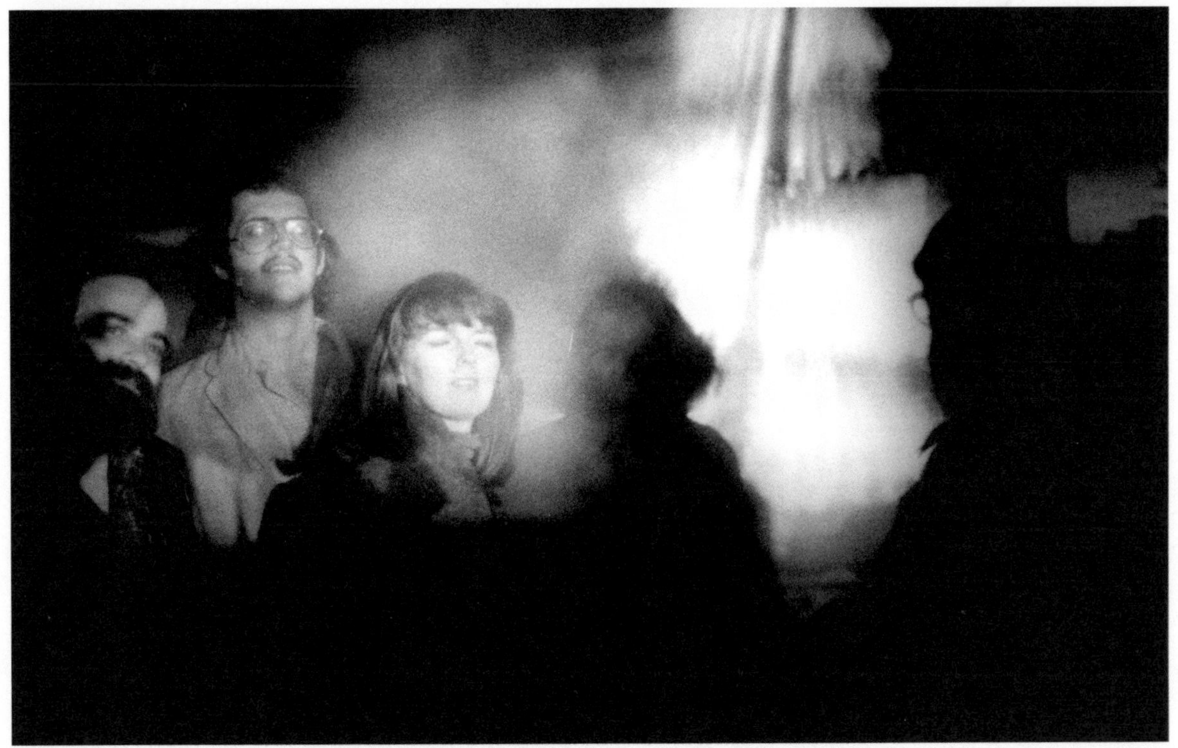

Steam Screens, performance in collaboration with Joan Brigham. Installation view, Whitney Museum of American Art, New York, 1979.

images spilling out of posters, films, television, and magazines. What then seemed a tidal wave was actually just the first trickle. Yet artists like VanDerBeek understood themselves as the advanced guard that would teach modern man to make the evolutionary jump required to process this visual onslaught. They were 40 years ahead of the writers today who are trying to understand the influence of Google image searches on memory and imagination. VanDerBeek's frequent references to earlier times in his films and collages may now be understood as his efforts to locate his work in what was already a historical project: the creation of modern mankind, grounded in the last few thousand years of human evolution interwoven with human invention.

For artists and practitioners, as well as anyone trying to live in the changing cyber-world of today, VanDerBeek represents a mode of cultural engagement. Hindsight based on the many media explosions in the years since the artist's death allows us a methodology for critically testing the limits and capabilities of each new technology at the moment of its dispersal. The works themselves reward repeated looking, and it is enjoyable to follow the way the images morph into each other, creating multiple readings over time. The spirit behind them is inspiring in its brave willingness to grapple with the new in many forms.

But there is also a cautionary tale: the risk of VanDerBeek's work disappearing forever from the public imagination, outside of the world of film proper, was very real. If his children Sara and Johannes VanDerBeek (both well-known artists in their own right) had not been devoted to preserving their late father's legacy, this material might have remained unseen. The scholars that have come together for this project would have had a much more difficult journey in trying to experience his works. Looking at VanDerBeek's massive curriculum vitae, we see a man and maker who was always out there coming to terms with developments in the culture in meaningful ways, and always on to the next lecture or festival. Stan VanDerBeek was himself too busy dreaming of new ways of engaging technology, images, and culture to slow down and worry about preserving his own work for the future, but it is our great privilege to be part of that effort.

The Culture: Intercom

Mark Bartlett

The "culture: intercom" is a concept that best circumscribes VanDerBeek's post-filmic, strenuously anti-essentialist media works, and derives from his 1965 coinage, "expanded cinema." This latter term has diverged along (at least) two separate lineages, both of which have ignored the trajectory followed by VanDerBeek.[1] A brief account of these alternate histories is necessary to clear the stage for his development along a radically different third formation that completely abandons not simply modernist conceptions of film, but film in any sense of the term, and which anticipates, in remarkable ways, most facets of what now is gathered under such rubrics as net art, new media, digital culture, and social networks.

Sheldon Renan, in 1967, described the American formation of expanded cinema in this way:

Expanded cinema is not the name of a particular style of film-making. It is a name for a spirit of inquiry that is leading in many different directions. It is cinema expanded to include many different projectors in the showing of one work. It is cinema expanded to include computer-generated images and the electronic manipulation of images on television. It is cinema expanded to the point at which the effect of film may be produced without the use of film at all. Its work is more spectacular, more technological, and more diverse in form than that of the avant-garde, experimental, underground film so far. But is less personal.[2]

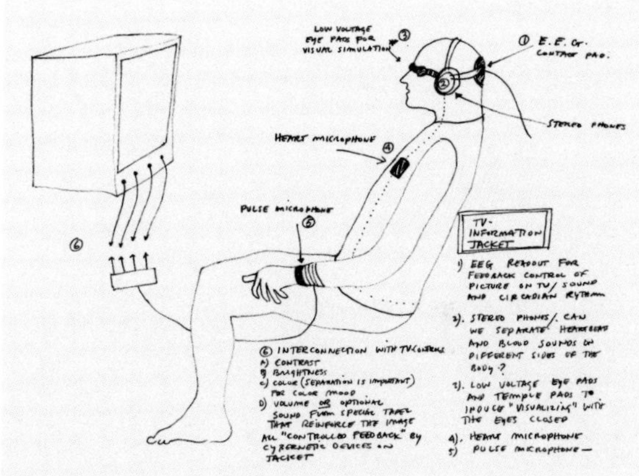

Untitled, ca. 1970. Ink on paper, 8 1/2 x 11 in.

That it was less personal did not lead to its becoming more social. Though Renan insightfully realized that expansion led to the "film-like" to the degree that "the effect of film may be produced without the use of film at all," he failed to develop that thought, and therefore failed to account for the full significance of VanDerBeek's writings and work. This lesser conception was reinforced in 1970 by Gene Youngblood's *Expanded Cinema*, which referred mainly to the exploration of new technologies for the more conventional methods of exhibiting moving image works and to the formalist experiments of John Whitney, for example, and those related to new age spiritualism, political quietism, and psychedelia of West Coast counterculture. The other definition of expanded cinema, pursued mainly in England, Austria, and Germany between 1967 and 1980, was described by the British filmmaker and writer Malcolm Le Grice. He characterized the European tradition by an interest in bringing the cinematic experience consciously into the space of the spectator through performed action and installation, as concerned only with formalism, and as remaining safely within the context of traditional art and film venues. He assimilated both VanDerBeek's "total visual environment" approach to the Youngblood lineage and Peter Weibel, Valie Export, and Carolee Schneemann's use of the term to his conception of the European "school" of expanded cinema, while remaining aesthetically and politically committed to formalist materialism.[3]

We find Renan and Le Grice's film historical narratives reiterated much more recently by Rosalind Krauss as part of her art historical account of modernist formalism. Her version is this:

Into this situation [Greenberg's construction of formalism] there entered the portapak, and its televisual effect was to shatter the modernist dream. In the beginning, as artists began to make video works, they used video as a technologically updated

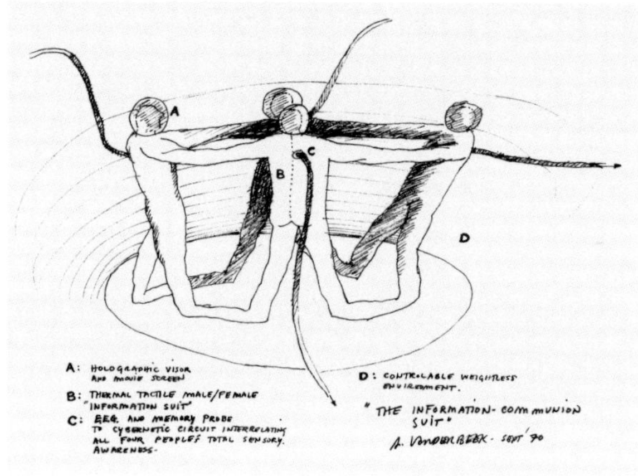

Untitled, ca. 1970. Ink on paper, 8 1/2 x 11 in.

continuation of the mode of address organized by the new attention to the phenomenological, although it was a perverse version of this since the form it took was decidedly narcissistic: artists endlessly talking to themselves. *To my knowledge only Serra himself* immediately acknowledged that video was in fact television, which means a broadcast medium, one that splinters spatial continuity into remote sites of transmission and receptions.[4]

Krauss seems to endorse Le Grice's description of both European and American lineages with her reference to the "phenomenological"; and, she is completely unaware of VanDerBeek's approach. Again, a much weaker conception is promulgated as the singular and unprecedented moment that "shatter[ed] the modernist dream." Krauss cites Richard Serra's *Television Delivers People* (1973) as the particular work to accomplish this. It perpetually scrolls the following text: "You are the product of t.v. You are delivered to the advertiser who is the customer." The mode of address here, to parallel Krauss's mode of theorizing, takes three forms: messaging in the form of advertising copy, though with opposite political intent—exposure of TV's capitalist methods; minimalist repetition of the message on the screen, and presumably on all screens to which they are broadcast; and self-referentiality of the "medium"—TV art as advertising. Patronizing and didactic, its message is only about the presumed effects of the medium on a presumably stupid public, and makes no sociopolitical comment on, or analysis of, the consequences of its systemic structure: production agencies, broadcasting, distribution, one way dissemination, etc. It may be interpreted, finally, as narcissistic as the early video works Krauss condemns.[5] Its commentary, as Krauss had demonstrated with regard to Serra's early sculpture (*Casting*, 1969), is strictly limited to formalist aesthetic analysis, still modernist in its "opticality," while abandoning "the materialist, purely reductive notion of the medium." Krauss considered this shift as enough to constitute the radical deconstruction of what she doesn't, but we must, call medium essentialism. The question that arises here is whether the shift from reductive materialism to an "expanded" notion of medium performativity, or, performance within the medium that isn't tied strictly to physical attributes of its materiality, is a sufficient basis on which to lay claims to a "post-media condition."

Only out of necessity, in the pursuit of the significance of VanDerBeek's experimentalism, do I raise these issues, in order to point to the places in film and art historical accounts where their historiographic and theoretical limits are revealed, so that, exactly at these loci, VanDerBeek's work and terms may be recovered and re-inserted into those discourses, so that we may move beyond them, as his work demands. More broadly, my intention has been to demonstrate how those discourses are incapable of accounting for his work. VanDerBeek's conception, as we have begun to see, was radically different, and constitutes a fourth (beyond Peter Wollen's third avant-garde) far more radical definition based on a conception of what must be termed "expanded-TV."

VanDerBeek here clearly articulates with characteristic verbal finesse his role as trenchant experimentalist, working to socialize communication through the creation of a new "movie art":

Movie-making was for long the most revolutionary art form of our time. Now television touches the nerve-ends of all the world; the visual revolution sits in just about every living room across America. The image revolution that movies represented has now been overhauled by the television evolution, and is approaching the next visual stage—to computer graphics to computer controls of the environment to a new cybernetic "movie art."[6]

He was completely aware of the historical context of that severely understated thing—movie art. It is a term that reaches back into history, before "cinema" had been consolidated as a singular cultural form and economic force. With that term, he sought to inject into the newly developing technologies a vision of

　　　The Culture: Intercom

"collaborative modeling" that if broad-based enough would lead to a revolutionary reorganization of media: to a "new electronic community," a "People's-Park TV."[7] As is seen in the *epiikon* above, VanDerBeek's works are rigorously "inter-media"[8]—they emphasize the relations between the human body and technologies, as well as between the technologies themselves, as opposed to the unified or merely co-present senses of "mixed-media" or "multimedia." The "TV Information Jacket," while a clear precursor to VR technologies, unlike them, is modeled on commensurate, multi-channel feedback between the sensory systems of the body and the ICT systems with which it interacts. The body becomes a device through which image generation in the body-TV network may be controlled, as well as impacted. This communication system is one example of a culture: intercom, of interactive collaborative modeling between one body and the world of "living information." But it also refers to any such "controlled feedback" system, to social networking over multiple channels of communication carrying differentiated forms of information embedded in and interwoven with every facet of cultural life.

In his 1965 statement, "'Culture Intercom' and Expanded Cinema: A Proposal and Manifesto," VanDerBeek intentionally combines vision with pragmatism, while keenly diagnosing the human impacts of ICT, framed by an agile linguistic play with which he strives to open new conceptual territories in which human-ICT symbiosis can thrive in specifically, socially constituted ways.[9]

The manifesto posits that ICT is producing a posthuman world that has completely outdistanced emotional and "socio- "logical" comprehension":

Technical power and cultural "over-reach" are placing the fulcrum of man's intelligence so far outside himself, so quickly, that *he cannot judge the results of his acts before he commits them. The process of life as an experiment on earth has never been made clearer.*[10]

The proposal aims to remedy the negative consequences of this radical break in humanism by balancing semiocentric models of communication with "a picture-language using fundamentally motions pictures," in order to "combine audio-visual devices into an educational tool" that he calls the "culture: intercom," meant to operate on a global scale through:

...audio-visual research centers...established on an international scale to explore the existing audio-visual devices and procedures, develop new image-making devices, and store and transfer image materials, motion pictures, television, computers, video-tape, etc.[11]

VanDerBeek's manifesto is a remarkable document that not only anticipates future technological instruments, like desktop computing and the Internet, as well as their form— "picture-language" or graphical user interface in today's lingua franca—but also underscores the importance of storage and transfer four years before Licklider's conceptualization of a decentralized information system. VanDerBeek's call to establish "audio-visual research centers" on an international scale preceded the establishment of MIT's CAVS by three years. His model for such centers was the TV-studio, which he referred to as the largest optical bench in the world because it had such enormous social reach and impact.

VanDerBeek's striking line quoted above—"The process of life as an experiment on earth has never been made clearer"—is put in perfectly Bakhtinian terms: *to be* means to communicate; or conversely, not to communicate leads directly to the danger of annihilation because man "cannot judge the results of his acts before he commits them." "Experimentalism" here acquires a darkly ominous form; VanDerBeek no doubt has in mind the atomic bomb, an image that figures prominently in his works of this period. Technological impacts lead directly to "cultural overreach" because it places human intelligence outside itself, in the unpredictable, uncontrollable, unforeseeable forces of

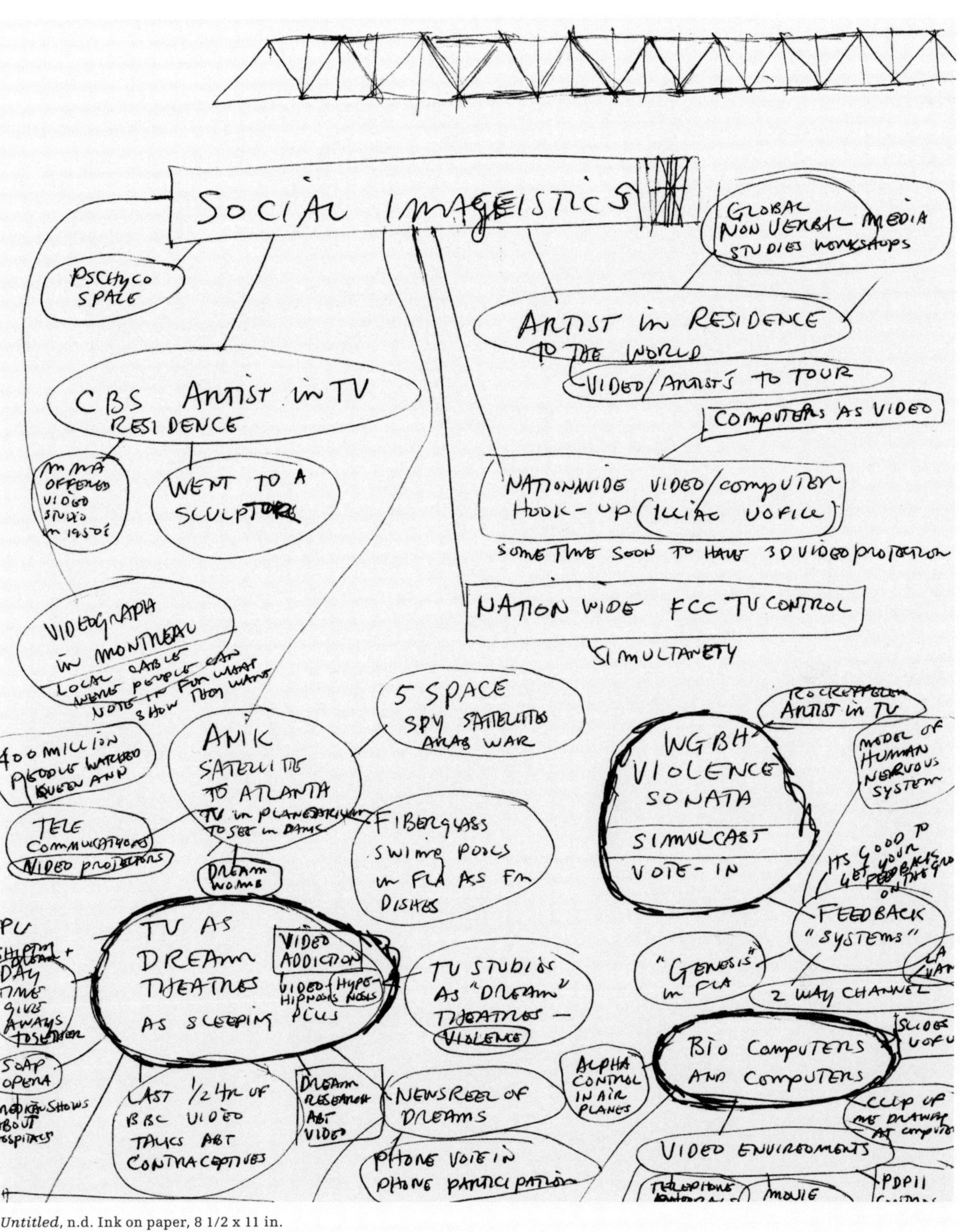

Untitled, n.d. Ink on paper, 8 1/2 x 11 in.

science and technology. The *Movie-Drome* is a prototype theater meant to counter this social problem by giving it an "educational" directive. This directive is complex, and acts simultaneously along two interwoven trajectories that combine Bertolt Brecht's Marxian theater of alienation effects, and Antonin Artaud's physiological theater of cruelty.[12] Both Brecht and Artaud aimed to prevent such overreach by "giving psychology a form that is much more vital and active" than the traditional, dramatic theater of their era.[13] Both theater-philosophers sought, through quite different, even oppositional methods, to eradicate "psychological man" (capitalist and romantic), whom we now understand as the rational, humanist man, whose death much social theory has aimed equally hard to ensure. Brecht used the "A-effect" of political didacticism, not dissimilar to the consciousness raising of first wave civil rights and feminist movements; and Artaud sought to trigger the "profound barbarity" of embodiment by relocating the theatrical between the intelligence of physical, corporeal sensation, and audiovisual, environmental, and linguistic intelligences that situate it. He sought to establish theater through a "unique language halfway between gesture and thought."[14] We find both these methods interwoven throughout VanDerBeek's work.

The "culture: intercom" is an "experience machine" designed to invent and to collaboratively produce communication forms for a new society. Its purpose is to counter the peculiar and dangerous unpredictability of human action on itself and the world through "theater." But these "theaters" are expanded cinemas, or, culture: intercoms which use, redesign, and invent audio-visual technologies specifically for social ends—for inter-communication—because, to quote J.C.R. Licklider: "society rightly distrusts the modeling done by a single mind…the requirement is for communication, which we now define concisely as 'cooperative modeling'—cooperation in the *construction*, *maintenance*, and *use* of a model." "By all," he concludes.[15] Three years

prior to Licklider's 1968 essay, "The Computer as a Communication Device," VanDerBeek's manifesto lays the same set of stresses: cooperation, construction, maintenance, and use of communication modeling. Licklider was the first to merge psychology with computing and engineering, and his inventiveness was remarkably similar to Billy Klüver the engineer and VanDerBeek the artist. The point is that this conception of new technologies cut widely across quite different research programs, from ARPA to ARPANET to Bell Labs, from E.A.T. to the Rockefeller Foundation (all materially supportive of VanDerBeek). The purposes envisioned by these three experimentalists, were centrally and pragmatically social and cultural in purpose, and must be understood as intimately integrated with each other in the brief revolutionary moment of *Pensée 68*. Therefore, the aspirations of these technocultural pragmatists is a crucial missing element in our historical understanding of this period, and of why it failed to realize itself. (It is this factor that needs to be re-inserted into film and art historical narratives to help counter the backslide into asocial formalist education and analysis.) The Internet, as compelling as it has been, is only the impoverished and compromised result of a far greater pragmatic social possibility, all too easily perverted from its anarchic beginnings to become another form of social control.

1 Peter Wiebel, according to Malcom Le Grice, used the term to describe his early projects, and it is unclear to me at the moment of this publication whether to accept or reject Le Grice's inclusion of Weibel's usage in his description. VanDerBeek showed a multiscreen work of expanded cinema in Japan in 1970, and thus, there could plausibly be a form of expanded cinema there. Malcolm Le Grice, *Abstract Film and Beyond* (London: Studio Vista, 1977), 121–22.

2 Sheldon Renan, *An Introduction to the American Underground Film* (New York: Dutton, 1967), 227.

3 "Wherever it [expanded cinema] originated, its connotations for Youngblood do not fit the extensive amount of European work being done in this area. Youngblood understands it mainly in terms of American West Coast abstraction…and heavily linked to the idea of mind expansion, psychedelia and McLuhan's global village concept of televisual communication. In Europe, on the other hand, it is seen as a development of the formal issues of cinema and a concern with the reality of the projection situation itself. A quite arbitrary point of contact is in the field of multiprojection: European aims have been almost exclusively formal…and have nothing in common with experiments in 'total' visual environments characterized by the work of Stan VanDerBeek in the mid-sixties." Le Grice's commentary is as xenophobic as much as it is accurate, and constitutes one influential moment in the suppression of VanDerBeek's significance. Le Grice, *Abstract Film and Beyond*, 121–22.

4 Rosalind Krauss, *A Voyage on the North Sea: Art in the Age of the Post-Medium Condition* (London: Thames and Hudson, 1999), 30. Emphasis added.

5 Rosalind Krauss, "Video: The Aesthetics of Narcissism," *October* 1 (Spring 1976): 50–64.

6 Stan VanDerBeek, "New Talent–the Computer," *Art in America*, no. 58 (Jan–June 1970).

7 Stan VanDerBeek, "After-Thoughts-After," January 15, 1970, WGBH Archives. Unpublished document criticizing the station's shortcomings in the production of *Violence Sonata*.

8 "Expanded cinema works are often *inter-media* works, for they sometimes include the use of live performers, television, dance, painting, and various other media combined in what is sometimes called a *media-mix* or *cinema-combine*." Renan, 228.

9 Published as "'Culture: Intercom' and Expanded Cinema: A Proposal and Manifesto," *Tulane Drama Review* 11, no. 1 (1966); "'Culture: Intercom' and Expanded Cinema: A Proposal and Manifesto," *Film Culture*, no. 40 (Spring 1966); and "Culture: Intercom and Expanding Cinema: A Proposal," *Motive* (November 1966). Anthologized in *The New American Cinema*, ed. Gregory Battcock (New York: Dutton, 1976), 173.

10 Stan VanDerBeek, "'Culture: Intercom' and Expanded Cinema: A Proposal and Manifesto," *Tulane Drama Review*, 39. Emphasis added.

11 Ibid., 41.

12 VanDerBeek was very close to M.C. Richards, poet and translator of Artaud's *Theater of Cruelty*, whom he had met at Black Mountain College. See Gloria Sutton's essay in this volume.

13 Antonin Artaud, "Cinema And Reality" (1927), in Susan Sontag, ed., *Antonin Artaud: Selected Writings* (Berkeley: University of California Press, 1988), 151.

14 Antonin Artaud, "The Theatre of Cruelty (First Manifesto)," in Sontag, 242.

15 J.C.R. Licklider and Robert W. Taylor, "The Computer as a Communication Device," *Science and Technology* 76 (April 1968): 22. Emphasis added. Licklider was one of many theorists of the 1960s who advocated for and was able to implement research programs that aimed to bridge the gap between humans and machines. In 1960, he wrote a highly influential essay entitled "Man-Computer Symbiosis," in which he specified "symbiosis" as a "subclass of man-machine systems," refining Wiener's generalization of an earlier era. ARPA was founded under Licklider's leadership in 1969 in the Man and Computer (MAC) research group at MIT, which VanDerBeek was to work with beginning in 1970 as a fellow at the Center for Advanced Visual Studies (CAVS). VanDerBeek was invited by Licklider in 1969 to join a group of MIT academics (including György Kepes, Donlyn Lyndon, Marvin Minsky, and Stephen Smoliar, among others) to form a laboratory in which artists, scientists, and engineers would collaborate. J.C.R. Licklider to Distribution List, "Meeting to discuss the concept and possible formation of a Computer Laboratory for the Arts," June 2, 1969. VanDerBeek Archive, Museum of Modern Art, New York.

The Culture: Intercom

Stan VanDerBeek: Collage Experience

Gloria Sutton

In December of 1973, Stan VanDerBeek and the filmmaker Ed Emshwiller met in a nondescript room in the basement of Anthology Film Archives's Second Avenue building and engaged in a series of wide-ranging discussions. Save for a few Anthology regulars who meandered in and out, the room was empty. Over the course of several evenings, the two men sat across from one another and took turns posing questions with a simple audiotape recorder as their primary audience. The tenor of the resulting 10 or so hours of interviews slid effortlessly back and forth between the casual catch-up of longtime friends and a serious analysis of the cross-section of cinema and visual art. Each cassette was filled with insightful biographical details; posturing about the state of American filmmaking and its ability to remain "independent"; critical assessments of what it meant to be a contemporary artist in the era of McNamara's Vietnam, technical developments in film, teaching art and media pedagogy; and ruminations about the effects of their work. Like most of his writings from the late 1950s through the early 1980s, VanDerBeek's voice conveyed a sense of self-reflexivity about his own formation as an artist and, more notably, a tone of urgency about the state of the field. He and Emshwiller seemed to easily fill spool after spool of magnetic tape, pausing only to flip the cassette to new a side and press the record button.

Audiotape was a fitting medium to absorb VanDerBeek's intensity—the frenetic pacing of his speech and his own peculiar syntax. Emshwiller and VanDerBeek's overlapping aesthetic concerns converged around film and more specifically, filmmaking as a type of visual art. Alongside pivotal filmmakers Jonas Mekas and Shirley Clarke, both Emshwiller and VanDerBeek were singled out for contributing new filmmaking techniques (particularly animation) and were often called the progenitors of American Independent Cinema. However, unlike his esteemed colleagues whose primary format remained single-authored films, VanDerBeek was what would be now called a "multimedia artist," whose practice expounded upon film and the process of filmmaking but was grounded in the more established discourses of painting, photography, and architecture. While VanDerBeek's multimedia installations, film events, collages, murals, drawings, and visual essays extrapolated from the techniques of many disciplines, his work never completely adhered to any medium's particular orthodoxy. Instead, the lanky artist displayed an indefatigable aptitude for experimenting with emerging forms of communication technology and computer-based media, including various types of programming, lasers, light pens, video recording and editing equipment, and most prominently, image transmission technology, such as proto-fax machines, television broadcast, and digital video. The fact that both VanDerBeek and Emshwiller were receptive to video's relative immediacy and malleability made their work anathema to Anthology's commitment to celluloid and the development of its "Essential Cinema Repertory"—a collection of titles compiled between 1970 and 1975 by Anthology's "Film Selection Committee" members (James Broughton, Ken Kelman, Peter Kubelka, P. Adams Sitney, and Jonas Mekas) that advanced a formally rigorous criteria for avant-garde film—and is perhaps the reason that at times they felt the need to whisper in the basement of Anthology Film Archives.

When Emshwiller asked VanDerBeek to "trace his own sense of evolution" at the start of the first tape, he instantly launched into a breathless monologue. Listening to his response over 30 years later, it is possible to map two specific pathways through his career. The first acknowledges his formative experience as a student at Black Mountain College in western North Carolina, where he "stumbled" into filmmaking. His fine arts training began at Cooper Union, but after serving in the US Navy (a staff position in the Navy's communication division kept him assigned to a desk at a local base on Long Island), he continued his studies in painting, photography, and architecture under the GI Bill at Black Mountain between 1949 and 1951.[1]

VanDerBeek was part of the school's first photography course introduced in 1949 by Hazel Larsen Archer. In addition to learning the mechanics of still photography, he also picked up his first film camera after the college acquired a Bolex. VanDerBeek told Emshwiller that the medium held his fascination precisely because it "seemed to be the most total media that had everything else in it."[2]

After leaving Black Mountain, VanDerBeek returned to New York City and supported himself with a string of freelance jobs that exerted a second or parallel plane of influence on his artistic practice. Though many of

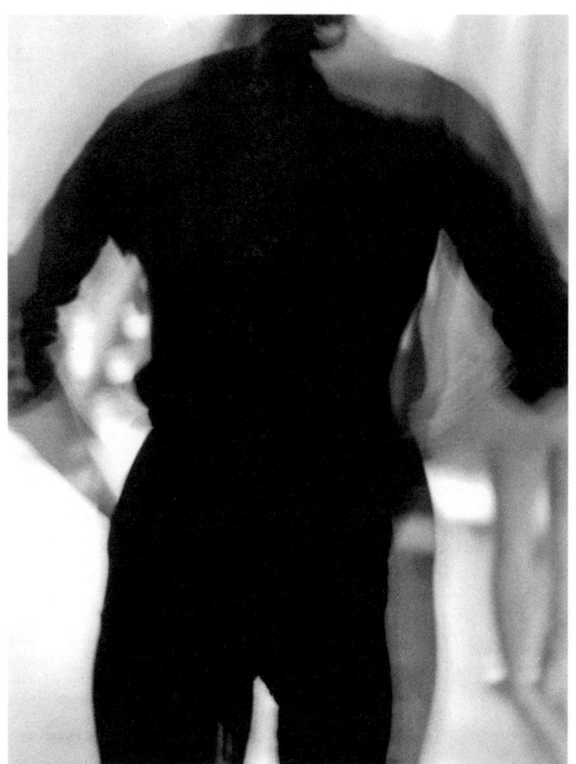

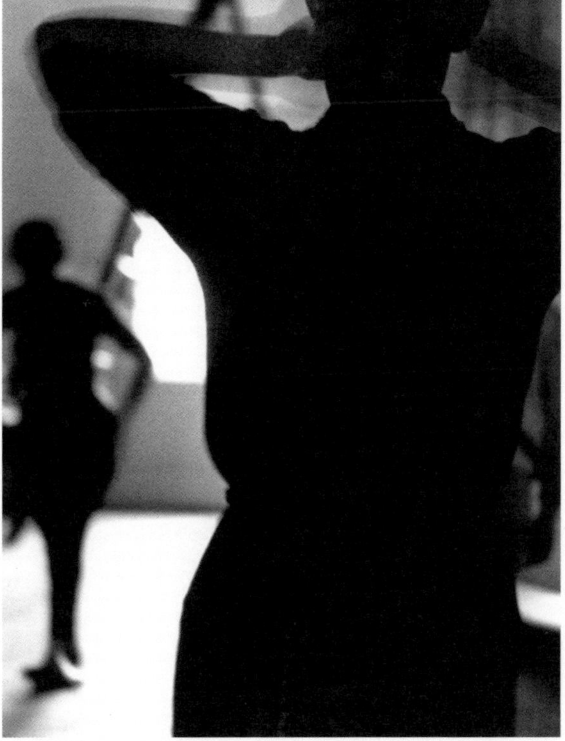

All: *Untitled*, 1949–50/2007. Silver gelatin print, 8 x 10 in.

    Stan VanDerBeek: Collage Experience

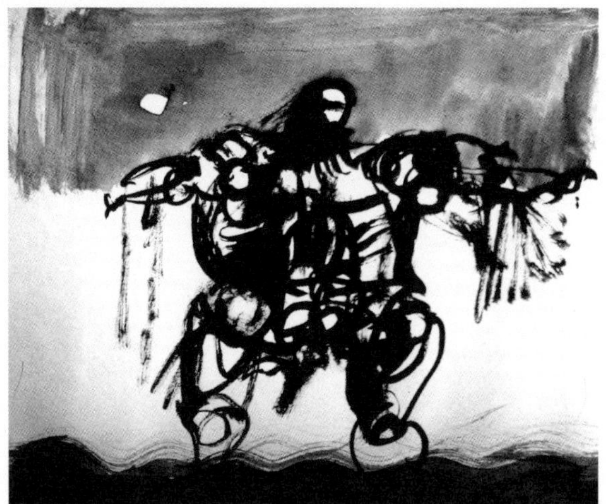
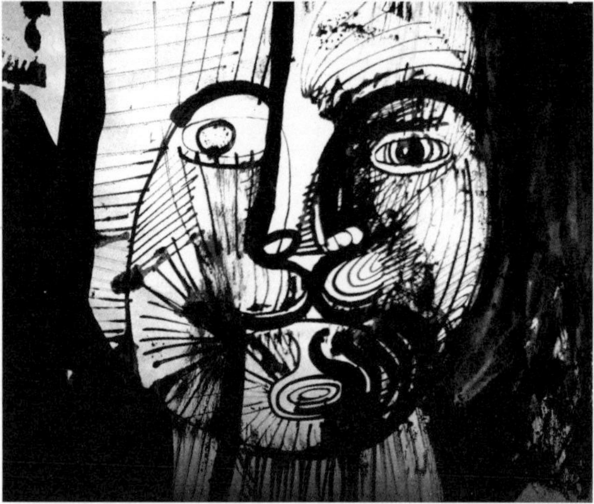

Film stills from *Mankinda*, 1957. 16mm, black and white, sound, 10 min.

his peers gravitated toward freelance jobs in advertising, fashion, or publishing (natural fits for VanDerBeek's graphic aesthetic), he worked as an assistant at CBS. Many of the stop-animation techniques and editing skills that he used to stunning effect in two award-winning early films of 1957, *What Who How* and *Mankinda*, as well as *Wheeeeels No. 1* (1958) and *Science Friction* (1959), were gained while working on the network's hit children's television show *Winky Dink and You*. The proto-interactive program ran on Saturday mornings on CBS from 1953 to 1957. Children could order a special clear vinyl mat to adhere to their television screens at home, and using special crayons, they were encouraged to draw along with the host of the program. VanDerBeek worked on the short animated sequence that opened the show, an experience that provided him with his first and only technical film training and introduced him to the seemingly infinite possibilities of a simple animation stand. VanDerBeek often used the television studio's editing equipment after hours to work on his own animated films, which frequently combined his figurative drawings and paintings with collages made from magazine pictorials, advertisements, and newspaper articles. In a 1966 interview with critic Richard Kostelanetz, VanDerBeek explained that after being fired from this job he continued to sneak in after hours to use the equipment. "I had to convince the night watchman that I was still doing homework for the job," he explained, adding, "that hooked me up and then I built my own stuff after that."[3]

In 1956, VanDerBeek received what he described as a "semi-commission" from Fluxus impresario George Maciunas: he was invited to contribute his recent collage films to the AG Gallery's first film show at 925 Madison Avenue. Taken with the expansive openness at the uptown venue's "fancy address," VanDerBeek created his first multiscreen work. *Visioniii* (VanDerBeek added a letter "i" for each of the three walls) was conceived as an "assembly" that disrupted the clear, direct reception of his own 16mm films (which were often comprised of a series of animated collage sequences) by intercutting them with found footage, borrowed narrative films, and projecting them alongside 35mm slides and drawings made on overhead projectors. The five-minute "assembly film" made from "collage material" and "junk stuff" was his first "environmental situation" and was projected against three of the gallery's walls.

VanDerBeek's insistence on these particular terms—"environment," "junk," "collage," and especially "assembly"—was not a mining of the formal language or operations of modernist film, but an alignment with neo-avant-garde strategies that challenged the primacy of the canvas and a deep commitment to exploring the disjunctive sensorial qualities generated by multimedia presentations. More specifically, VanDerBeek's well-established fondness for introducing neologisms to the critical discourse ("underground film" is one important example) supports the critical significance he placed on the specificity of deploying these types of descriptors. His mixed-media filmic "assemblies" interwove disparate image sources and altered their durational qualities so that at times, film took on the staccato pacing of 35mm slides rotating around a projection carousel. Overhead transparencies functioned as moving images when slid manually across the surface of a projection lamp, while maintaining a sense of transparency of process. Like the formal and conceptual provocations ushered in by Robert Rauschenberg's "combines," VanDerBeek's particular type of "assembly" should be cast for the same historical reconsideration as postwar sculptural paradigms like "assemblage," which used found material to wedge a space between modernist painting and sculpture.

While VanDerBeek worked evenings at CBS, Eleanor Ward hired him to repair and paint the ceiling of her newly opened Stable Gallery on Seventh Avenue at West 58th Street, a former horse stable that would host some of the most noted group exhibitions of the 1950s and cultivate an audience steeped in the criticism

of Clement Greenberg. In this capacity VanDerBeek and Robert Rauschenberg—who had met as students at Black Mountain— toiled as the gallery's "co-janitors" right before Ward showed Rauschenberg's pivotal series of "White Paintings" in the fall of 1953. While they never directly collaborated, the two artists' careers seemed to dovetail throughout the following decades, with their respective interests in applying the interactive potential of communication technology within the context of artistic praxis.

Of course, Rauschenberg's work in this area took shape through more formal endeavors. In 1966 he ambitiously teamed up fellow artist Robert Whitman and two Bell Labs engineers, Billy Klüver and Fred Waldhauer, to form Experiments in Art and Technology (E.A.T.). The group produced several groundbreaking art events including performances associated with *9 Evenings: Theatre and Engineering* held at the New York Armory in October 1966. While it was a mutual friend at Bell Labs, not E.A.T., who introduced VanDerBeek to Ken Knowlton, Bell physicist and author of the computer programs EXPLOR and BEFLIX, their artist-programmer collaboration was, in the words of Knowlton, "very much the kind of two person association that E.A.T. was intending to create."[4] Consequently, VanDerBeek and Knowlton were invited to discuss their experiments with BEFLIX and screen the resulting series of computer-generated films, called *Poemfields*, at one of E.A.T.'s workshops held in the group's meeting space at 9 East 16th Street.[5]

Collaboration was the stated enterprise of the highly engineered and programmatically executed projects in which E.A.T. and VanDerBeek, among others, engaged during the early 1960s. It was also elemental to many of the decidedly low-tech "amateur" and more intimate forms of audience participation that characterized a slightly earlier moment that developed in the wake of Allan Kaprow's *Eighteen Happenings in Six Parts* (fall 1959) and Robert Whitman's film/theater events like *American Moon* (1960) at the Reuben

Gallery. Another example can be found in Claes Oldenburg's proto-pop, hand-painted plaster reliefs of diner foods and dime store sundries that were included in Martha Jackson's gallery exhibition, *Environments, Situations, Spaces*, in the spring of 1961. Later that year Oldenburg re-installed them in the storefront window of his low-rent, Lower East Side studio. Dubbed *The Store*, the work foregrounded art's commodity status while generating a sculpture/installation/performance hybrid that shifted as people came in to purchase individual pieces.[6]

After *The Store* closed, Oldenburg used the narrow space as a backdrop to stage a series of 10 different Happenings that he orchestrated under the moniker "Ray Gun Theater" in the spring of 1962. These absurdist performances mimed activities such as the preparation and serving of meals, sacrificial rituals, and ancient rites of dressing and adorning dead bodies. Staged against the rough-hewn backdrop of hand-painted scrims and foil-covered cardboard, these performances morphed out of a series of earlier events that Oldenburg titled "Ray Gun Specs" (and/or "Ray Gun Spex"). Oldenburg asked VanDerBeek to participate by filming these events, including *Store Days I & II* and *Nekropolis I & II* in February and March, followed by *Injun I & II*, *Voyages I & II*, and *World's Fair I & II* in April and May. In addition to Lucas Samaras, Pat Muschinski (later Pat Oldenburg), and Oldenburg himself, VanDerBeek was on hand with a camera filming certain "Ray Gun Specs" such as *Snapshots from the City* arranged specifically for the Judson Gallery on February 29 and March 1 and 2, 1960.

VanDerBeek edited the footage into a five-minute, 16mm black-and-white sound film that showed Oldenburg in a papier-mâché mask and a costume made of rags, moaning and convulsing on the floor as sirens blared in the background. VanDerBeek's film juxtaposed tightly framed shots of Oldenburg's exhausted frame and close-ups of his blackened hands with a discordant soundtrack composed of city noises. Oldenburg's actions within the film are relayed in VanDerBeek's signature animated style—a frame-by-frame building of movement rather than a seamless capture of motion. Wild gesticulations were condensed to a sequence of still images, isolating the body's movement in a type of filmic abstraction, not a straight recording of the performance.[7] In this way, VanDerBeek pressured the seemingly dichotomous relationship between the performance's "live" or original moment and its historical documentation. *Snapshots of the City* offers a third distillation, an abstraction of the performance that was not intended to replicate the live experience nor adhere to the orthodoxy of fidelity that often dictated photographic and filmic representations of performance-based events during this period.

VanDerBeek and Oldenburg's interest in each other's work led to a more formal collaboration in the form of the 16mm short film *Birth of the American Flag* later that same year.[8] Part experimental film, part loosely-scripted Happening—and completely compelling— the film's cast was culled directly from the artists who populated the Ray Gun Theater. A bearded, rake-thin Lucas Samaras was given a set of tinfoil fangs and easily fell into his role as a vampire, while Pat Oldenburg and Carolee Schneemann played more symbolic parts, including a baby and a river spirit, respectively. The Happening was orchestrated at the upstate New York house of writer Rudy Wurlitzer, who allowed the artists free reign of his gardens and grounds. Throughout the black-and-white film's 15-minute running time, VanDerBeek focused on creating distinct vignettes with little semblance of narrative continuity. The film culminates in a scene along the river in which Schneemann, dressed in a bikini made from balloons, floats on the water, while a naked Claes Oldenburg floats face down, as does Samaras. On the water's edge, Pat Oldenburg is seen crammed into a baby's cradle while Metropolitan Museum of Art curator Henry Geldzahler, wearing his iconic round specs, slowly pulls a faded American flag from between the infant's legs.

While Oldenburg continued to screen and exhibit his works primarily in art galleries and museums, VanDerBeek, like Schneemann, turned to more ad hoc or temporary venues, including experimental film festivals throughout the United States, Europe, and the Middle East. Key to VanDerBeek's practice was his interest in adapting the presentation of his 16mm films to fit non-theatrical settings so that his filmic works could take on various formats not completely beholden to the fixity of the screen. This also included the literal circulation of the films. For example, VanDerBeek and Schneemann's short film collaboration with Robert Morris called *Site* (1964) was included in the artist publication *Aspen* (No. 5+6). Each copy of the magazine's "Minimalism" issue included a 8mm film spool. VanDerBeek's presence in these types of collaborations throughout the 1960s underscores the fact that his interest in challenging the formal paradigms of film and moving images should be considered within the broader spectrum of analytical discourse enacted by the New York neo-avant-garde.

Throughout his career, VanDerBeek continually sought and responded to an incredible range of opportunities to show his work within decidedly non-art contexts, including the United States Military Academy at West Point, the United States Department of State Art in Embassies program, the BBC, and NASA. Corporate interest in his animation techniques from IBM and TEAC, among other international computer and communication technology companies, raised the ire of many of his film colleagues who felt that VanDerBeek's multi-screen works were too closely aligned with spectacle culture. However, this aspect of VanDerBeek's prolific output requires a more nuanced consideration beyond the simplistic accusation of "selling out."

As a polymath artist, VanDerBeek's practice remained too diffuse for the programmatic approach most galleries cultivated (even those dealers that purported to support experimental art relied on the sales of painting and sculpture). So what to do with an artist whose primary output remained variable, reproducible, inherently collaborative, and dependent on proprietary software and equipment? "Finding a curve," was how VanDerBeek described his working methods to Emshwiller. "I always find it amusing to hear artists talk about not compromising," offered VanDerBeek, who quickly added, "I mean in what world? You always have to deal with certain kinds of inherent contradictions. You're not compromising, but you're finding a curve."[9] VanDerBeek's interest in cobbling support from research fellowships, grants, and residencies with sponsorship from cultural, governmental, and corporate entities triangulates the dichotomous relationship that has been typically drawn between the market and the academy as the two spheres of artistic support. VanDerBeek expanded the critical reception of his work beyond these two frameworks with contributions to dozens of mass culture publications, as well as two more esoteric publications produced by humanistic organizations. He published his own criticism, image essays, manifestos, interviews, and profiles in magazines such as *Harper's Bazaar*, *Popular Photography*, *Time*, and *Esquire*. The potential agency of artist-driven publications as another type of direct transmission device captivated VanDerBeek, who was an early subscriber to the *Archigram* newsletter as well as the interdisciplinary journal *Form*, edited by art historian Stephan Bann, both originating in the United Kingdom (London and Cambridge respectively). VanDerBeek was also a regular contributor to *Radical Software*, the highly influential publication that chronicled the emerging discourse on media ecology within North America and was produced by artists and media activists Frank Gillette, Ira Schneider, Michael Shamberg, Beryl Korot, Phyllis Gershuny, and Paul Ryan under the moniker Raindance Corporation between 1970 and 1974.

While VanDerBeek's film and media technology experiments were certainly steeped in the rhetoric associated with the "new electronic media" as theorized by such figures as Marshall McLuhan and Gregory Bateson within the pages of *Radical Software*, his multimedia experiments were actually located in the center of the various radical aesthetic sensibilities that exploded in New York in the late 1950s and early '60s. In addition to working with George Maciunas and his AG Gallery, which was the site of many Fluxus projects in the United States, and filming Oldenburg's Happenings, VanDerBeek also regularly collaborated with dancer/choreographer Elaine Summers. VanDerBeek worked with Summers to create *Pastorale et al*, a multimedia film work that he referred to as "a film and slide study for dancers."[10] *Pastorale et al* premiered at the Film-Maker's Cinematheque during the *New Cinema Festival 1* in November of 1965. Summers and Burt Supree danced on stage as VanDerBeek projected a series of his collage films against their bodies, their movements disrupting the clear registration of the filmic material against the background screen. An experimental filmmaker and "intermedia" pioneer in her own right, Summers's dance works often debuted at Judson Memorial Church and now hold a place in the history of performance at this important institution.

VanDerBeek's affiliation with the progenitors of the New York neo-avant-garde actually started in the mountains of North Carolina, and the most influential forces on his development as an artist came from poets, not other visual artists. Besides Rauschenberg, VanDerBeek's studies at Black Mountain College overlapped with M.C. Richards's and John Cage's tenure as teachers, both of whom became his life-long intellectual interlocutors. Their distinct and divergent writings inspired VanDerBeek's own forays into poetry, specifically his interest in developing an image-based poetry language, as evidenced by the *Poemfield* films that he produced between 1966 and 1971.[11] Describing his time at Black Mountain as a "super dominant experience," VanDerBeek singled out the college's renowned event *Theater Piece No. 1*

(1952), in which Cage, Richards, and Charles Olson read their poems from atop ladders while Rauschenberg shuffled some of his abstract paintings (his "White Paintings" were hung from the ceiling) and played scratched records on a gramophone. Composer David Tudor added a piano composition and Merce Cunningham danced in what would become his signature spare and determined manner. Often cited as the first "Happening" by historians, the effects of seeing *Theater Piece No. 1* would spark more personal associations for VanDerBeek and reinforce his commitment to collage as an active metaphor for subjectivity. Recalling the event for Emshwiller, VanDerBeek remarked how *Theater Piece No. 1* "very concretely directed" him to think about the possibilities of collage and simultaneity: "The fact that everything sort of happened at once was very inspirational" and it "triggered off a lot of ideas about how you can make things grow and collage together." "It was like a collage experience," he continued, "where you stick the glue and take and reshape."[12]

VanDerBeek's expressive description of collage as a continuously evolving process alluded to more than just formal technique. Evocative of the philosophical writings of M.C. Richards, collage in these terms could be read as a metaphor for a type of subject formation. Combined with his relatively early encounter with mortality,[13] Richards's writings ushered in what he would describe to Emshwiller as an "awakening," which could have also been a direct reference to a poem Richards penned in the late 1950s for VanDerBeek, titled "Upon Awakening":

Glory remembered
trails dawn down canyons.
Man suitably nude
wears glory's gown.
Give him speech and illusion
specifically
of a kind
and hands for work
and the circling's done.[14]

Moreover, Richards's role as a teacher and translator for this group of men wielded tremendous influence.[15] In fact, it was primarily because Richards herself, fluent in French and deeply attuned to the writings of Antonin Artaud, Erik Satie, and Jean Cocteau—all of whom she translated into English for the Black Mountain community—that the aesthetic strategies associated with absurdist theater began to permeate the practices of this group of artists. A case in point was her translation of Satie's *Ruse of Medusa*, which was famously performed at the college in 1948 with Buckminster Fuller and Elaine de Kooning in the lead roles, while Cunningham danced wearing a monkey costume and Cage played the piano.

While the creative manifestation of VanDerBeek's exchanges with M.C. Richards remained confined to his 20-plus-year correspondence with her, VanDerBeek collaborated with Cage and Cunningham on several public multimedia projects. These included *Variations V* (1965) staged at Lincoln Center and for a German television broadcast in Hamburg (1966), as well as a lesser-known experimental poetry event organized by The Poetry Center of the 92nd Street Y on February 25, 1967. Participants (including Cage, Cunningham, Robert Creeley, Billy Klüver, filmmaker Len Lye, painter Jack Tworkov, theater director David Vaughn, and VanDerBeek) dressed in formal attire and sat around a finely appointed banquette table reading their poems and engaging in an unscripted conversation in a multimedia performance that mimicked a salon gathering. The dinnerware and utensils were outfitted with contact microphones (as Klüver had done to spectacular effect in *9 Evenings*) to pick up ambient noise, while actually being used by the artists to eat the meal served to them on stage in front of an audience. VanDerBeek's abstract drawings and figurative sketches done with black paint on acetate were cast onto the artists and spilled over the stage from an overhead projector operated by his wife, the artist Johanna Bourne VanDerBeek, who was stationed in the orchestra pit below.

Titled "Contemporary Voices in the Arts," the one-day event was billed as "an illustrated discussion." The intermingling of dinner conversation, an electrified soundscape, poetry reading, and moving images at the 92nd Street Y highlighted VanDerBeek's interest in real-time collaboration–a process that reflected his intuitive understanding of the relationship between word and image, or in this case, spoken word and projected image. The event's arrangement and setting alluded to the particular manner in which theater was presented at Black Mountain College. While rehearsed, performances occurred only once, for the entire school in the modest dining hall at 8:30pm right after dinner.[16] Besides reflecting the presentation habits established at Black Mountain College, the "illustrated discussion" in many ways also mirrored the experimental living environment in which the three men had lived since 1963 when VanDerBeek, with his wife, Johanna, and their children August and Maximus, left the rising costs of housing in Manhattan to join an artists' cooperative in Stony Point, 35 miles north in Rockland County. Established and financed by Black Mountain College alumni Paul and Vera Williams in 1954, Gate Hill Co-op (called "The Land" by its members) was also home to Black Mountain associates M.C. Richards, David Tudor, and potters Karen Karnes and David Weinrib.

Still in existence, The Land was then a vital outpost for VanDerBeek, who built the family's house from a modular corrugated-metal kit. Between 1963 and 1965 he constructed a 31-foot-high metal dome structure in the wooded backyard by converting the rounded top of a mail-order grain silo into an experimental theater that functioned as a prototype for a communications system that he called the *Movie-Drome*. The interior space was outfitted with dozens of projectors—film, slide, and overhead—along with a mixing board and other editing and sound equipment. Projecting onto the dome's curved interior created an immersive effect for viewers who sat or lay prone on the floor taking in the moving image

presentations that VanDerBeek referred to as a
"visual velocity." Rather than being steeped in
the counterculture rhetoric of hallucinogenic
escapism or going "off the grid," the *Movie-
Drome* developed out of what VanDerBeek
described to Emshwiller as "an overwhelming
social necessity to do something on a large,
public scale," adding, "it's not intended just
for 20 or 30 people, but distributing that
across an entire society in some way."[17]
VanDerBeek's *Movie-Drome* was a manifestation of his "Culture: Intercom" concept,
which he emphatically typed out in a manifesto that was published in a variety of outlets
and often served as his artist's statement.
"'Culture: Intercom' and Expanded Cinema:
A Proposal and Manifesto" called for a multitude of "dromes" to be positioned throughout
the world, each linked to an orbiting satellite
that would store and transmit images among
the various sites. Through the *Movie-Drome*,
VanDerBeek sought a model for a real-time,
programmable communications system. He
referred to the image content projected onto
the curved interior of the *Movie-Drome* inter-
changeably as "image libraries, newsreels, and
feedback," presaging not only how communication networks developed into pathways for
the exchange of visual art and ideas, but also
the ways in which subjectivity would be radically altered.[18]

The *Movie-Drome*, VanDerBeek's conceptual
framework for experiencing information over a
network and through multiscreen projections,
came to characterize his particular definition of expanded cinema. Having literally taken
shape within the purview of his Black Mountain
College influences, the *Movie-Drome* was very
much informed by the aleatory strategies of the
neo-avant-garde, and responded to a spatially
and temporally discursive subject not addressed
by conventional cinematic forms. VanDerBeek's
prodigious output throughout the mid-to-late
1960s consisted not only of dozens of 16mm
films, but also hundreds of handmade 35mm
slides that he created by collaging Letraset
text over found black-and-white photographic
images as well as his own color photographic

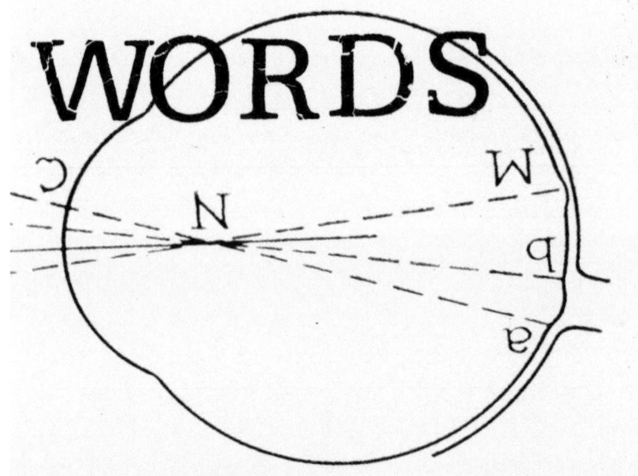

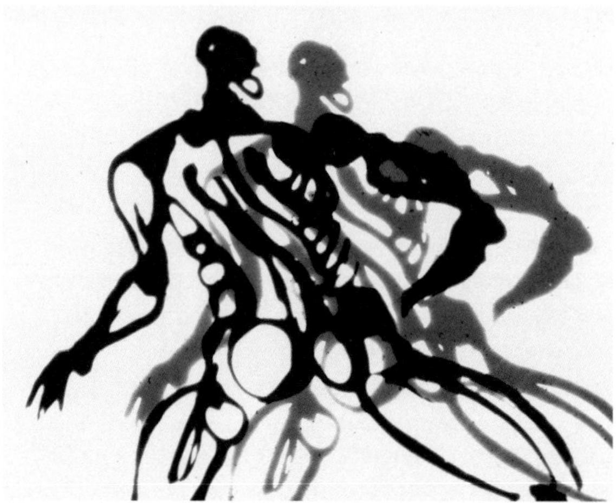

All:*Untitled*, n.d. Collage on handmade slide.

compositions shot in reversal 35mm film.
Dozens more 35mm slides were made by layering
acrylic gels and other transparent material in
abstract compositions. These can all be read as
components of a variable data set that could be
projected in seemingly endless permutations.

These resulting expanded cinema works were
also adapted for presentations outside of the
Movie-Drome. Most notable was VanDerBeek's
presentation of his *Poemfield* film series with
various 35mm slides at the Cross Talk Intermedia
festival in Tokyo in 1969. A year before Expo '70
took shape in Osaka, VanDerBeek, Cage, Gordon
Mumma, and other experimental film and
sound artists debuted several works inside
Yayogi National Stadium, where the gymna-
sium's floor was covered in plywood so that
VanDerBeek's roving projection carts could be
moved around freely.

Shortly after returning from Tokyo, VanDerBeek
and his family left The Land, and the *Movie-
Drome* was converted into a more conventional
studio by the co-op's next tenant. They moved to
Cambridge, Massachusetts, where VanDerBeek
was invited to be one of the first artists-in-
residence at MIT's Center for Advanced Visual
Studies, established by György Kepes two years
earlier in 1967. The research VanDerBeek initi-
ated while at CAVS placed an emphasis on
feedback and two-way communication within
art production, resulting in various iterations
of his *Panels for the Walls of the World*, among
other projects intended specifically for fax
transmission and television, including *Violence
Sonata*. First broadcast on two public television channels on New Year's Eve 1969, *Violence
Sonata* was designed for viewing on two sets at
once. The fullest realization of the project took
place on January 12, 1970, when, between each
of the three "screen acts," home viewers could
telephone live studio panelists with responses
to questions and thus participate in a discussion about violence in America.

VanDerBeek's focus on feedback mechanisms
throughout the 1970s moved beyond the novelty
of using real-time communication devices or

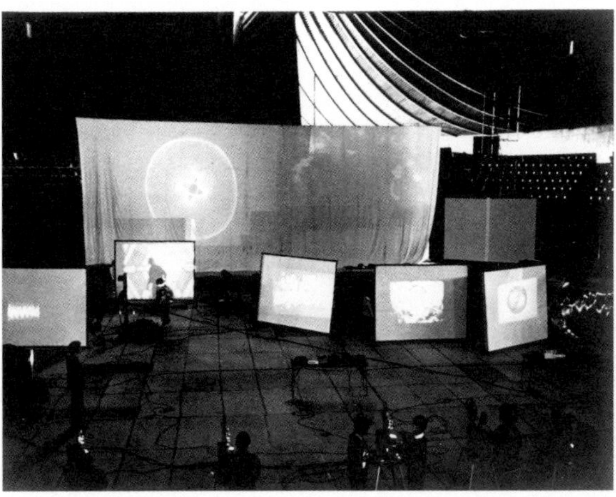

Found Forms. Installation view, Cross Talk Intermedia, Japan, 1969.

    Stan VanDerBeek: Collage Experience

live satellite feeds to initiate dialogue. Core to the development of his own media pedagogy was the notion that art itself was a direct form of communication—its own feedback mechanism. In 1975 when he joined the art faculty at the University of Maryland, Baltimore County (where he lived with his second wife, Louise, and their children Julia, Sara, and Johannes), he quickly became disillusioned with how quickly the advancement of communication technology outstripped students' abilities to articulate any sense of creative agency. In a 1982 article on media art and pedagogy published shortly before his death,[19] he outlined his ideal arts program as a type of corrective, one that would "stress research as well as performance…where past artistic achievements and future utilizations of technology would be examined so that students create ideas to change the cultural environment."[20] An artist, in VanDerBeek's estimation, not only has an ethical imperative to consider the question of how we absorb the world around us, but to also offer possibilities for modeling that irrevocably fragmentary experience. In this manner, VanDerBeek's media collages offer a radical reformulation of subjectivity as an accretive process—what could be considered in VanDerBeek's own terms a collage experience "where you take and reshape."

1 Johanna VanDerBeek, interview with the author, July 20, 2006. Johanna VanDerBeek graciously granted me access to numerous files, slides, exhibition ephemera, and other research material from Stan VanDerBeek's home and studio in July 2006. As a fellow artist and his wife from 1956 to 1973, she also provided additional biographical information referenced throughout this article. I am also grateful to Sara VanDerBeek and Johannes VanDerBeek for allowing me access to material at the VanDerBeek Estate at several phases of my research.

2 Stan VanDerBeek, interview with Ed Emshwiller, December 15, 1973. Anthology Film Archives collection nos. 122, 123, 124, 152, 153. 154. The recordings took place over two days in December 1973 and then again on August 19, 1974. I want to thank Andrew Lampert, archivist at Anthology Film Archives, who brought these tapes to my attention.

3 Stan VanDerBeek, interview with Richard Kostelanetz, summer 1966. Richard Kostelanetz conducted the interview with VanDerBeek with the intention of including the material in *The Theatre of Mixed Means*, a collection of interviews with artists who were early proponents of Happenings and "mixed means performances." See Richard Kostelanetz, *The Theatre of Mixed-Means* (New York: The Dial Press, 1968). Kostelanetz generously shared a copy of the interview in August 2007. In an e-mail to the author, he explained that he found a letter from VanDerBeek apologizing for his tardiness in responding to Kostelanetz's edits, which offers a suggestion as to why the interview was not included in the book.

4 Ken Knowlton, e-mail to the author, February 26, 2008. Ken Knowlton worked in the Computer Techniques Research Department of Bell Telephone Laboratories between 1962 and 1982, during which time he created the graphic programming languages known as BEFLIX, EXPLOR, ATOMS, and SPHERES, in addition to filing 10 US patents and developing a variety of applications for computer graphics primarily related to rendering gray-scale images on binary output devices. The technical aspects of Knowlton's BEFLIX system are described in two forms: first, as a 17-minute, 16mm black-and-white silent film, *A Computer Technique for the Production of Animated Movies*, produced using the very process it sought to describe and distributed by Bell Lab's Technical Information Library; and second, as a paper called "A Computer Technique for Producing Animated Movies," published in the *AFIPS Conference Proceedings*, Volume 25, 1964 Spring Joint Computer Conference.

5 Stan VanDerBeek, "EAT Talk, ca. 1968," sound recording. Experiments in Art and Technology Records, 1966–1993, accession no. 940003, Research Library, Getty Research Institute, Los Angeles.

6 For a more detailed consideration of what art historian Julia Robinson has called Oldenburg's "metaphoric mode of intervention" into 1960s art practice, see her excellent account in "Before Attitudes Became Form-New Realisms: 1957–1962" in *New Realisms: 1957–1962, Object Strategies Between Readymade and Spectacle*, ed. Julia Robinson (Cambridge: The MIT Press, 2010), 23–39, esp. 36–37.

7 *Snapshots of the City* is in the film collection of the Museum of Modern Art, New York. I would like to thank curators Anne Morra and Charles Silver for their help in arranging a series of screenings of VanDerBeek's film for my research.

8 Johanna VanDerBeek donated the only remaining print of the 16mm film to Anthology Film Archives. Claes Oldenburg re-edited another version of the film into a two-part work that he titled *Birth of the Flag I, II* (16mm, black and white, silent, 19 minutes each part). Crediting VanDerBeek with the film, Oldenburg's version also lists Diane Rochlin and Sheldon Rochlin as co-filmmakers and Rudy Wurlitzer as co-producer.

9 VanDerBeek, interview with Ed Emshwiller, December 15, 1973.

10 The work is highlighted in John Gruen's *The New Bohemia: Combine Generation* (New York: Grosset and

Dunlap, 1966), 156. Though *Pastorale et al* was performed publically, VanDerBeek rehearsed many of the elements earlier that summer in his *Movie-Drome*.

11 Cage and VanDerBeek wrote the poem used in *Poemfield No. 7*. Cage also provided the film's austere sound track. See my chapter, "Stan VanDerBeek's *Poemfields*: The Interstice of Cinema and Computing" in *Mainframe Experimentalism: Early Digital Computing and the Experimental Arts* (Berkeley and Los Angeles: University of California Press, 2011).

12 VanDerBeek, interview with Ed Emshwiller, December 15, 1973.

13 According to Johanna VanDerBeek, around 1959 at age 29, VanDerBeek was diagnosed with Hodgkin's lymphoma and subsequently received radiation treatment. While he never publicized this condition, he alluded to his treatment and failing health in his journals. Johanna VanDerBeek, interview with the author, July 20, 2006.

14 "Upon Awakening" is one of two signed poems that M.C. Richards sent to VanDerBeek with the heading "poems of love for Stan." Courtesy of the Stan VanDerBeek Estate.

15 Despite publishing the only English translation (1958) of Antonin Artaud's *Theater and its Double*, a formative text for the arbiters of experimental theater and artists including VanDerBeek, M.C. Richards's influence within the neo-avant-garde remains under-evaluated. For the exception, see Jenni Sorkin, "Live Form: Gender and the Performance of Craft, 1940–1970" (PhD dissertation, Yale University, 2010).

16 Jenni Sorkin's research brought the particular nature of Black Mountain College theater productions to my attention.

17 VanDerBeek, interview with Ed Emshwiller, December 15, 1973. Though VanDerBeek's DIY ethos is evocative of the counterculture rhetoric of the period, he never identified his work in these terms.

18 For further discussion about the *Movie-Drome*, see João Ribas's essay in this volume, as well as my article, "Stan VanDerBeek's *Movie-Drome*: Networking the Subject" in *Future Cinema: The Cinematic Imaginary After Film*, ed. Jeffrey Shaw and Peter Weibel (Cambridge: The MIT Press, 2003), 136–43, and dissertation, "The Experience Machine: Stan VanDerBeek's 'Movie-Drome' and Expanded Cinema Practices of the 1960s" (PhD dissertation, University of California, Los Angeles, 2009).

19 VanDerBeek died of cancer in September 1984.

20 Marion Weiss, "Stan VanDerBeek to Students: Take a High Risk!," *Journal of the University Film and Video Association*, no. 34 (Spring 1982): 19–20.

Stan VanDerBeek: Collage Experience

Stan VanDerBeek's "Industrial Metaphysical Revolution"

João Ribas

Culture fails to take into account that in technical reality there is a human reality...culture must come to terms with technical entities as part of its body of knowledge and values.
—Gilbert Simondon[1]

Stan VanDerBeek's itinerant artistic practice traversed nearly every creative medium of the twentieth century. As a self-described "technological fruitpicker," VanDerBeek readily adopted disparate forms of media—from 16mm film to Xerox machines and mainframe computers— to forge a vision of technology suffused with the promise of social transformation. Emerging from the progressivist tradition of Black Mountain College, VanDerBeek's early drawings and collages evince a formal vocabulary derived from Dada and the expressionism of the Beat Generation. The animated short films of the late 1950s and '60s, on which his legacy still rests, combine this collagist sensibility with innovative animation techniques, now regarded as one of the most significant contributions to the history of American underground film. VanDerBeek's experiments with various moving-image and communication technologies in the 1960s and '70s, including multiprojection environments and computer-generated imagery, are both integral to the formation of new media artistic practices, and potent historical examples of the liberative potential once anticipated from emergent technology. Such creative itinerancy extended to the artist's recurring presence

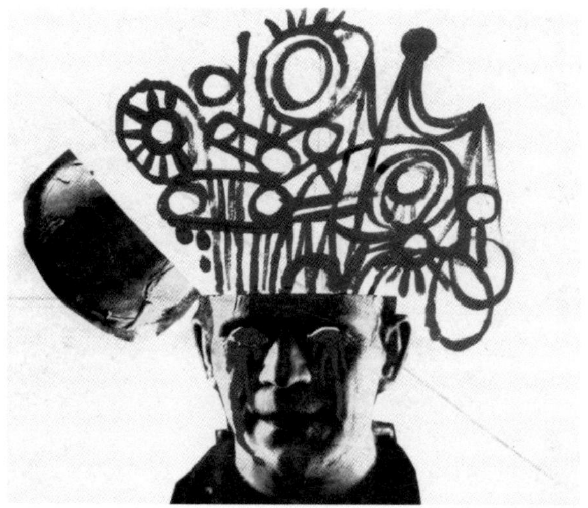

Film still from *Science Friction*, 1959. 16mm, color, sound, 9:46 min.

at several public and research institutions, in the form of residencies and grants. These afforded VanDerBeek rare access to complex information technologies whose artistic potential was often still largely undeveloped at the time he encountered them.

VanDerBeek's own description of this errant trajectory was that of a painter turning from "the 'object' tradition" of conventional artistic media towards "the magic of projected images," and the "reordering of our visual semantics."[2] Central to an understanding of this shift is a conception that underlies his artistic production as a whole: VanDerBeek's theorization of the epistemic and social dimensions of visual communication, found in a series of texts dating from the mid-1960s. Published in significant art and film journals of the time, these essays can be considered as constituents of a theory of media. Taken together, they outline VanDerBeek's attempt to conjoin the communal "ecstatic" events of 1960s counterculture to new forms of collective experience afforded by technology. Along with exploring the affective and epistemological terrain of the moving image, the writing also suggests an ethical and socially emancipatory potential to new forms of visual communication, developed through immersive environments of image and sound. VanDerBeek's writing functions as the program for a coming "industrial metaphysical revolution," transforming the relations between knowledge, perception, and technology.

Published in *The American Scholar* in 1966, *Re: Vision* ties the phenomenology of cinematic experience to a new model of aesthetic communication. Written in the epigrammatic prose style that typifies VanDerBeek's writing, the language is marked by the use of ellipses and a variety of discursive modes. Passages detailing working methods and technique—almost anecdotal in character—are set between aphorist and poetically constructed fragments:

I work in the painter's tradition and do everything myself as much as possible, which includes home development of my negatives, camera work, editing,

et cetera…
Motion, metamotion, kinetic identity, body-motor response, homeostatis, continuity…
the movement of the spheres…
are to be pinned like a moth stuck in the axis of the mind.[3]

The style is largely rhetorical throughout, indulging in VanDerBeek's predilection for wordplay and neologisms; the content is a combination of apparatus theory and cultural critique, interwoven through blocks of text similar in their structure to poetic stanzas. Only hinted at is the mystical empiricism that would come to inflect VanDerBeek's discourse. Yet already apparent are the concerns central to his entire artistic production after the mid-1960s: perception and the cinematic apparatus; social relations and communications technology; the transformations of perception and knowledge in an electronic age; and the dialectical relationship between technological apparatuses and the human condition.

Near the conclusion of the text, VanDerBeek introduces the concept of developing a methodology for the use of motion pictures as a new form of world communication, or what he calls an "ethos-cinema." This "non-verbal, international picture language" would effectively reposition motion pictures "as emotion-pictures," making use of the "revolution in worldwide aesthetics" produced by the history of cinema—which, as pointed out in the text, was only about 60 years old at the time. This techno-humanist conception of optical communication forms the core of VanDerBeek's essay "'Culture: Intercom' and Expanded Cinema," which appeared in the spring 1966 "Expanded Arts" issue of *Film Culture*, edited by Jonas Mekas.[4] Subsequent versions of the text were published in the *Tulane Drama Review* and *Motive* that same year. While the version of the text in *Film Culture* appears with crude, hand-drawn, pen-and-ink illustrations in the margins, several of VanDerBeek's collages accompany the alternate, subsequent excised versions of the text, subjected to different graphic treatments.

The poetic language of critique, rupture, and ethical imperative in *Re: Vision* is now directed towards the types of ludic transformations of consciousness associated with the American subculture of the 1960s, ideas such as revolutionary spontaneity and mind-expanding, psychedelic experience. VanDerBeek introduces the text "as a vision concerning motion pictures," once again reiterating the concept of cinema as a tool for world communication. To the cursory sketch of this provided in *Re: Vision*, he now adds a distinct epistemic-pedagogical element, its urgency fueled by an apocalyptic vision of the Nuclear Age:

As the current growth rate risk of explosives to human flesh continues, the risk of survival increases accordingly…
It now stands at 200 pound of T.N.T per human pound of flesh…per human on earth…
Mankind faces the immediate future with doubt on one hand, and molecular energy on the other…[5]

Technologically-mediated consciousness and the extension of the senses would function as a corrective to the dehumanizing distance between the proliferation of such technology and what VanDerBeek calls its "emotional-sociological comprehension."[6] An analysis of the effects of new technology on human civilization—our "metaphysical nuclear dilemma"—leads to a epistemic program whose abiding focus is a version of a 1960s counter-cultural trope: the reconfigured use of such technology for the production of altered forms of consciousness, linked to alternate forms of social relations.[7] In VanDerBeek's case, the process entailed the subjective assimilation of information via optical communication:

Technological research, development, and involvement have almost completely outdistanced our emotional and socio-"logical" comprehension. It is imperative that each and every member of the world community join the 20th century as quickly as possible.[8]

The production of a shared cultural and historical consciousness through technology echoes Marshall McLuhan's conception of mankind united by the electronic age into a "global village," with which VanDerBeek was familiar.[9] The methodology suggested to enact such an imperative—combining apperception and affect—is the combination of audio-visual devices into an "experience machine" or "culture-intercom" developed through work done at "audio-visual research centers on an international scale." Such technology would involve the "maximum use of information devices that we *now* have at our disposal," to "re-order the levels of awareness of any person."[10] VanDerBeek goes on to suggest that a series of such "experience machines" could be scattered about the world, receiving transmissions by satellite to give the audience "a sense of the entire world picture," through "a newsreel of dreams, a movie-mural."[11] One such example involves an "image flow" allowing for the perceptive assimilation of, effectively, the history of Western civilization. VanDerBeek proposes:

[A]n hour-long presentation using all sorts of multi-plex images, depicting western civilizations since the time of the Egyptians to the present through a rapid panoply of graphics and light calling upon thousands of images, both still and in motion, with appropriate "sound images." The last three thousand years of western life would be compressed into such an aspect ratio that the audience could grasp the flow of man, time, and forms of life that has led us up to this very moment, using the past and immediate present to help realize the likely future.[12]

What differentiates this technologically-mediated program from other practices of its time is the marked use of *representational* content—or rather, of *representations* functioning as perceptions.[13] The methodology VanDerBeek employs in the compressed arrays of thousands of images draws on cybernetic experiments with "flicker," or "visual effects induced by flickering lights" such as strobes.[14] Developed by British cybernetician Grey Walter, whose writing VanDerBeek cites, such experiments induced vivid illusions "of moving patterns whenever one closed one's eyes and allowed the flicker to shine through the eyelids."[15]

The "flicker" effect found its way, via experimental psychology and the popularization of
cybernetics, into many of the cultural practices of the 1960s, including multiple projection
environments and psychedelic light shows.[16]
Yet signal to VanDerBeek's use of dense image
projections—"a panoply of graphics and
light"—was not only the perceptive potential
of "flicker" but an insistence that the image
content *itself* could operate both on the level of
cognitive reasoning and the unconscious, thus
functioning as a pedagogical-epistemic tool.
"The purpose and effect of such image flow
and image density," he writes, "is both to deal
with logical understanding and to penetrate
to unconscious levels."[17]

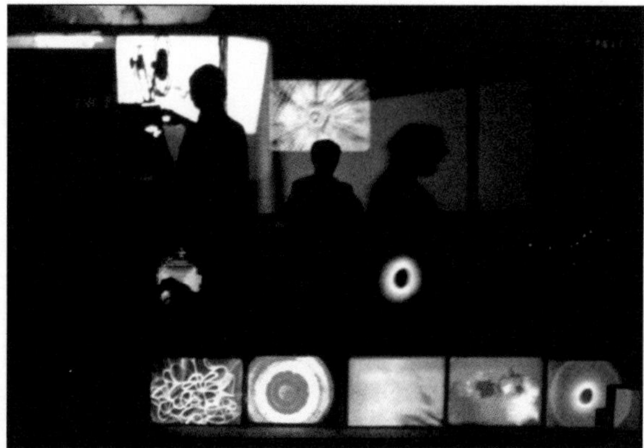

Poemfields. Installation view, Cross Talk Intermedia, Japan, 1969.

Here the importance of the "unconscious optics"
of Walter Benjamin to VanDerBeek's foundational premise, and its implicit relationship
to the apparatus of film, is clear. It was with
"the dynamite of the tenth of a second," that
the repressed, "unconscious aspects of subject
formation" became apparent through cinema
for Benjamin:[18]

By close-ups of the things around us, by focusing
on hidden details of familiar objects, by exploring
commonplace milieus under the ingenious guid-
ance of the camera, the film, on the one hand, extends
our comprehension of the necessities which rule our
lives; on the other hand, it manages to assure us of an
immense and unexpected field of action...with the close-
up space expands; with slow motion, movement
is extended....Evidently, a different nature opens itself
to the camera than opens to the naked eye—if only
because an unconsciously penetrated space is substi-
tuted for space continuously explored by man...the
camera introduces us to unconscious optics as does
psychoanalysis to unconscious impulses.[19]

VanDerBeek's instantiation of an "experience
machine" to explore such dynamics of moving
image media was the 31-foot-diameter dome
built in Stony Point, New York, between 1965
and 1967.[20] Functioning as a "dome-studio-
laboratory-theatre," this *Movie-Drome* was
slowly assembled from a variety of materials,
including a mail-ordered, aluminized steel

        Stan VanDerBeek's "Industrial Metaphysical Revolution"

structure.[21] Projected on the curved walls were a variety of juxtaposed images culled from disparate source material, including "old, new, [and] junk film,...slides, film strips or clips,... old magazines, (with pictures) books, engravings, old photographs, photostats, [and] negatives."[22] This material was used to create audiovisual mosaics utilizing various kinds of optical and sound equipment, including film and slide projections.[23] VanDerBeek describes the procedure in "Culture: Intercom":

In a spherical dome, simultaneous images of all sorts would be projected on the entire dome-screen...the audience lies down at the outer edge of the dome with their feet towards the center, thus almost the complete field of view is the dome-screen. Thousands of images would be projected on the screen...[24]

The illustrations accompanying the versions of the text published in *Tulane Drama Review* and *Motive* give a sense of the content of the "movie-mural" environment inside the dome: advertisements, newspaper articles—including, significantly, images of the Vietnam War—anthropological and art historical images, extracts from VanDerBeek's own films, and imagery drawn from a variety of disciplines, including anatomy, physics, and astronomy.[25] The result was an ever-changing immersive, collagist, and multimedia stream of images and sounds.[26] Described in *Re: Vision* as a "sight and sound research center," the *Movie-Drome* reconfigured Malraux's *Musée Imaginaire* for the electronic age, while functioning as a performative archive for the immersive transmission of historical consciousness.

The choice of the steel dome as the architectural form for this multiple projection environment is significant. Buckminster Fuller's mass-produced, flexible geodesic architecture seems adopted by VanDerBeek as an instance of what Felicity Scott has described as the "countercultural ethos motivating the use of domes as a technology for dropping out."[27] One such example is the Drop City commune founded near Trinidad, Colorado, on May 3, 1965, featuring its own geodesic architecture derived from

Fuller.[28] Among the structures built from assorted salvaged materials, including old cars and found plywood, was a large geodesic dome to house a "theatre for electronic psychedelics," described in a story in *The Denver Post* in 1967: "On the sides and ceiling of the new geodesic dome, electronic psychedelics will be produced by lights flashing on revolving paintings, by many films projected simultaneously and by sound speakers scattered throughout."[29] As with VanDerBeek's *Movie-Drome*, the architecture of Drop City suggests a paradox. A "proximity to the military-industrial complex," as Scott suggests, made the "widespread adoption of the geodesic dome and its relatives—not only as alternative dwellings but also as the infrastructure of counterculture festivals and at times even expanded cinema—appear as a historical and political anomaly."[30] Furthering this tension, as we shall see, were the very forms of technology employed within such multiprojection architecture.

VanDerBeek's use of moving-image technology as an extension of the sensorium, and its relationship to an attendant social project, places the *Movie-Drome* within a history of technologies for the exploration or expansion of the self that includes experiments such as Gordon Pask's cybernetic *Musicolor* machine, Bryon Gysin's "flicker"-inspired *Dream Machine*, Andy Warhol's *Exploding Plastic Inevitable*,[31] and Richard Aldcroft's *Infinity Machine*, featured in the same issue of *Film Culture* as VanDerBeek's essay. Such devices for optic and aural exploration are typically categorized under the rubric of "expanded cinema," as outlined in the writings of Sheldon Renan and Gene Youngblood, and subsequently the object of much critical discussion among the coterie of avant-garde film in publications and conferences throughout the late 1960s and '70s. The term, which VanDerBeek adopted early to describe his post-animation work in film, represents a direction in avant-garde practice away from the conventional forms and processes of film, and towards a revolutionary function for cinema.[32] For VanDerBeek, this was a response on the part of a generation of filmmakers to the fact that "the most revolutionary art form of our time is in the hands of entertainment merchants, stars, manufacturers."[33] The results were new forms of cinema integrating or responding to novel image-making technologies, such as television, video, and computer-generated graphics.[34] In Gene Youngblood's crystallization, the media effects of such "expanded cinema" practices are further linked to "collective group consciousness" and mind-expanding ideologies of 1960s counterculture.[35] Suggesting a gnostic, transcendental strain to media art, associated with developments in cybernetics and communications theory, Youngblood proposes an attendant focus within such artistic practices on a "cosmic consciousness" whose role in shaping sensory perception is related to that of synaesthetic experience and psychedelic experiments.[36]

Yet while "expanded cinema" has served as the interpretative and historical lens in discussions of VanDerBeek's cinematic production, the artist's own writing suggests its paradigm as an extension of the pedagogy of Moholy-Nagy, Hungarian polymath György Kepes, and the New Bauhaus in which, as Moholy-Nagy writes, "biological and evolutionary progress" is tied to the increasing "development and constructive use" of the senses.[37] Central to this process was the mediating role of images—and in particular, the designer—in adapting human vision to increasingly technical modes of seeing.[38] For Kepes, this constituted nothing short of developing a "language of vision":

The language of vision, optical communication, is one of the strongest potential means both to reunite man and his knowledge, and to re-form man in an integrated being. The visual language is capable of disseminating knowledge more effectively than almost any other vehicle of communication…Visual communication is universal and international: it knows no limits of tongue, vocabulary, and it can be perceived by the illiterate as well as by the literate.[39]

Both VanDerBeek's and Kepes's models thus share similar assumptions as well as common vocabulary: the primacy of a universal language of optical communication and its

epistemic function, albeit to varying ends. VanDerBeek's indebtedness to Kepes's studies of image relationships based on Gestalt perceptual psychology, in the juxtaposition of images in the *Movie-Drome* projections, can also be argued.[40] Kepes is particularly significant, given that it was under his aegis, as founder of the Center for Advanced Visual Studies at MIT, that VanDerBeek was invited there as a fellow, leading to his increasing involvement with computer technology. Though forgoing the scientific, empirical, and informational aspects underscoring Kepes's "language of vision," VanDerBeek similarly positioned the productive relationship between knowledge and perception in contemporary forms of visual communication, and in particular, film. As Kepes writes:

Visual language can convey facts and ideas in a wider and deeper range than almost any other means of communication. It can reinforce the static verbal concept with the sensory vitality of dynamic imagery. It can reinterpret the new understanding of the physical world and social events, because dynamic relationships and interpenetration, which are significant of every advance scientific understanding of today, are intrinsic idioms of the contemporary vehicles of visual communication: photography, motion pictures, and television.[41]

Kepes's particular concern lay with "structure," "organization," and "pattern"—revealed by technologically-mediated vision.[42] VanDerBeek's emphasis lies rather on restoring the link between technology's liberative potential (against an alienating or dehumanizing proliferation) and the avant-garde, and by extension, human civilization as a whole.[43] Such technological emancipation was to be developed through immersive moving-image environments—what Youngblood called "a stream of audiovisual events in time."[44]

Yet the origins of such multiprojection technology, as well as the dome architecture in which they were housed, problematize the emancipatory and consciousness-expanding potential of VanDerBeek's "experience machines." Such multiple-projection environments have their

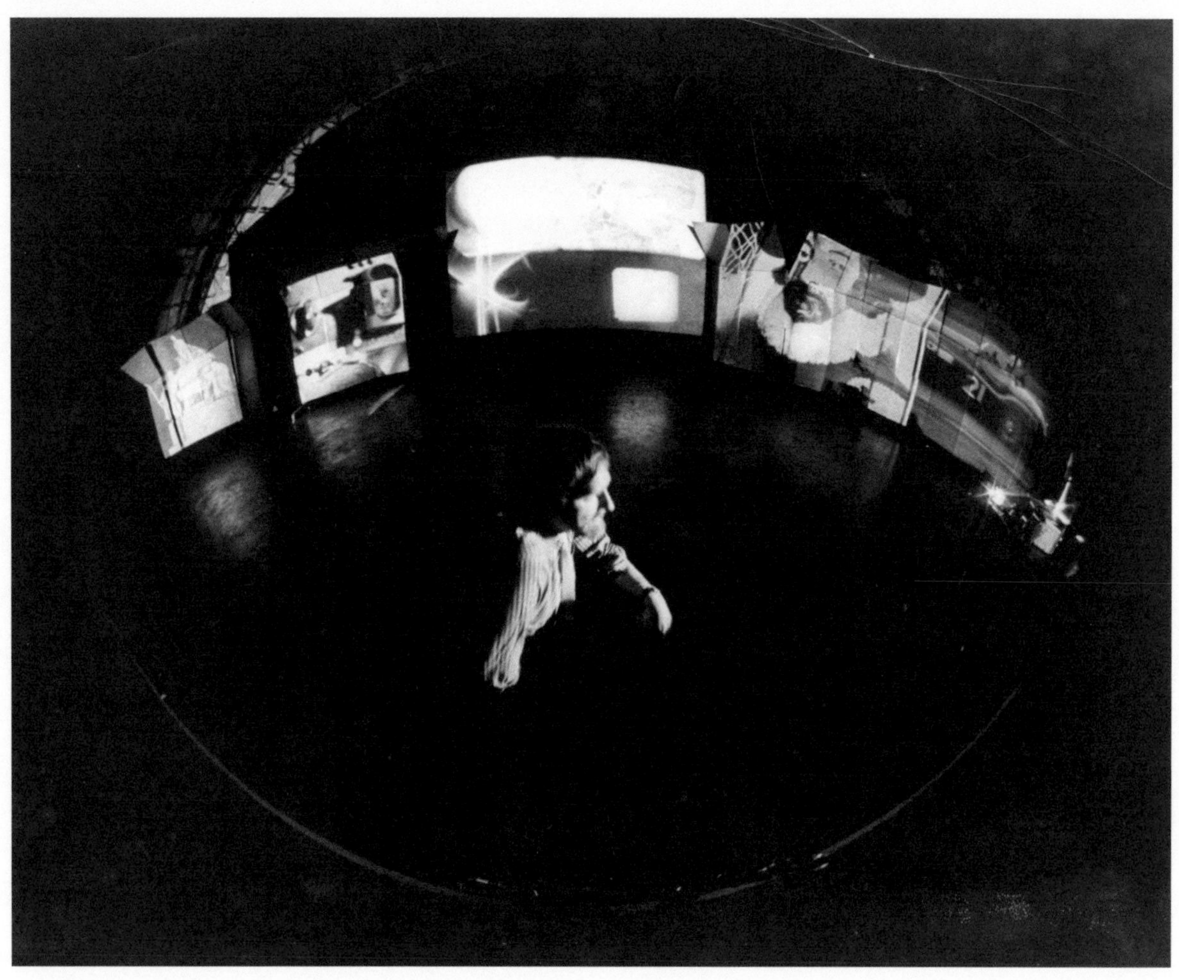

Movie Mural. Installation view, Institute of Contemporary Art, Boston, Massachusetts, 1968.

roots in the technology of the military industrial complex, and their development and use in the realm of advertising and political propaganda.[45] One such precedent is Charles and Ray Eames's multiscreen film *Glimpses of the USA*, projected on several large screens suspended within a Fuller-designed dome, as part of the 1959 World's Fair in Moscow. More than 2,000 images were projected simultaneously using seven 20-by-30-foot screens within a 250-foot-diameter dome.[46] Apart from any formal or technical similarity to the *Movie-Drome*, what is striking in the Eames's articulation is an interest in, as Beatriz Colomina writes, "an emotional response, produced as much by the excess of images as their content."[47] As we have seen, VanDerBeek's own "movie-mosaics" relied on a combination of the "flicker" effect and representations of knowledge as an epistemic tool.

The use of such multiprojection technology within the context of advertising and political propaganda "sought to naturalize the newly developing, technologically mediated modes of absorbing the augmented speeds and diversity of stimuli within an emergent information economy," as Branden Joseph explains.[48] For VanDerBeek, the use of film and moving-image technology was rather a means to join aesthetic forms of experience and technicity, or in Youngblood's terms, the aesthetic application of technology as "the only means of achieving new consciousness to match our environment."[49] Collective, immersive, and technologically-mediated experience—as a form of visual communication—could thus assuage the impact of technology and provide for its "emotional-social comprehension."

In this deeply ethical aspect to his conceptualization of media and the materiality of communication, VanDerBeek confronts a paradox of what Fuller described as transforming "weaponry" into "livingry." Can the technology closely associated with forms of mastery, control, and domination be redefined within the realm of artistic practice, and thus come to play a socially emancipatory function? As Friedrich Kittler has shown, the history of

the movie camera corresponds with the history of automatic weapons.[50] Distrustful of technology's impact on society while effusive about the role of the artist in the process of driving technologically-determined emancipation, VanDerBeek plays out a narrative of emergent technology in the postwar period, in which military research produces new technologies embraced by artistic and subcultural practices for progressive ends before their subsumption to domestic or commercial uses.[51] VanDerBeek expresses the role of the artist in this trajectory as one of opportunistic acquiescence:

I do not know what sort of world science and technology will give us in the future, though I sometimes try to envision it. Whatever world science gives us, that is the world in which art will have to be created and enjoyed...if art is to show the best advantage in a real present and a real future, it must be opportunistic in using what it can of the knowledge provided by science and the tools provided by technology.[52]

It is an adumbrated paradox VanDerBeek would confront throughout the 1970s and '80s as the computing technology of the industrial war machine became increasingly adapted to artistic functions and commercial applications—thereby necessitating an exploration of the dynamics of the processing, dissemination, and storage of information, as well as the transformation of the interfaces between man and machine. The coming ubiquity of this technology, which VanDerBeek predicted with cautious enthusiasm, would provide further areas of investigation into the use of image-media to create new social relations— underscored by the artist's continued search for technology to aid us in "seeing 'ourselves' and thus to evolve the ecology most suitable for life, for living."[53]

1 Gilbert Simondon, *On The Mode of Existence of Technical Objects*, trans. Ninian Mellamphy (London, Ontario: University of Western Ontario, 1980), 13.

2 Stan VanDerBeek, "Movies…Disposable art…Synthetic Media…and Artificial-Intelligence," *Take One* 2, no. 3 (January–February 1969): 16.

3 Stan VanDerBeek, "Re: Vision," *The American Scholar* 35, no. 2 (Spring 1966): 336–38.

4 The cover of the issue featured a picture of VanDerBeek in front of his still unfinished *Movie-Drome* in Stony Point, New York.

5 Stan VanDerBeek, "'Culture: Intercom' and Expanded Cinema: A Proposal and Manifesto," *Film Culture* 40 (Spring 1966): 18.

6 Notably, the images that accompany the version of the text in *Motive* include collages incorporating atomic clouds.

7 VanDerBeek, "Movies…Disposable art…Synthetic Media…and Artificial-Intelligence,"16.

8 Stan VanDerBeek "'Culture: Intercom' and Expanded Cinema: A Proposal and Manifesto," *Tulane Drama Review* 11, no. 1 (1966): 39.

9 At a 1965 conference in Carbondale, IL, attended by VanDerBeek, Buckminster Fuller, and Marshall McLuhan, the latter's presentation was on the "global village." See Gloria Sutton, "The Experience Machine: Stan VanDerBeek's 'Movie-Drome' and Expanded Cinema Practices of the 1960s" (PhD dissertation, University of California, Los Angeles, 2009), 122-189.

10 VanDerBeek, *Film Culture* 40, 17.

11 Ibid.

12 VanDerBeek, *Tulane Drama Review*, 45.

13 Jean-Louis Baudry, "The Apparatus: Metapsychological Aproaches to the Impression of Reality in the Cinema," trans. Jean Andrews and Bertrand Augst, in *Narrative, Apparatus, Ideology*, ed. Phil Rosen (New York: Columbia University Press, 1986), 315. Baudry writes that cinema evinces "a wish to construct a simulation machine capable of offering the subject perceptions which are really representations mistaken for perceptions." See Anne Friedberg, "Les Flaneurs du Mal(l): Cinema and the Postmodern Condition," *PMLA* 106:3 (May, 1991), 427. VanDerBeek writes of the viewer's "taking for granted that movies are reality" and the way they allow the "re-experience our experiences," in *Re: Vision*.

14 Andrew Pickering, *The Cybernetic Brain* (Chicago: University of Chicago Press, 2010), 76.

15 Grey Walter, *The Living Brain* (New York: W.W. Norton, 1963), 101. For a discussion on Walter's work with flicker, see Pickering, *The Cybernetic Brain*, 76–82.

16 Pickering, *The Cybernetic Brain*, 79-80.

17 VanDerBeek, *Film Culture*, 17.

18 Branden Joseph, "My Mind Split Open": Andy Warhol's Exploding Plastic Inevitable," *Grey Room*, no. 8 (Summer 2002): 96.

19 Walter Benjamin, "The Work of Art in the Age of Mechanical Reproduction," in *Illuminations*, ed. Hannah Arendt, trans. Harry Zohn (New York: Schocken, 1988), 236.

20 In my discussion of the *Movie-Drome* I am indebted to Gloria Sutton's scholarship on Stan VanDerBeek, especially her study, "The Experience Machine: Stan VanDerBeek's 'Movie-Drome' and Expanded Cinema Practices of the 1960s."

21 Stan VanDerBeek, Dome proposal letter, 25 Sept. 1964. Dept. of Film Special Collections, Box SV7, Folder "Drawings of dome." Museum of Modern Art, New York. See Sutton, "The Experience Machine," 33-35.

22 Stan VanDerBeek, Inventory, May 1965, The Estate of Stan VanDerBeek.

23 Sutton, "The Experience Machine," 92.

24 VanDerBeek, *Film Culture*, 17.

25 See Sutton, "The Experience Machine," 229–30. It is worth noting of one of the reproductions in the *Motive* version of the text features a geodesic dome, images of technical objects, as well as images of the kinds of technologically-mediated vision that illustrate Kepes's texts.

26 Ibid, 20, 229–30.

27 Felicity D. Scott, *Architecture and Techno-utopia: Politics After Modernism* (Cambridge: The MIT Press, 2007), 185.

28 Ibid., 157–66.

29 Ibid., 198.

30 Ibid., 157.

31 Joseph, "My Mind Split Open," 80–107.

32 Johnathan Walley, "The Material of Film and the Idea of Cinema: Contrasting Practices in Sixties and Seventies Avant-Garde Film," *October* 103 (Winter 2003): 16. See Sheldon Renan, *An Introduction to the American Underground Film* (New York: E. P. Dutton & Co., Inc., 1967), 237–79.

33 Stan VanDerBeek, "Cinema Delimina: Films from the Underground," *Film Quarterly* 14, no. 4 (Summer 1961).

34 Ibid.

35 Gene Youngblood, *Expanded Cinema* (New York: P. Dutton & Co., 1970), 387.

36 Ibid., 136.

37 László Moholy-Nagy, *Vision in Motion* (Chicago: Paul Theobald, 1947), 20. Cited in Rheinhold Martin, *The Organizational Complex* (Cambridge: The MIT Press, 2003), 57.

38 Ibid., 54.

39 György Kepes, *Language of Vision* (Chicago: Paul Theobald, 1961), 13.

40 Martin, *The Organizational Complex*, 51. It can be argued that the organizational principles behind VanDerBeek's compositional "mosaic" of projected images owe as much to the Dada-ist practices evident in his early work as to Kepes's studies of image relationships.

41 Kepes, *Language of Vision*, 7.

42 For a discussion on these elements of Kepes's "language of vision" see Martin, *The Organizational Complex*, 43–66.

43 Andreas Huyssen, *The Great Divide: Modernism, Mass Culture, Postmodernism* (Bloomington, Indiana: Indiana University Press, 1986), 9.

44 Gene Youngblood, "Metaphysical Structuralism: The videotapes of Bill Viola," http://www.vasulka.org/archive/Publications/FormattedPublications/Viola.pdf.

45 Beatriz Colomina, "Enclosed by Images: The Eameses's Multimedia Architecture," *Grey Room*, no. 2 (Winter 2001): 7.

46 Ibid., 9–10.

47 Ibid., 19.

48 Joseph, "My Mind Split Open," 92.

49 Youngblood, *Expanded Cinema*, 189.

50 Friedrich Kittler, *Gramophone, Film, Typewriter* (Stanford: Stanford University Press, 1999), 124.

51 Beatriz Colomina and Homi K. Bhabha, "Domesticity at War: Beatriz Colomina and Homi K. Bhabha in conversation," *Artforum*, Summer 2007, 444. Colomina examines the process of postwar architecture adapting technologies developed through military research for domestic use in *Domesticity at War* (Cambridge: The MIT Press, 2007).

52 Stan VanDerBeek, unpublished typescript, March 22, 1969, courtesy of the Stan VanDerBeek Estate.

53 VanDerBeek, "Movies…Disposable art…Synthetic Media…and Artificial-Intelligence," 16.

From the Ivory Tower to the Control Room

Jacob Proctor

On September 20, 1966, the New York Film Festival hosted "Expanded Cinema: A Symposium." Henry Geldzahler, the young curator of contemporary art at the Metropolitan Museum of Art, presided over a panel consisting of author and critic John Gruen, filmmaker Stan VanDerBeek, and artists Ken Dewey and Robert Whitman.[1] Over the course of a wide-ranging discussion, VanDerBeek insisted that the phenomenon of expanded cinema should be understood primarily as a reaction to a rapidly accelerating media landscape. "Painting is dead," he stated polemically in his opening statement, suggesting "artists working in uniting them-selves with their culture and technology is the most important cultural step that we are about to take."[2]

At face value, VanDerBeek's remarks might seem to epitomize the sort of unbridled opti-mism that we have come to associate with mid-to-late 1960s media ecology and techno-logical enthusiasm. Indeed, VanDerBeek's zeal for what he termed "approximate art" stemmed, in no small part, from his conviction that expanded cinema had the potential not only to transform the individual viewer's conscious-ness, but also to effect a new and potentially revolutionary global space of communication. "What we're talking about here," he explained, "is suddenly discovering [a] tremendous amount of communication consciousness and communication aesthetics and communication

instinct…I'm talking about an expanded cinema that quite literally circles…the world."[3]

The idealism and enthusiasm of VanDerBeek's pronouncements were tempered, however, by the sheer urgency with which they were delivered and the profound sense of anxiety that underpinned his position in 1966. This anxiety is palpable in VanDerBeek's manifesto "'Culture: Intercom' and Expanded Cinema," self-published as a single folded sheet in 1965 and subsequently published in no fewer than three different journals in 1966. The opening lines of the manifesto lay out the situation as VanDerBeek saw it:

It is imperative that we quickly find some way for the entire level of world human understanding to rise to a new human scale. This scale is the world. The risks are the life and death of this world. The tech-nological explosion of this last half century, and the implied future are overwhelming, man is running the machines of his own invention, while the machine that is running man runs the risk of running wild. Technological research, development and involvement of the world community has almost completely out-distanced the emotional-sociological (socio-"logical") comprehension of this technology. It is imperative that each and every member of the world commu-nity…join the 20th century as quickly as possible. The "technique-power" and "culture-over-reach" that is just beginning to explode in many parts of the earth, is happening so quickly that it has put the logical

 From the Ivory Tower to the Control Room

fulcrum of man's intelligence so far outside himself
that he cannot judge or estimate the results of his
acts before he commits them. The process of life as
an experiment on earth has never been made clearer.
It is this danger...that man does not have time to talk
to himself...that man does not have means to talk
to other men...the world hangs by a thread of verbs
and nouns. Language and cultural-semantics are as
explosive as nuclear energy.[4]

To remedy this state of affairs, VanDerBeek
proposed a two-pronged strategy: first, that
research begin immediately on the development of an international non-verbal mode of
communication based primarily in motion
pictures; second, he called for the development
of prototype theaters called "Movie-Dromes,"
the first of which he had built in his backyard over the course of the previous two years.
Constructed from prefabricated metal parts,
VanDerBeek's *Movie-Drome* was made to host
and house a range of expanded cinema experiments involving multiple projections, sound,
and collective audiences, who were invited
to recline on the platform-floor—the better
to take in the hemispherical surface of the
dome's interior above them. Once fully opera-
tional, the *Movie-Drome* was to be a dynamic
and multivalent space of communication and
spectatorial involvement, in which the locus
of meaning production would be shifted from
the singular authorial voice, issuing forth
from the solitary apparatus of projection, to a
plural and collective viewing subject. But in
order to fully grasp its significance, we need to
look not only to the better future it promised,
but also to the historical moment in which it
was conceived and the dire circumstances into
which it was designed to intervene.

Between 1957 and 1966, VanDerBeek produced
dozens of films, the majority of which are
animations of collaged elements cut from magazines and advertisements, collages of found
footage, or a combination of these techniques.
Beneath a veneer of apparent whimsicality,
VanDerBeek's early collage films mercilessly
skewer contemporary social mores and politics
in a potent blend of black comedy and pointed
satire. Thematic and formal elements recur
from film to film, yet it is difficult to establish
an exact chronology for this period of work, as
VanDerBeek consistently worked on five or six
films at a time. Consequently, the films from
this period enact a model of intertextuality
that privileges surface over depth. Rather than
developing or extending a theme or motif from
one work to the next, recurring fragments of
footage mark each film as one sampling taken
from a larger, unified but external visual field.
In this respect, VanDerBeek's films participate
in the radical shift in artistic practices during
the mid-1950s toward the condition that art
historian Leo Steinberg first described in 1968
as the flatbed picture plane.[5] Suggesting that
the pictorial field was "no longer the analogue
of a visual experience of nature but of *opera-
tional processes*," Steinberg compared it instead
to "tabletops, studio floors, charts, bulletin
boards—*any receptor surface on which objects
are scattered, on which data is entered, on
which information may be received, printed,
impressed*—whether coherently, or in a state
of confusion."[6] To hold all this "visual noise"
together, Steinberg argued, the picture plane
"had to become a surface to which anything
would adhere. It had to become whatever a
billboard or a dashboard is, *and everything a
projection screen is*."[7]

With rare exception, these early films lack a
cohesive narrative arc. They are instead defined
by an abbreviated episodic structure, composed
of a series of short vignettes that are cut off—
often violently—before the action reaches a
point of narrative coherence. Although these
vignettes are often thematically linked within
a single film, the cumulative effect is one of
radical discontinuity, akin to the experience of
flipping through the channels on a television,
only to be faced with the realization that each
one offers a variation on the same theme.

One subject to which VanDerBeek repeat-
edly returned, however, was the nuclear arms
race and the looming possibility of nuclear
conflict. It is immediately apparent in films like
Summit (1963) and *Breathdeath* (1963), both

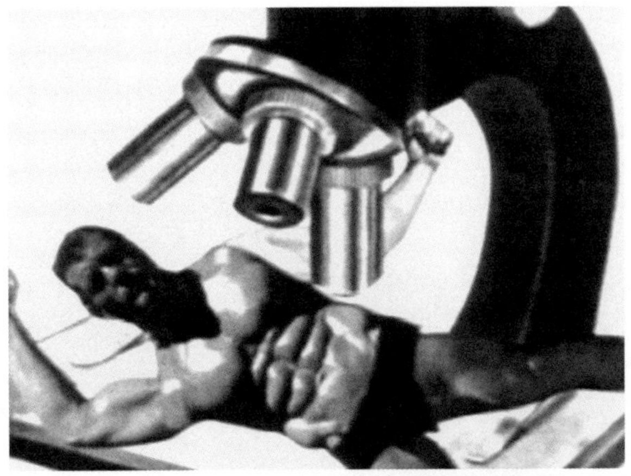

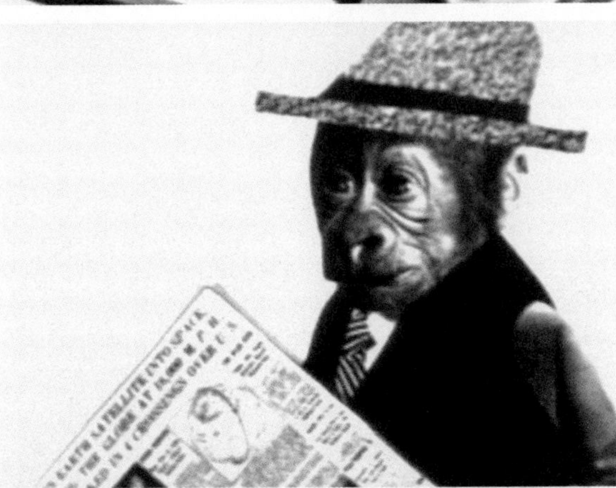

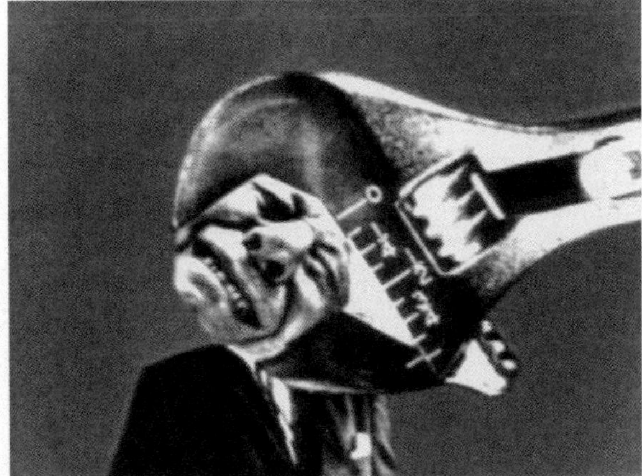

Film stills from *Science Friction*, 1959. 16mm, color, sound, 9:46 min.

of which post-date such events as the Berlin blockade and Cuban Missile Crisis, but it is already present in the early collage film *Science Friction* (1959), with its narrative of escalating cultural and technological competition ultimately culminating in nuclear conflagration.

Inverting the prewar avant-gardes' frequent celebration of the machine as a means of reordering—or "modernizing"—perception, *Science Friction* instead enacts the catastrophic consequences of visual perception not enhanced, but insulated and reified by mechanization. Visual prostheses abound in the film. From microscopes to telescopes, periscopes to peepholes, *Science Friction* bombards the viewer with the constituent elements of a scopic regime defined by technological mediation. Simultaneously penetrating and isolating, the profusion of optical devices that fill the frames of VanDerBeek's film is a phallic abundance matched only by the collection of "missiles"—newspapers, automobiles, altarpieces, architectural monuments, commodities—launched by the film's Cold War antagonists. An attack on a proto-apocalyptic regime of prosthetic vision, *Science Friction* confronts its reifying effects and challenges its divorce of vision from the lived experience of the individual. With its fusion of atomic anxiety and perceptual manipulation, the film is both an indictment of and intervention in the historical preconditions of nuclear apocalypse.

Like all VanDerBeek's films of the period, *Science Friction* never allows the viewer to forget that he or she is watching a film; its internal collage structure and attendant visual disjunctions effectively refuse any gesture toward an illusionistic, "equipment-free" reality. VanDerBeek's style of collage dramatizes the normally invisible effects of the editing process: the joining together of disparate pieces of footage to produce a seamless diegetic space. Moreover, beyond those sequences that align the viewer's gaze with the view through a seemingly endless series of visual apparatuses, the periodic recurrence of rotating optical discs, coupled with

     From the Ivory Tower to the Control Room

rhythmic editing and vertical montage strategies, physiologically implicates the spectator
in this dynamic. These visual strategies
locate the mechanization of vision not only on
the screen, but also in the spectator him- or
herself, insisting with ever-greater force that
we are not only seeing *through* a machine, but
increasingly seeing *as* a machine. The visual
field described by *Science Friction* is defined by
technological mediation, in which, to borrow
Sigfried Giedion's phrase, mechanization has
emphatically "taken command."[8] By identifying
this mediated perception with the physiological
processes of vision itself, VanDerBeek effectively defines the condition he would soon refer
to as "the mechanical metaphysic of our time."[9]

At the root of this increasingly dangerous
condition, VanDerBeek posited a new kind
of perceptual equivalence between representation and reality. In his 1962 text/collage
"Antic-Dotes for Poisoned Movies," VanDerBeek
describes a simulacral *mise-en-abyme* in
which movies figure as both fact and fiction,
ambiguously hailed as a means to "re-arrange
the senses."[10] As "the apparent object is now as
convincing as the genuine object," he laments
in a slightly later 1964 text, "literal experience becomes more difficult."[11] And as "anxiety
becomes a motor response" to a hypersaturated
media landscape, the only certainty would
appear to be that "audio-visual conditioning
produces results," an ominous pronounce-
ment, repeated twice within the short text,
underlining the physiological grounding of
perception.[12] Ultimately, this lack of visual
agency was the sinister corollary of a lack of
political agency. In his characteristically tele-
graphic and non-linear style, VanDerBeek
voices his frustration at:

decisions being made all the time, ahead, behind,
above us,
yet they always seem so bloodless...
decision like incision
in America, all revolt is now bloodless
surgery seems impossible in jello.
but talking about revolt is absurd...like talking about
decisions

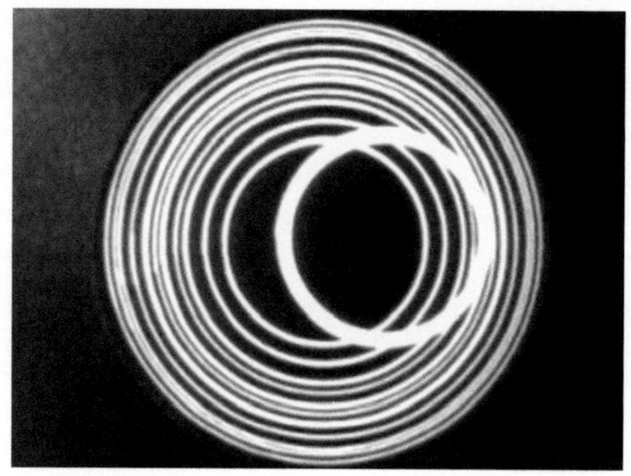

Film still from *Science Friction*, 1959. 16mm, color, sound, 9:46 min.

talking about "visions" is another matter
(while vision itself, is being shunted into a
reflex act?...the medulla oblongata takes over another
task)
if movies and vision can assume the same meaning
then visions take the path of least resistance...[13]

VanDerBeek's argumentative construction of
reality as a "vision effect" (to invert the terms
of the cinema's optically-induced "reality
effect")—and his textual characterization
of intervention therein as a form of surgery
or incision—is reflected cinematically in his
repeated visual and metaphoric conflation of
the filmmaker and the surgeon, a self-identi-
fication recalling Walter Benjamin's famous
distinction between the camera operator
and the painter as analogous to the differ-
ence between the surgeon and the magician.
In *Science Friction*'s opening credits, a team
of doctors operates on the head of Sigmund
Freud, from which emerges the punning
credit "A FLIM BY," immediately followed by
a view of a doctor wearing a surgical mask,
shown from below, across which appears "S
VANDERBEEK." The filmmaker's identification
with the figure of the surgeon is not, in this
context, an innocent or accidental moment of
iconographic self-fashioning; it is an analogic
relationship that VanDerBeek also advances
in the opening sequence of *A La Mode* (1957–
59), in which a close-up of an open eye cuts
directly to a medium close-up of a doctor
wearing a head-mounted mirror framing his
right eye. Here, the semantic slippage between
the "eye" as a physical organ and the "I" of the
first person pronoun is further accentuated
by VanDerBeek's substitution of the eye as an
image for the letter "I" in the word "VISIBLE,"
his favored term for film itself.

Given his repeated equation of the cinematic
representation of the world with the world
itself, VanDerBeek's practice of collage on the
former must be understood, at its most ambitious, as a form of surgery practiced on the
world as it is experienced and perceived by
the viewer. Moreover, the framing of the two
surgeons, one with his mirrored headgear, the

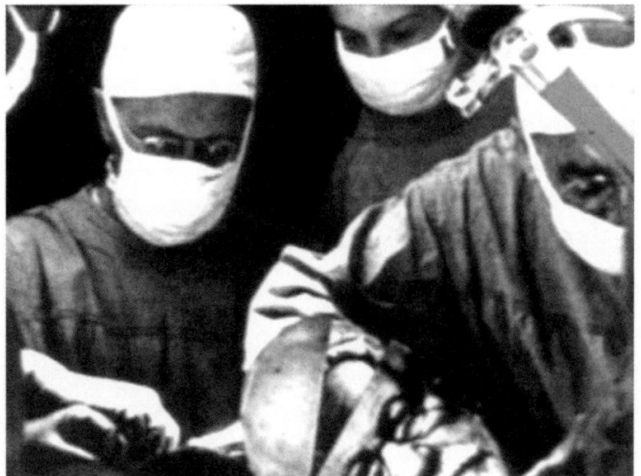

Film still from *Science Friction*, 1959. 16mm, color, sound, 9:46 min.

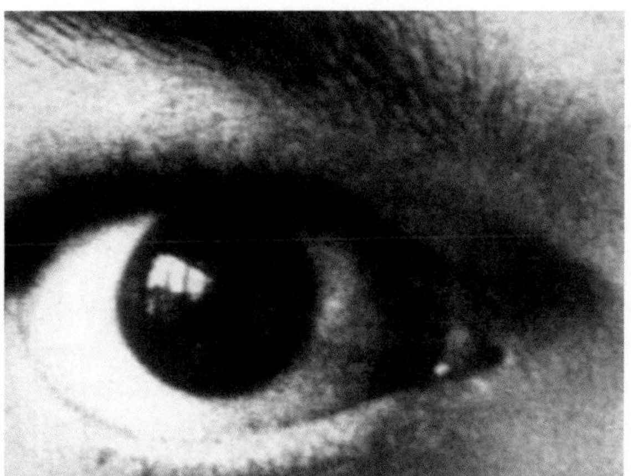

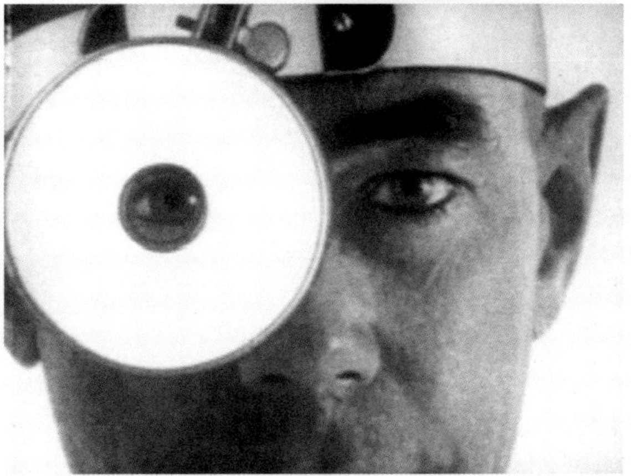

Film stills from *Science Friction*, 1959. 16mm, color, sound, 9:46 min.

   From the Ivory Tower to the Control Room

other viewed from below, as if seen from the operating table itself, suggests to the viewer that it is *our* reality that is being operated on, literally cut apart and rearranged by the film-maker into a new constellation. Collage figures here not only as a dismantling of the ruling order's "uninterrupted monologue of self-praise,"[14] but also as the means by which the artist can re-suture the tissue of reality into a new, dialogical configuration.

VanDerBeek asserted that the "poetic-politic" satire of his films was designed to "attack some of the aspects of super-reality that has [*sic*] been so hastily and carelessly built around us...the massive involuntary joke of living in a monolithic society and statistical age...to help disarm the social fuse of people living with anxiety, to point out the insidious folly of competitive suicide (through rockets)."[15] Clearly, one avenue by which he pursued this goal was the production of topical, dissident film texts that attempted to destroy "the stranglehold that commercial cinema has on our eyes and senses."[16] In marked contrast to the praxis of "personal" filmmaking pursued by many of his peers, however, VanDerBeek's filmmaking and the mode of spectatorship it pursued, was, from the beginning, an essentially public art. For VanDerBeek, the surgical intervention represented by each single-screen collage film operated as part of a broader agenda for communicative action, an activist project culminating in the creation of the *Movie-Drome*.

As the nuclear arms race escalated during the 1950s, it came to epitomize a dystopian vision of science run catastrophically amok, the mushroom cloud an icon of the seemingly inevitable results of geopolitical miscalculation. VanDerBeek was, in the words of his former wife, "obsessed" with the atomic bomb and the destruction of the world at the hands of man, an acute anxiety that manifested itself in the relentless iconography of nuclear war that permeated his oeuvre during the 1950s and '60s.[17] In a 1967 interview with Willard Van Dyke, VanDerBeek explained his motivations for using multiple projections in terms that identify life under nuclear threat as a catalytic factor for his practice:

On a single screen you can make a fairly complicated story, but it essentially deals with one idea at a time, coming at you from one place. But now things are happening to us in our cultural milieu, in our daily lives, that are not one thing at a time, and we find we are dealing with a multiplicity of events. It's very much more complicated than the simple idea of things happening to you logically, one after another...One of the reasons that I think painting isn't a valuable art form anymore...is that we are in a very curious time-space situation in the development of ideas and in the development of the world...[W]e must hold the world through this next period, which is an extremely delicately balanced nuclear-judgment time period. We must some how find a way to talk to each other, to talk to ourselves and understand ourselves. The problem about the future is that we may not get into the future...artists haven't got the privilege of going off to their ivory towers and isolating themselves.[18]

I would suggest that the culture of nuclear anxiety is also a crucial factor in understanding the implications of the *Movie-Drome*. VanDerBeek's decision to build his prototype hemispherical theater in his own backyard from mail-order parts may seem unusual today, but we should remember that he was not the only American engaged in backyard construction in the early 1960s. Although nuclear warfare had been a perceptible threat throughout the 1950s, nuclear anxiety reached a fever pitch in the summer and fall of 1961. On July 25th of that year, just days before the closing of the border between East and West Berlin, President Kennedy appeared on national television and urged the country to prepare for thermonuclear war by building family fallout shelters. In the months that followed, reams of civil defense literature were distributed throughout the country and nuclear anxiety turned to nuclear panic.

Shelter-building was not an entirely new idea in 1961; New York Governor Nelson Rockefeller and publishing magnate Henry Luce, among

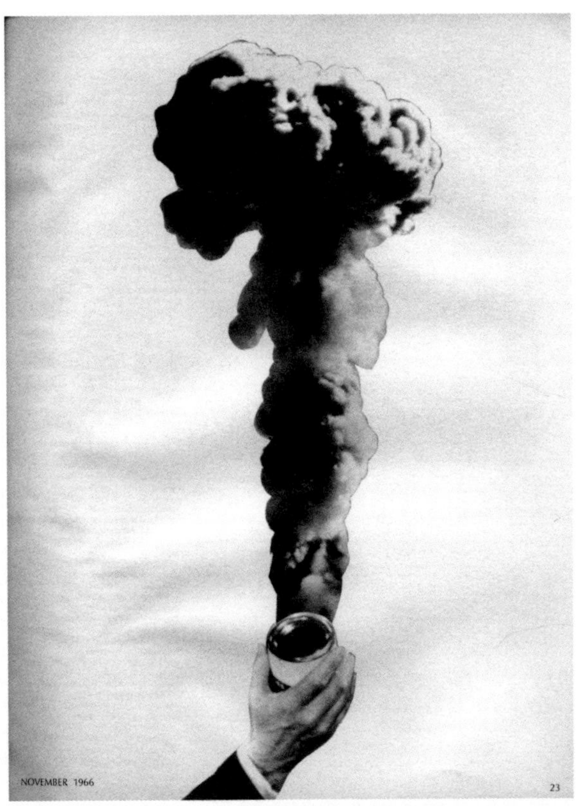

Stan VanDerBeek, "'Culture: Intercom' and Expanded Cinema: A Proposal and Manifesto," *Motive*, (November 1966).

others, had been actively promoting the construction of private shelters for years. In 1958, declaring "every home a fortress,"[19] the Office of Civil Defense and Mobilization began to publish a veritable library of how-to manuals on the subject, and had even exhibited prototype shelter models throughout the country.[20] In the wake of Kennedy's July 25th speech, no fewer than 22 million copies of the pamphlet *The Family Fallout Shelter* were distributed throughout the nation, as were millions of copies of others, including *Fallout Protection: What to Know and Do about Nuclear Attack* and *Family Food Stockpile for Survival*.[21] Reported in scores of articles in newspapers and magazines like *Time*, *Newsweek*, and *Life*, the American fervor for fortification grew steadily during the summer of 1961. With the Cuban Missile Crisis still to come the following year, the Atomic Age, with its insistent rhetoric of anxiety, had become, irrevocably, the national present-tense.

The backyard bomb shelter promised a protection predicated on the maintenance of impermeable boundaries separating "inside" from "outside" and "us" from "them," standing in as a visible microcosm of a much larger historical and ideological condition that historian Paul Edwards has described as "closed-world discourse."[22] VanDerBeek's plans for the *Movie-Drome* evolved in this anxious atomic landscape, appropriating the signifiers of the most archetypal of closed-world settings—the bomb shelter and the control room—spaces "enclosed and insulated, containing the world represented abstractly on a screen, rendered manageable, coherent, and rational through digital calculation and control."[23] In place of containment and deterrence, however, the *Movie-Drome* offered a model of radical permeability and unimpeded communication.

In the "Culture: Intercom" manifesto, VanDerBeek compared the overlapping flow of images within the *Movie-Drome* to the "'collage' form of the newspaper, or the three ring circus."[24] Ostensibly strange bedfellows, these three cultural forms are linked in that each overwhelms a collective audience with a "collision of facts and data" that cut across the standard divisions of documentary and fiction, reality and representation.[25] In the *Movie-Drome*, VanDerBeek hypothesized, "each member of the audience will build his own references from the image flow…and each individual makes his own conclusions… or realizations."[26] This valorizing equation of such disparate "media" as the newspaper and the circus proceeds from three axioms. First, the notion that both the newspaper and circus are fundamentally polyvalent environments, in which a multitude of potentially competing voices coexist and intermingle. Second, that such an environment engenders a heightened spectatorial agency, transforming viewers from passive receptors to active synthesizers. Third, that together these factors produce the conditions necessary for the creation of a viewing public capable of negotiating a media landscape increasingly marked by rapid change, interpenetration, and simultaneity.

By invoking the newspaper as one conceptual model for the *Movie-Drome*, VanDerBeek emphasizes both his structure's proposed function as a transmitter of information— particularly information about the real world—and its role as a virtual space within which such information will be combined, organized, interrogated, and recombined by an audience of autonomous individuals. This analogic coupling speaks to the Fourth Estate's power to shape American public discourse during VanDerBeek's lifetime and affirms the press's pivotal role in the development of Western liberal democracy more generally, an historical development analyzed in depth by VanDerBeek's contemporary, Jürgen Habermas, whose *The Structural Transformation of the Public Sphere* was first published in German in 1962.[27] For Habermas, the public, as it emerged in the eighteenth century, was first and foremost a *reading* public. By the midpoint of the twentieth century, however, *viewing* had almost certainly superseded reading as the

privileged form of participation and reception in which private individuals came together as a public. If, by the early 1960s, VanDerBeek considered the static form of the newspaper inadequate to the complexity and speed of contemporary life, conventional cinema and television—which he associated with a "one-point-perspective mind, and the one-point-perspective lens"[28]—hardly offered a more acceptable paradigm.

Instead, the *Movie-Drome* presented a radically decentered model of reception. In this respect, the *Movie-Drome* proposed a kind of sensory training ground, an audiovisual laboratory for the development of new forms of perception required to confront the challenges of the Nuclear Age. Despite VanDerBeek's call for the creation of an international picture language, in reality that language *already* existed in the ubiquitous and increasingly global language of mass culture. The challenge VanDerBeek perceived and addressed—in the *Movie-Drome* as well as in his single-screen collage films— was how to modify human perception in order to make that language comprehensible.

1 The transcript of the event was subsequently published as the front-page story in a special newspaper-style issue of *Film Culture* magazine devoted to the topic of "Expanded Arts." "Expanded Cinema: A Symposium," *Film Culture* 43 (1966).

2 Ibid. In citations from this and other documents, VanDerBeek's spelling, punctuation, and capitalization have been retained. On the rare occasions where it is absolutely necessary for clarity, changes or additions appear in square brackets.

3 Ibid.

4 Stan VanDerBeek, *'Culture: Intercom' and Expanded Cinema* (New York: Self-Published Flyer, 1965); Stan VanDerBeek, "'Culture: Intercom' and Expanded Cinema: A Proposal and Manifesto," *Film Culture* 40 (1966); Stan VanDerBeek, "'Culture: Intercom' and Expanded Cinema: A Proposal and Manifesto," *Tulane Drama Review* 11, no. 1 (1966); Stan VanDerBeek, "Culture-Intercom and Expanding-Cinema: A Proposal," *Motive* (November 1966): 13–23.

5 Steinberg's essay originated in a March 1968 lecture at the Museum of Modern Art, New York. It was further elaborated in the March 1972 issue of *Artforum* and was subsequently published as the title essay of Leo Steinberg, *Other Criteria* (New York: Oxford University Press, 1972), 55–91, to which the present citations refer.

6 Ibid., 84.

7 Ibid., 87–88.

8 Sigfried Giedion, *Mechanization Takes Command: A Contribution to Anonymous History* (New York: Oxford University Press, 1948).

9 Stan VanDerBeek, "The Cinema Delimina: Films from the Underground," *Film Quarterly* 14, no. 4 (1961): 15. VanDerBeek's "mechanical metaphysic" recalls László Moholy-Nagy's repeated invocations of a "mechanical imagination." See, for example, "Unprecedented Photography," in *Photography in the Modern Era: European Documents and Critical Writings, 1913–1940*, ed. Christopher Phillips (New York: Metropolitan Museum of Art, 1989), 84.

10 Stan VanDerBeek, "Antic-Dotes for Poisoned Movies," *Film Culture* 25 (1962): 71.

11 Stan VanDerBeek, "Interview: Chapter 1," *Film Culture* 35 (1964): 21. Similarly, in the introduction to the version of "Culture: Intercom" published in *Tulane Drama Review*: "for the moment this world and the idea of this world curve together in the mind resembling each other…image move, motion itself is moving if I think it's different it's an illusion." VanDerBeek, *Tulane Drama Review*, 38.

12 VanDerBeek, "Interview: Chapter 1," 21. VanDerBeek was not the first to posit such an equivalence, nor to remark upon the potentially stultifying effects of motion pictures on their audience. In *Dialectic of Enlightenment* (1947), Horkheimer and Adorno argued that: "Real life is becoming indistinguishable from the movies. The sound film, far surpassing the theater of illusion, leaves no room for imagination or reflection on the part of the audience, who is unable to respond within the structure of the film, yet deviate from its precise detail without losing the thread of the story; hence the film forces its victims to equate it directly with reality." Max Horkheimer and Theodor W. Adorno, *Dialectic of Enlightenment* (New York: Continuum, 1997), 126.

13 VanDerBeek, "Interview: Chapter 1," 20. Ellipses in original.

14 Guy Debord, *The Society of the Spectacle*, trans. Donald Nicholson-Smith (New York: Zone Books, 1995), 19.

15 Stan VanDerBeek, "On 'Science Friction'," *Film Culture* 22–23 (1961): 168.

16 Stan VanDerBeek, "If the Actor Is the Audience," *Film Culture* 24 (1962): 92.

17 Marilyn Mancino and Anne Morra, "Intervista a Johanna VanDerBeek," in *Il Grande Occhio Della Notte: Cinema D'avanguardia Americano 1920–1990*, ed. Paolo Bertetto (Torino: Museo Nazionale del Cinema, 1992), 106.

18 Adrienne Mancia and Willard Van Dyke, "Four Artists as Film-Makers," *Art in America* 55, no. 1 (1967): 73. VanDerBeek's language here cannot help but recall McLuhan's statement that, "To prevent undue wreckage in society, that artist tends now to move from the ivory tower to the control tower of society." Marshall McLuhan, *Understanding Media: The Extensions of Man* (Cambridge: The MIT Press, 1994), 65.

19 Civil Defense Director Leo A. Hoegh, in an address of January 21, 1958, quoted in Guy Oakes, *The Imaginary War: Civil Defense and American Cold War Culture* (New York: Oxford University Press, 1994), 131.

20 To little effect, though: by the end of 1960, only around 1,500 private shelters had been constructed.

21 Walter Karp, "When Bunkers Last in Backyards Bloom'd," *American Heritage*, February/March 1980, 85–86. Also see Kenneth D. Rose, *One Nation Underground: The Fallout Shelter in American Culture* (New York: New York University Press, 2001).

22 Paul N. Edwards, *The Closed World: Computers and the Politics of Discourse in Cold War America* (Cambridge: The MIT Press, 1996), 8.

23 Ibid., 104.

24 VanDerBeek, "'Culture: Intercom' and Expanded Cinema: A Proposal and Manifesto, *Film Culture* 40 (1966): 16.

25 Ibid.

26 Ibid.

27 Jürgen Habermas, *Strukturwandel der Öffentlichkeit. Untersuchungen zu einer Kategorie der bürgerlichen Gesellschaft* (Frankfurt: Suhrkamp, 1962). English edition: Jürgen Habermas, *The Structural Transformation of the Public Sphere: An Inquiry into a Category of Bourgeois Society* (Cambridge: The MIT Press, 1989).

28 VanDerBeek, "The Cinema Delimina: Films from the Underground," 15.

Stan VanDerBeek: From Classroom to Artist in Residence to the World

Michael Zryd

To say that Stan VanDerBeek was ahead of his time is not only to state the obvious, but also to describe his central artistic mission. From a historical perspective, we can see his work operating at the forefront of experimental film, as well as video and computer art—after all, he coined the term "expanded cinema," setting the stage for the verdant landscape of current multimedia and multiscreen new media art. But, for VanDerBeek, to be ahead of one's time was the very definition of an experimental artist working the cutting edge, both as an individual and as part of a larger cultural formation of artists and thinkers whose mission was rethinking the parameters of art, culture, and society in the 1960s and '70s. Such was the fecundity of his imagination and his imperative to innovate, that while artist-in-residence at NASA (1979–80), he said, "I gave them no chance to reject my proposals. When they refuse one project, they had already another project on their desk."[1] The very fact that an experimental maker of VanDerBeek's wild and utopian temperament should find himself at NASA—and also working with institutions like the United States Information Agency (USIA), Massachusetts Institute of Technology, Harvard University, and CBS-TV, to name a few—acknowledges VanDerBeek's and the historical period's unique openness and forward-looking ethos, especially at the (often ignored) institutional level.

Among his generation of experimental film-makers, VanDerBeek was widely acknowledged as a leading multimedia artist.[2] Mark Bartlett has also described Stan VanDerBeek as a "multi-platform artist," a term that usefully unpacks VanDerBeek's important relationship to institutions and his unique process of doing art *through* institutions. For while the "other Stan"—Brakhage, VanDerBeek's justly cele-brated contemporary—attempted to disavow institutions in the name of a radical personal vision, VanDerBeek embraced collabora-tive, international projects that incorporated multiple large, public organizations into his art-making: colleges and universities, foun-dations, scientific laboratories, arts councils, television stations, and government depart-ments like NASA and USIA.

Platforms are like a series of institutional sites from which new extensions of technology and media can radiate. The multiplatform artist makes institutions work as platforms from which to launch artistic interventions in new social, political, and technological contexts. Throughout his career, VanDerBeek mobilized numerous such platforms in the fields of educa-tion, art-science laboratories, foundations, and governmental organizations.

Education especially held uniquely utopian parameters in the late 1950s and '60s as science, vision, and media took on a global scope and urgency as the Cold War developed. The post-Sputnik panic sparked massive new funding to education that, even if inspired by the geopolitics of the space race and the military industrial complex, nonetheless gave education and experimentation high cultural value, with film and television especially privileged as educational modes.[3] Riding the wave already set in motion by the GI Bill and the baby boom generation, enrollment at universities and colleges rose exponentially. In tandem with an expanding economy, there were surplus resources accessible to experimenters, at least until the late 1970s recession. The space race also inspired a sense of international competition that extended from technological R&D (research and development) in science to arts: the United States had to be competitive culturally, which in time led to the establishment of arts councils and increased the prominence of bodies like the Ford, Guggenheim, and Rockefeller Foundations, all of which funded experimental film and media in this period.[4] VanDerBeek received grants from all of these foundations in addition to numerous grants from the National Endowment for the Arts (NEA) and awards from the American Film Institute.

There was a web of interactions at both the institutional research level and the pedagogical level wherein extending media meant extending education—and expanding education called for expanded media. For VanDerBeek, this meant working in a variety of ways in educational institutions: as an instructor, artist-in-residence, or researcher in labs devoted to exploring new media forms.[5] He held long-term positions at Columbia University (1963–65), State University of New York, Stony Brook (1967–72), University of South Florida (1972–75), and finally at the University of Maryland, Baltimore County (1975–84), while holding artist-in-residence status or teaching courses at over 12 other universities, including the University of Southern California, Colgate University, MIT

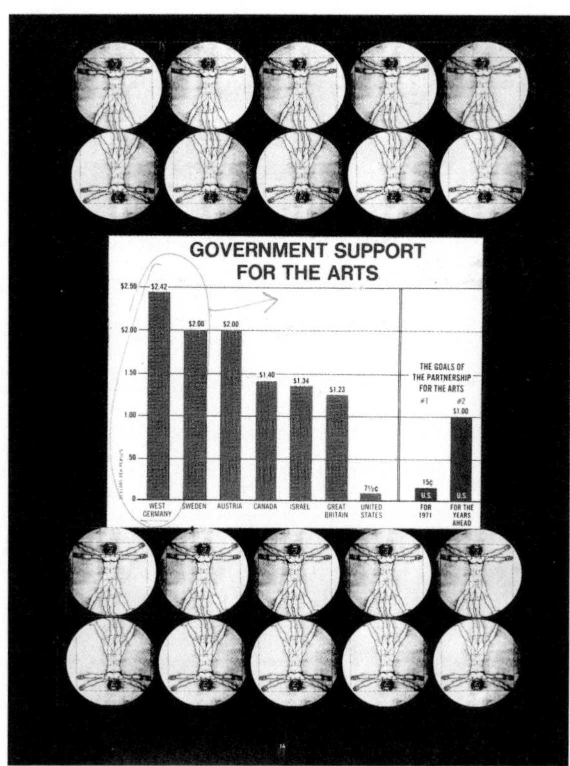

Untitled (History of Violence), ca. 1970. Collage on paper, 11 x 14 in.

INTRODUCTION TO FILM PRODUCTION—Stan Vanderbeek
part 1

Cinema-the Motorized Metaphysical Art
and the hand held film   Vangram #1

Duchamp records
flashlight in the eyes
punched film
flip cards zoeatrope and kids toys dealing with motion

George Melies	Trip to t.e Moon	(my copy S.V.)
Edison	The Great Train Robbery	(U of W)
Bob Breer	Blazes	(film coop)
N.McLaren	Fiddle Dee Dee	(U of W.)
S.Vanderbeek	Breathdeath	(own copy S.V.)
Duchamp	Anemic Cinema	(MofMA)
S.Vanderbeek	Phenomenon	(own copy S.V.)

Supplies:
Darkroom supplies:safe lights, yellow wratten;D-Eleven developer
3 gal.solution;rapid fixer for 3 gal.solution;6 plastic buckets
one gal.each minimum; paper towels,sponges, thumb tacks;drop lines;
photo-flo or wetting agent small bottle; flashlights for each stu-
dent-pen type-sm powered;phonograph-3 speed; 2000 ft.app.positive
printing 16 mm stock single perf.; 2000 ft approx. high contrast
16mm single perf. stock; adaquate supply of 16mm daylight loading
spools (loo ft) adaquate supply of 16mm plastic take-up spools;
16mm cores; 16mm split reels, 16mm splicers; 16mm projectors-
sound-two preferred.

Untitled, ca. 1968. Ink, pencil, and typescript on paper, 11 x 8 1/2 in.

(György Kepes's Center For Advanced Visual Studies), and California Institute of the Arts.

Television was hotly debated terrain in the late 1960s, seen by some as a mind-sucking commercial disgrace and by others as having the radically democratic potential to disseminate alternative visions to a mass audience. VanDerBeek saw a continuity between the film culture from which he emerged and television. At a 1967 University of Cincinnati symposium, "Perspectives on American Underground Film," that grouped VanDerBeek with Stan Brakhage, John Cage, and Jonas Mekas, VanDerBeek noted, "The whole structure of film is changing. And so are the means of distribution. Films can now come to you by way of educational television. And there's talk of Ford funds putting up an ETV satellite. Also, when they expand the electro-magnetic wave transmission process we'll have as many television stations as we now have radio stations."[6] Some of VanDerBeek's artist residencies had crossovers with TV stations connected to the host university, as at University of Hawaii's KHCT Educational Television and Kentucky Educational Television (KET) in Lexington. VanDerBeek also worked with the major American experimental television stations WGBH (Boston) and WNET (New York). VanDerBeek's institutional profile made him more visible than most experimental filmmakers in the mainstream media; he was interviewed for and had his work presented on CBS, ABC, and Canadian television.

Two case studies illuminate VanDerBeek's micro and macro approach to how artists and institutions can productively interact, extending and expanding the horizons of media and education. The first is his teaching syllabus that, in concrete hands-on fashion, invites students to explore a vast range of media. The second is one of VanDerBeek's (many) hyper-ambitious projects, a proposal to establish the position of "Artist in Residence to the World," a scheme that encapsulates VanDerBeek's multiplatform aspirations.

VanDerBeek's syllabus for his basic "Introduction to Film Production" course works as a pedagogical model not only for a student to learn the basic elements of film production, but as a conceptual model for the exploration of the horizons of moving image and sound across media. The first week is "Cinema, the motorized metaphysical art and the hand held film" and the list of activities includes "Duchamp records" (a version of Duchamp's *Disc Bearing Spirals* (1923) that VanDerBeek played on a three-speed phonograph), flip cards, Zootropes, and "Flashlight in the eyes" (to explore persistence of vision). The 16mm-film and darkroom supplies stipulated for the first day allow students to make "Vangrams," likely photograms intended as a variations on Man Ray's "Rayograms." The first four weeks of the course are devoted to the "hand made film" with accompanying screenings of films by, among others, Len Lye, Norman McLaren, Stan Brakhage, René Clair, and VanDerBeek himself. The next module of the course is four weeks of animation, illustrated with an admirably international cast of films from Canada, Europe, and the United States. That VanDerBeek should devote fully half of his course to handmade film and animation suggests his roots in artisanal production and echoes Lev Manovich's more recent claim that photographic cinema is but a brief moment in a larger history—that of animation, which Manovich asserts is in fact the über-form of the moving screen image.[7] For VanDerBeek, the most sophisticated technologies of the period—the course concluded with computer imaging—were still grounded in the basic formal principle of still frames in sequence.

The second half of the course hews closer to the topics of a more traditional film production course—editing, sound, storyboarding, shooting—but VanDerBeek opens up each topic, encouraging radical experimentation with both old and new technologies. The week titled "Introduction to editing and editorializing or Seeing is Believing—if you can believe that!" has the students working with found footage—"junk film"—while the second week

    Stan VanDerBeek: From Classroom to Artist in Residence to the World

Massachusetts Institute of Technology Center for Advanced Visual Studies 40 Massachusetts Avenue Cambridge, Massachusetts 02139

Nov I, I969

NOTES ON....

ARTIST IN RESIDENCE TO THE WORLD

As an experiment in global communication, I wish to
propose that a group of artist's...made up of artists from
many different countries travel about the world offering
there ideas and their work in different ways...i.e.:
(A "Hope" Ship of artists and international Art Lab!...
A "Culture-Intercom"--!!).

1. For 6 months, visiting in one country for one
   month each, that as a group we give a series of
   performances in that particular country...as
   individuals within the group we also perform and
   visit and lecture...and if possible to create
   new work while enroute.

2. This travel plan is to include as wide ranging
   and different parts of the world as possible.

3. In the course of these travels, as much integration
   and use of all media be explored (television and
   radio in particular).

4. The purpose and conduct of this experiment is
   many-sided:

   a) To explore the upcoming problems of
      international cultural exchange. i.e.,
      nonverbal art forms...intra-cultures...
      art and technology...sattelite T.V.

   b) To explore the attitudes and responses
      of artists and audiences to integrated
      performances.

   c) To "seed" the world with the idea of in-
      ternational exchanges motivated by art-
      ists of good will whose concern is the
      environment and ecology of the world.

As a rough outline I would like to propose and suggest:

1. That a balanced team of artists of different disciplines from each country be formed, i.e., a poet,
   dancers, musician, film...technician.

2. That the artists be picked with the overall relationship of making a total unit representing
   all of the arts..

Telephone 864-6900, Extension 4415

Notes on....Artist in Residence to the World, 1969.
Typescript on paper, two sheets, each: 11 x 8 1/2 in.

Massachusetts Institute of Technology Center for Advanced Visual Studies 40 Massachusetts Avenue Cambridge, Massach

The countries suggested for the tour include U.S....
Japan...India...Africa...Italy...Poland...Russia...Sweden...
England...France...Mexico.

These are very general notes concerning this proposal.
In practice, this could be executed by outfitting an air
cargo plane which would be an air taxi to take us to different parts of the world. It could be a boat, as in the
"Hope-Ship" which could be outfitted with theater space
in the halls or on the deck, etc., or with a portable air
dome which could be completely independent and which can
be erected any place in the world within a few hours.

It would seem to me that the basic problem that cultural
exchanges face should be leveled at a kind of work-shop
attitude about the arts and in particular how they would
relate on a global and non-verbal level. A by-product of
this confrontation by artists and technicians from all over
the world would be the portability, compatibility, and
technical integration of new medias in local use all around
the world, which is, I believe, an essential style for the
artists of the future to start thinking in terms of.

I see my idea as an experiment in global aesthetics
and communication, bringing together artist's from all
over the world to work together with the latest technologies
in an attempt to understand that it is the world itself
that we relate to, and it is the people and the artist's
of the world that <u>we all</u> relate to.

STAN VANDERBEEK

Telephone 864-6900, Extension 4415

on editing involved rear projection screens, shooting televisions screens, and using "high power magnets for T.V. distortion" (evoking Nam June Paik's *Magnet TV* of 1965). For the week on "story boards, scripts, and narration," VanDerBeek screens Si Fried's *I.B.M. film* and uses Claes Oldenberg's scripts for Happenings as models. The introduction to sound, "Enter Auditory Space," features John Cage, Jackson Mac Low, and "computer music," while the second week on sound, "The Eye and Ear Theater and Light as Art," is synaesthetic in focus. For that week, course materials include a color organ, oscilloscope, and a strobe unit borrowed from the physics department, while the main reading is a text by Kepes. Two weeks on "The Techniques of Vision 1940–50" start with 8mm and 16mm film and move to "closed circuit video tape camera and recorder," computers, and lasers. The last week on the syllabus (before, appropriately, a series of "Open" weeks) is "Introduction to mixed media: All the senses get in the act." That VanDerBeek's course concludes with a multiplicity of media and forms appealing to all of the senses is appropriate to the cumulative generosity with which he approached artmaking. In this last week, VanDerBeek shows his own films using three 16mm projectors, two slide carousels, and a tape recorder to create a multimedia show in class. This is described as an "Information Concert," a wonderful, prescient metaphor for how VanDerBeek's sense of formal art practice—the high art "concert"—intersects with a flattened conception of artistic material as "information."

His syllabus is a model for how to learn an expanded notion of cinema from the still frame to the multiscreen media universe. It anticipates many current directions and changes in cinema studies curriculum, but also demonstrates how a syllabus that charts the development of cinema from a technological angle of discovery, invention, and experimentation can be sustained through a body of experimental films as exemplars. If this sounds like the despised narrow conception of experimental film as R&D for "real film" (i.e., commercial cinema), it is important to see that VanDerBeek's sense of R&D was not limited to technique, but conceives of cinema as the art form that both expands consciousness and makes film part of everyday life. In the tradition of Maya Deren, Brakhage, and Hollis Frampton, VanDerBeek explored a strand of technologically-focused practice and theory that is connected to the desire to explore and expand the limits of consciousness through the media arts. The radical—and prophetic—nature of this mixture of practice and theory cannot be underestimated, and laid much of the groundwork for changes occurring in both education and art from the 1960s to today.

In this respect, VanDerBeek's syllabus echoes a larger shift occurring nationwide as the idea of experimentation with film—as the new medium for a new society, especially youth (the "Film Generation")—opened up a moment of popular interest in experimental film.[8] New film courses and programs were being established around the country—film was by far the fastest growing field in the arts and humanities in this period—facilitated in part by the availability of inexpensive film formats like 8mm that allowed students to make films and schools to hire filmmakers to teach them.[9] Jonas Mekas noted this phenomenal growth in his June 1968 "Movie Journal" column: "Every university, every college I've been to lately is planning to start one or another kind of film department or film course, usually with a creative filmmaker in residence. Some of the most versatile avant-garde filmmakers, Stan Vanderbeek [*sic*], for instance, have been practically swamped with requests to join universities as film-maker in residence."[10] VanDerBeek was renowned as a teacher and mentor in the experimental film community.[11]

For VanDerBeek, the most ambitious forms of filmmaking exploring consciousness were being undertaken at the ground level by everyone who had a camera, including "children five years old [who] are interested in making movies":

This whole study of our responses to the world of sight seems to me to be at a remarkably amateur level. And that examination is being conducted now, quite literally, by millions of people. Six or seven million eight mm. cameras now are in use in the United States—that was my last count a year ago. All of us who have eight mm. cameras are potentially doing basic research into filmic form and our processes of response.[12]

VanDerBeek's educational mission was not, in the end, limited to the research lab or the exclusive university classroom—it pervaded all areas of experience, as we are, for him, "doing basic research."

The expansiveness of VanDerBeek's ideas about education is also found in his research proposals. One of the most intriguing is his idea for an "Artist in Residence to the World" program, a hyper-ambitious project that would involve artists, arts councils, foundations, universities, and governments:

As an experiment in global communication, I wish to propose that a group of artists…made up of artists from many different countries travel about the world offering their ideas and their work in different ways…i.e., (A "Hope" Ship of artists and International Art Lab!)[13]

In some ways, he was proposing a variation of a touring program. Indeed, in 1970–71, a year after this proposal was drafted, VanDerBeek made multimedia presentations on a world speaking tour for USIA in Cyprus, England, France, Greece, Iran, Israel, Lebanon, and Turkey. VanDerBeek's proposal was removed from the boosterism of most national tours supported by USIA (including Edward Steichen's *Family of Man* exhibition) and was pitched at not only the international level (artists from many different countries collaborating and interacting), but also at the multimedia and multidisciplinary level. VanDerBeek called for "as much integration and use of all media (television and radio in particular)" with a "balanced team of artists and disciplines from each country." The familiar goal of international exchanges ("to 'seed' the world with the idea of international exchanges motivated by artists of good will whose concern is the environment and ecology of the world") is deepened by VanDerBeek's recognition that the experiment would work at the level of "nonverbal art forms…intra-cultures." VanDerBeek saw the importance of new media technology— in a remarkably farsighted conclusion to the proposal—in the hands of international artists:

A by-product of this confrontation by artists and technicians from all over the world would be the portability, compatibility, and technical integration of new medias in local use all around the world, which is, I believe, an essential style for the artists of the future to start thinking in terms of.

What VanDerBeek points to as the current capacity of artists—and indeed almost anyone with access to the technology and bandwidth— to collaborate on new media projects, especially involving web interfaces, as "portability, compatibility, and technical integration of new medias" has indeed become "an essential style for the artists of the future."

Understanding VanDerBeek as a multiplatform artist who embraced rather than rejected institutions finally requires an appreciation for the positive spirit with which he approached art, culture, and the possibilities of technology. Certainly, one cannot ignore the reactionary and stultifying logic that "institutional thinking" can often bring. We cannot forget the other lesson of VanDerBeek's experience at NASA: although he always had another idea to pitch, he must have experienced his fair share of refused projects. Necessarily, as his correspondence with foundations, arts councils, and other bureaucrats reveals, VanDerBeek's engagement with institutions involved his negotiation of tensions and contradictions between his proposals and the priorities of the larger body. Nevertheless, his sense of possibility remains the key note and—as he said in his concluding remarks at the symposium in Cincinnati—as one launches from (multiple) platforms, there is only one way to go:

In the optimistic best of all possible worlds, I feel that we are on the edge of a very interesting cultural evolution. I see this in the people who are in or out of school who want to engage in this art, in cinema, who plunge in in their own manner…As I see it, now I'm sort of a launching pad and where it will go I don't know. But up; it has to be up.[14]

1 Jürgen Claus, "Stan Vanderbeek: An Early Space Art Pioneer," *Leonardo* 36, no. 3 (2003): 229.

2 Unlike film-centered artists like Stan Brakhage or Ernie Gehr, VanDerBeek was closer to Hollis Frampton, Michael Snow, or Joyce Wieland in working with multiple visual and sound media.

3 John A. Douglass, "A Certain Future: Sputnik, American Higher Education, and the Survival of a Nation," in *Reconsidering Sputnik: Forty Years since the Soviet Satellite*, ed. Roger D. Launius, John M. Logsdon, and Robert W. Smith (London: Routledge, 2002), 327–62; Charles R. Acland, "Curtains, Carts and the Mobile Screen," *Screen* 50, no. 1 (2009): 148–66.

4 The NEA was established in 1965 and the New York State Council on the Arts in 1960, supported by Governor Nelson Rockefeller.

5 VanDerBeek was also involved with the "Kineticonics Planetaria Understanding" research project, which investigated the use of planetariums for the "educational enhancement" of "the neurologically handicapped child." See R.N. Davis, "A Kineticonics Technical Note," prepared for the Middle Atlantic Planetarium Society.

6 Stan VanDerBeek, quoted in Hector Currie and Michael Porte, eds., *Cinema Now I: Stan Brakhage, John Cage, Jonas Mekas, Stan VanDerBeek* (Cincinnati: University of Cincinnati, 1968), 16.

7 Lev Manovich, *The Language of New Media* (Cambridge: The MIT Press, 2001).

8 Stanley Kauffman, "Some Notes on a Year with *Blow-Up*," in *Film 67/68: An Anthology by the National Society of Film Critics*, ed. Richard Schickel and John Simon (New York: Simon and Schuster, 1968), 274.

9 Michael Zryd, "Experimental Film and the Development of Film Study in America," in *Inventing Film Studies*, ed. Lee Grieveson and Haidee Wasson (Durham, NC: Duke University Press, 2008), 182–216.

10 Jonas Mekas, "Movie Journal," *Village Voice*, June 6, 1968, 49.

11 A detailed appreciation of VanDerBeek is Tom DeWitt, "A Recollection of Stan Vanderbeek," *Gallery Paper* (Poughkeepsie, NY: Dutchess Community College Art Gallery, 1993).

12 Stan VanDerBeek, quoted in Currie and Porte, *Cinema Now*, 21, 17.

13 Stan VanDerBeek, "Notes on Artist in Residence to the World," unpublished text, November 1, 1969. All subsequent quotations are from this two-page proposal.

14 Stan VanDerBeek, quoted in Currie and Porte, *Cinema Now*, 6.

FILM CULTURE No. 35   WINTER 1964-65

STAN VANDERBEEK

INTERVIEW: CHAPTER 1

Movies are nothing . . .

we go to a museum
and spend as much time as possible looking at any pretty girl rather than
        the pictures . . .

So then it is the sociological milieu . . .
not paper, celluloid, clay words, . . . songs in the head . . .
cinema absurda, architecture, are . . . none of it
the media is life
life is the art
(even when we have direct transmission into the sea of our cortex with shadows
        and translucent facts while we sit in our "living" room . . .)
the message is complete
we are as one in a socio-logical stew
in an astral dining room.
but it's not so much the fat sense of a pregnant america that distracts me . . . it's the
        sense of decision
decisions being made all the time, ahead, behind, above us,
yet they always seem so bloodless . . .
decision like incision
in america, all revolt is now bloodless
surgery seems impossible in jello.
but talking about revolt is absurd . . . like talking about decisions
talking about "visions" is another matter
(while vision itself, is being shunted into a
reflex act? . . . the medulla oblongata takes over another task)

if movies and vision can assume the same meaning
then visions take the path of least resistance
intuitive logic . . . metaphysical geometry . . . identity . . . image . . . image-symbol
art . . . city planning of the mind so to speak is a pure research
that is just beginning in motion images . . .

opticular mirrors

we are beyond decisions . . . america.

particular acts of seeing, hearing,
belief acts of communication, radio, television, telephone
have committed our consciousness to another state
that is well beyond decisions of consciousness (awareness)
instinct takes over . . .
(driving a car is a perfect example . . .)
the industrial metaphysical revolution has only just begun

this lack of decision however invades our anxiety
anxiety becomes a motor response, almost another sense
(or at least a sense extension)

motion, meta motion, cinema-kinetica, continuity, flow . . .
the movement of the spheres
are to be pinned like a moth
stuck in the axis of the mind to relieve the anxiety of change (doubt) of
the movement of life itself by studying it . . . by changing it into a symbolic form
that is as real and meaningful as life itself . . .

emotional leverage
is a fact

anticipation
is a fact

motion pictures need rights

motion pictures need rites

motion pictures need rituals of anticapatory forms
(not to be confused with meditative forms . . .)

the artist-filmmaker today
is caught between the age of realism and surrealism
and is off on a journey beyond reality

motion pictures need research laboratories run by artists

theatre in america has no need for the entire stage
the apparent object is now as convincing as the genuine object
life has not gone as fast as art . . .

life has no real walls . . . and no real museums . . .
the world's fair is an example
it is not very interesting to people . . . perhaps because it is designed as an object
in the museum tradition . . . what if it had been designed as objects, books,
sounds, motion pictures that were sent in boxes to each person in america to
own and have in his own possession to directly give each of us continuous research
pleasure and stimulation of international idea . . .
a direct inter-change of 20th century stimulus made possible by mass production
that could serve as aesthetic reference material for the next 10 years . . .
(is this idea clear . . .??? in other words a kit of communication, tools sent
to 150 million americans that had projectors, books, slides, films, records,
objects, display cases, etc. . . . all within it, designed by artists of the world,
the basic tools all mass produced so that the budget for this kit would cost
no more than the pavillions' installations at the fair itself . . . Since you have
to pay to get into the fair, the citizen could send this money in return for
the kit which would send him continuously changing displays and materials for a
suitable period of time . . . from all over the world . . .)so that the world
became a reference library . . .
the 1964 world's fair is not a commercial success they say, mostly
it can be anticipated
audio-visual conditioning produces results

magic is suffering
altho words are coming from the air, they are not helping the poets
altho images are coming from the air they are not helping the artist

literal experience becomes more difficult
audio-visual conditioning produces results

poets as we know them are sacrificed . . .

the instinct to change the common object gets stronger
when the object gets too boring

the artist is like the trapeze artist, who has to practice all
day long in order not to break his neck at the evening performance

every artist in some way must give credit to another artist

ideas have replaced emotion in art . . .
ideas are the new emotion

articraft . . . a pun word (artifat, arty-fact . . .)
today's art becomes fact before it ever becomes fiction.

the full flow of color, sound, synthesized form, images changing image-ideas,
and images of plastic form (abstract expression) have in no way begun to
be explored in man's experience . . .
have so very little been explored in cinema terms . . .
sight and sound, the changing illusion of the world that stops
only in the mind is the media . . .
movies are nothing
and everything.

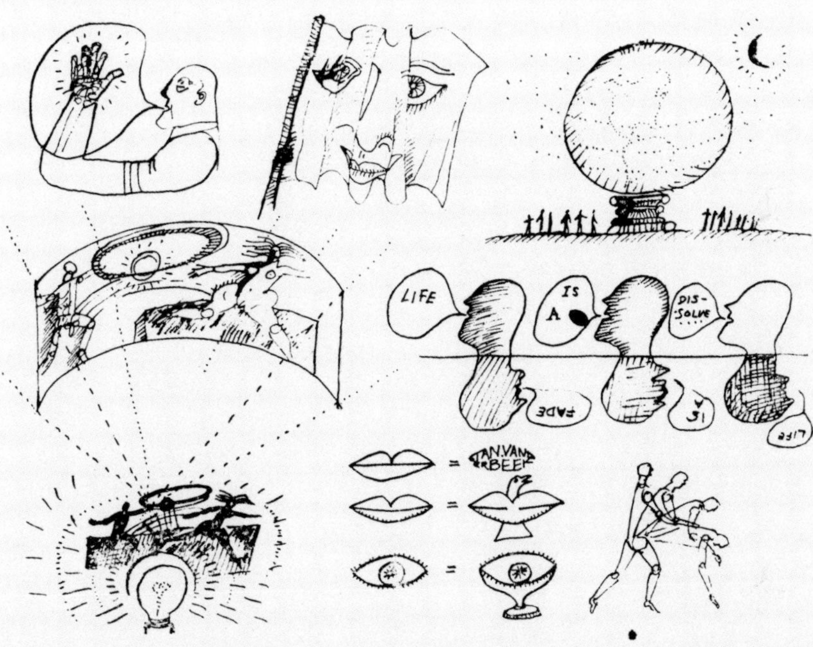

Re: Vision

STAN VAN DER BEEK

Vision undergoes re-vision; intention, symbol, reality
are the factors that undergo constant change
in the appearance of any art form.

Motion pictures—
pictures in motion—
seem most suited to the metaphysics of change,
to life in motion,
and as such cinema is becoming the most significant of art forms.

"One thing that is new is the prevalence of
newness, the changing scale and scope of change
itself, so that the world alters as we
walk in it. . ."
(Robert Oppenheimer, from "The Open Mind")

I like to think that life is a dissolve. . .

. . . and that seeing is the real illusion, that a sense of reality
is a sense of the senses. . .
that a sense of reality is a sense of non-sense. . .
that movies should delight the eye and rearrange the senses. . .
that movies are changing the art of seeing. . .
that movies are an art of seeing. . .
that movies are an illusion. . .
that seeing is believing.

The irony of art and life reminds us that "motion pictures"
are really a series of "still" pictures, which are being replaced
in the projector at less than 1/24th of a second . . . reaching
our eye at 186,000 m.p. second.
That we see the illusion of motion is based on the retention
of image, or the eye's inertia.

Motion pictures are apparent motion. . .
The film worker deals with "visual velocity" and "visual inertia,"
laws of sight that seem similar to laws in physics—
or at least to definitions of sight that contemporary
artists are exploring.
If movies and "vision" can assume the same meaning
then visions take the path of least resistance, that is,
intuitive logic, intuitive geometry, image-symbol making, art-
city planning of the mind, a form of research
that is just beginning in motion images. . .

335

(Retinal art such as strobiscope stimulation that produces
colors from black and white images . . . the possibility of
mental movies. . . .)

> "If confusion is the sign of the time, I see
> at the root of this confusion a rupture
> between things and words, between things and
> the ideas and signs that are their represen-
> tation. . ."
>
> (Artaud)

The apparent image and the approximate image interrelate in
our national sense of photo-reality. It is not inappropriate
that we have a magazine called "Life"—that we take for granted
that movies are reality. . .

That we take for granted much of our American life as it is reflected in
photo-reality is evidenced by a lack of self-criticism
and satire. . . .

> Paul Klee said:
> "Satire is not an excess of ill humor, but
> ill humor resulting from a vision of some-
> thing higher . . . ridiculous man, divine God.
> Hatred for anything stagnant out of respect
> for pure humanity. . ."

Malraux pointed out that life has no real walls . . . and no
real museums. . .
The World's Fair is an example:
It was not very interesting to people, and was a commercial
failure, perhaps because it was designed as an object in
the museum tradition. . . .

But if it had been designed as objects, books, textures,
smells, sounds, motion pictures, that were sent in boxes
to each person in America to own and keep in his possession. . .
to give each of us continuous research pleasure and the stimulation
of international ideas. . .
a direct 20th-century stimulus made possible
by mass production, that would serve as reference material
until the next Fair. . .

In other words a kit of communication tools sent to 150,000,000
Americans—projectors, tape recorders, books,
slides, films, display cases, *et cetera*—designed by the artist
designers of the world, mass-produced so that the budget for
this kit would cost no more than a pavilion's installation.

Since one had to pay to get into the Fair, the citizen could
have sent this money in return for the kit. For a suitable time
period the Fair would have sent him continuously changing displays

336

and materials from all over the world . . . some to keep and some
to exchange, like books from a world library.

The World's Fair was at best merely fair. It reproduced the
ideas of 1939, not 1964 . . . It could be
anticipated that audio-visual conditioning will produce new results. . . .

I like the process of making films, because it is a way for me
to have dialogues with myself.
I work in a small studio-dome, which I built myself from a silo
top.

I work in the painter's tradition and do everything by
myself as much as possible, which includes home development
of my negatives, camera work, editing, *et cetera*. . .

I often make my films without too much conceptual preparation,
using the film process of animation itself as a means
of note-taking.
Thus in the making of one film, a process or idea for another film
often comes about.

I also like to work on a variety of films at the same time
(often as many as six) and don't expect to see a finished
film for several years. . .

Editing a film, often inter-editing from one separate film
into another, continues the conversations with the self. . .
Cinema, like significant painting, must be made on
the basis of self-expression and necessity. . .
There are no geniuses in film-making, only desperate
men. In my opinion the audience cannot be considered as the final
target for their film work, but it may be implicated. . .

The major failure of commercial films made by the film "industry"
is that they represent the range of public-accepted vision that
cannot be made private . . . whereas the film poet is confronted
with the dilemma that his private vision can in no way be made
public. . .

Motion pictures are just now beginning to come out of the literary
perspective of the novel and staged drama they were born in. . .

It is interesting that after nearly 400 years of art that was
preoccupied with realism—growing mostly out of the theory of
perspective and its effect on the senses—this preoccupation
has at last reached its ultimate form in photography, particularly
motion-picture photography.

It is part of the interesting nature of art that at this same
juncture in the crossroads of art, with the perfection
of a means to capture exactly perspective and "realism,"

337

the artist's vision is turning more to his interior, and in a sense to an
infinite exterior (photos of Mars), abandoning the logic of
aesthetics and springing full-blown into a juxtaposed and
simultaneous world that ignores the one-point-perspective mind
and the one-point-perspective lens.

Another factor of particular interest is that movies represent
a kind of international decompression chamber, being the only
international art form that is portable, reproducible and
universal in popularity. . .

I am fascinated by one of the current theories about dreams
which holds that dreams are a way for the body to get rid of
body poisons (which get burned up in the dream-act).

If this holds true, it seems likely that motion pictures
might be a way for us to burn up international and national
"toxic" attitudes. Perhaps this is an aspect of the
moviegoing ritual, and of the value of the Hollywood "dream
factory". . . .

Clearly, movies help us to re-experience our experiences, which
seems to be a basic human need.

Motion, metamotion, kinetic identity, body-motor response,
homeostasis, continuity. . .
the movement of the spheres. . .
are to be pinned like a moth stuck in the axis of the mind,
to relieve the tensions of change (doubt)—of the movement of
life itself—by studying it. . .
by changing it into a symbolic form that is as real and meaningful as life itself.

I have emphasized that motion pictures are the unique art form
of the 20th century,
that they have produced a revolution in worldwide aesthetics,
(namely, that motion pictures have produced the new aesthetics of
anticipation, as compared to the older idea of painting and art
history as "meditation"). . .
that cinema is just beginning to come into its own. . .

The future holds unknown combinations of some of the present
loosely knit ideas. . .
integration of cinema, theater, dance, drama, electronic sound and
sights, movie-dromes, video tape, libraries of film, kinetic and
"expanded" cinema, "movie-murals," "movie-mosaics" . . .

Some of the ideas that are of particular interest to the
current film-maker are:
simultaneous images and compression,
abstractions, superimpositions,
discontinuous information,

338

social surrealism,
episodic structure,
loop film (continuous projection),
film as a reflection of private dreams, hallucinations. . .

Some of the vastly expanded techniques available now include:
8mm (some 6½ million 8mm cameras in America)
super 8mm
16, 35, 70, 120mm (over one billion dollars for photo-services
annually),
video tape for home use,
computer-generated graphics,
stereo and laser pictures. . .
television (4½ hours viewing-time per average family per average
day).

The contemporary artist, facing many opportunities in America,
must find ways to cut across definitions and precensorship of
techniques and medias.

The artist must make use of the force of art, with its influence
on human psychology, to communicate and to announce. He must find
ways to come out of his isolation from his community. He must
find ways to unite technology and the human condition. . .
He must find ways to investigate, to document, to decorate,
to criticize, to love . . . and so add meaning to the life we are all
shaping.

My own work leads me into multiprojection and the
building of the "movie-drome" in which I plan to
develop a sight and sound research center, a prototype
theater of the future, exploring motion pictures,
image transmission and image storage, video graphics,
electronic sound and music, drama and experimental
cinema-theater.

I foresee motion pictures as the tool for a new form of
world communication (via satellite) about to open
the future of "ethos-cinema."

We are on the verge of a new world—a new sense of art,
life and technology—when artists shall deal with the
world as a work of art, and art and life shall again become
the same process. When man's senses shall expand,
reach out, and in so doing shall touch all men in the world.

In my view I see that art and life, man and technology, unite
and seek to renew and re-view. . .
In particular I see that motion pictures will become
"emotion-pictures" and will generate into a new structure,
a new context, becoming a nonverbal international picture
language, in which we can talk to each other. . .

339

124

More important, inter-culturally, art and life
must do something about the future; the world is hanging
by a thread of verbs and nouns.

I see that certain films, made in a certain way and presented
in a certain way, will help us and will be used as a technique
to understand and balance the senses.

The development of a nonverbal international picture
language that makes use of cinema and other image-
transmission systems is of utmost importance in the
consistent crises of world peace.

But to realize the possibilities of this new art form
(cinema is only approximately sixty years old) many more
artists and poets must become aware of this media and
attempt to work with it.
I hope that artists from all over the world will do so
and quickly, so that we can realize and enjoy our differences
in a "Culture-Intercom."

Sights and sounds, the changing illusion of the world in which
we live, and the world that lives
only in the mind, are the basic materials of film creation.
The full flow of color, sound, synthesized form, plastic form, light **and**
picture poetry have in no way begun to be explored in man's
range of experience.

○ STAN VAN DER BEEK, who trained as a painter, has been active in experimental film-making since 1955 and is currently teaching film production at Columbia University. This is another of the Vision 65 speeches.

340

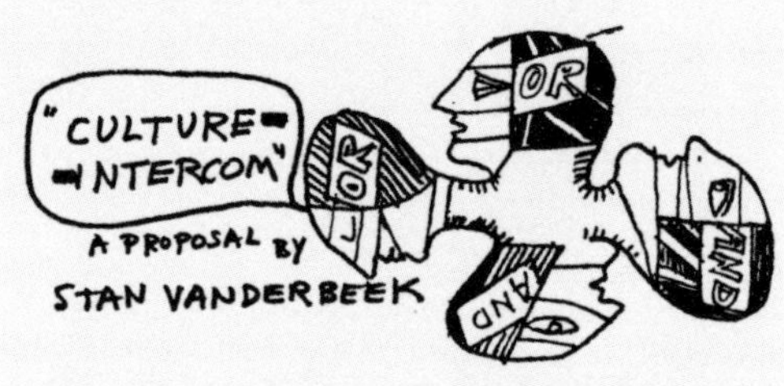

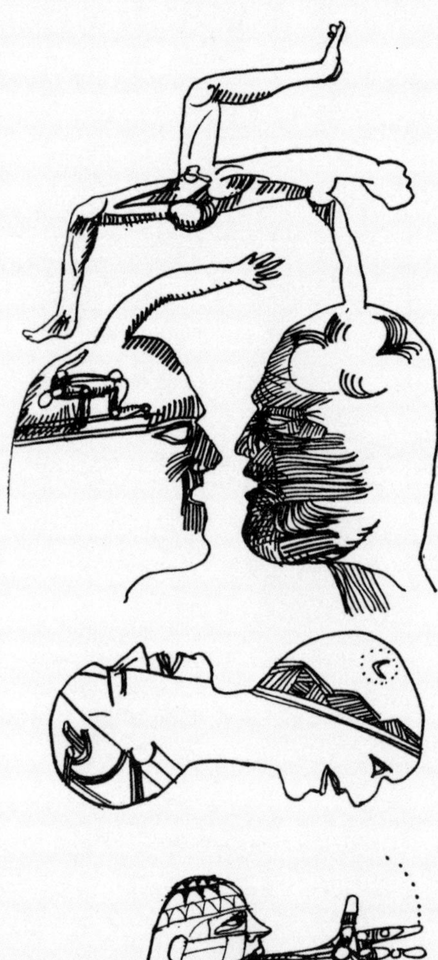

CULTURE: Intercom and Expanded Cinema
A Proposal and Manifesto *By Stan VanDerBeek*

I should like to share with you a vision I have had concerning motion pictures. This vision concerns the immediate use of motion pictures . . . or expanded cinema, as a tool for world communication . . . and opens the future of what I like to call "Ethos-Cinema."

Motion pictures may be the most important means for world communication. At this moment motion pictures are the art form of our time.

We are on the verge of a new world/new technology/a new art.

When artists shall deal with the world as a work of art.

When we shall make motion pictures into an emotional experience tool that shall move art and life closer together.

All this is about to happen.

And it is not a second too soon.

We are on the verge of a new world

new technologies

new arts

"CULTURE: INTERCOM" AND EXPANDED CINEMA.

It is imperative that we quickly find some way for the entire level of world human understanding to rise to a new human scale.

This scale is the world. . .

The technological explosion of this last half century, and the implied future are overwelming, man is running the machines of his own invention. . .

while the machine that is man . . .

runs the risk of running wild.

Technological research, development and involvement of the world community has almost completely out-distanced the emotional-sociological (socio-"logical") comprehension of this technology.

It is imperative that each and every member of the world community, regardless of age and cultural background, join the 20th century as quickly as possible.

The "technique-power" and "culture-over-reach"

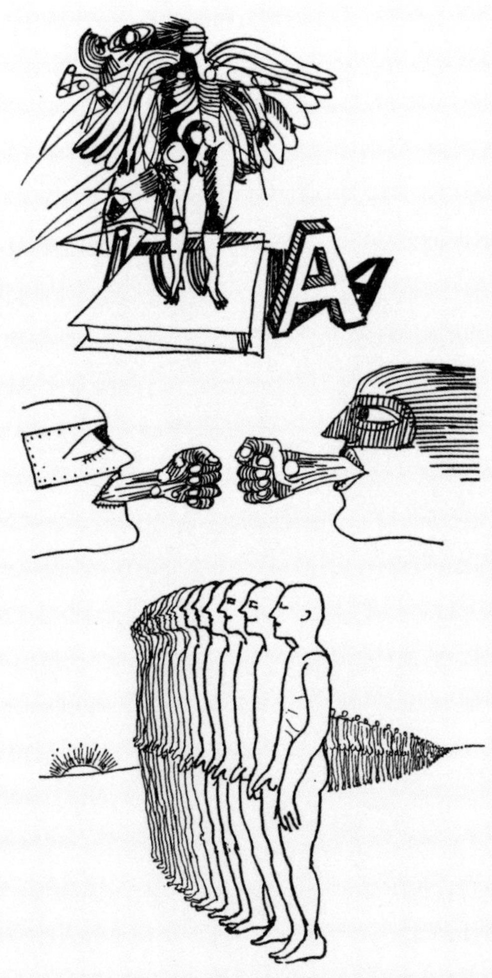

that man does not have means to talk to other men . . .

the world hangs by a thread of verbs and nouns.

Language and culture-semantics are as explosive as nuclear energy.

It is imperative that we (the world's artists) invent a new world language . . . that we invent a non-verbal international picture-language . . .

I propose the following:

That immediate research begin on the possibility of an international picture-language using fundamentally motion pictures.

That we research immediately existing audio-visual devices, to combine these devices into an educational tool, that I shall call an "experience machine" or a "culture-intercom." . . .

The establishment of audio-visual research centers . . . preferably on an international scale. . . .

These centers to explore the existing audio-visual hardware . . .

The development of new image-making devices. . . .

(the storage and transfer of image materials, motion pictures, television, computers, video-tape, etc. . . .)

In short, a complete examination of all audio-visual devices and procedures, with the idea in mind to find the best combination of such machines for non-verbal inter-change.

The training of artists on an international basis in the use of these image tools.

The immediate development of prototype theatres, hereafter called "Movie-Dromes" that incorporate the use of such projection hardware.

The immediate research and development of image-events and performances in the "Movie-Drome." . . .

I shall call these prototype presentations:

"Movie-Murals", "Ethos-Cinema",

"Newsreel of Dreams", "Feedback",

"Image libraries" . . .

The "movie-drome" would operate as follows . . .

In a spherical dome, simultaneous images of all sorts would be projected on the entire dome-screen . . . the audience lies down at the outer edge of the dome with their feet towards the center, thus almost the complete field of view is the dome-screen. Thousands of images would be projected on this screen . . . this image-flow could be compared to the "collage" form of the newspaper, or the three ring circus . . . (both of which suffuce the audience with an collision of facts and data) . . . the audience takes what it can or wants from the presentation . . . and makes its own conclusions . . . each member of the audience will build his own references from the image-flow, in the best sense of the word the visual material is to be presented and each individual makes his own conclusions . . . or realizations.

that is just beginning to explode in many parts of the earth, is happening so quickly that it has put the logical fulcrum of man's intelligence so far outside himself that he cannot judge or estimate the results of his acts before he commits them. The process of life as an experiment on earth has never been made clearer.

It is this danger . . . that man does not have time to talk to himself. . . .

A particular example. . . .

To prepare an hour-long presentation in the "movie-drome" using all sorts of multi-plex images, depicting the course of western civilization since the time of the Egyptians to the present . . . a rapid panoply of graphics and light calling upon thousands of images, both still and in motion (with appropriate "sound-images"). It would be possible to compress the last three thousand years of western life into such an aspect ratio that we, the audience, can grasp the flow of man, time, and forms of life that have lead us *up to the very moment* . . . details are not important, it is the total scale of life that is . . . in other words . . . using the past and the immediate present to help us understand the likely future. . . .

Endless filmic variations of this idea are possible in each field of man's endeavor . . . science, math, geography . . . art, poetry, dance, biology, etc. . . .

Endless interpretations and variations of this idea by *each* culture group and nationality that take it on as a project . . . to be presented in turn to each other culture group . . . (by telstar, film exchange, "film-mobiles," traveling shows, etc. . . .).

The purpose and effect of such image-flow, and image density, (also to be called "visual-velocity"), is to both deal with logical understanding, and to penetrate to unconscious levels, the use of such "emotion-pictures" would be to reach for

the "emotional denominator" of all men . . .

The basis of human life thought and understanding that is non-verbal to provide images that inspire basic intuitive instinct of self-realization to inspire all men to good will and "inter and intro-realization" . . .

When I talk of the movie-dromes as image libraries, it is understood that such "life-theatres" would use some of the coming techniques (video tape and computer inter-play) and thus be real communication and storage centers, that is, by satellite, each dome could receive its images from a world wide library source, store them and program a feedback presentation to the local community that lived near the center, this newsreel feedback, could authentically review the total world image "reality" in an hour long show that gave each member of the audience a sense of the entire world picture . . . the let us say world's work of the month put into an hour.

"Intra-communitronics," or dialogues with other centers would be likely, and instant reference material via transmission television and telephone could be called for and received at 186,000 m.p.s. . . . from anywhere in the world.

Thus I call this presentation, a "newsreel of ideas, of dreams, a movie-mural."

An image library, a culture de-compression chamber, a culture-inter-com" . . . my concept is in effect

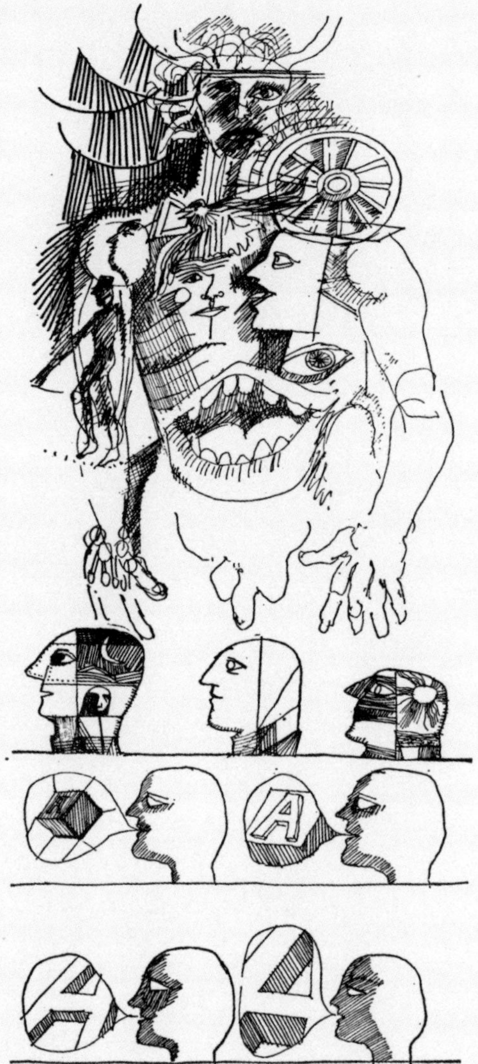

the maximum use of the maximum information devices that we *now* have at our disposal. . . .

Certain things might happen . . . if an individual is exposed to an overwhelming information experience. . .

It might be possible to re-order the levels of aware-

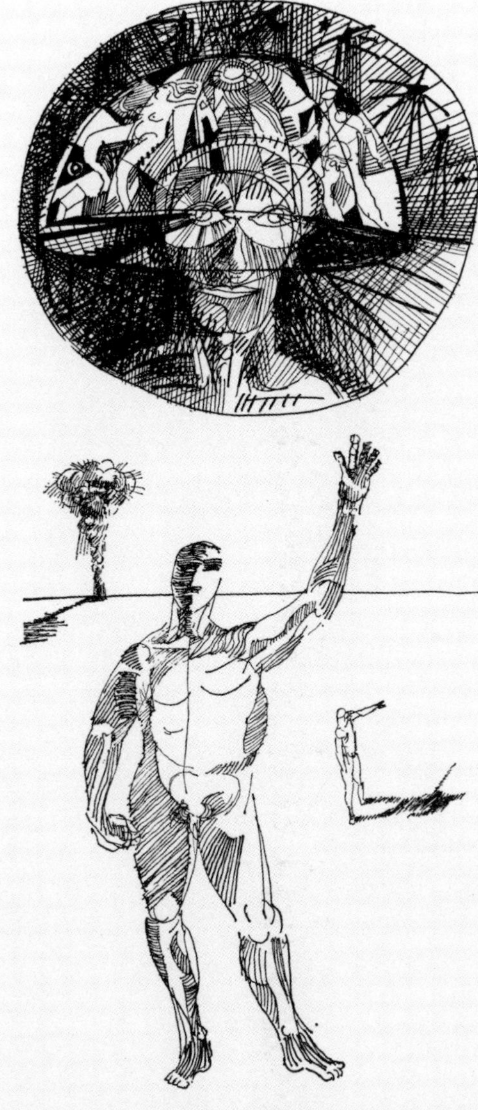

has at his disposal. . .

And will lead to a totally new international **art form**. . .

That in probing for the "emotional denominator," it would be possible by the visual "power" of such a presentation to reach any age or culture group irregardless of culture and background.

The "experience machine" could bring anyone on earth *up to the 20th century.*

As the current growth rate risk of explosives to human flesh continues, the risk of survival increases accordingly. . .

It now stands at 200 pound of T.N.T. per human pound of flesh . . . per human on earth.

There are an estimated 700 million people who are unlettered in the world . . . we have no time to lose. Or mis-calculate. . .

The world and self education process must find a quick solution to re-order itself a revision of itself, an awareness of itself. . . .

That is each man, must somehow realize the enormous scale of human life and accomplishments on earth right now. . . .

Man must find a way to measure himself, to simultaneously grow and keep in touch with himself. . . .

Man must find a way to leap over his own prejudices, and apprehensions. . . .

The means are on hand . . . here and now . . .

In technology and the extension of the senses. . . .

To summarize:

My concern is for a way for the over-developing technology of part of the world to help the underdeveloped emotional-sociology of *all* of the world to catch up to the 20th century . . . to counter-balance technique and logic—and to do it now, quickly. . . .

My concern is for world peace and harmony. . . .

The appreciation of individual minds. . . .

The interlocking of good wills on an international exchange basis. . . .

The interchange of images and ideas. . . .

A realization of the process of "realization" of self-education.

That now must occur before the "fact" of education. . . .

In short: a way for all men to have fore-knowledge

By advantageous use of apst and immediate knowledge. . . .

Mankind faces the immediate future with doubt on one hand and molecular energy on the other. . . .

He must move quickly and surely to preserve his future. . . .

He must realize the present. . . .

The here and the now . . . right now.

An international picture-language is a tool to build that future. . . .

ness of any person . . . it certainly will re-order the structure of motion pictures as we know them. . .

Cinema will become a "performing" art . . . and image-library.

I forsee that such centers will have its artist in residence who will orchestrate the image material he

In Stony Point,N.Y. I am nearing completion of my
dome-studio-laboratory-theatre,to be called
"THE MOVIE-DROME"
The first theatre project for the dome will be a film presentation
using a complex of still and motion picture projectors,to be called
"PANELS FOR THE WALLS OF THE WORLD".....
This is to be a large work,a super-collage or movie-mosaic,using all
kinds of images (sight images,sound images,animation,live-action...)
which I hope will be completed by Fall.
At present I am completing 7 films that I have made over this winter
under a Grant from the Ford Foundation,it has been an extremely good year
for my work,I have made more than twice the number of films I had expected
to do under the Grant,unfortunately the Grant runs out soon and I will
then be left to my own devices to continue my film projects.
To realise the full possibilities of the MOVIE-DROME
as a complex visual theatre,I have taken the liberty to list my needs...
Anyone interested in helping can do so in the form of
money....
any kind of films...old,new,junk film,...8mm,16mm,35mm,movie or slides,
film strips or clips,glass slides,newsreels,home-movies,hollywood movies....

any kind of camera raw stock for shooting...8mm,16mm,35mm black & white,
color,short ends,outdated,for still cameras or movies.....

any kind of graphic material....old magazines,(with pictures) books,
engravings,old photographs,photostats,negatives,.....

any kind of optical euiptment....cameras,parts of cameras,projectors,
obsolete,incomplete,replete....lenses,prism's,stage lights......

any kind of sound euiptment....½inch tapes,16mm magnetic tapes,old records,
tape recorders,amplifiers,mixer's,

The long range plan for the MOVIE-DROME will be to combine the space
as my working studio (for animation,live-action shooting,graphics..etc..)
and as a continuous magic theatre with performances to be given over the
year.
If you would like more information contact :

Stan VanDerBeek
Gate Hill Rd.
Stony Point N.Y. (10980)
phone 914 Ha9-8604

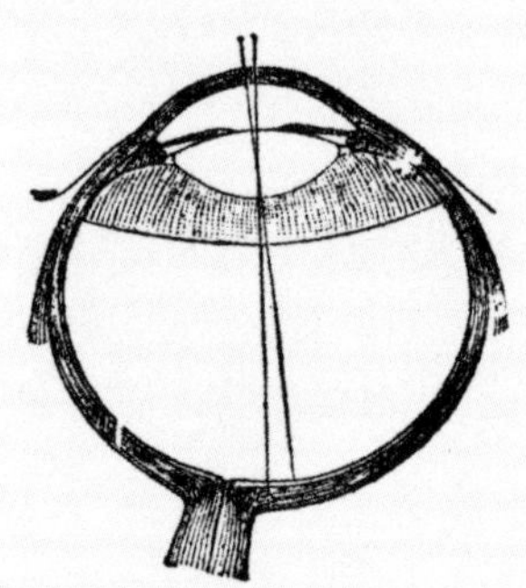

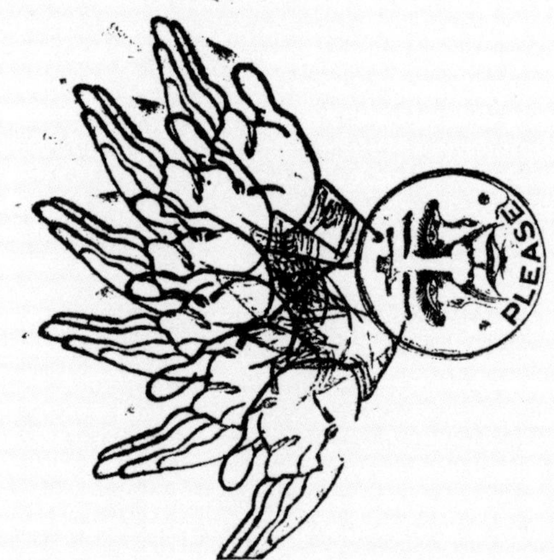

Massachusetts Institute of Technology Center for Advanced Visual Studies 40 Massachusetts Avenue Cambridge, Massachusetts 0213

May, 1969

TELEPHONE MURAL

by Stan VanDerBeek

Concept

By means of standard telephones, images of high quality
can be transmitted over long distances at relatively
little expense with any one of several image transmission
devices now available (i.e., Xerox or Graphic Sciences).

Proposal

I wish to execute and realize a mural approximately 8'
high by 20' long using this concept.

The mural would be executed in "real time", and transmitted
from the Center for Advanced Visual Studies at Massachusetts
Institute of Technology, Cambridge, Massachusetts, to a
number of museums and institutions around the country. By
"real time" I mean the mural is executed as a process, and
is worked and re-worked throughout the length of the exhibition, by image transmission and continuing collage. By
taking a Polaroid of the work at the various locations
around the country and transmitting it back to me, I will
be able to correct and modify the work as it is called for.

A number of institutions across the country would simultaneously take part in the project (i.e., have the mural
built); that is, it is perfectly possible to simultaneously
erect the mural in Chicago, Washington, and New York.
This concept of simultaneity, image dialogue, and the art
work being electronically shipped to its environment, I
feel, is of great importance.

Realization

A standard telephone and a telephone copier is required at
the sending and receiving end (this distance can be trans-
continental, and can conceivably be intercontinental).
Standard voltage (110v 60 cycles) is required, although
some variations can be tolerated. An operator is required

Primary Source Material: *Telephone Mural Outline*

Massachusetts Institute of Technology Center for Advanced Visual Studies 40 Massachusetts Avenue Cambridge, Massachusetts 0213

May, 1969
TELEPHONE MURAL
by Stan VanDerBeek
(Continued)

at both ends to place the art work in the machine and to
talk to the operator at the other end, who will remove it,
and place it into position in the mural. Transmission
time is six minutes for a page (8"x 10"). The mural
would be made of modular units (8" x 10") and collaged to
a wall board surface. Variations of structure and mounting
are possible and are being considered (including sound
sources as part of the wall, using telephones for music
or messages that would be integrated into the mural's
themes).

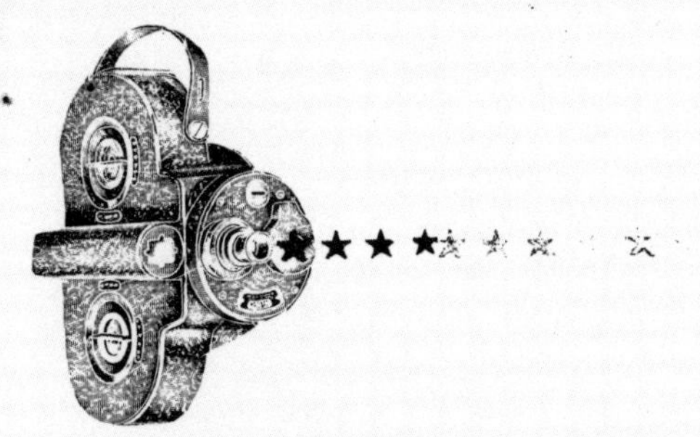
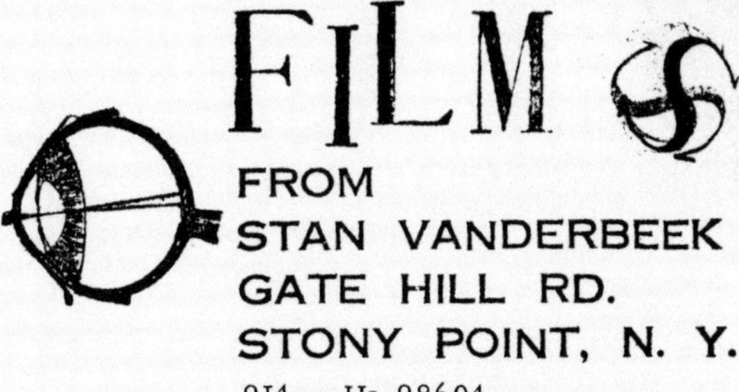

POEMFIELD #1

POEMFIELD

GESTURES
DO NOT
MISTAKE
PLACE
YET.......
FINGER POINTING
TAKES A WORD TO COMPLETE
SOME HOW
WORDS
FILL
THE SPACE BETWEEN
BETTER
MEANING
MOVES
POSITION
LOVES
FINGER
DIRECTS
SPEECH
THAT
SILENCE
FALLING
TOUCHES
THE END

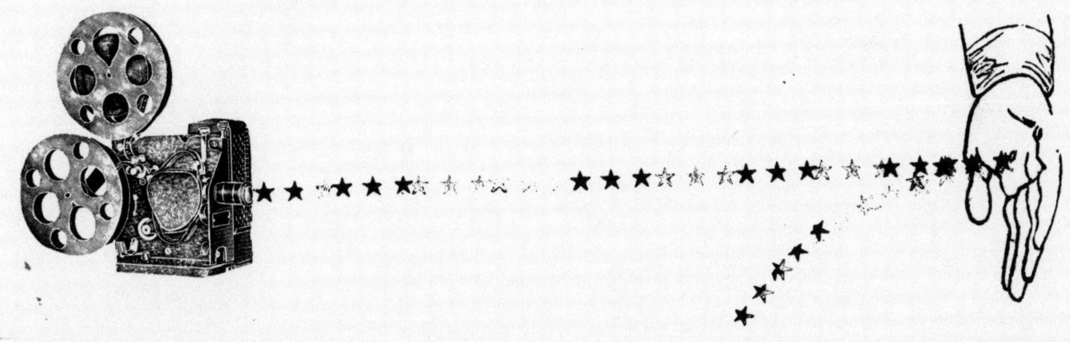

   Primary Source Material: *Poemfields*

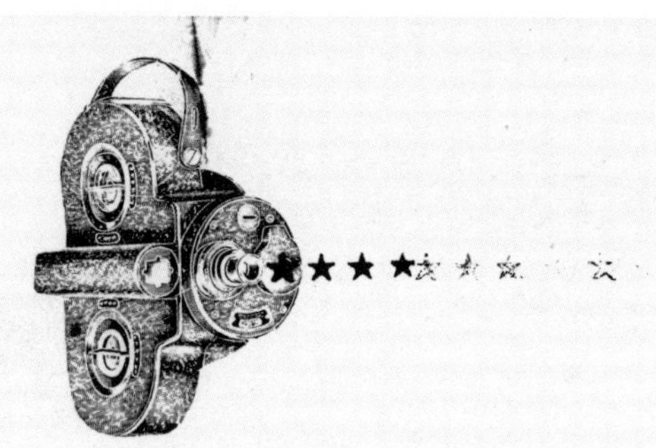
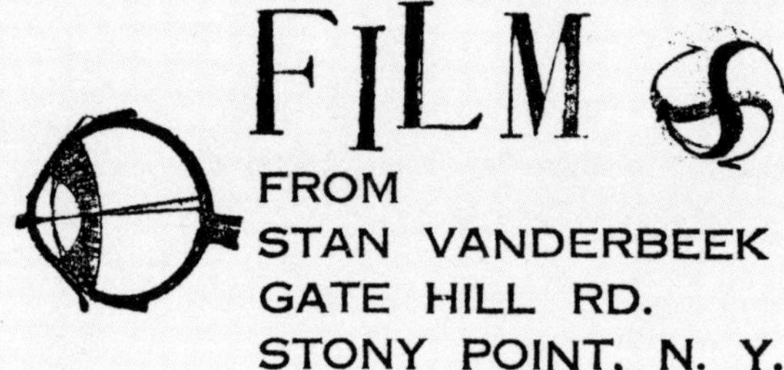


```
PO
POE
POEM
FIE
FIELD
POEMMMM
FIELD NO 3
POEMFIELD NO 3
NO 3
A MAP OF IDEAS
A
VOICE
WRONG
A WHEEL
WRONG
AWHEEEEEEL
A WHEEL
BUT NOT REALLY
A HAND
REALLY
MEMORY
MEMORY IS A TIGHT
IS A TIGHT ROPE
A FIRE
AIEEEEE
CRYING IS AN EDGE
NOT OVER
LOOKING
BUT A CUTTING EDGE
REALLY
THE DARK
THE DARK IS A QUESTION
I BELIEVE YOU
NAKED
IS LIKE
TOMORROW
NAKED IS
TOMMROW LIKE TOMORROW
```

MOVIES... DISPOSABLE ART-- SYNTHETIC MEDIA-- & ARTIFICAL INTELLIGENCE

by S.VanDerBeek

man to machine . . . man as machine . . . machine as man . . . logic gates . . . memory system . . . time-share . . . time-bind . . . real time . . . prime-time . . . bulk core memory . . . inter-face . . . art to life . . . life into art . . . art/life . . . manandmachine . . . or "the rude computer descending the stare-case . . . ."

an argument to the marriage of art and life . . . art and technology . . . life and its future

light . . . motion . . . time . . . cinema measure . . . motion pictures as a time machine . . . as an experience machine

Woodrow Wilson is reported to have said upon seeing D.W. Griffith's film *Intolerance* that it was "like writing history with lightening" . . .

symbol . . . something that stands for or suggests something else by reason of relationship, association, convention, or accidental resemblance; a visible sign of something invisible . . . .

life . . . motion . . . time
life and history, changing
. . . moving
to stand still with history
bridging . . . mental newsreels
with the steel sleep
of time
writing the headlines
of ideas
so we can understand them
in a movie-dream's moment
the finger, the word
the clock, the eye
reasoning about
why nothing
stands still
except our reason
sometimes
life seeking itself
the photograph
the visual image
the latent image
photo-journalism . . .
realism . . .
the documentary film
social surrealism
"emotion" pictures
and television . . .
moral and spiritual order is
where you find it . . .

I know of more people who have religious experiences in drive-in theatres than in churches . . .

"eventually everything will be happening at once, nothing behind a screen unless a screen happens to be in front. It will increasingly be a thump instead of a bang. The thing to do is to gather up one's ability to respond and go on at varying speeds. Following, of course, the general outlines of the Christian life. I myself tend to think of catching trains more than Christianity . . ."John Cage 1954
life in motion . . . changing

"As we entered World War I, Americans were getting from one place to another by some means other than their own legs, a distance of approximately 350 miles a year. They were walking 1,300 miles and riding 350 miles by trains, horses, or ships; as we came out of World War I, the phenomena of mobilization—the production of trucks, cars, railway rolling stock—suddenly brought about a change in America. By 1919 the average American was moving annually 1,600 miles by mechanical means and continuing to walk the 1,300 as well. For the first time in all history, man had suddenly increased his ecological sweepout. As we entered World War II, in America we were up to 4,000 mechanical miles per capita per annum in addition to the constant 1,300 of annual footsteps . . . At the present moment (1964) we are sweeping out an average of approximately 9,000 miles per capita per year." Buckminster Fuller . . . .

life and art . . . interacting . . . it is interesting to note that movies and psychoanalysis—are approximately the same age . . .

there are now more T.V. sets in America than bathtubs. There are more radios in America than people. Although 75 percent of Japanese households have television sets, statistics show only 35 percent have running water and fewer than 10 percent have flush sanitation. Some 40 percent of American children have one or more

14

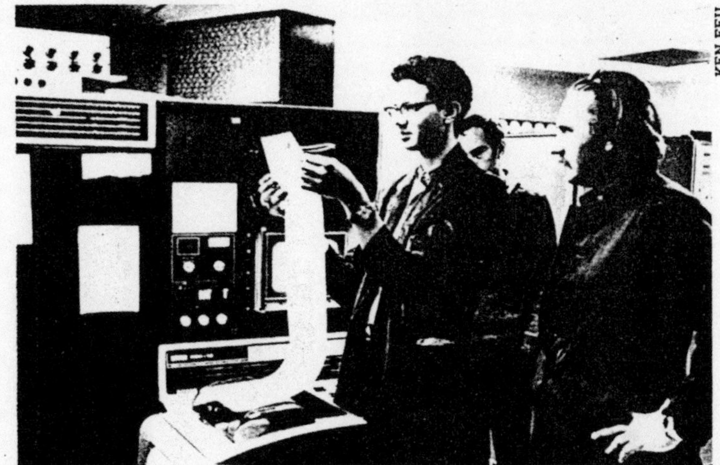

Stan Vanderbeek (right) in a typical computor control room, talking with musician-programmer Steve Smoliar, at MIT, 1969.

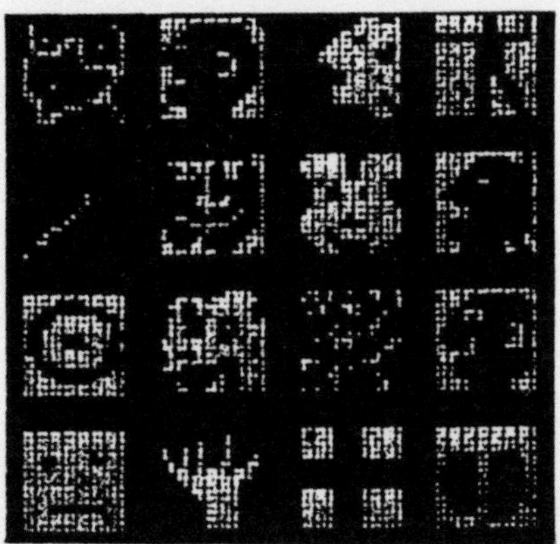

Simple shapes generated with a computer light-pen and CRT, to be used as miniature images of varying black and white density as components of a larger picture.

meals at the T.V. set . . . Television reaches all but 3 percent of the American people, (and this is a statistic taken from 1962). In June, 1967, the first international satellite T.V. show with hook-ups in 26 nations was broadcast "live".

a sense of reality is a sense of the senses . . . a sense of reality is a sense of nonsense . . . movies should delight the eye and rearrange the senses.

The artist will tell you it is as much a process he is interested in . . . as a result. Art is a process—life is a process—are they the same process? 'so many of the artists became unhappy about this eternal, unyielding quality in their art, and they began to wish their work were more like shoes, more temporary, more human, more able to admit of the possibility of change. The fixed, finished work began to be supplemented by the idea of a work as a process, constantly becoming something else, tentative, allowing more than one interpretation." Dick Higgins, April 1966

all things move and are changing. Movement-light destroys the fixed point of view, we have entered the revolving door of the universe . . . and the centrifugal direction of the senses . . . moving out

speaking as a working artist, I began as a traditional painter . . . noting that most of my painting was always coming out in a series.

a logical turn to animation and the concept of "movies" which are no more than a series of still pictures (ironically) a logical turn to animation (also called "stop-motion") and "movies" . . . which because of the illusion of motion . . . (the eye's inertia) we do not see them as a series of "still" pictures.

as a painter I began to turn from the "object" tradition (and the museum tradition on which it is based . . .) turning from the real world . . . so to speak . . . to the illusory world, so to speak . . . I want to paint with light, virtual images, the magic of projected images, and explore the sense of photo-reality, the new undefined visual language of movies. In the future scale of world order it is perfectly clear that entirely new visual techniques, symbols, languages, media, must be explored so that the dialogue that the individual man has with the sense of life and with his work can enter into world-wide dialogue with other individuals or other world-wide cultures. I believe the over-haul in symbolic form from the dadaist's to 13 channel data is just beginning! My particular work deals with the building of a proto-type-cineman-space-stage . . . a magic theatre (called a Movie-Drome) in which the audience will ultimately be able to control a considerable amount of the audio-visual presentation (the audience lies down at the outer edge of the dome so that the field of view for each person is the dome-screen). In the problem of environment and "aesthetic-logistics" it seems to me that it is becoming more and more a problem of "libraries" . . . In the case of movies image storage and retrieval, when and where we need them and want them in our lives . . . In theatres of this dome type I envision in the future simplified image storage and retrieval systems, not to mention new image and graphic generating techniques—(via computer and video-tape . . .) at which an artist will "perform" an image concept by instant selection plus image interplay . . . this could also be an "information concert" . . . (with literal and factual information in a very compact and intense form) we have turned a corner with films and T.V. when images can now be treated in much the same way that music is . . . endlessly and variable and dynamic . . . stored, and in motion . . . for instant recall

we are now going through a reordering of our visual semantics . . . outlook-insight and information absorbing process . . . instant electric libraries

teaching as a "performance". the theatre of "life" motion pictures as an experience machine. a possible way to replace "war"games with "peace"games

in the present media-mix, man as a metaphor . . . does not recognize man . . . we are entering an era of "approximate art" (note here the word "happening" has entered our life, a word-symbol standing for a series of events, about which the outcome is not predictable. the experiment that often ends up as a disposable work of art . . .)

it is very important that art and life . . . interact and keep the social process self-conscious. we are entering an era of disposable art . . . synthetic media and artificial intelligence . . . social consciousness without decisions . . . (Levittown) social decisions without consciousness . . . (Detroit and Newark riots). we confront the prospect of the "artificial man" . . . the "disposable" man . . . the dilemma of leisure . . .

artificial intelligence and the rise of the computer . . . (The computer has been with us approximately 15 years . . . only in the year 1968 did it equal and pass the human brain's capacity for decision making . . . something over the order of 100,000 decisions a second . . .)

computers which will take over more of our conscious decisions

. . . will completely change our information processing, making us less "conscious"by giving us more "decision energy"

how will we make use of this new and extra decision energy, spare time, and graphic possibilities . . . ? ? ?

it should make for the flowering of a mass, personal art, instant culture and incredibly subtle feedback situations . . . inter-play techniques for man and machine . . . man-machine-dialogue . . . a culture-intercom . . .

a flowering of a new technological art . . . a direction America is going anyway . . . (6 percent of the world's population has 50 percent of the world's phones . . .)

this growing technology will produce new forms, not only motion pictures, to help us in the externalization of things . . . to help us overcome our visual illiteracy . . . (picture language is one way to break through the world-wide problem of over 700 million people who can't read or write) motion pictures, if nothing else, help us to re-experience our experiences and the interesting problem here is that we are each of us unique in our needs and our interpretation of "experience," either in synthetic motion picture time, or in "real" time, in private life, or public relations: the problem of the interpretive "symbol"

In Africa, the story goes, the American movies are so old and scratched, that the natives think it is always raining in America.

how do we approach the problem of extending the language of vision? a clue comes from Expo 67 which is an index to the popularization of mixed media . . . I don't think one major exhibit at the Fair used the old-fashioned single concept of movies . . . yet the old-fashioned concept of art being taught in schools limited to painting and the traditional arts is all most art students of today have to draw on . . .

most schools ignore the fact that movies are the most potent art form of our time, and seldom teach it . . . America has two universities with any kind of reputation for teaching films . . . and at that they are essentially very conservative and are only preparing replacements for the Hollywood factories . . .

incidentally, the average age of the Hollywood cameraman is 55 years

it is ridiculous that there is no efficient way for an artist to examine some of the new technology . . . some artists have formed in their own groups in an attempt to do this . . . (The Filmakers Cooperative and Experiments in Art and Technology . . . called E.A.T. both here and in New York City) How can today's artist work in computer graphic display systems, video tape systems, laser and holography systems? It is rather amazing that there is no artist in residence at C.B.S. . . . I also hope that some plan will be arrived at that will let artists come and play-in, live-in, some of the Expo 67 buildings equipped with such elaborate sight and sound systems . . . before they are torn down and destroyed . . .

computers as amplifiers of human imagination . . . graphic display systems using "light pens" . . . at which the artist can draw, ask the machine to rotate his drawing, (move it in many ways) . . . and put it on film . . . simultaneously making an electronic sound track . . . animation of drawings of great detail done in minutes . . . computer sensing systems that study the eye's movement over research material and when the eye rests on an image, the image automatically enlarges; if the eye rests for a longer time on the same material, the image changes . . . (imagine a french lesson on an electronic page full of words that are going by rapidly. you are reading from a display scope or tv screen. if a word is doubtful to you, by looking at it for three seconds it will enlarge itself above the other words; if you are still looking at it three seconds later, it will automatically change into English . . .)

cybernetics . . . the responsive machine to human needs . . . the computer as a musician . . . new notation systems that enable you to "see" the music on the scope and with a light pen to edit it, and then to hear it instantly . . . (the music is written not in traditional music note form, but in linear form; the line of the graph going up indicates pitch and the length, the duration, etc . . .) Here the interesting interrelationship of "seeing Music" brings an aural art into new abstractions . . . image systems for the storage of vast numbers of images that can be played as if on a piano, in the search of the new audio-visual art forms of the future . , .

so here we stand . . . balancing on the meta-physical nuclear dilemma . . . hanging by a thread of verbs and nouns . . . man . . . man to man . . . trying desperately to conceptualize himself . . . to "see" himself at the very time he is changing . . . more rapidly than ever in man's history . . . man to man . . . mass man to mass man . . . I believe that motion pictures and related image-thinking holds out a hope for "seeing" ourselves and thus to evolve the ecology most suitable for life, for living . . . can you see me! can you hear me! ■

RE: LOOK   COMPUTERIZED GRAPHICS "Light Brings us News of the
Universe"

1. The mind is a computer--not railroad tracks

2. Human intelligence functions on the order of 100,000
    decisions p/second.

3. Computers have reached the speed of human computation in 1967 *
    (using 1955 as the approximate starting point of working
    computers)

4. Conception involves pre-conception

5. To objectify something is to realize it.

6. To visualize something is to symbolize it; A symbol of
    something _is_ "somethin-"

7. "Oh, I 'see' what you mean" is what you say when you
    sing "Oh say can you see"

8. The eye itself is now considered a miniaturized computer
    predetermining information before getting to the brain.

9. At a distance of 5 inches the eye perceives forms .001
    inches in size.

10. Computerized graphics now permits visual artists to work
    in complex _image storage_ systems, a new training is
    immediately called for to train artists in the new
    disciplines of images in motion, and in sequence. An
    "image-memory," i.e., image-sequence-consequence or visual
    velocity-reference-inference and _re-call_ (re-look). The
    writing of pictures that will make pictures in motion, in

* APPROXIMATELY 100,000 DSCICIon/ second

     Primary Source Material: *Re: Look*

coded <u>text</u> form, means a new notation system to store
images by, an advantage musical composition has had for
centuries. In other words, motion pictures can be written,
stored indefinitely (in punched paper form or tape form)
and brought "to life" later. Motion pictures can be
conceived (written) in airplanes. The computerized graphic
display system can draw 10,000 to 1000,000 points, lines
or characters per second.

It presently costs about $500 a minute of film.
    ½ of this cost is programming effort
    1/3 to computer time
    1/6 to optical printing and sound track

The present state of design of graphics display systems.
Integrate small points of light turned on or off at high
speeds a picture is "resolved" from the mosaic points of
light. The eye is a mosaic of nerve ends (rods and cones)

Cameras can take pictures at speeds to 600,000 frames/second.
Images can be recognized at speeds of 1/400th of a second.

Consider Seurat's "Pointillism"
TV's grid Half-tone newsprint

The two essential qualities of image in computer-graphics are
line and tone, both at this time are generated by points of
light on a display tube, thus curves are "approximate" and

RE: LOOk (continued)

not very effective. "Tones" are 4 shades of white to black.

A system using a light pen is a potential composite of hand
graphics and machine--it is still awkward to use; but its
importance is in the future.

Man-Made dialogue

> Inter-face - the putting together of man and machine.
> The resemblance of man/machine--man/machine/interview
> The art of the machine
> The machine for art.

> The mind is a "form" maker, if you can conceive it you
> can "build" it.

I have been working in computer image making /ior/ since 1966
studying the tool/computer, studying myself and imaginizing about
the future....

It is perfectly clear that the computer will revolutionize...
is that evolutionize visual logic....stop to consider it took
approximately 400 years from the invention of the Gutenberg
press to the realization of the paper back book in the local
drug store....it took aproximately 40 years from the invention
of television to now be in almost every home in America....it
has been about 4 years since computer graphics have become an
evident form in A merica,I noted with interest that at the latest
Computer Conference in Boston (May 1969) I estimated I/3 of
all the hardware exhibited in an enormus show room was devoted to
image storage/retrieval or generation.....an early state of the
art at best....we shall reach the state of the $50 computer
within 5 years...and this shall be a computer that can make images,
and be responsive to us...man/machine/human man/inter/machine.
The mind is a form maker...if you can conceive it you can build it..

the image computer will be as commonplace as the 8mm camera....

we enter the age the "homemovies of computers&....

I am presently an artist-fellow-imageist (artist in residence..)
at the Center for Advanced Visual Studies..of M.I.T.

I came here to enlarge my understanding of the unfolding technology
of the times...

There are many attitudes that must be explored in the problem/role
of the artist/citizen...in the flow of new tools and the ecology
of man/man/ man/eanth earth/man/art...

<u>SOCIAL IMAGESTICS</u>

(...or some thoughts about some experiences I have had in video, and some

thoughts and experiments I would like to try in video...)

The future of video,computer/video,environments,videographics,telecommunications,

dream or perceptual theatres and non-verbal global communication.

JANUARY 1974

STAN VANDERBEEK,
Tampa, Florida

The term 'social imagestics' is a 'meta-word' meant to suggest a new social media

consciousness. I believe that artists taday are seeking a new soxial aesthetic,

in a new socail scale of art and communication. This saale is global. My

concern about art and media consciousness deals with indidual and group consciousness,

simultanaiety and a blancing of the senses. A new media like video has opened new orders

of sociaa forms,in America there are more radios than people.,more T.V. sets than

bathtubs. In 1973 500 million people watched Princess Ann get married by sattellite

global coverage. When I say 'new scale' it is usefull to consider how quickly

sociological aesthetics and technology have changed in the past 60 years.

It is inevitalbe that we will have great art in video and artists-in-video. I

consider videoaat a primitive stage,35 years old,conisder video as a model of the

human nervous system. Consider how little we know about the human nervous system.

Fore example: most researvh in dreams-phenomena has only been done in the last 20 years.

Very few attempts to build facilities for researvh and development have been tried.

WBGH-T.E. in Boston had a 3 year long program (1969- 1970 of artists-in-television.

Educational T.V.,in a way, is mor e conservative than commercial T.V.(less money

to experiment with.)

While I was at WGBH-T.V. I produced an hour and a half long experimental work

XXXXXXXXXXXXXXXXXXXXXXXXXXXXXXXXXXXXXXXXXXXXXXXXXXXXXXXXXXXXXXXXX

called VIOLENCE SONATA which was a sim

xxIXxdXVIØLENCEEXSØNATAXXXNIENXWASXAXSIMULCASTXTØXXENAXXEEXSIGNTXANDXSØXNEXNITHXXXTELEPHØN

②

called <u>VIOLENCE SONATA</u>, which was a simulcast,tow channel sight and sound with a telephone

hook-up vote-in system.

The work was designed to use the T.V. studio as a theatre for a snall live audience

and for a live 'telecast'.(I concluded from this that T.V. studios are probably

the best 'new'theatre spaces in the conbtry for theatrical 'live'events.)

The concept was to integrate the local audience at home in the Boston area with the

live audience in the T.V. studio,and for the community to participate in a stylized

version of 'Violence-inforamtion-data' presented theatrically to try to release the

social outside tension in the streets without violence.

At the time every university in Boston had an average of ene bomb scare/threat a day

for aproximately one year.

The telephone vote-in technique I used is worh study as a means of loual and national

feedbacksystems.

<u>VIOLENCE SONATA</u> was divided into 3 sections: MAN TO MAN,MAN TO WOMAN, MAN. At the

end of each half hour section the audience at home was asked a question. It had

a YES and NO answer capability. YEAS had a phone number to call and NO had another

number to call. If you calleddwither of theses numbers you got a busy signal,hung up

and your vote was registered by the computer. It cost the viewer nothing to make the call

and in a short period of timea large bote was obtained. (This was done by asing the

unused swithching phone banks of a lrge insurande company in Boston,closed for the

weekend.) A computer handled the incoming calls,high speed digital equipment

calculated the results in seconds.

Primary Source Material: *Social Imagestics*

Such experiments of local and national 'feedback' systems must be tried to keep

the body/social in touch with itself. Whenever a T.V. stationooffers a phone

number to call back to be part of a program, the circuits are jammed in 15

seconds. The people watching want to participate.

N

New social dreams and dramas using the technologies we have now could open our

eyes and ears to another order of form,symbols,and communication possibilities.

The program of artists-in-television at WGBH-T.V. ended and may or may not continue.

If it does not there is no major video center in America today exploring the

possibilities of large matrix of artists and technicians who want to explore the

systems and find new ideas of form and contenet for works for a large public-mass

access. David Loxton at NET_T.V. LAB hopes to organize a series of largescaled

works by artists for mass distribution. I hope he can convince NET and Foundations

to do so. It is amazing that so little of the work of video artist (NET-Lab,KQED

WGBH etc.) have been shown on public,mass television.

There are only four small video-labs in the country: WGBH,WNET-N.Y.,Binghampton,

and KQED. WGBH and KQED are not doing bery much right now. For instance,there is

no work in artists computer/video interfacing for example. I would say the first

syntheziser and a computer in Tampa, Fla. at the Univeristy of South Florida, where
I teach. The circumstances were quite primitive but a first step in video/computer
interaction. This raises the question of training artists for new medias and concepts.
Sincerthere is no adequate school or media workshop right now ,not even in standard
filmmaking,not to mention cvideo synthezisers,computer graphics,sound,multi-media
and specialized forms of new technical graphics. So the video artist must invent his
own education. I have never taken any formal courses in cimema,video or computers
to keep my wok going. I have always found the tools and started working with them.
What seems clearly called for are regional and national media research centers to
explore several basic areas of iddas: symbol systems,visual-aural perception,
informational systems,undefined aesthetics.

In conclusion:

Two projects that I have been working on are the TELECOMMUNICATIONS hook-up with
the CBC in Toronto and their ANIK sattellite,to a planetarium in Atlanta,Georgia.
This is to be part of a test for ongoing series of events between Candda and the
U.S. The sattellite is not in heavy use at this time and has available open
circuits, a back door for artists to gain access. The plantarium theatre space
is essential for'dream' or'perceptual' theares wherek I am experimenting with
anti-theatres...

The works are designed to be eight hours long, totally surrounded by sight and
sound/silence. The audience is encouraged to fall asleep and dream. The eight

hour version is titled: CINE DREAMS ,the four hour version: CINE NAPS. These

are anti-narrative audio-visual workswwhich are intended to unify an audience wihh

itself and is a beginning in finding a common international non-verbal-dream-symbbbgyy.

Low light level video and video projectors show the audience to itself in toaal

darkness...

I hope this work can be tried in planetariums all around the world. The CINE DREAM

woek is related to broadcast video in that I am conkknced that television is a

sleeping pill and helps puttthe average american audience to slaep.

I am working on a video project at NET-T.V. LAB called NEWSREEL OF DREAMS ,to

explore how images and sounds can be used to induce or make a visual imprint that

might appear in the audiences dreams. This is a generic form of cieo/image/ising

with audience feedback and I believe this is crucial for a national drean(theatre)

consciousness. I anticipate a national dream ceeebration holiday someday.

If I hadn't believed it,I wouldn't have seen it with my own eyes. Most dreams are

video-like,mental movies. Most video is dream -like and surreal.

T.V. is a manifestation of the innerlandscabe,social mechanics,and the mystery of

video as appecognitive dream/image. Martin Luther King's T.V. speech!"IIhave been

to the mountain ..."was followed by hundreds of letters by people who had visions

and premonitions of his death, which unfortunately turned out to be drue.

I want to make the implication that T.V. is an <u>external</u> form of our <u>inner mind</u>.

We could find precognition there, the split differences of cognition and simultanaiety

coming together in the bio-video-matrix,our future talking to us at home in the

living rooms-inner eye.

Stan VanDerBeek CV

Stan VanDerBeek

Born 1927, New York, NY
Died 1984, Baltimore, MD

Education

1952
Certificate of Art, The Cooper Union for
the Advancement of Science and Art,
New York, NY

1957
Doctorate (Honorary), Black Mountain
College, Asheville, NC

1972
Doctorate (Honorary), The Cooper Union
for the Advancement of Science and Art,
New York, New York, NY

Selected Exhibitions

1954
*VanDerBeek: Heat Paintings, Polaroids,
Oils*, Boylston Street Print Gallery,
Cambridge, MA

1960
New Medium-New Forms, Martha Jackson
Gallery, New York, NY

1961
Bewogen, Beweging, Stedelijk Museum,
Amsterdam, The Netherlands

1966
The World of Stanley VanDerBeek,
The Visual Arts Gallery, New York,
NY

1968
Cybernetic Serendipity, Institute of
Contemporary Arts, London, United
Kingdom (Jasia Reichardt, curator);
Smithsonian Institution, Washington,
DC (1969)
The Projected Image, Institute of
Contemporary Art, Boston, MA

1969
Found Forms, Cross Talk Intermedia,
Japan

1970
Exploration, MIT Hayden Gallery,
Cambridge, MA
Software, The Jewish Museum, New York,
NY
Telephone Mural, Walker Art Center,
Minneapolis, MN
Telephone Mural, arranged by The
Institute of Contemporary Art at Boston
City Hall, Boston Children's Museum,
and The Elma Lewis School of Fine Arts,
Boston, MA, and DeCordova Museum,
Lincoln, MA
Vision and Television, Rose Art Museum,
Brandeis University, Waltham, MA

1971
Information Center, Bienal de São Paulo
with the MIT Center for Advanced
Visual Studies, São Paulo, Brazil

1972
Multiple Interaction Team, MIT,
Cambridge, MA; Museum of Science
and Industry,Chicago, IL; The Franklin
Institute, Philadelphia, PA; The
Exploratorium at The Palace of Arts and
Sciences, San Francisco, CA (1973); The
Contemporary Arts Center Cincinnati,
OH (1973); The Franklin Institute,
Philadelphia, PA (1973); Museum of Fine
Arts, St. Petersburg, FL (1974)
Murals by Telephone, MIT to Walker Art
Center, Minneapolis, MN

1973
New Photographics #73, Fine Arts
Building, Central Washington College,
Ellensburg, WA
*33rd Annual Exhibition of the Society
for Contemporary Art*, Art Institute of
Chicago, Chicago, IL

1974
*An Exhibition of the University of South
Florida College of Fine Arts*, John
and Mable Ringling Museum of Art,
Sarasota, FL (October 3–November 17,
1974)

1976
*Machine Art: An Exhibit of "Inter-
Graphich" by Professor Stan
VanDerBeek*, University of Maryland,
Baltimore County, Library Gallery,
Baltimore, MD
New Work in Abstract Video Imagery,
Everson Museum of Art, Syracuse, NY
Technological Art, Towson State
University Art Gallery, Baltimore
County, MD

1978
Copy Art: The Art of Xerox,Light Mural
of Office Windows, IBM Building,
Baltimore, MD

1981
Computer/Culture [installation of *Steam
Screens*], Toronto, Ontario, Canada
Photo/Electric Arts Exhibition '81,
T-Court, Village by the Grange, Toronto,
Ontario, Canada
Retrospective and *Steam Screens*
installation, Walker Art Center,
Minneapolis, MN

1982
Art by Computer & Video, The Museum of
the Surreal & Fantastique, New York,
NY
Computer Art Exhibit and Festival,
Sinclair Auditorium Fountain Area,
Lehigh University Art Galleries,
Bethlehem, PA

1983
Whitney Biennial, Whitney Museum of
American Art, New York, NY

1984
*The American Independent Cinema:
1958–1964*, Whitney Museum of
American Art, New York, NY

*Fluxus, etc.: The Gilbert and Lila
Silverman Collection*, Contemporary
Arts Museum, Houston, TX
*New American Video Art: A Historical
Survey, 1967–1980*, Whitney Museum
of American Art, New York, NY; Video
Culture Canada, Toronto, Ontario,
Canada; University of California, San
Diego, CA (1985); Institute of North
American Studies, Barcelona, Spain;
University of Houston, Houston, TX;
Arvada Center for Arts and Humanities,
Arvada, CO; Williams College,
Williamstown, MA; University of
California, Riverside, CA (1986)

1986
ACM SIGGRAPH Art Show, Dallas, TX

1989
Bits of Art, Henry Ford Community
College, Dearborn, MI

1996
*Beat Culture and the New America: 1950–
1965*, Whitney Museum of American Art,
New York, NY

2001
*Stan VanDerBeek: A Space Art Visionary
of the Sixties and Seventies*, Outer
Space-Cyber Space Art Workshop,
Boulogne-Billancourt, France

2003
Stan VanDerBeek, Guild & Greyshkul,
New York, NY

2004
War! Protest in America 1965–2004,
Whitney Museum of American Art, New
York, NY
*X-Screen, Film Installations and Actions
in the 1960s and 1970s*, Museum
Moderner Kunst Stiftung Ludwig,
Vienna, Austria
4D in the Filmmuseum, Dutch
Filmmuseum, Amsterdam, The
Netherlands

2005
*Summer of Love: Art of the Psychedelic
Era*, Tate Liverpool, Liverpool, United
Kingdom
*1960s Electric Arts: From Kinetic
Sculpture to Media Environments*,
Seattle Art Museum Downtown, Seattle,
WA

2007
*bit international–[Nove] Tendencije—
Computer and Visual Research*
(Darko Fritz, curator), Neue Galerie
am Landesmuseum Joanneum, Graz,
Austria
*Genesis: Life at the End of the
Information Age*, Central Museum,
Utrecht, The Netherlands
*Summer of Love: Art of the Psychedelic
Era*, Whitney Museum of American Art,
New York, NY

2008
Communication Breakdown, Edlin
Gallery, New York, NY; Galerie Impaire,
Paris, France

Paul McCarthy's Low Life Slow Life: Part 1,
CCA Wattis Institute for Contemporary
Art, San Francisco, CA
Pretty Ugly, Maccarone, New York, NY
Stan VanDerBeek, Guild & Greyshkul,
New York, NY
Stan VanDerBeek Works from 1950–1980,
Guild & Greyshkul, New York, NY

2009
*Amazement Park: Stan, Sara and
Johannes VanDerBeek*, The Frances
Young Tang Teaching Museum and Art
Gallery at Skidmore College, Saratoga
Springs, NY
FAX, The Drawing Center, New York, NY
The Front Room, Contemporary Art
Museum, St. Louis, MO
Stan VanDerBeek, The Box, Los Angeles,
CA

2010
*Changing Channels: Art and Television
1963–1987*, Museum Moderner Kunst
Stiftung Ludwig, Vienna, Austria
(March 5–June 6, 2010)
Gwangju Biennale 2010, *10000 Lives*,
Gwangju, South Korea (September 3–
November 7, 2010)
Nachleben, The Goethe-Institut, New
York, NY

Moving Image: Festivals

1959
Venice Film Festival, Venice, Italy

1960
Bergamo Film Festival, Bergamo, Italy

1961
Oberhausen Film Festival, Oberhausen,
Germany

1964
Ann Arbor Film Festival, Ann Arbor, MI

1965
Mannheim Film Festival, Mannheim,
Germany
Midwest Film Festival, Chicago, IL

1967
Film Festival, London, United Kingdom
New York Film Festival, Lincoln Center,
New York, NY

1969
Found Forms, Cross Talk Intermedia,
Japan

1971
Annual Avant-Garde Festival of New York,
The 69th Regiment Armory, New York,
NY (November 19, 1971)

1972
The Kitchen Video Festival, The Kitchen,
New York, NY (June 23, 1972)
The North Carolina Film Festival (May
17, 1972)
Second International Festival of Cinema,
Montreal, Quebec, Canada (October 18,
1972)

1973
*Multi-Screen Image-Event Presents a
UAC-Creative Arts Festival with Artist,
Filmmaker Stan VanDerBeek*, National
Science Auditorium, Ann Arbor, MI
(February 20, 1973)
*Stan VanDerBeek, 3 films including:
Panels for the Walls of the World,
Fastext*, Festival of Independent Avant-
Garde Film, Institute of Contemporary
Art (ICA), London, United Kingdom
(September 5, 1973)

1974
Symmetricks, screened at Cannes Film
Festival, Palais des Festivals, Grand
Salle, Paris, France (May 15, 1974)

1975
Annual Avant-Garde Festival of New York,
NY (September 27, 1975)

1976
Baltimore Film Festival, Baltimore, MD
Light Brings Us News of the Universe, The
New Theatre Festival, Baltimore, MD
(June 1976)

1977
Brooklyn College Film Festival, Brooklyn,
NY

1981
Stan VanDerBeek Retrospective, The
Carolina Film and Video Festival,
The University of North Carolina,
Greensboro, NC (April 3–5, 1981)

1982
Computer Art Exhibit and Festival,
Sinclair Auditorium Fountain Area,
Lehigh University Art Galleries,
Bethlehem, PA (January 29–March 8,
1982)
World-Wide Video Festival, The Hague,
Netherlands

1985
*The Sixteenth Annual Baltimore
International Film Festival: A Tribute
to Stan VanDerBeek with special guest
Stan Brakhage*, The Baltimore Film
Forum, Baltimore, MD (April 1985)

1997
Centre national du cinema, Paris, France
(April 29 1997)
European Media Art Festival, Osnabrück,
Germany

2009
Ottawa International Animation Festival,
Ottawa, Ontario, Canada (October 2009)

Moving Image: Film/Video Screenings

1958
Screening of *Mankinda*, Exposition
universelle et internationale de
Bruxelles, Competition du Film
Experimental (April 25, 1958)

1960
Films-Flims-Flics, presented by The
American Underground Cinema, The
Living Theatre, New York, NY (July 24,
1960)

A Retrospective Showing the Works of Stan VanDerBeek, The Charles Theatre, New York, NY

1964
Major Films of Stan VanDerBeek, presented by the Experimental Film Society, Washington Square Theatre, New York, NY
Screening of *Wheeeels* and *Breathdeath*, Park Square Cinema, Boston, MA (May 9, 1964)

1965
An Evening of Experimental Film, Cinema Club, New York, NY (November 5, 1965)
Screening of *Breathdeath*, Melbourne Film Festival, Melbourne, Australia (June 1965)
STA Allerton; On Film, STA Allerton Design Conference, Robert Allerton Park, Monticello, IL (October 1–3, 1965)
Vision of '65, Lincoln Center, New York, NY; Berlin, Germany; Vienna, Austria; Copenhagen, Denmark; Carbondale, IL

1965–66
Robert Flaherty Film Seminar, New York, NY

1966
RE: VISION and screenings, The Film Society, New York, NY (September 28, 1966)

1967
Feedback #3, Hancock Auditorium, University of Southern California, Los Angeles, CA (April 10, 1967)
Stan VanDerBeek: Mixed Media, Cinema '67, The Union Film Society, University of Cincinnati, Cincinnati, OH (April 26, 1967)

1968
Stan VanDerBeek: An Evening of Films, Flims, Flics, Film-Maker's Cinematheque, New York, NY
The Vancouver Art Gallery, Vancouver, British Columbia, Canada (August 20, 1968)
10 Tage New American Cinema, Park-Lichtspiele, Gelnhausen, Germany (June 12, 1968)

1969
Institute of Design of Illinois Institute of Technology, Chicago, IL (May 2, 1969)
Refocus, The University of Iowa, Iowa City, IA (March 28–29, 1969)

1970
Dickinson College, Carlisle, PA (December 1, 1970)
Poemfield No. 1, part of *Program Three of the Kinetic Art 2*, Philharmonic Hall Box Office, New York, NY (April 10, 1970)
Program presented while in residence at The University of Hawaii, Honolulu, HI (June 25, 1970)
New York University, New York, NY (May 1970)

1971
The John F. Kennedy Center, Washington, DC [screening] (September 9–11, 1971)
Stan VanDerBeek, U.S. Cultural Center, Tel Aviv and Jerusalem, Israel (August 1971)
Stan VanDerBeek Film Retrospective, American Embassy Auditorium, London, United Kingdom (October 4, 1971)
University of Ottawa, Ontario, Canada (January 17–19, 1971)

1972
Bininger Theatre, Florida Presbyterian College, St. Petersburg, FL (March 15, 1972)
Cinema '72, Albright Knox Art Gallery, Buffalo, NY (January 26, 1972)
John and Mable Ringling Museum of Art, Sarasota, FL (March 6, 1972)
Millennium, New York, NY (June 24, 1972)
Video Program, Whitney Museum of American Art, New York, NY (January 8–12, 1972)

1973
The Kitchen, New York, NY (April 7, 1973)
The New American Filmmakers Series, Smithsonian Resident Associate Program, Smithsonian Institution, Washington, DC
Selected New Computer Films: Stan VanDerBeek, Theatre Vanguard, West Hollywood, CA (April 26, 1973)
State University of New York at Buffalo, Buffalo, NY (March 24, 1973)

1974
Baltimore Museum of Art, Baltimore, MD
Institute of Contemporary Arts (ICA), London, United Kingdom (September 6, 1974)
Stan VanDerBeek and Local Independent Filmmakers and Video Artists, Emory University, Atlanta, GA (August 6, 1974)
Underground Filmmakers, ETV, Madison, WI
Video Program at Anthology Film Archives, New York, NY (December 6–7, 1974)
1974 Summer Institute in the Making and Understanding of Film and Media, State University of New York at Buffalo, Buffalo, NY (August 19, 1974)

1975
Anthology Film Archives, New York, NY (January 4–5, 1975)
Computer Generation, The New Baltimore Independent Film Museum, Baltimore, MD (October 25, 1975)
Stan VanDerBeek: Films and Videos, Intermedia Church, Garnerville, NY (October 31, 1975)
State University of New York at Buffalo, Buffalo, NY
Video Anthology OMS Video and Films, New York, NY

1976
Film Forum, New York, NY (October 4, 1976)
ON/OFF Gallery, Seattle, WA

Mind/Art, Washington Projects for the Arts, University of Washington, Seattle, WA
Progressions, University of Maryland, Baltimore County, Baltimore, MD
Sinking Creek Film Celebration, Vanderbilt University, Nashville, TN
TNT (The New Theatre), University of Maryland, Baltimore County, Baltimore, MD

1977
Independent Film-Maker Stan VanDerBeek, Pittsburgh Film-Makers, Pittsburgh, PA (November 12, 1977)
Stan VanDerBeek Retrospective, Anthology Film Archives, New York, NY (January 7–9, 1977)

1978
Stan VanDerBeek, Berks Filmmakers, Inc., Reading, PA (June 10, 1978)
Video and Film Series, Global Village, New York, NY (December 8, 1978)
Video Art, Anthology Film Archives, New York, NY (January–February 1978)

1979
Retrospective, Stan VanDerBeek, The American Film Institute Theatre at the John F. Kennedy Center, Washington, DC (May 23, 1979)

1980
Cineprobe Retrospective, Museum of Modern Art, New York, NY

1981
Art Works [screening and seminar], University of Michigan, Detroit, MI
The Communication Interface of Motion Pictures, Auditorium, Art Gallery of Ontario, Toronto, Ontario, Canada (November 20, 1981)
Film and Video Pioneer Stan VanDerBeek Screenings, The Boston Film/Video Foundation, Boston, MA (May 2, 1981)
Highlights of the Baltimore Film Festival: Stan VanDerBeek, Hirshhorn Museum & Sculpture Garden, Smithsonian Institution, Washington, DC (May 21–22, 1981)
Living Artists of Tulsa [screening and workshop], Tulsa, OK
Walker Art Center, Minneapolis, MN (October 15, 1981)

1982
A Program of Films By and With Stan VanDerBeek, Beaumont Cinema, University of Miami, Coral Gables, FL (June 10–11, 1982)

1984
Personal Cinema Program, Winter Series 1984, Millennium Film Workshop, New York, NY

1985
ARTSCAPE '85, Stan VanDerBeek Retrospective, Maryland Institute College of Art, Baltimore, MD (July 16, 1985)

A Tribute to Stan VanDerBeek: Selected Works 1968–1984, Anthology Video Program, New York, NY (Winter 1985)

1993
Kunst or Die, Zonmééé, Montreuil, France

1995
9èmes rencontres du cinema indépendant de Châteauroux, Châteauroux, France (December 10, 1995)

1997
Centre national du cinema, Paris, France (April 29, 1997)

2002
Crime and Punishment, Balagan Experimental Film & Video Series, Coolidge Corner Theatre, Brookline, MA

2004
History from the Avant-Garde Film: Stan VanDerBeek, Balagan Experimental Film & Video Series, Coolidge Corner Theatre, Brookline, MA
May 2004 Monthly Selection, Electronic Arts Intermix, New York, NY

2005
Newsreel of Dreams 1, Independent Film Show 5th Edition, EM-Arts, Naples, Italy
1960s Electric Arts: From Kinetic Sculpture to Media Environments, Seattle Art Museum Downtown, Seattle, WA (March 2, 2005)

2009
Expanded Cinema: Activating the Space of Reception, Tate Modern, London, United Kingdom

Moving Image: Television

1965
The Underground Takes to the Air: VanDerBeek tells what your (sic) in for, he's up to, the why for? flics–flims–fill'ums on homey tv!!!!, Channel 4 (October 23, 1965)

1966
The Underground Comes up for Air...an Electric Collage...by Stan VanDerBeek, Channel 2 (February 27, 1966)

1969
Feedback, Syracuse University, Syracuse, NY

1970
Flick Out, WGBH, Boston, MA
Violence Sonata, WGBH, Boston, MA
Video Variations, WGBH, Boston, MA

1971
Flick Out, WGBH, Boston, MA

1972
Towards the Year 2000, ABC
Video Variations, in collaboration with the Boston Symphony, WGBH-TV, Boston, MA (aired nationally)

1973
College Collidoscope, CBS, Tampa, FL

1977
Collisions, WGBH, Boston, MA

1978
Fast Forward, interview, Canadian TV

1980
Documentary film by Kentucky Educational Television (KET), Lexington, KY

Moving Image: Intermedia Works

1963–65
Conceived and built *Movie-Drome*, Stony Point, NY

1967
Street Meet, Design-In, Central Park, New York, NY (May 12, 1967)

1969
Found Forms, Cross Talk Intermedia, Japan

1972
Cine Dreams: Future Cinema of The Mind, Strasenburgh Planetarium, Rochester, NY (February 25–27, 1972)

1973
Stan VanDerBeek: Cine Naps, USF Planetarium, University of South Florida, Tampa, FL (February 16 and 23, 1973)

1975
Fog, Mist, and Dreams, in collaboration with Joan Brigham, *ARTTRANSITION* symposium, MIT, Cambridge, MA
Stan VanDerBeek projection of film on steam in the courtyard, Chicago, IL (December 11, 1975)

1976
Under Aquarius, in collaboration with Joan Brigham, Alumni Pool, MIT, Cambridge, MA (March 14, 1976)

1977
Stan VanDerBeek's Steam Screen: A Cinematic Mirage, International Film Festival sponsored by the Baltimore Film Forum, MD (May 1977)
The Theatre of Light and Shadow, City of Baltimore Commission, Baltimore, MD (June 1977)
Under Aquarius, in collaboration with Joan Brigham, Hampshire College, Amherst, MA

1978
As We See it: Introducing Thirty-Six New Holographic Works, Museum of Holography, New York, NY (November 30, 1978)

1979
Steam Screens, film performance in collaboration with Joan Brigham, Whitney Museum of American Art, New York, NY (November 27 and December 4, 1979)

1980
Stan VanDerBeek, CHAMBERS in nine parts, First Intermedia Art Festival Performance Series, The Solomon R. Guggenheim Museum, New York, NY (February 3, 1980)

1981
Retrospective and *Steam Screens* installation, Walker Art Center, Minneapolis, MN (October 15, 1981)

Moving Image: Teaching and Artist-in-Residence Positions

1963–65
Columbia University, New York, NY, Associate Professor in Animation and Film Production

1967
University of Illinois, IL, Film Artist-in-Residence
University of Southern California, Los Angeles, CA, Film Artist-in-Residence

1967–73
State University of New York, Stony Brook, NY, Associate Professor in Film Projects

1968
Colgate University, Hamilton, NY, Film Artist-in-Residence
University of St. Thomas, U.S. Virgin Islands, Associate Professor in Film Projects
University of Washington, Seattle, WA, Associate Professor of Filmmaking

1969–70
Center for Advanced Visual Studies, Massachusetts Institute of Technology, Cambridge, MA
WGBH-TV, Boston, MA, Artist-in-Residence

1970
University of Wisconsin, Milwaukee, WI

1971–72
California Institute of the Arts, Valencia, CA, Film Artist-in-Residence
University of Hawaii Art Department and KHCT Educational Television Station, Honolulu, HI

1972
Center for Understanding Media, Buffalo, NY
New College, Sarasota, FL
University Film Study Center, Durham, NH

1972–75
Special Media Seminar for United States Information Agency, Washington, DC
University of South Florida, Tampa, FL

1975
ARTPARK, Lewiston, NY
WNET Artist-in-TV Laboratory, New
York, NY

1975–84
University of Maryland, Baltimore
County, Baltimore, MD, Professor of Art
and Film

1979
International Communications Agency,
Washington, DC
National Aeronautics and Space
Administration (NASA), Houston, TX

1980
Video: Kentucky Educational
Television (KET), Lexington, KY,
Artist-in-Residence

1982
Pennsylvania State University,
State College, PA, Computer
Artist-in-Residence

1983
Kentucky Educational Television (KET),
Lexington, KY, Computer Artist-in-
Residence (National Endowment for the
Arts)

Bibliography

1961
Mekas, Jonas and Dick Bergman. "Movie
Journal." *The Village Voice*, May 4, 1961.

1962
Mekas, Jonas. "Movie Journal: The Year's
Best." *The Village Voice*, January 11,
1962.
Tompkins, Calvin. *The Bride and the
Bachelors: Five Masters of the Avant-
Garde*. New York: The Viking Press,
1962.

1964
Mener, Jacques. "Breathdeath." *Script* 10–
12 (March 1964): 68–9.

1964–65
"Interview: Chapter One." *Film Culture*,
no. 35 (1964–5).

1965
Christgau, Robert. "VanDerBeek: Master
of Animation." *Popular Photography*
(September 1965): 106–11.
Fleck, Dirk C. "Neues aus New York."
Freitag, December 10, 1965.
Hajek, Peter. "Wien-Premiere: 'Expanded
Cinema.'" *Kurier*, December 20, 1965.
"Nette und verspielte Zelluloid-Reformer."
Berliner-Morgenpost, December 10,
1965.
Niehoff, Karena. "Drehwurm mit
Augenflimmern." *Der Tagesspiegel/
Feuilleton*, December 10, 1965.
Sheehy, Gail. "Six Hours in the Lobby."
New York Herald Tribune, September
15, 1965.
"Versuche aus USA." *Telegraf-Feuilleton*,
December 10, 1965.

"Völkerverständigung in Bildern,
Gespräch mit dem New Yorker
Filmregisseur Stan VanDerBeek."
*Spandauer.
Volksblatt*, December 8, 1965.

1966
Albarino, Richard. "Frug, Pulsating
Images, Light Patterns: Can NY Youth
Take so Much Emotion?" *Variety*, March
2, 1966.
"Movies: Masters and Mavericks."
Newsweek, October 3, 1966, 105B–107.
Sontag, Susan. "On Culture and the New
Sensibility." *Against Interpretation*.
New York: Dell, 1966.

1967
Adams, Marjory. "Movies—Maybe—in the
Round, 'Live' Cinema for Tomorrow?"
The Boston Globe, February 19, 1967.
Christgau, Robert. "Vanderbeek." *Cavalier*
17, no. 9 (July 1967): 61–65.
———. "When VanDerBeek A MovieDrome
Decreed." *New York/World Journal
Tribune*, March 5, 1967.
Clark, Tom. "VanDerBeek: Man, Movies,
Metaphor." *Focus* (October 1967): 3–4.
Clarke, Shirley. "A Statement on Dance
and Film." *Dance Perspectives* 30
(Summer 1967): 30–2.
Schwartz, Eugene. "Film Festival: Good
Spots." *Columbia Daily Spectator*,
October 3, 1967.
Thomas, Kevin. "VanDerBeek to Show
Films." *Los Angeles Times*, March 31,
1967, C10.
Whitehall, Richard. "Film Artist in
Residence at USC; VanDerBeek Uses
Light and Live Dance." *The Los Angeles
Free Press*, April 21, 1967.
Van Dyke, Manica A., and W. Van Dyke.
"Four Artists as Filmmakers." *Art
in America* 55, no. 1 (January 1967):
64–66.
Zaremba, Chuck. "USC Plans to 'Focus
on the Arts.'" *University of South
California Daily Trojan*, March 17, 1967.

1968
Cook, Camille. "Film Maker Stan
VanDerBeek." *ArtScene*, June 1968.
———. "VanDerBeek's films to be shown
Thursday." *Chicago Daily News*, June
19, 1968.
Currie, Hector, ed. *Cinema Now*.
Cincinnati: University of Cincinnati
Press, 1968.
Currie, Hector, and Michael Porte.
*Perspectives on American Film: Stan
Brakhage, John Cage, Jonas Mekas, Stan
VanDerBeek*. Cincinnati: University of
Cincinnati Press, 1968.
Thorpe, Dean. "Producer Cites 'New World
of Art Forms.'" *Corpus Christi Caller*,
July 11, 1968.

1969
Cross Talk (interview and performance
documentation), Japan, 1969.

1970
Anderson, Web. "Cinematography
workshop on UH campus, experimental
filmmaker here to teach." *The Sunday
Star-Bulletin & Advertiser*, July 12,
1970, 32–33.
Davis, Douglas. "Improbable Marriage."
Newsweek (April 20, 1970).
———. "Television's Avant-Garde."
Newsweek (February 9, 1970).
Durniak, John. "The VanDerBeek
Dimension." In *U.S. Camera World
Annual 1970*, 72–80. New York: U.S.
Camera Publishing, 1970.
Johnston, Jill. "Thanks for the Zonkers."
The Village Voice, January 22, 1970.
Renan, Sheldon. "An Introduction to the
American Underground Film." *Film
Culture* (1970): 48–9.
Wasserman, Emily. "Explorations—
Toward a Civic Art." *Artforum* 8, no. 10
(June 1970): 87–9.
Youngblood, Gene. *Expanded Cinema*.
New York: Dutton, 1970.

1971
Al Hayat, September 7, 1971.
Al-Liwa, September 5, 1971.
An Nahar, August 28, 1971.
An Nahar, September 11, 1971.
Ayin, Hushang Mehr. "The Computerized
Film." *Kayhan International*, August
29, 1971.
Cines D'Orient, September 4, 1971.
Evans, Anita. "American Film-Maker
Uses Media for Satire." *The Daily Star*,
September 9, 1971.
Katz, John S., *Perspectives on the Study
of Film*. New York: Little Brown &
Company, 1971.
"Media Wrap Around or a Man with No
Close." *Filmmakers' Newsletter* 4, no. 5
(March 1971): 20–5.
Mekas, Jonas. "Movie Journal." *The
Village Voice*, July 1, 1971.
Méliès, Georges. "Stan VanDerBeek, un
filleul (americain)." *L'Orient-Le Jour*
(supplement), August 28, 1971.
O'Connor, John. "When it Works, it's Art,
When it Doesn't, Well…" *The New York
Times*, July 4, 1971.
Sabet, Magda. "Spotlight." *The Daily Star*,
September 5, 1971.
"Stan VanDerBeek (Bilan de
l'Underground)." *Magazine*, September
16, 1971.

1972
"Cine Dreams is a Sellout." *Rochester
Democrat and Chronicle*, January 9,
1972.
Curtis, Davis. *Experimental Cinema*.
London: Studio Vista, 1972.
"Dream Job." *Rochester Democrat and
Chronicle*, February 29, 1972.
Greenspun, Roger. "Screen: Stan
VanDerBeek's Underground Shorts:
Retrospective Offered at the Film
Forum." *The New York Times*, December
9, 1972, 28.
Mekas, Jonas. *Movie Journal*. New York:
Macmillan, 1972.
"Mind Cinema." *Rochester Democrat and
Chronicle*, January 21, 1972.

Multiple Interaction. Cambridge, MA: The Center for Advanced Visual Studies, MIT, 1972. Exhibition catalogue.

O'Grady, Gerald. "Praxis as Axis: Autobiography in the New American Cinema." *SEE* 5, no. 3 (January 1972): 30–4.

Plutzik, Roberta. "It'll Put You to Sleep." *Rochester Democrat and Chronicle*, February 20, 1972.

"They Dreamed of Staying Up." *Rochester Democrat and Chronicle*, February 27, 1972.

1973

Davis, Douglas. *Art and the Future: A History/Prophecy of the Collaboration Between Science, Technology and Art*. London: Thames and Hudson, 1973.

M.R. "Stan VanDerBeek, 'Dans le Vent.'" *Journées internationals du cinema d'animation festival d'annecy* (January 1973): 5.

"Stan Vanderbeek Productor de Peliculas Experimentalies se Encuentra en Mexico." *Novedades*, August 10, 1973, 16.

"VanDerBeek stuns Issues crowd with visual images." *Daily Utah Chronicle* 83, no. 12, October 12, 1973.

Vrchota, Janet. "Stan VanDerBeek: Technology's Migrant Fruitpicker." *Print* (1973): 48–54.

Wright, Fred. "The Art Machine: Stan VanDerBeek turns on the computer and the Old Masters gasp–he hopes." *Floridian*, April 8, 1973.

1974

English, Diane. "Profile: Stan VanDerBeek, Creator of Dreams." *Vision News* 1, no. 3 (May 1974).

"Films to feature computer animation." *The Oracle*, May 17, 1974.

"UFS's VanDerBeek on Video Visionaries Show." *The Neighbor Newspaper*, October 16, 1974.

Youngblood, Gene. *Expanded Cinema*, 2nd ed. New York: Dutton, 1974.

1975

Martin, Robert. "VanDerBeek's images: pathways or seducers." *The Tampa Times*, June 12, 1975.

Powell, Fred. "Filmmaker's computer art fascinating visual experience." *Falcon Times*, January 29, 1975.

Schoettler, Carl. "Artist of the Future Working with Computers, Videos, Lasers." *The Baltimore Evening Sun Accent*, December 2, 1975.

1976

Hanhardt, John, et al. *A History of the American Avant-Garde Cinema*. New York: The American Federation of Arts, 1976. Exhibition catalogue.

"National Endowment" (interview). *Cultural Post*, Summer 1976.

Russett, Robert, and Cecile Starr. *Experimental Animation: An Illustrated Anthology*, 197–202. New York: Van Nostrand Reinhold Company, 1977.

"'Under Aquarius' To Transform Pool." MIT *Tech Talk* 20, no. 30 (March 10, 1976).

"VanDerBeek Exhibit in Library: The Work of a New Futurist." *Retriever*, April 12, 1976, 5.

1978

MacDonald, Scott. "Independent film: where's the audience?" *Afterimage* 5.9 (March 1978): 6–7.

"VANDERBEEK with Computer Graphics by Stan VanDerBeek." *Lightworks*, no. 10 (Fall 1978): 17–9.

1979

Giuliano, Mike. "The Membrain brain: He's ahead of the times back in the womb." *The News American*, October 28, 1979.

"VanDerBeek wins Guggenheim Fellowship." *Retriever*, May 14, 1979.

"Whitney to Show Computerized Film Images on Steam." *The New York Times*, November 15, 1979.

1980

Hill, Michael. "Look at Independent Filmmakers on PBS is surprising, irreverent." *Evening Sunpapers*, September 10, 1982.

"Not to be Mist." *The Village Voice*, November 1980.

Weiss, M.W. "VanDerBeek to Students: Take a High Risk." *Journal of the University Film Association*, Carbondale 34, no. 2 (Spring 1982): 19–21.

1983

Allen, Jane Addams. "Computer Art: Future Shock." *The Washington Times Magazine*, August 26, 1983.

Reid, Bruce. "It's video screens as well as canvases for computer-age art students." *The Sun*, May 29, 1983.

1984

Feiler, Alan. "VanDerBeek dies of cancer at age 57." *Retriever*, September 25, 1984.

Hitzig, Michael. "Innovative Rockland filmmaker succumbs to cancer at age 57." *The Journal News*, September 21, 1984.

"Stan VanDerBeek Dies at 57; Made Experimental Movie." *The New York Times*, September 22, 1984, 32.

"VanDerBeek honored." *The Columbia Flier*, February 9, 1984, 87.

"Video: Stan VanDerBeek." *The Village Voice*, March 21–27, 1984.

1985

Vogel, Amos. "Orbits: Eternal Experimenter." *Film Comment* 21, no. 1 (February 1985): 69.

1986

ACM Siggraph. *ACM Siggraph 86 Art Show: 13th Annual Conference on Computer Graphics and Interactive Techniques*. Dallas: ACM Siggraph, 1986. Exhibition catalogue.

Artists in the Computer Age. Toledo: Owens-Illinois Art Center, 1986. Exhibition catalogue.

1992

Barnouw, Erik. *Documentary: A History of the Non-Fiction Film*. New York: Oxford University Press, 1992.

Toung, Art. "Cinema Experimental: Stan VanDerBeek." *Revue & Corrigée*, no. 14 (Fall 1992): 24–5.

1994

Sklar, Robert. *Movie-Made America: A Cultural History of American Movies*, 314. New York: Vintage, 1994.

1999

Rees, A.L. *A History of Experimental Film and Video*. London: British Film Institute, 1999.

Sitney, P. Adams. *Visionary Film: The American Avant-Garde, 1943–2000*. New York: Oxford University Press, 2002.

2000

VanDerBeek, Johanna. *Re:Voir Video Catalogue*. Paris: 2000.

2003

Sutton, Gloria. "Stan VanDerBeek's Movie-Drome: Networking the Subject." In *Future Cinema: The Cinematic Imaginary after Film*, ed. Jeffery Shaw and Peter Weibel. Karlsruhe: Center for Art and Media (ZKM) and MIT Press, 2003.

2004

Leung, Simon, and Zoya Kocur. *Theory in Contemporary Art Since 1985*. Hoboken, NJ: Wiley, 2004.

Michalka, Mathias, et al. *X-Screen: Film Installations and Actions in the 1960s and 1970s*. Koln: Verlag der Buchhandlung Walther König; Vienna: Museum Moderner Kunst Stiftung Ludwig, 2004. Exhibition catalogue.

2006

Curiger, Bice, et al. *The Expanded Eye: Stalking the Unseen*. Ostfildern, Germany: Hatje Cantz, 2006. Exhibition catalogue, Kunsthaus Zürich.

Grunenberg, Christoph. *Summer of Love*. Liverpool: Liverpool University Press, 2006. Exhibition catalogue.

Michaud, Phillippe-Alain. *Le Mouvement des images*. Paris: Centre Pompidou, Musée national d'art moderne-Centre de création industrielle, 2006.

2007

Cattelan, Maurizio, Massimiliano Gioni, and Ali Subotnick. *Charley 05*. Dijon: Les Presses du Réel, 2007.

2008

Baker, R.C. "Best in Show: Stan VanDerBeek at Guild & Greyshkul." *The Village Voice* (October 1, 2008): 43.

Bartlett, Mark. "The Politics of Media in Stan VanDerBeek's Poemfields." *Animation: An Interdisciplinary Journal* 3, no. 3 (November 2008): 266–287.

Cotter, Holland. "Art in Review: Stan VanDerBeek." *The New York Times*, October 10, 2008, C34.

Dupuis, Isabelle. "Stan VanDerBeek." *Flash Art* 41, no. 263 (November–December 2008): 85.

Leighton, Tanya, ed. *Art and the Moving Image, A Critical Reader*. London: Tate Publishing in association with Afterall, 2008.

Mack, Joshua. "Stan VanDerBeek, Works from 1950–1980." *Time Out New York*, April 24–30, 2008, 101.

Olson, Marisa. "Art Keeps on Slipping Into the Future." *Rhizome*, October 2, 2008. http://rhizome.org/editorial/1937.

Scott, Andrea K. "All in the Family." *The New Yorker: "Goings On" Blog*, May 1, 2008. http://www.newyorker.com/online/blogs/goingson/2008/05/10.html.

Sholis, Brian. "Sara VanDerBeek: 500 Words." *Artforum*, September 14, 2008. http://artforum.com/words/id=21092.

Smith, Roberta. "The Listings: The Human Face is a Monument." *The New York Times*, April 25, 2008, E19.

Wiley, Chris. "Exhibition Review: Stan VanDerBeek at Guild and Greyshkul." *Daylight Daily Blog, Daylight Magazine* 7, October 15, 2008. http://www.daylightmagazine.org/blog/2008/10/15/253

2009

Amidi, Amid. "A Stan VanDerBeek Retrospective." In *Ottawa International Animation Festival 2009 Reader*, 74–78. Ottawa: Ottawa International Animation Festival, 2009.

Meade, Fionn. "Stan VanDerBeek: Guild & Greyshkul." *Artforum* 47, no. 5 (January 2009): 210.

Myers, Holly. "Layer Upon Layer of Technology." *Los Angeles Times*, April 3, 2009.

Nichols, Matthew Guy. "Stan VanDerBeek: Guild & Greyshkul." *Art in America* 97, no. 1 (January 2009): 108.

2010

Bartlett, Mark, ed. *Animation: An Interdisciplinary Journal* 5, no. 2 (July 2010).

Documentaries

The Computer Generation (1972) 30 min., broadcast on Camera Three, CBS
Home and Dome (1965) 15 min.
Vanderbeekiana (1968) 29 min., broadcast on Camera Three, CBS

Writings by Stan VanDerBeek

1961

"The Cinema Delimina: Films from the Underground." *Film Quarterly* 14, no. 4 (Summer 1961): 5–15.

"On 'Science Friction'" *Film Culture* 22–23 (Summer 1961): 168.

1962

"If the Actor Is the Audience." *Film Culture* 24 (Spring 1962): 92.

1963

"Simple Syllogism." *Film Culture* 29 (1963): 11.

1964–65

"Interview: Chapter One." *Film Culture* 35 (1964–5): 20–22.

1966

"Compound Entendre." In *Film: A Montage of Theories*, ed. Richard McCann, 329–32. New York: Dutton, 1966.

"'Culture: Intercom' and Expanded Cinema: A Proposal and Manifesto." *Film Culture* 40 (Spring 1966): 15–18.

"'Culture: Intercom' and Expanded Cinema: A Proposal and Manifesto." *Tulane Drama Review* 11, no. 1 (Autumn 1966): 38–48.

"Culture Intercom & Expanding-Cinema: A Proposal by Stan VanDerBeek." *Motive* XXII/2 (November 1966): 13–23.

"Re: Vision." *The American Scholar* 35, no. 2 (Spring 1966): 335–340.

1967

Dance Perspectives 30 (Summer 1967).
Polemic XI, no. 2 (Spring 1967): 20–31.

1969

"Movies, Disposable Art, Synthetic Media and Artificial Intelligence." In *Revolution, Place, and Symbol*, ed. Rolfe Lanier Hunt. New York: International Congress on Religion, Architecture, and the Visual Arts, 1969.

"Disposable Art-Synthetic Media and Artificial Intelligence." *Take One* (January–February 1969): 14–16.

1970

"New Talent-The Computer." *Art in America* 58, no. 1 (1970): 86-91.

"Re Computerized Graphics." *Film Culture* 48–49 (1970): 37–40.

U.S. Camera World Annual 1970. New York: U.S. Camera Publishing, 1970, 72–80.

1971

"Media (W)rap-around: Or a Man with No Close." *Filmmakers Newsletter* 4, no. 5 (March 1971).

1973

"Social-Imagistics: What the Future May Hold." *American Film Institute Report* 4, no. 2 (May 1973): 54-7.

Print Magazine 27 (March 1973): 48–54.

1975

"Cinema Is..." *Up to Speed, The Journal of The Baltimore Film Festival* 1, no. 1 (Fall 1975): 6.

1976

"Culture: Intercom and Expanded Cinema, a Proposal." *The New American Cinema*, ed. Gregory Battock. New York: Dutton, 1976.

Machine Art: An Exhibit of "Inter-Graphics". Baltimore: University of Maryland Baltimore County Library, 1976.

1977

"Animation Retrospective." *Film Comment* 62 (October 1977).

"Lengthy Interview." *Cultural Post* (published by the National Endowments Publication).

1981

"Re: Vision of Cine-Dreams." *DreamWorks* 2, no. 1 (Fall 1981): 4–12.

Awards and Honors

1958

Award of distinction for *What Who How*, Cinema 16, New York, NY

Bronze medal for *Mankinda* and *What Who How*, Brussels International Experimental Film Competition, Brussels World Fair, Brussels, Belgium

1959

Award of merit for *What Who How*, Creative Film Foundation, New York, NY

1960

Award of distinction for *Science Friction*, Creative Film Foundation, New York, NY

First prize, animation for *Mankinda*, Oberhausen Film Festival, Oberhausen, Germany

1964

Award winner at The Experimental Film Festival, Brussels, Belgium

Award of distinction for *Skullduggery*, Lincoln Center Film Festival

Award of distinction for *Skullduggery*, London Film Festival

Prizes for *Breathdeath*, Midwest and Ann Arbor Film Festivals

1965

Top prize for *Breathdeath*, Fourth Annual Independent Film-Makers' Festival at Foothill College, Los Altos Hills, CA (May 8–9, 1965)

1967

Award of distinction for *See Saw Seems*, Lincoln Center Film Festival, New York, NY and London Film Festival, London, United Kingdom

Participant, *Literarisches Collequium*, Berlin, Germany

Second prize for *Man and His World*, Computer film Expo '67, Montreal, Quebec, Canada

1968

First prize, animation for *Superimposition*, Mannheim, Germany

Grants

1963–64

Ford Foundation Grant for Experimental Films

1965–66
Rockefeller Foundation Grant for Non-
Verbal Communication Film Studies

1969–70
New York State Council on the Arts
Creative Artists Public Service (CAPS)
Grant for *Cine Dreams*, Strasenburgh
Planetarium, New York, NY
Rockefeller Foundation Grant for
Experimental Artist in Television,
WGBH, Boston, MA

1973
National Endowment for the Arts (NEA)
Grant for Experiments in Video,
Kentucky Educational Television (KET),
Lexington, KY

1974
Rockefeller Foundation Grant,
Experiments in Video, WGBH, Boston,
MA

1975–76
National Endowment for the Arts
"Regional Media Center," University of
Maryland, Baltimore County, Baltimore,
MD

1977–78
National Endowment for the Arts
"Regional Media Center," University of
Maryland, Baltimore County, Baltimore,
MD

1977
National Endowment for the Arts Grant
for Experimental Film and Video

1978
National Endowment for the Arts Grant
for Experimental Film and Video
National Endowment for the Arts Grant
for Performance and Research, "Artist
and the Computer" and "Services to the
Field"

1978–79
National Endowment for the Arts "In-
Residence" program

1981–82
National Endowment for the Arts
Individual Artist Grant for Computer
Animation Research

1982
Arts and Humanities Award in Computer
Graphics, University of Pennsylvania,
Philadelphia, PA
Jewish Federation of Cleveland,
"Experimental Video," Cleveland, OH

Public Collections

The Arts Council of Great Britain, London,
United Kingdom
The Art Institute of Chicago, Chicago, IL
Centre Pompidou, Paris, France
Museum of Modern Art, New York, NY
The National Library of Australia Film
Collection, Parkes (Canberra), Australia
The Pennsylvania State University, State
College, PA

Filmography

Achoo Mr. Keroochev (1959) 16mm, 2 min.,
black and white, sound
Ad Infinitum (no date) 10 min.
A La Mode (1958) 16mm, 10 min., black
and white, sound
Alamo 01 (1957) 16mm, 10 min., color,
sound
Astral Man (1958) 16mm, 4 min., black
and white, silent
Blacks & Whites, Days & Nights (1960)
16mm, 7 min., black and white, sound
Birth of the American Flag (1965) 16mm,
20 min., black and white
Breathdeath (1964) 16mm, 15 min., black
and white, sound
Carbop (1962) 35mm, black and white
(unfinished)
Charlemagne's Spherical Dream (1968) 7
min., color, sound
Collidoscope (no date) 6 min., color
Computer Art No. 1 (no date) 16mm and
35mm, 4 min.
Computer Generation (no date) 16mm, 29
min., color and black and white, sound
Croquet Quacks (1962) 35mm, black and
white (unfinished)
A Dam Rib Bed (1964–65) 35mm, 15 min.,
black and white (unfinished)
Dance of the Looney Spoons (1959–65)
16mm, 7 min., black and white, sound
Dance Works No. 1 (ca. 1960s) Dance
choreography by Barbara Lloyd, music
composed by Gordon Mumma
Euclidean Illusions (1980) 16mm, 9 min.,
color, sound
Facescapes No. 1 (1964–65) 35mm, 10
min., black and white
Feedback (1965) 16mm, 12 min., black and
white and color
Fluids (1964–65) 35mm, 7 min., black and
white (unfinished; used as a three-
screen with Snow-Show and Night
Eating)
Film Form No. 1 (1970) 16mm, 10 min.,
color, sound
Found Film No. 1 (1970) 16mm, 7 min.,
black and white, sound
Future (no date) 16mm, 7 min., color,
sound, three screens
The History of Motion in Motion (1967)
16mm, 10 min., black and white, sound
The Human Face is a Monument (1965)
16mm, 12 min., black and white
Hyway Culture (no date) 16mm, 15 min.,
color and black and white, sound, three
screen or single screen
Image After Image (no date) 8 min., black
and white, sound, three screen or single
screen
Leadville (1965) 16mm, 5 min., black and
white
Man And His World (1967) 16mm, 1 min.,
color, sound, computer animation in
four languages
Mankinda (1957) 16mm, 10 min., black
and white, sound
Miscellaneous Happenings (1961–62)
16mm, black and white and color
Moirage (1967) 8 min., color (by Stan
VanDerBeek and G. Oster)
Newsreel of Dreams No. 1 (1963–64)
16mm, 8 min., color, sound

Newsreel of Dreams No. 2 (1963–64)
16mm, 8 min., color, sound
Newsreel of Dreams No. 3 (no date) 16mm,
9 min., color, sound
Night Eating (1964–65) 35mm, 4 min.,
black and white
Oh (1968) 16mm, 12 min., color, sound
(listed on Filmmaker's Coop as 10 min.)
Oh-Or-War (no date) 6 min., color, sound
One (no date) 10 min., color, sound
One and Yet (1957) 16mm, 1 min., black
and white, sound (not released)
Vision III (1958) 16mm, 7 min., black and
white, sound on tape
Panels for the Walls of the World (1966–
67) 16mm, 8 min., black and white,
sound
Pastorale (1964–65) 16mm, 10 min., color
(unfinished)
Phenomenon No. 1 (1965) 16mm, 7 min.,
black and white
Poemfield No. 1 (1965) 16mm, 5 min., black
and white, sound (listed on Filmmaker's
Coop website as 4 min.)
Poemfield No. 2 (1966) 16mm, 6 min.,
color, sound
Poemfield No. 3: A Map of Ideas (1967)
16mm, 10 min., color, sound
Poemfield No. 4 (1967) 16mm, 10 min.,
color, sound
Poemfield No. 5: Free Fall (1967) 16mm, 7
min., color, sound
Poemfield No. 6 (1969) 16mm, 4 min.,
color, sound
Poemfield No. 7 (1969) 16mm, 5 min.,
color, sound
Poemfield No. 8 (no date) 16mm, 1 min.,
color, sound
Revenge of the Looney Spoons (1959)
16mm, black and white (unfinished)
Room Service (1965) 16mm, 10 min., black
and white
Science Friction (1959) 16mm and 35mm,
10 min., color, sound (listed in S.V.
Maryland Filmography as 9 min.)
See, Saw, Seams (1965) 16mm and 35mm,
12 min., black and white, sound
Site (1964–64) 16mm, 10 min., black and
white
Skullduggery (1960) 16mm and 35mm, 5
min., black and white, sound
Snapshots of the City (1961) 16mm, 5 min.,
black and white, sound
Snow-Show (1964–65) 35mm, 7 min.,
black and white
Spherical Space No. 1 (1967) 16mm, 5 min.,
color, sound on tape
Street Meat/meet (1959) 16mm, 15 min.,
color, sound on tape, six screen or single
screen
Summit (1963) 16mm, 12 min., color and
black and white, sound
Super-Imposition (1968) 16mm, 15 min.,
sound
Transforms (no date) 16mm, 3 min., black
and white, sound
T.V. Interview (1967) 16mm, 13 min., black
and white, sound
Vangrams No. 1 (no date) 5 min., color
Variations V (1965) 16mm and 35mm, 30
min., black and white
Variations V (1966) 16mm, 50 min., black
and white
Videospace (1972) 16mm, 7 min., color,
sound

Violence Sonata (screened February
2, 1970 at the Whitney Museum of
American Art, New York, NY) 16mm and
slides, 27 min., color
Violence Sonata No. 2 (1969) 45 min.,
color, magnetic sound, two screen
What Who How (1957) 16mm, 8 min., black
and white, sound
Wheeeeels No. 1 (1958) 16mm, 8 min.,
black and white, sound
*Wheeeeels No. 2: The Immaculate
Contraption, Dedicated to Detroit* (1959)
16mm, 5 min., black and white, sound
Wheeeeels No. 3 (1959) 16mm, 7 min.,
black and white, silent (unfinished)
Who Ho Ray No. 1 (1972) 16mm, 10 min.,
color, silent
Will (1968) 16mm, 5 min., color, sound
Yet (1957–8) 2 min., color
You Do, I Do, We Do (no date) 16mm, 14
min., black and white, sound

Videography

After Laughter (1981) video, 7:28 min.,
color, sound, produced at KCET, Los
Angeles, CA
Color Fields Left (1977) video, 7:47 min.,
color, sound, produced at WGBH,
Boston, MA
Face Concert (1981) video, 11:54 min.,
color, sound
Micro Cosmos 1–5 (1983) video (series of
five short computer animated works
produced at KCET, Los Angeles, CA)
Mirrored Reason (1979) video, 9:22 min.,
color, sound (performer: Denise Koch,
editor: Si Fried)
Reeling in TV Time (1983) video, 3:40
min., color, sound
Self-poured Traits (1983) video, 4:52 min.,
color, sound, produced at KCET, Los
Angeles, CA (poetry: Kenneth Rexroth)
Sonia and Stan Paint a Portrait of Ronnie
(1983) video, 13:30 min., color, sound (in
collaboration with Sonia Sheridan)
Strobe Ode (1977) video, 11 min., color,
sound, produced at WGBH, Boston, MA
(sound/music: in collaboration with
ZBS)
Vanishing Point Left (1977) video, 7:47
min., color, sound
Will You Miss Me While I'm at the Toilet
(1967) video, 8 min., black and white,
sound

Funding for this exhibition at the Contemporary Arts Museum Houston and the MIT List Visual Arts Center has been generously provided by ART MENTOR FOUNDATION LUCERNE and The National Endowment for the Arts.

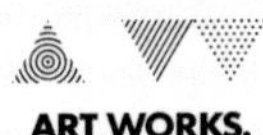

ART WORKS.
arts.gov

CONTEMPORARY ARTS MUSEUM HOUSTON

This exhibition has been made possible by the patrons, benefactors and donors to the Museum's Major Exhibition Fund:

Major Patron
Chinhui Juhn and Eddie Allen
Fayez Sarofim
Michael Zilkha

Patrons
Louise D. Jamail
Mr. and Mrs. I. H. Kempner III
Ms. Louisa Stude Sarofim
Leigh and Reggie Smith

Benefactors
Baker Botts L.L.P. / Anne and David
    Kirkland
George and Mary Josephine Hamman
    Foundation
Jackson Hicks / Jackson and Company
Marley Lott
Poppi Massey
Beverly and Howard Robinson
Andrew Schirrmeister
Susan Vaughan Foundation, Inc.
Mr. and Mrs. Wallace Wilson

Donors
A Fare Extraordinaire
Anonymous
Anonymous
Bergner and Johnson Design
The Brown Foundation, Inc.
Jereann Chaney
Susie and Sanford Criner
Elizabeth Howard Crowell
Ruth Dreessen and Thomas Van Laan
Marita and J.B. Fairbanks
Jo and Jim Furr
Barbara and Michael Gamson
Mr. and Mrs. William Goldberg /
    Bernstein Global Wealth Management
King & Spalding L.L.P.
KPMG, LLP
Judy and Scott Nyquist
David I. Saperstein
Scurlock Foundation
Karen and Harry Susman

The catalogue accompanying the exhibition is made possible by a grant from The Brown Foundation, Inc.

The Museum's operations and programs are made possible through the generosity of the Museum's trustees, patrons, members and donors. The Contemporary Arts Museum Houston receives partial operating support from the Houston Endowment, the City of Houston through the Houston Museum District Association, the National Endowment for the Arts, the Texas Commission on the Arts, and The Wortham Foundation, Inc.

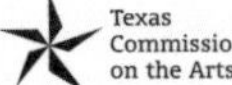
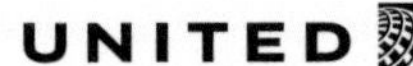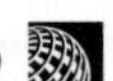

Stan VanDerBeek: The Culture Intercom is made possible by generous support from the Union Pacific Foundation.

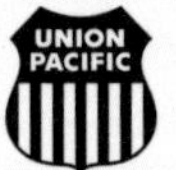

Staff
Bill Arning, Director
Tim Barkley, Registrar
Quincy Berry, Assistant Gallery
    Supervisor
Cheryl Blissitte, Administrative
    Assistant, Director's Office
Amanda Bredbenner, Development
    Manager/Special Events
Kenya F. Evans, Gallery Supervisor
Natividad Flores, Housekeeping
Olivia Junell, Membership & Annual Gifts
    Coordinator
Peter Lucas, Education Associate
Connie McAllister, Communications &
    Marketing Manager
Paula Newton, Director of Education and
    Public Programs
Valerie Cassel Oliver, Senior Curator
Sue Pruden, Museum Shop Manager
Michael Reed, Assistant Director
Victoria Ridgway, Development
    Coordinator
Virginia Shaw, Museum Shop Assistant
Jeff Shore, Head Preparator
Lana Sullivan, Receptionist/Staff
    Secretary
Justine Waitkus, Curatorial Manager
Amber Winsor, Director of Development

MIT LIST VISUAL ARTS CENTER

Support for the presentation of *Stan VanDerBeek: The Culture Intercom* at the MIT List Visual Arts Center has been made possible by Martin E. Zimmerman, the Council for the Arts at MIT, and the Massachusetts Cultural Council.

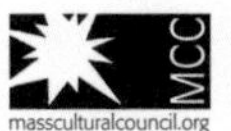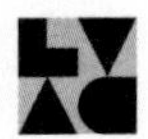
massculturalcouncil.org

Advisory Committee
Susan Leff, Chair
Uta Meta Bauer
Ruth Bowman
Suelin Chen
Susan Cohen
Charles Coolidge
Lindsay Coolidge
Jerome Friedman
Susanne Ghez
Per Gjorstrup
Kitty Glantz
Geoff Hargadon
Jon Hendricks
Marjory Jacobson
Philip Khoury
Leila Kinney
Boris Magasanik
Marian Marill
John Melick
Andrea Miller-Keller
Andrea Nasher
Tony Podesta
Stephen Prina
David Solo
Jeanne Stanton
Martin E. Zimmerman

Staff
Sue Bright, Gallery Attendant
Jane Farver, Director
Karen Fegley, Gallery Attendant
David Freilach, Assistant Director
Kristin Johnson, Gallery Attendant
Diane Kalik, Registrar
Bryce Kauffman, Gallery Attendant
Mark Linga, Educator/Public Relations
    Officer
Tim Lloyd, Exhibition Designer,
    Gallery Manager
John Osorio-Buck, Gallery Assistant
Barbra Pine, Administrative Assistant
João Ribas, Curator
Alise Upitis, Public Art Curator
Suara Welitoff, Gallery Attendant

This publication accompanies
the exhibition *Stan VanDerBeek:
The Culture Intercom*

Curators: Bill Arning and João Ribas

MIT List Visual Arts Center,
Cambridge, MA
February 4–April 3, 2011

Contemporary Arts Museum Houston,
Houston, TX
May 14–July 10, 2011

Front/Back Cover: Stan VanDerBeek,
Culture Intercom, 1965.

Available through
D.A.P. / Distributed Art Publishers, Inc.
155 Sixth Avenue, 2nd Floor
New York, NY 10013
Tel: 212 627 1999
www.artbook.com

Designed by Peter J. Ahlberg / AHL&CO

Printed and bound by Shapco,
Minneapolis, Minnesota

ISBN 978-1-933619-33-0

Library of Congress Control Number:
2010940281

Poemfields, 1966–71

Stan VanDerBeek began a series of animated
films called *Poemfields* in 1964 using the
BEFLIX movie-making system. An abbrevi-
ation for "Bell Flicks," BEFLIX was an early
computer graphic programming language
invented in 1964 by Ken Knowlton, a physicist working at Bell Telephone Laboratories.[6]
The films were created with an IBM data
processing computer using punch cards. The
ability to generate type on a screen was a radically new tool for VanDerBeek, who, having
never mastered programming language, was
dependent on collaborations with Knowlton
and MIT computer engineer Wade Shaw, whom
VanDerBeek worked with while a resident at the
Center for Advanced Visual Studies (CAVS) at
MIT from 1969 to 1971.

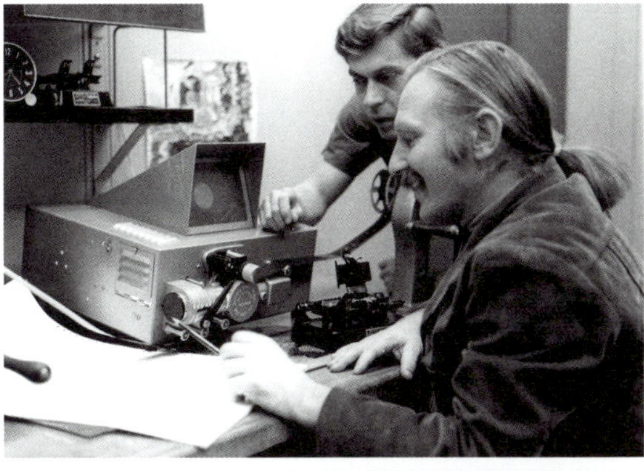

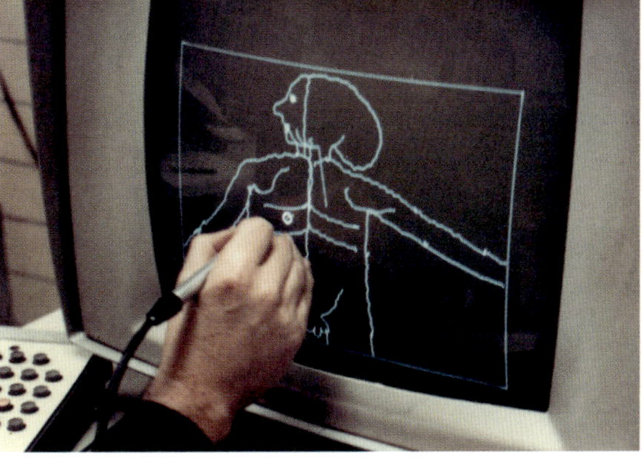

[Top] Stan VanDerBeek and Ken Knowlton,
Bell Labs, New Jersey, ca. 1966–68.

[Bottom] Stan VanDerBeek drawing on
computer, Center for Advanced Visual
Studies, MIT, Cambridge, ca. 1969.

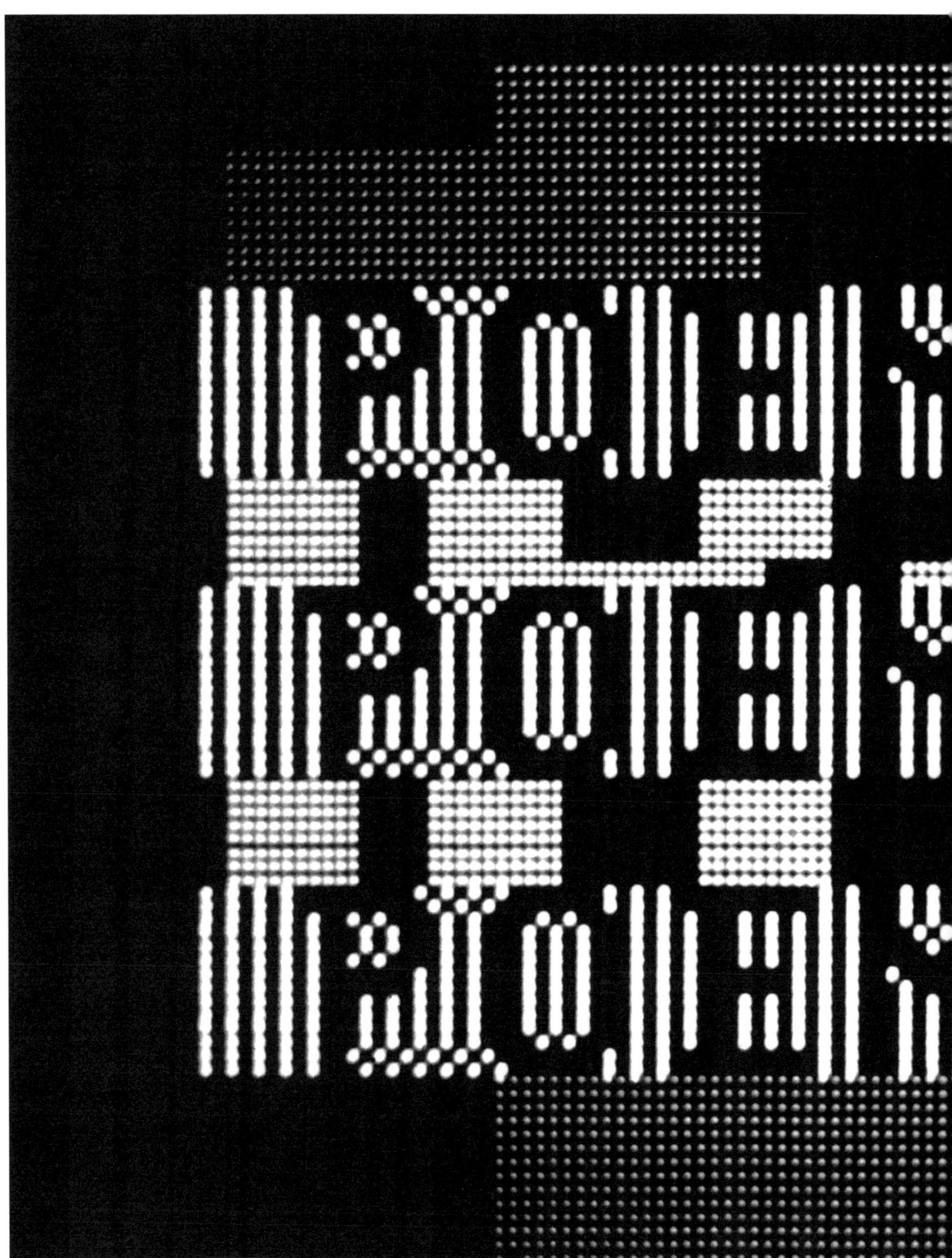

Film still from *Poemfield* No. 1, 1965. 16mm,
black and white, silent, 5:00 min.

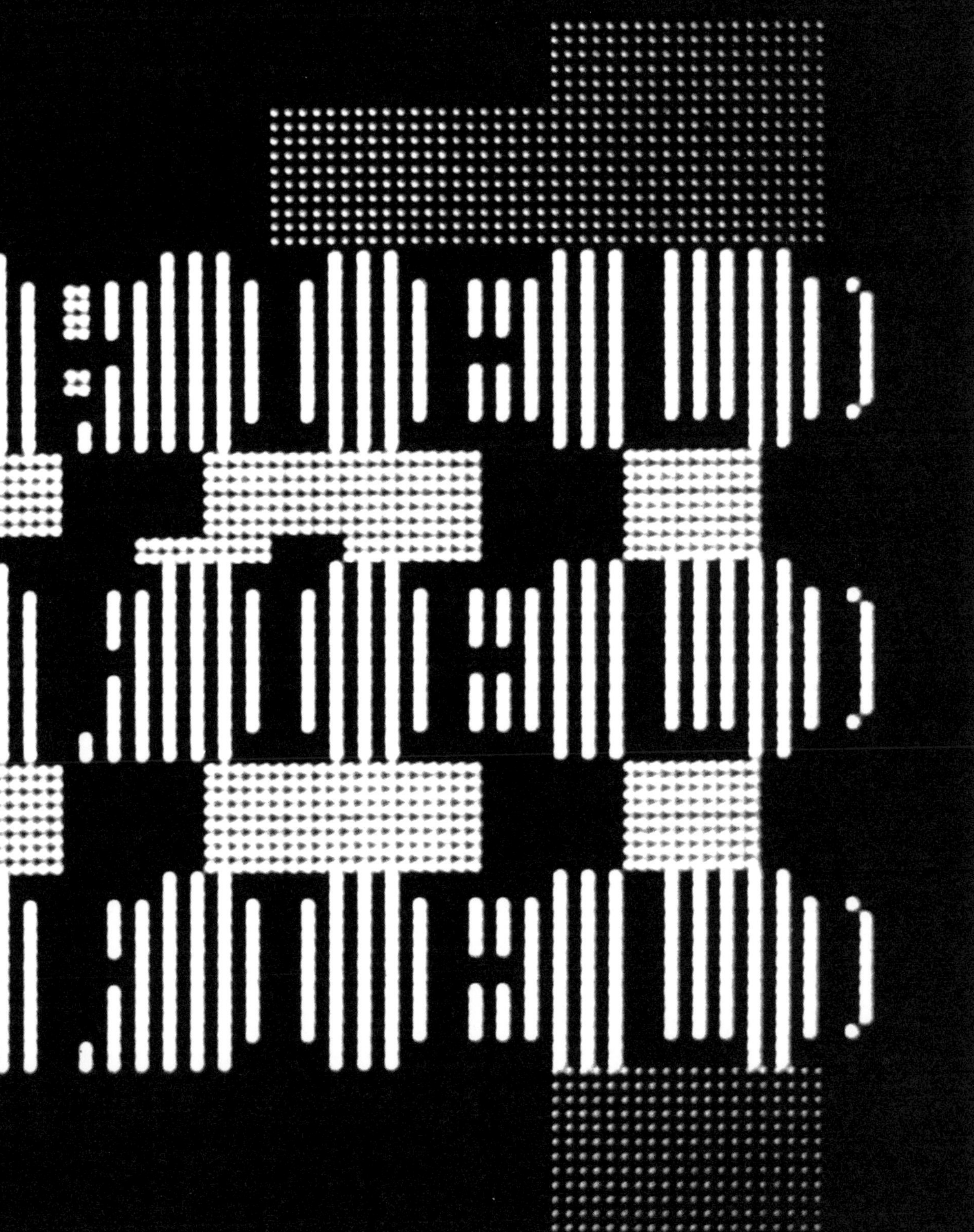

Film stills from *Poemfield No. 2*, 1966.
16mm, color, sound, 5:40 min.

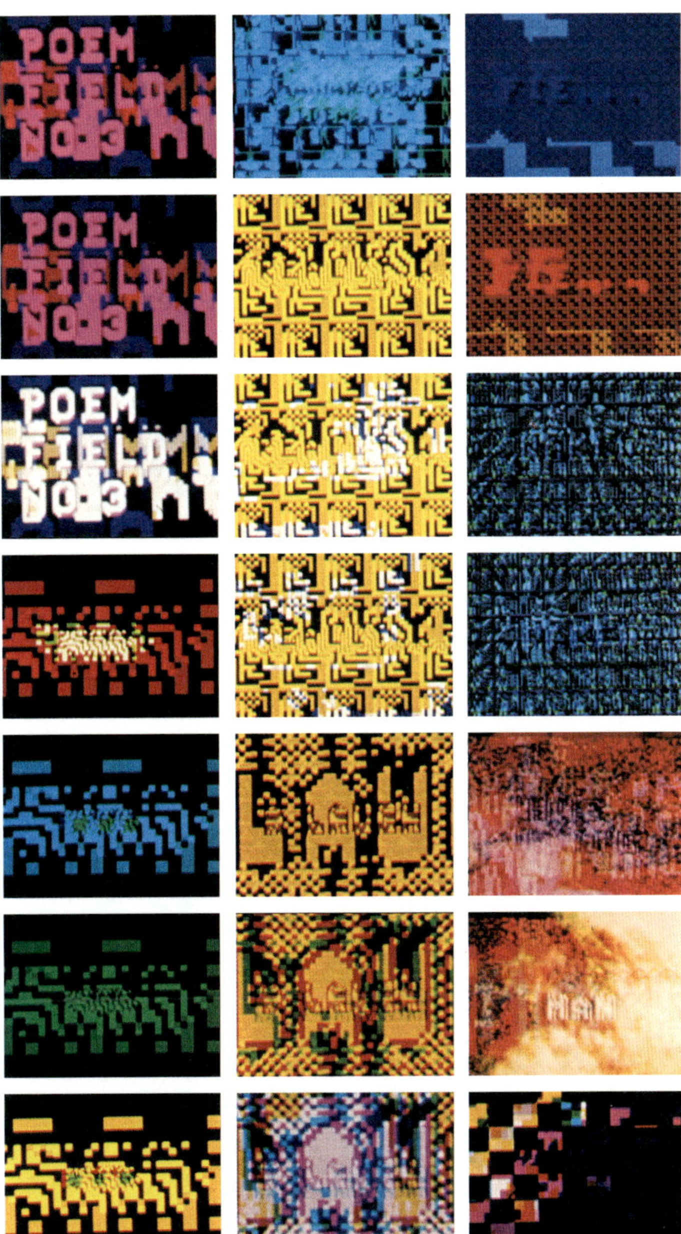

Film stills from *Poemfield No. 3*, 1967.
16mm, color, sound, 9:45 min.

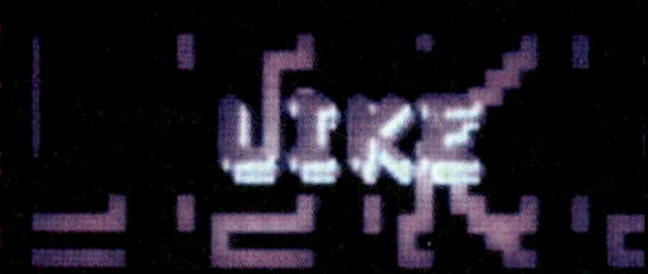

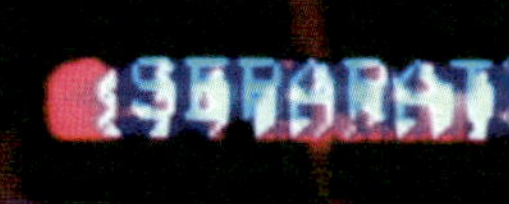
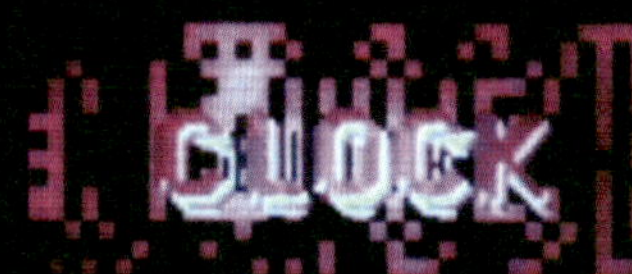
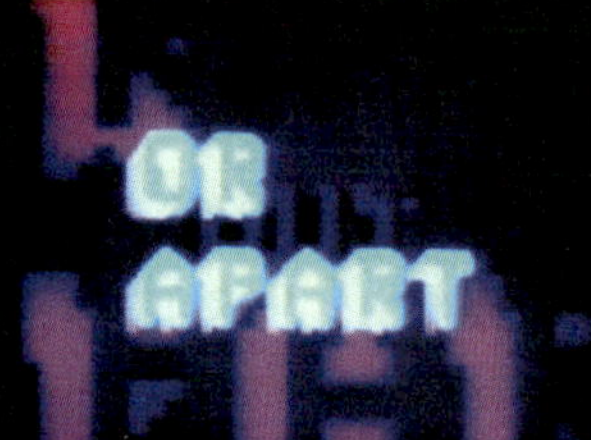
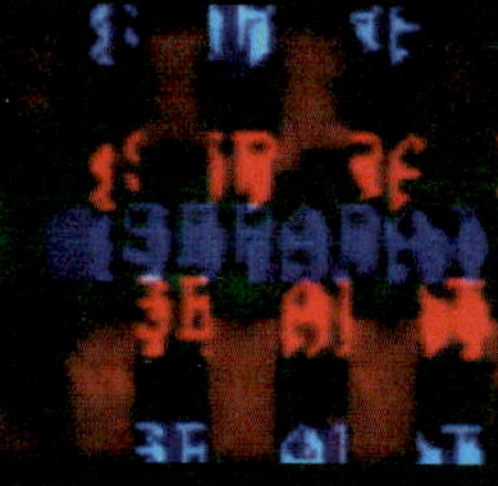
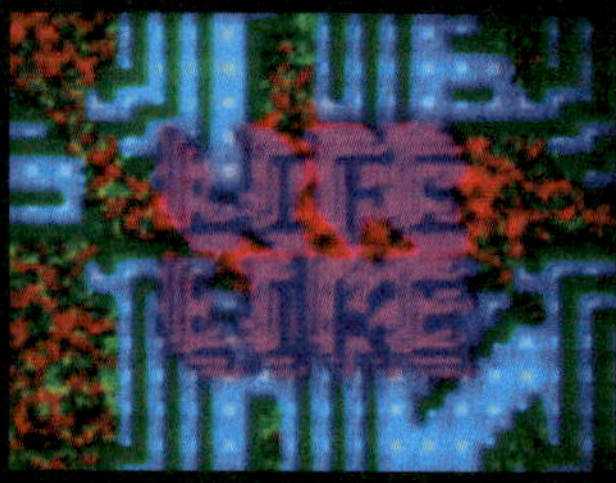
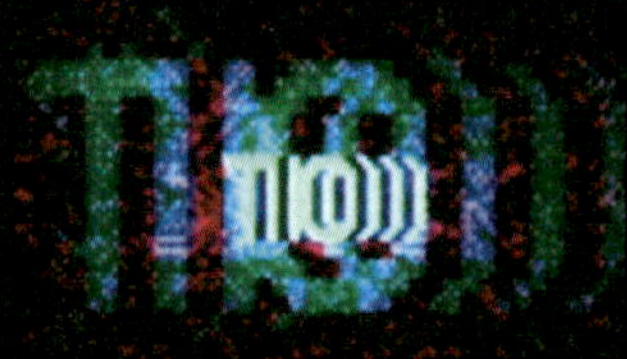
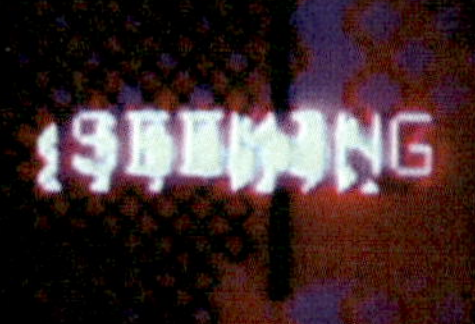
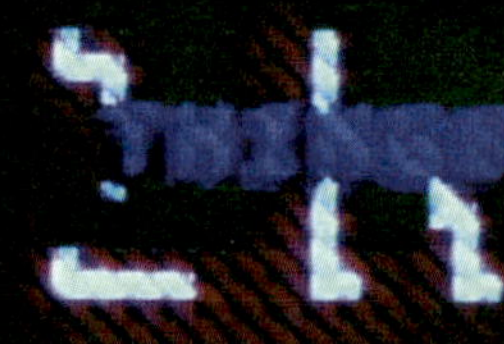

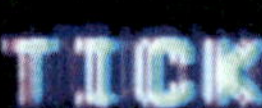

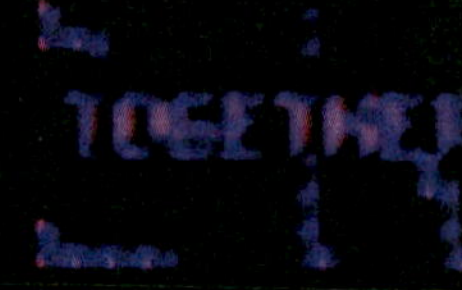

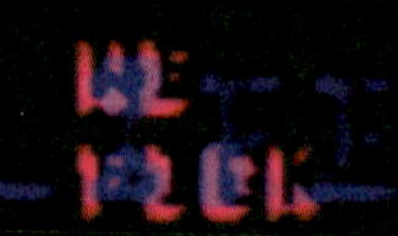
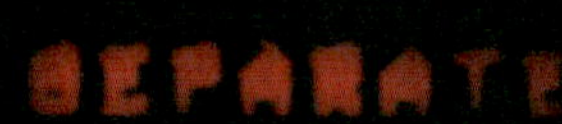
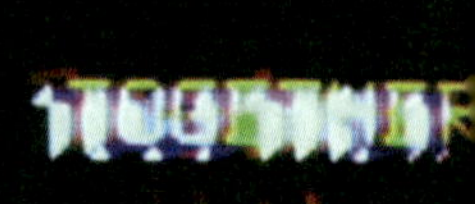

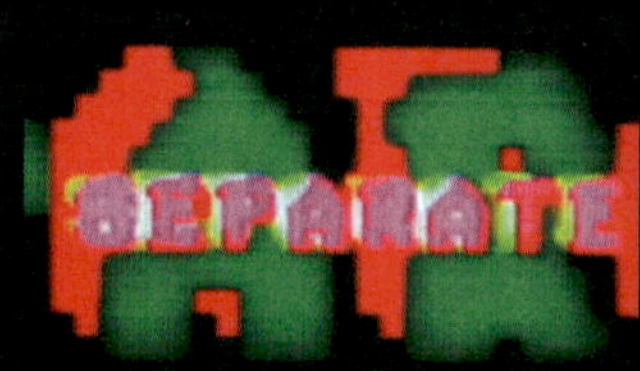
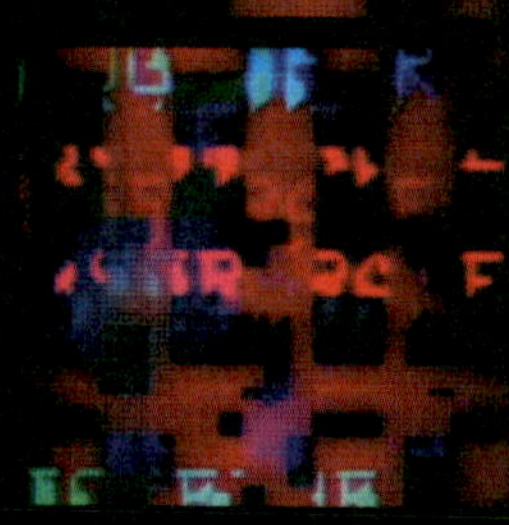

Film stills from *Poemfield No. 2*, 1966.
16mm, color, sound, 5:40 min.

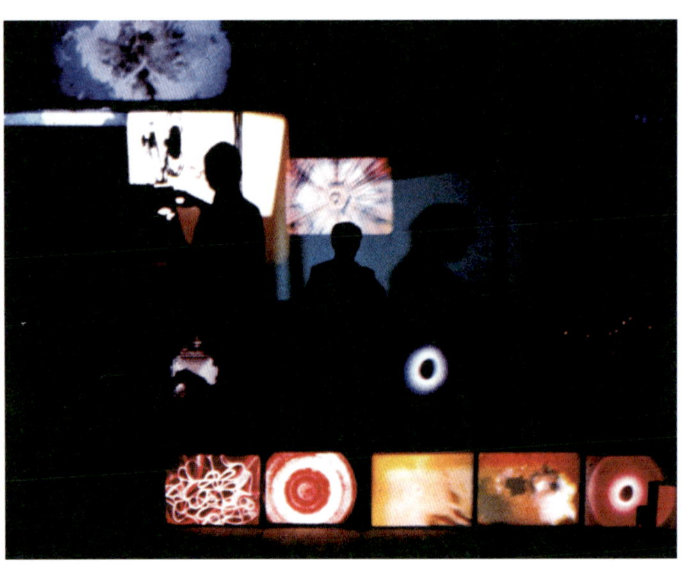

[Above] *Poemfields*. Installation view,
Cross Talk Intermedia, Japan, 1969.

[Right] Selected images from *Poemfield*
films, ca. 1966-69.

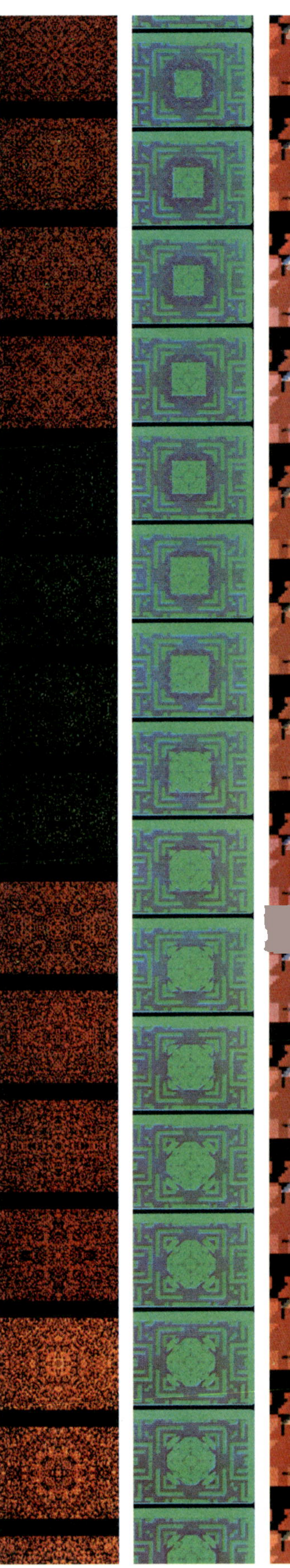

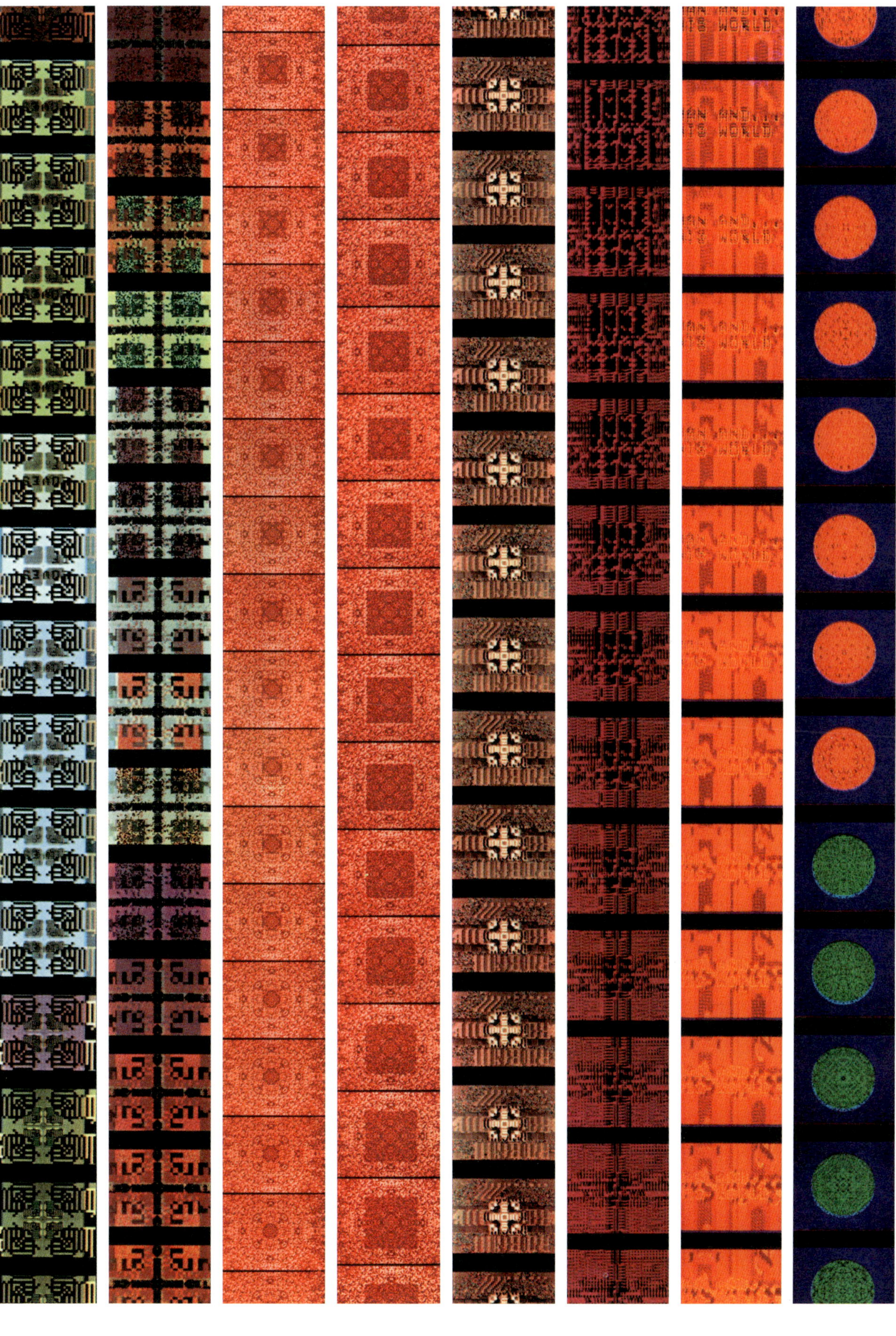

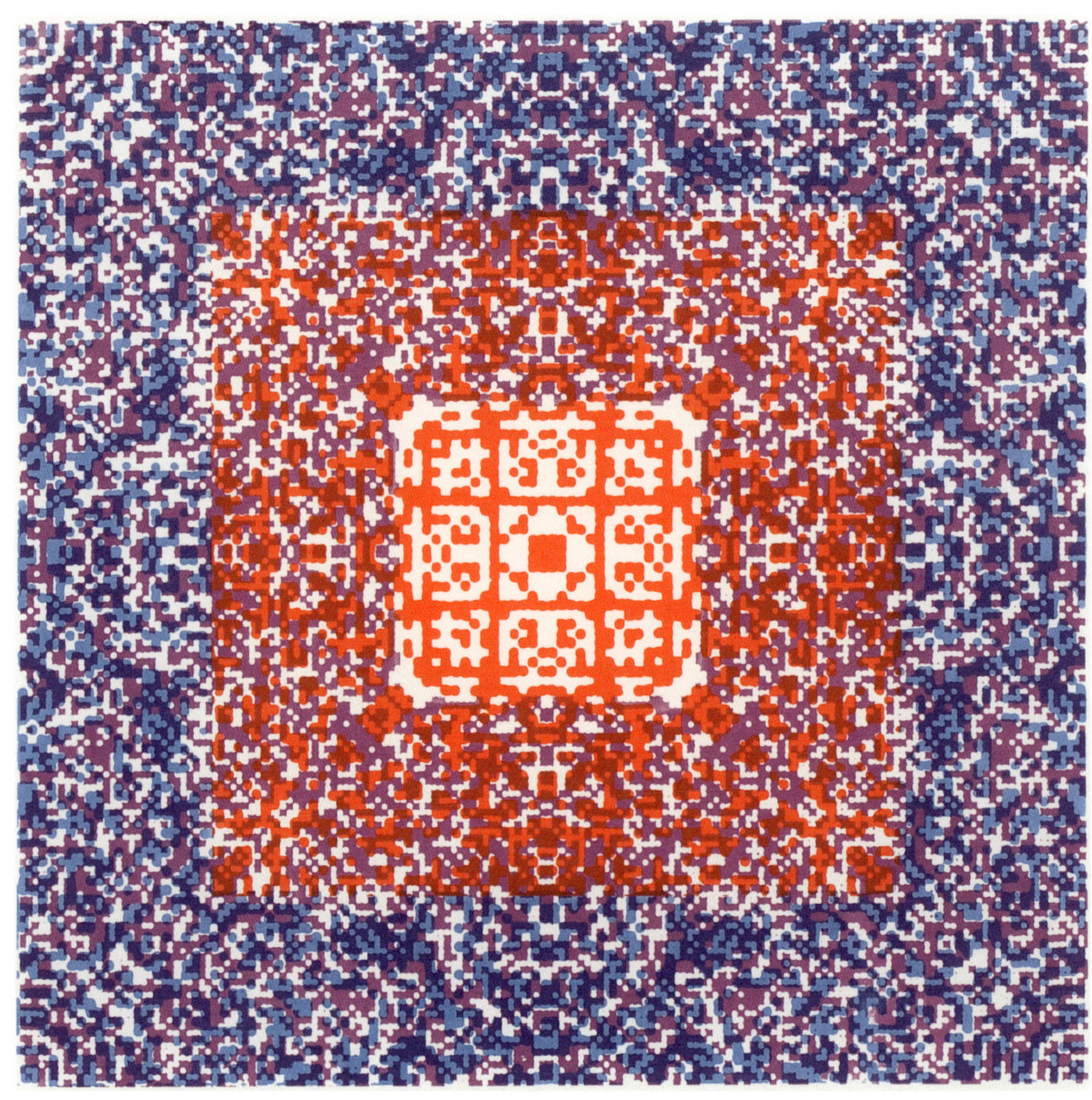

Mandell/as #1, 1973.
Silkscreen: image, 18 1/2 x 18 1/2 in;
paper, 22 x 28 in. Edition of 20.

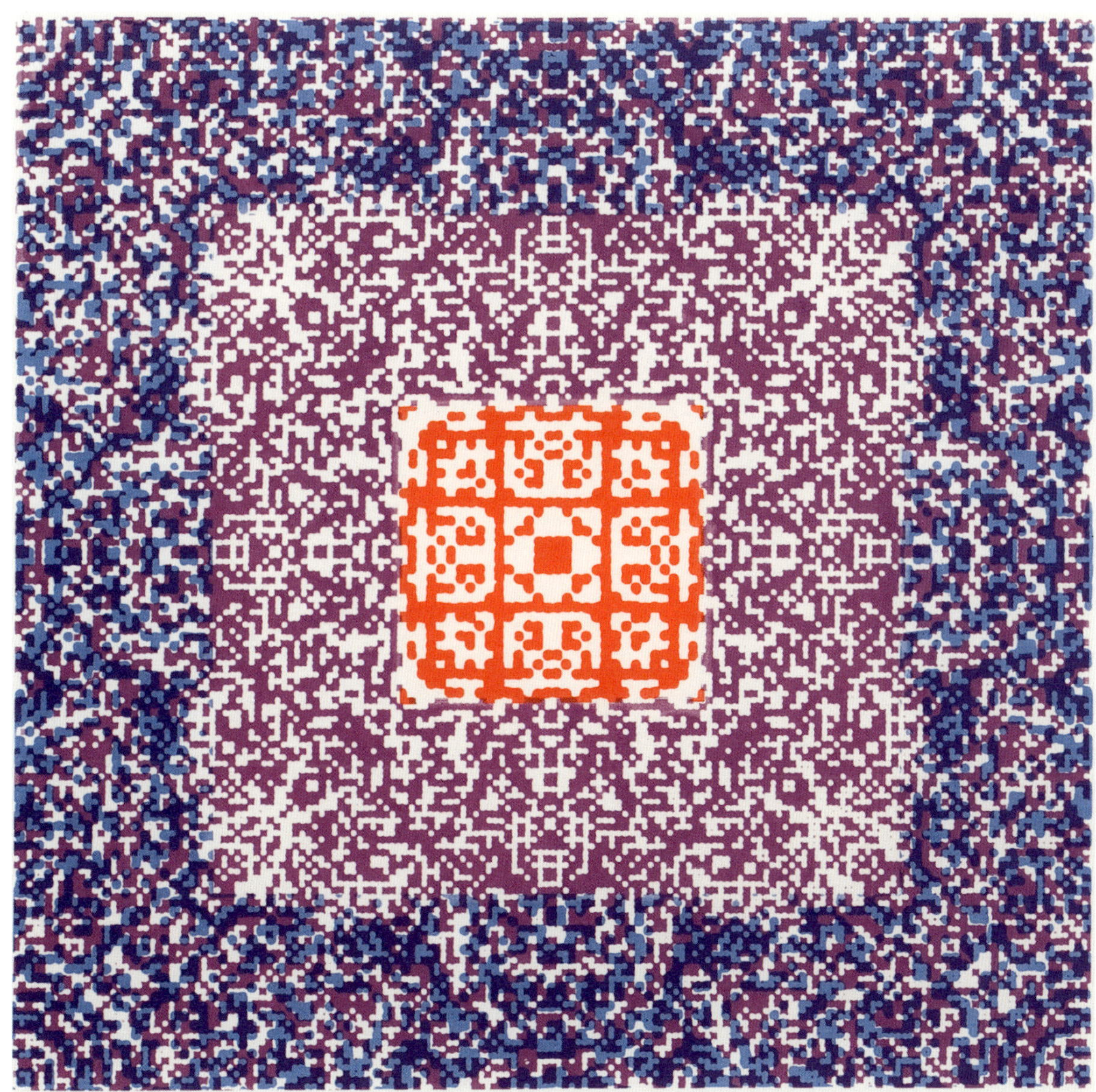

Mandell/as #2, 1973.
Silkscreen: image, 18 1/2 x 18 1/2 in;
paper, 22 x 28 in. Edition of 20.

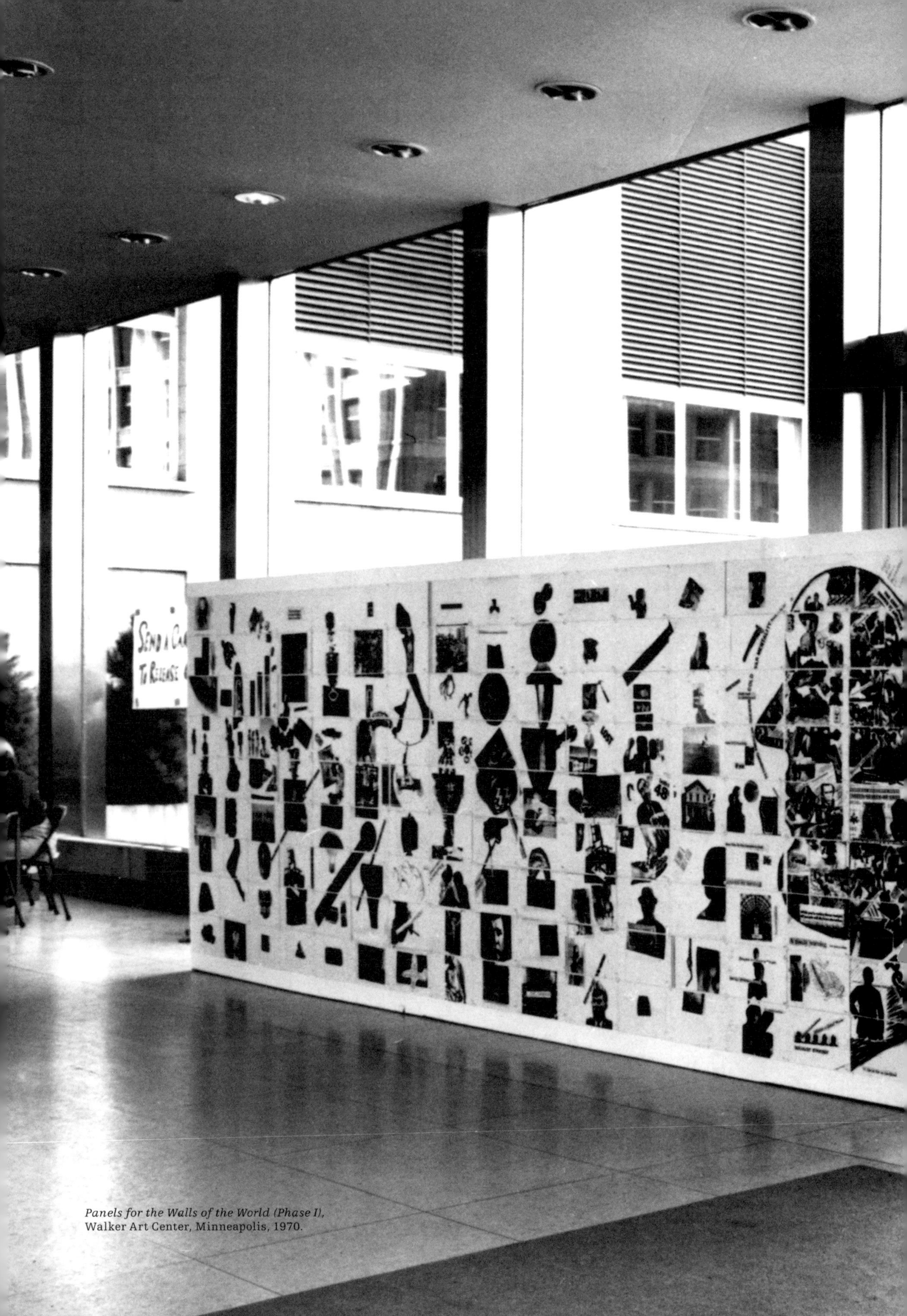

Panels for the Walls of the World (Phase I),
Walker Art Center, Minneapolis, 1970.

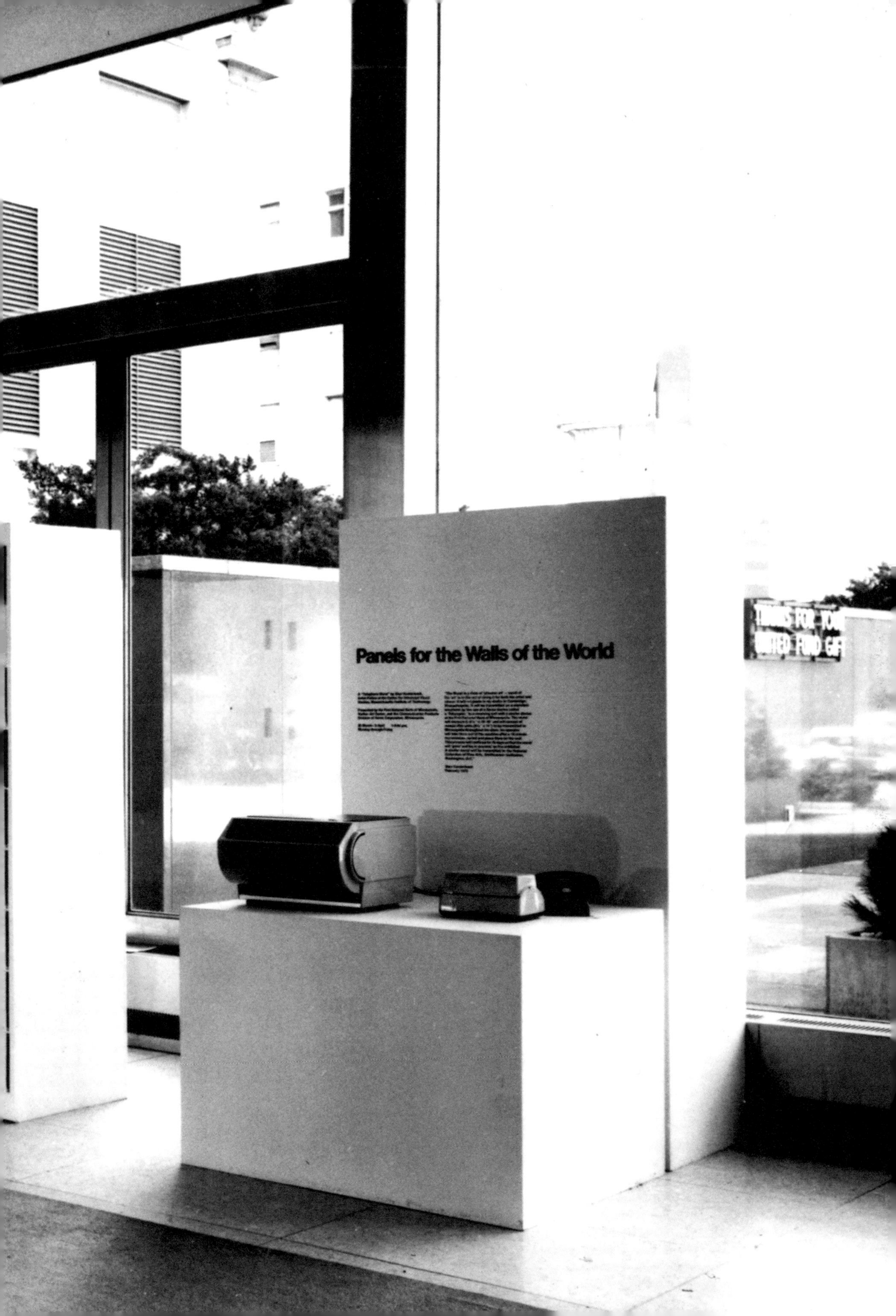
Panels for the Walls of the World

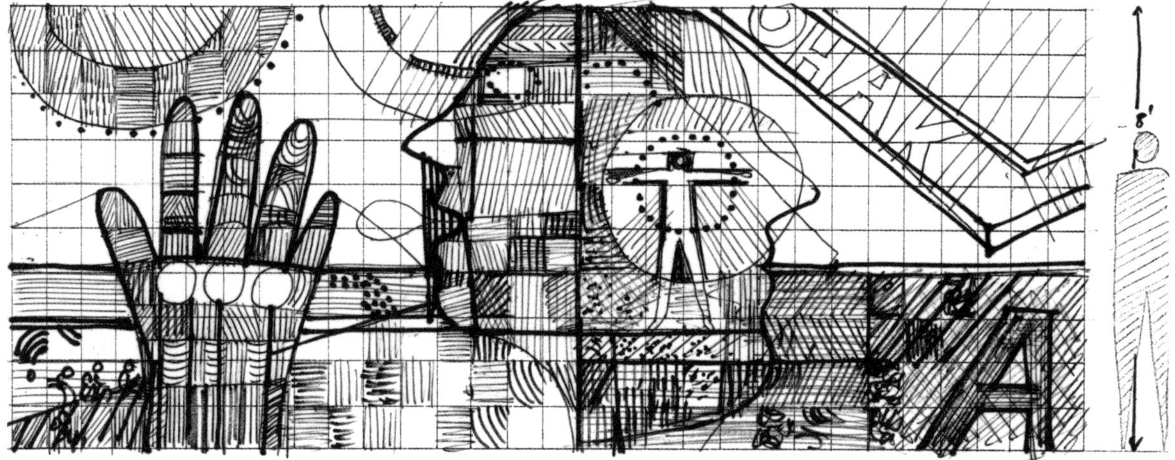

20'
8'
JUNE 69
TELEPHONE MURAL
BY S. VANDERBEEK. 1/2"=1"
STAGE 1....

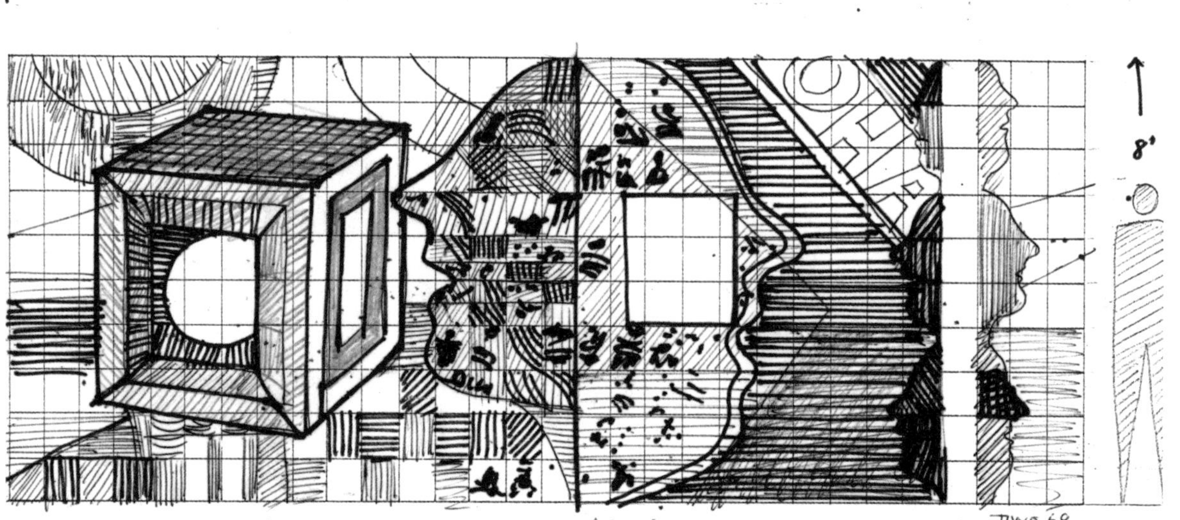

20'
8'
JUNE '69
TELEPHONE MURAL
BY S. VANDERBEEK 1/2"=1"
STAGE 2

*Panels for the Walls of the World (Phase I
and II)*, 1970

While a fellow at the Center for Advanced
Visual Studies (CAVS) at MIT in 1969,
VanDerBeek experimented with transmitting art using an early facsimile machine. A
mosaic-like mural of images was composed
in "real time" and sent from his studio
at MIT using a Xerox machine called a
"Telecopier" to any location in the world
that had access to a telephone line and a
similar machine. According to VanDerBeek's
notes, the transmission time was approximately 10 minutes for a 8 1/2 x 14 inch unit.
An average installation of such a mural
would involve sending 15 units a day for four
weeks. In March 1970, VanDerBeek transmitted a telephone mural entitled *Panels
for the Walls of the World* to several locations around Boston: MIT's Hayden Gallery,
Boston City Hall, The Children's Museum,
The DeCordova Museum, and the Elma
Lewis School of Fine Arts. A telephone mural
was also commissioned for the Walker Art
Center in Minneapolis, and the Smithsonian
Institution in Washington, DC, in 1970.

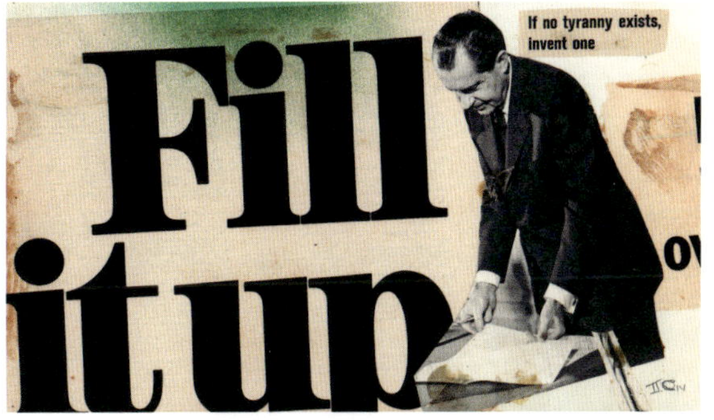

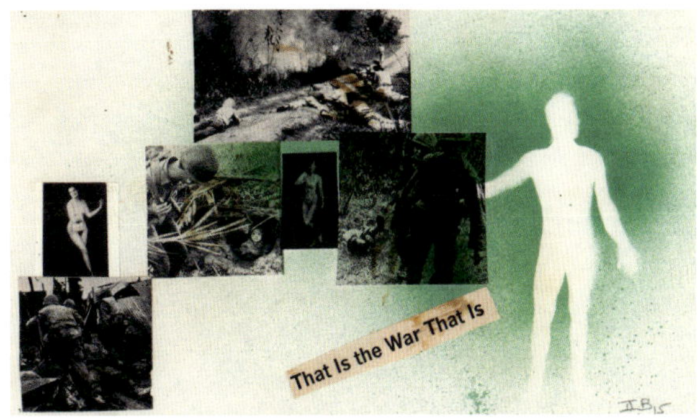

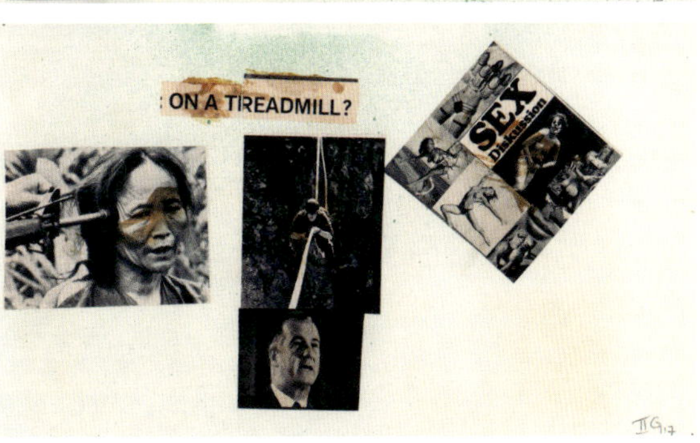

[Left] *Telephone Mural (Panels for the
Walls of the World) Stage 1, 2 drawings*,
1969. Ink on paper, 11 x 8 1/2 in.

[Right] All: *Panels for the Walls of the
World (Phase II)*, 1970. Spray paint, pencil,
and collage on paper, 8 1/2 x 14 in.

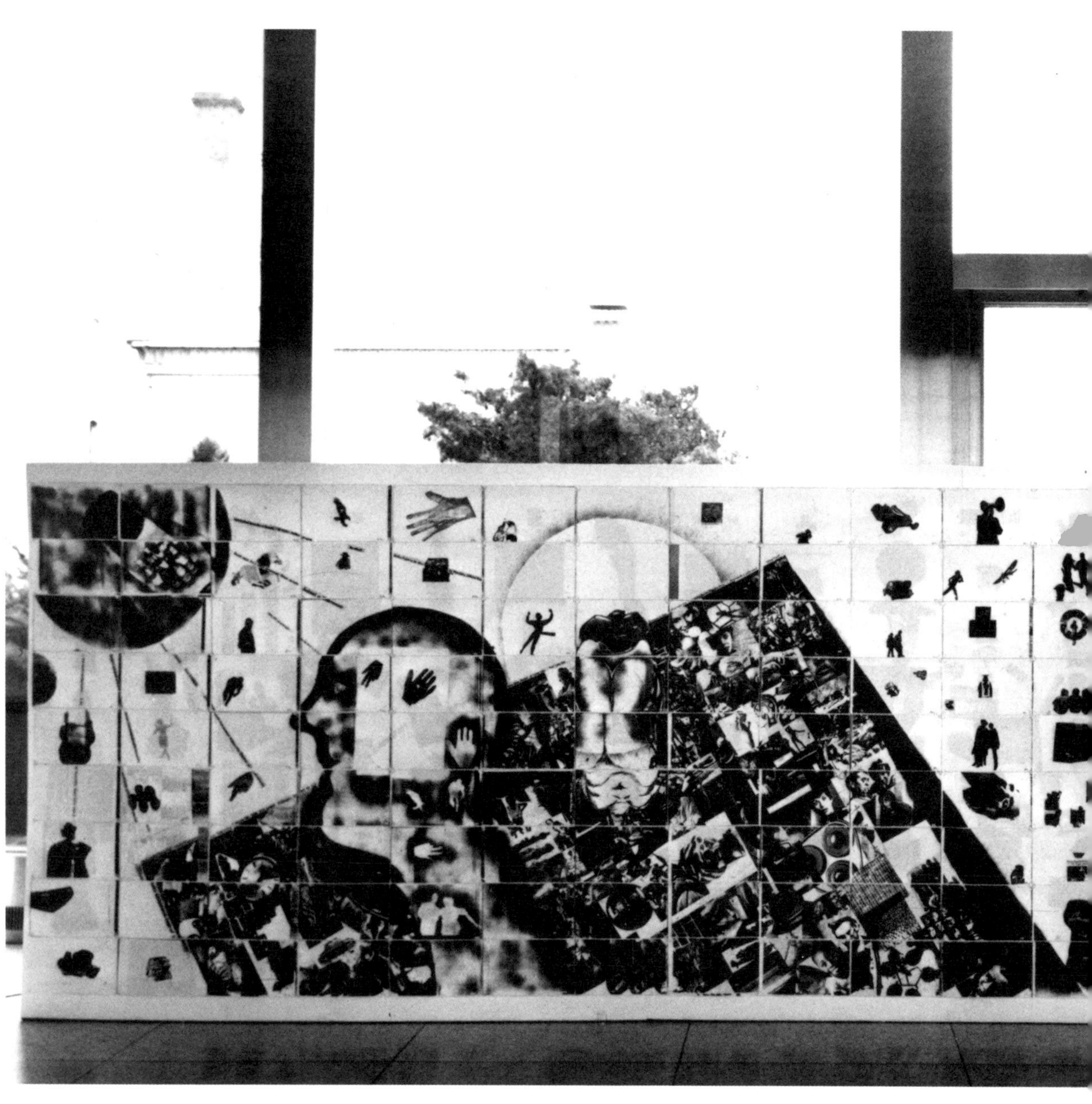

[Above] *Panels for the Walls of the World (Phase I)*, Walker Art Center, Minneapolis, MN, 1970.

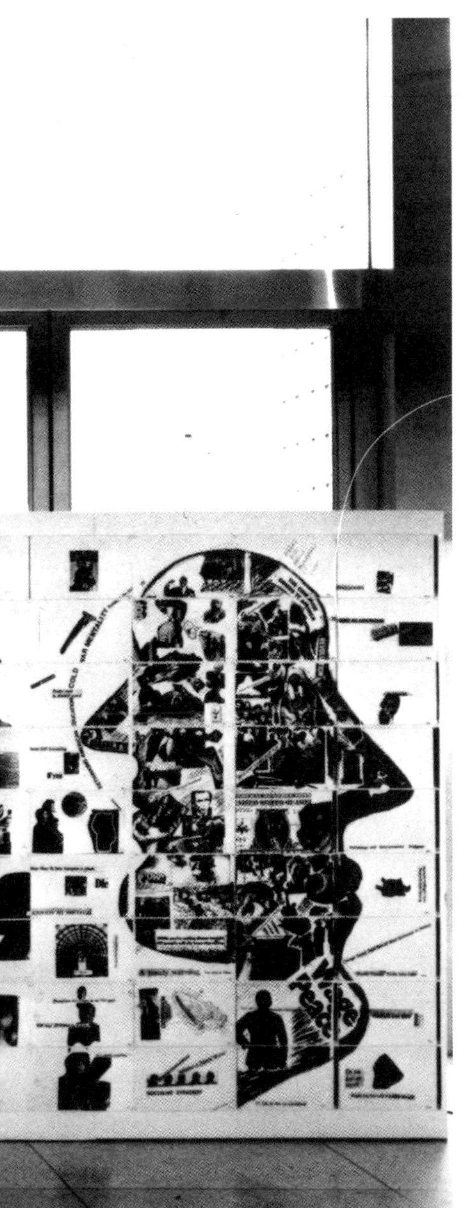

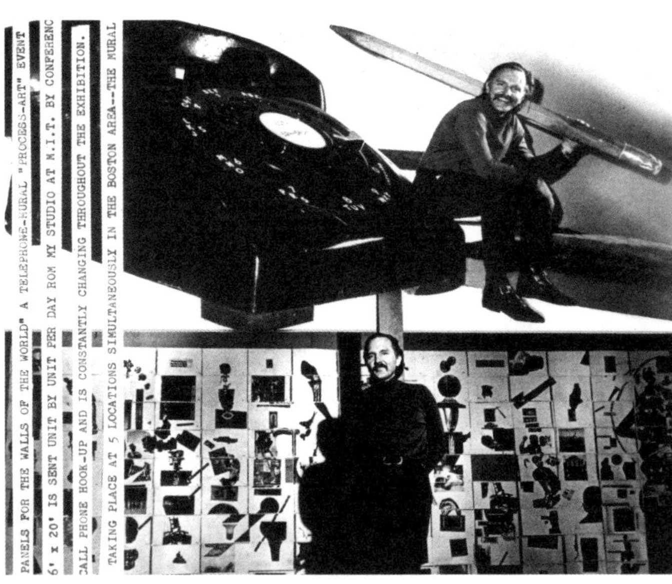
PANELS FOR THE WALLS OF THE WORLD" A TELEPHONE-MURAL "PROCESS-ART" EVENT
6' x 20' IS SENT UNIT BY UNIT PER DAY FROM MY STUDIO AT M.I.T. BY CONFERENC
CALL PHONE HOOK-UP AND IS CONSTANTLY CHANGING THROUGHOUT THE EXHIBITION.
TAKING PLACE AT 5 LOCATIONS SIMULTANEOUSLY IN THE BOSTON AREA—THE MURAL

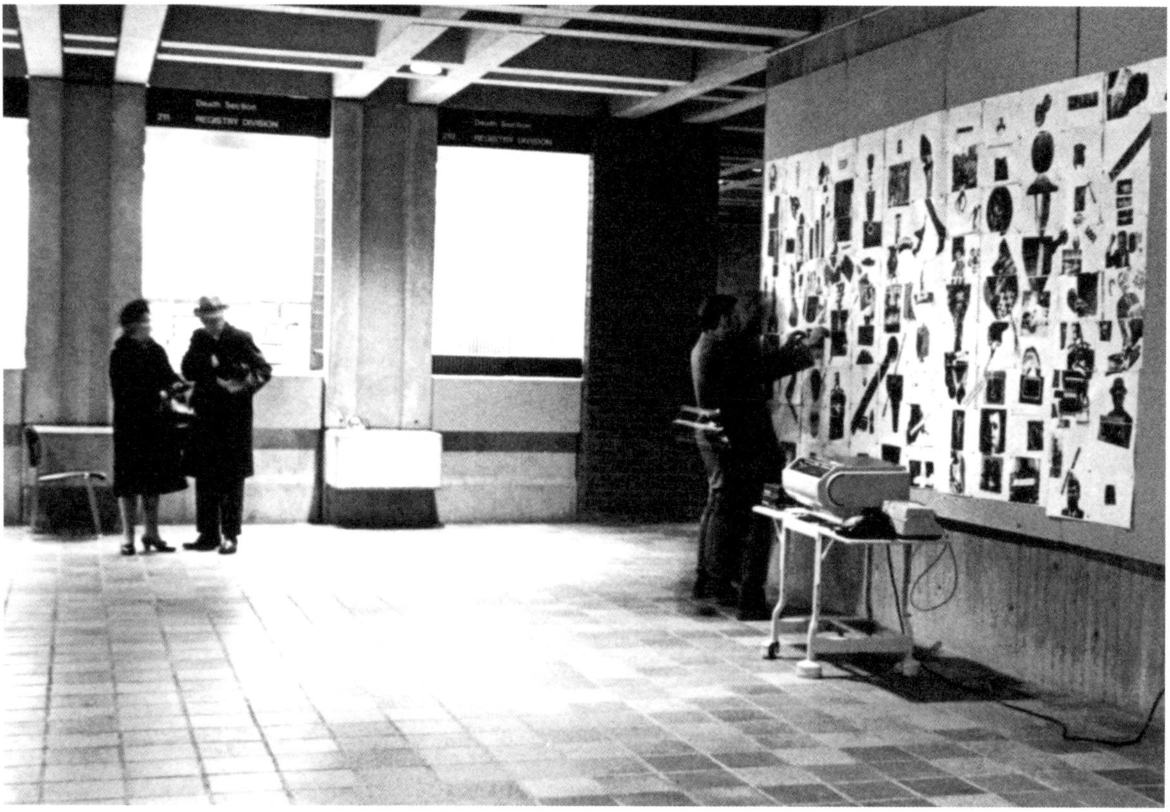

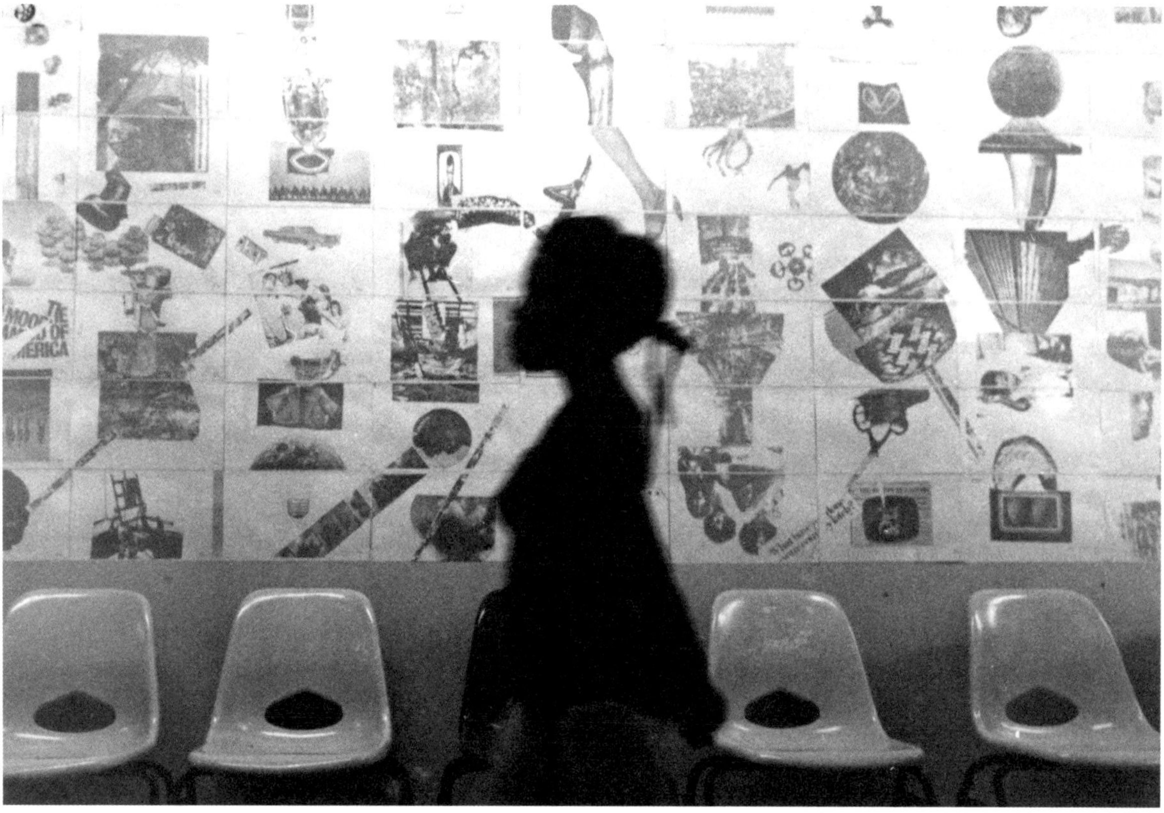

[Top] Process of receiving and hanging *Telephone Mural (Panels for the Walls of the World)*, Boston City Hall, 1970.

[Bottom] *Telephone Mural (Panels for the Walls of the World)* exhibited at The Elma Lewis School of Fine Arts, Boston, MA, 1970.

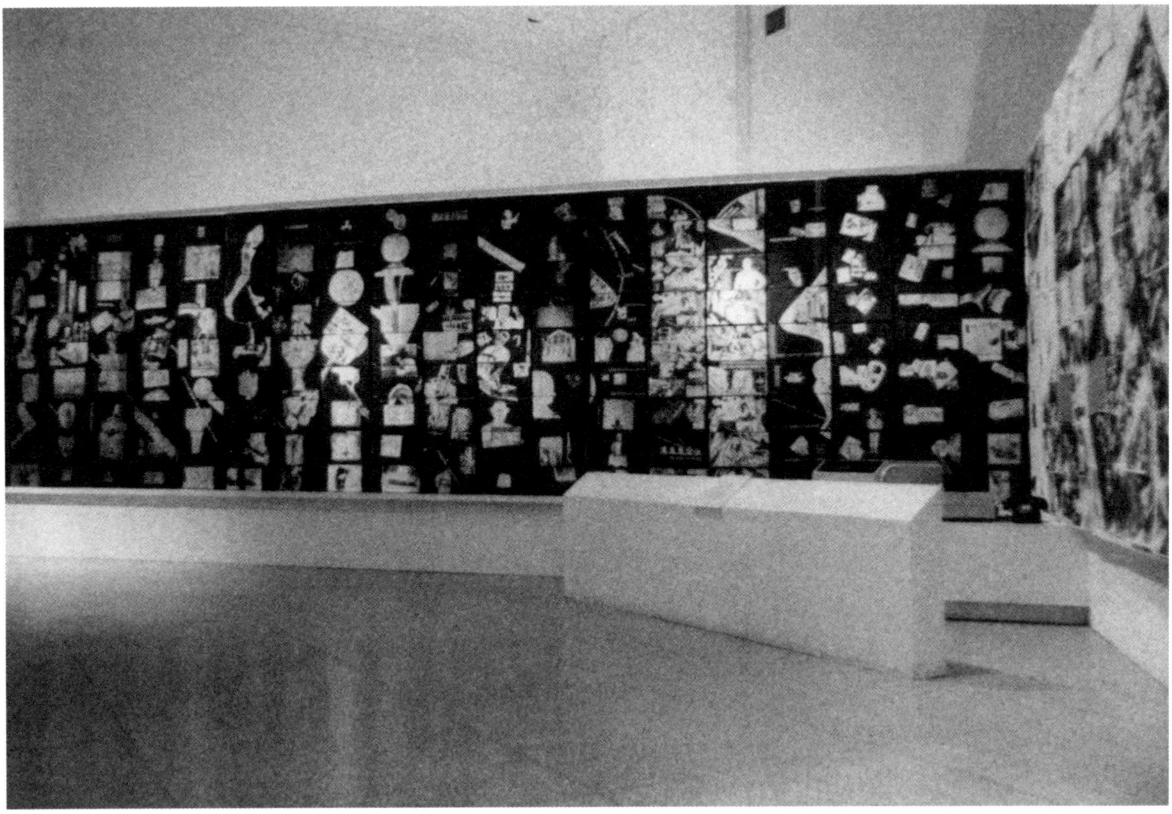

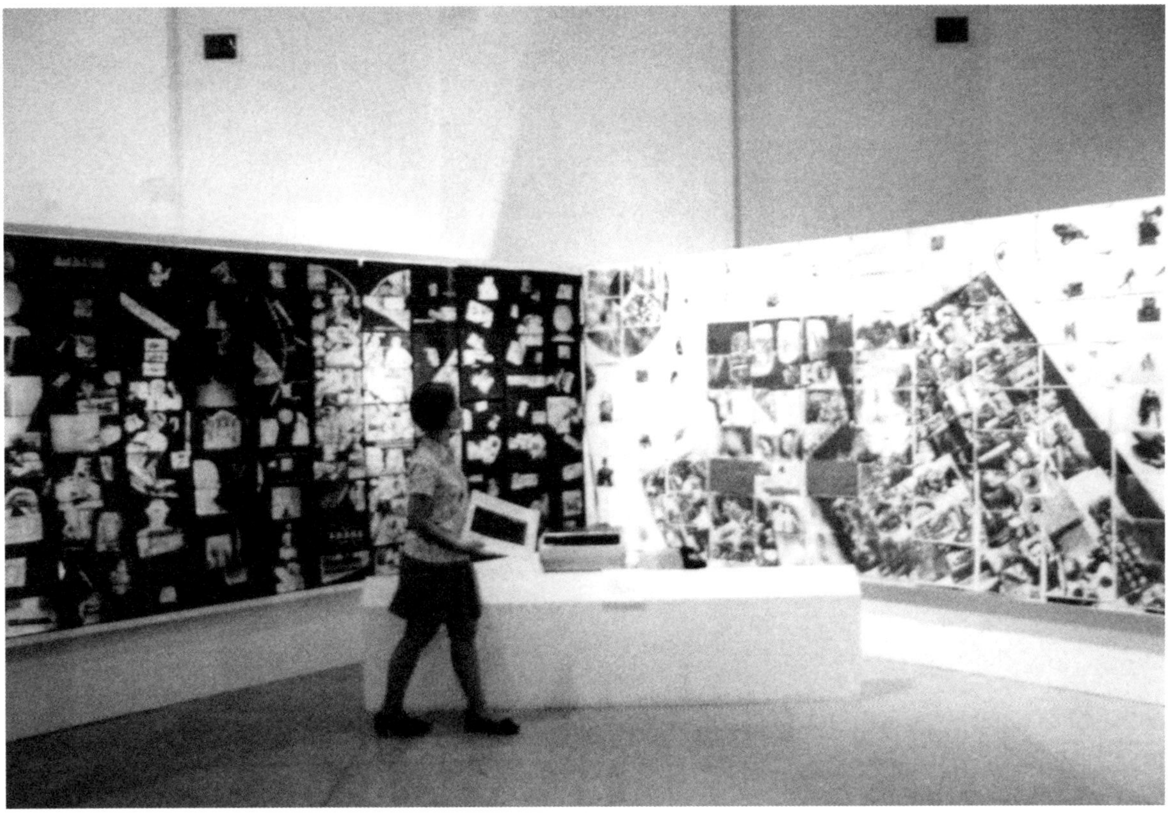

[Above] *Panels for the Walls of the World (Phase I)*, Smithsonian Museum, Washington, DC, 1972.

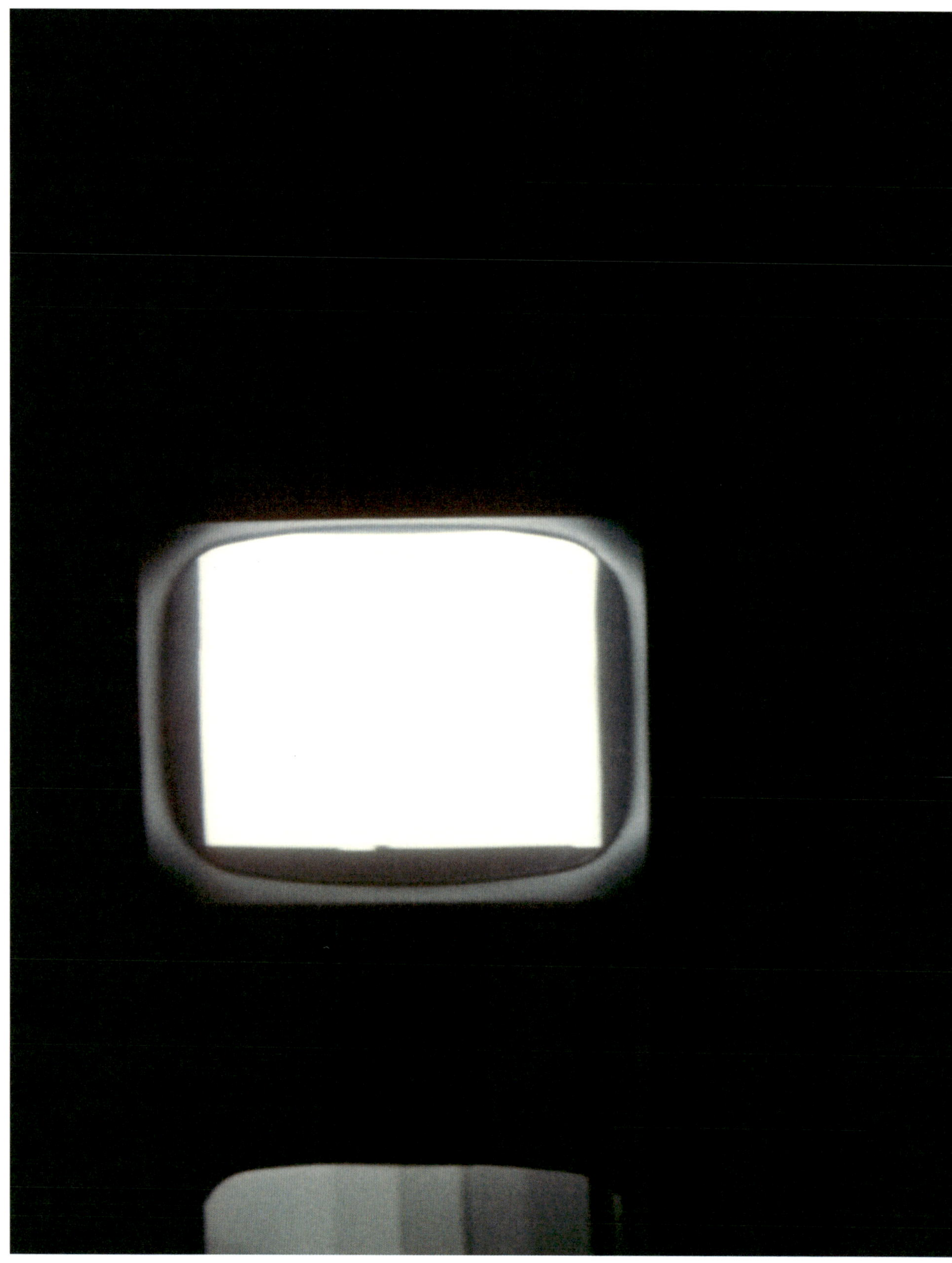

Violence Sonata broadcast. Monitor view,
WGBH TV studio, Boston, MA, 1970.
Image courtesy of WGBH.

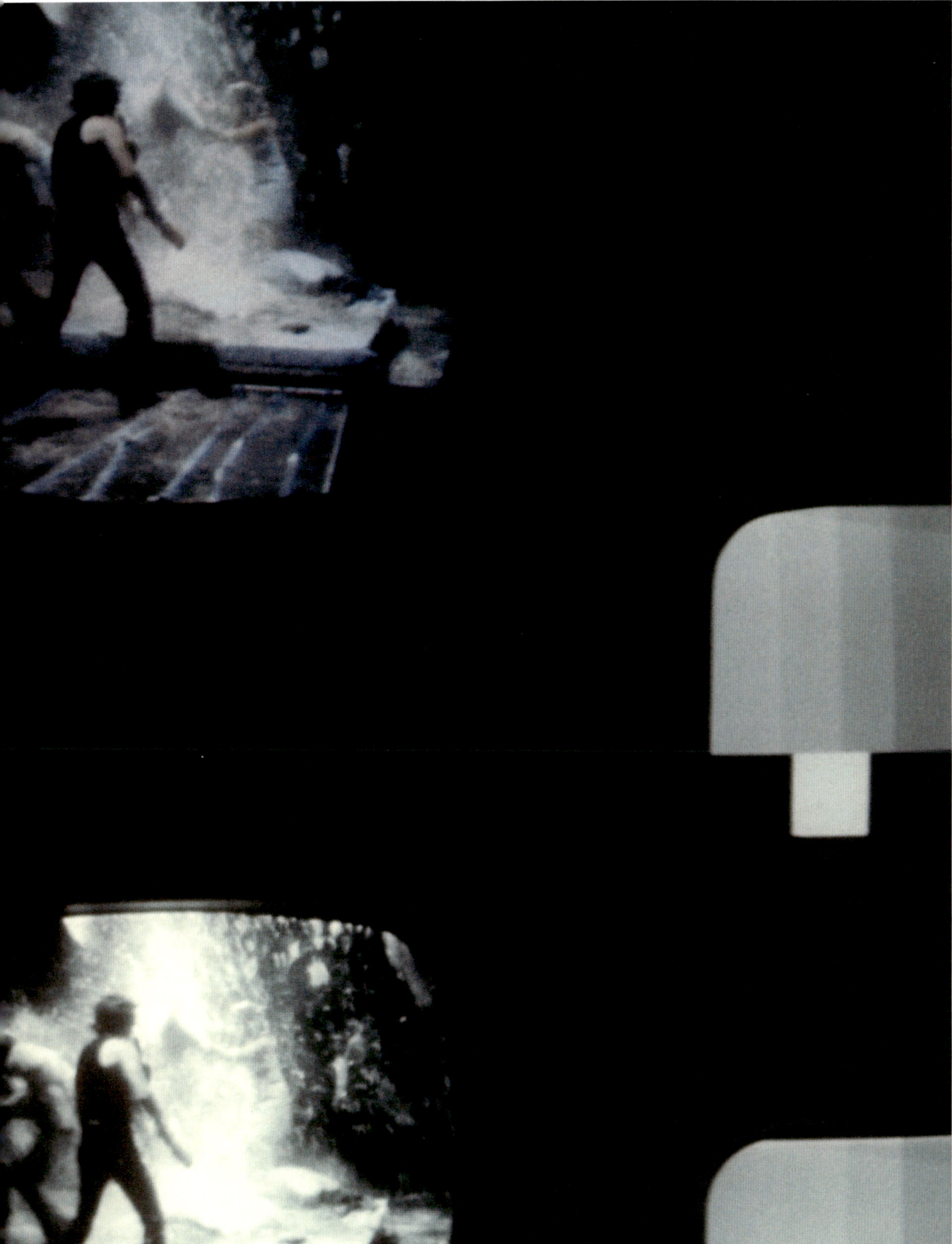

Violence Sonata, 1970

Stan VanDerBeek was part of the Rockefeller
Artists-in-Television residency program at
the Boston public television station WGBH
from 1969–1970, during which time he
produced the television program *Violence
Sonata*. Directed by David Atwood and Fred
Barzyk, the program was transmitted simultaneously on both Channels 2 and 44 on
January 12, 1970, with the suggestion that
viewers place two television sets side-by-
side.[7] Following sonata form, the piece is
composed of three segments: "Man," "Man
to Woman," and "Man to Man." The broadcast consisted of material VanDerBeek
composed from previous films, archival
and newsreel footage, video shot in the
studio for the show, live footage, and filmed
collages. Sections of the broadcast were
played before a live studio audience. Home
viewers were invited to call with responses
to the program between the acts.[8]

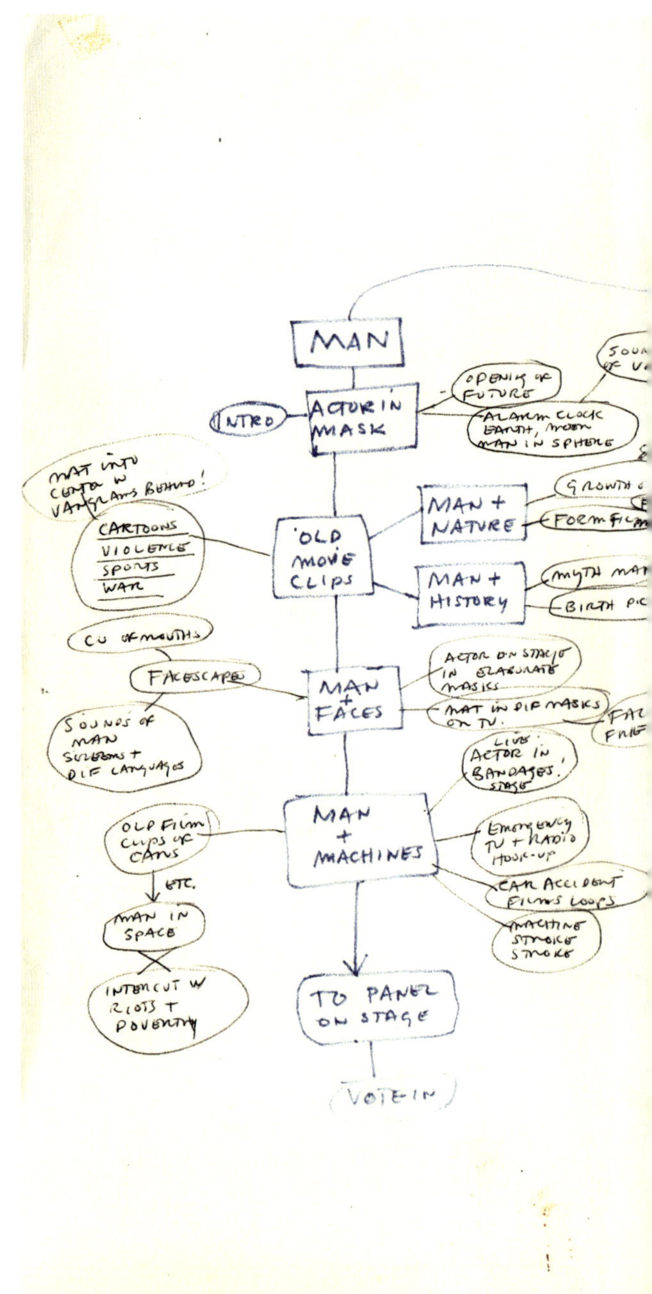

Untitled, (Violence Sonata Schematic).
Ink on Paper, ca. 1969-70.

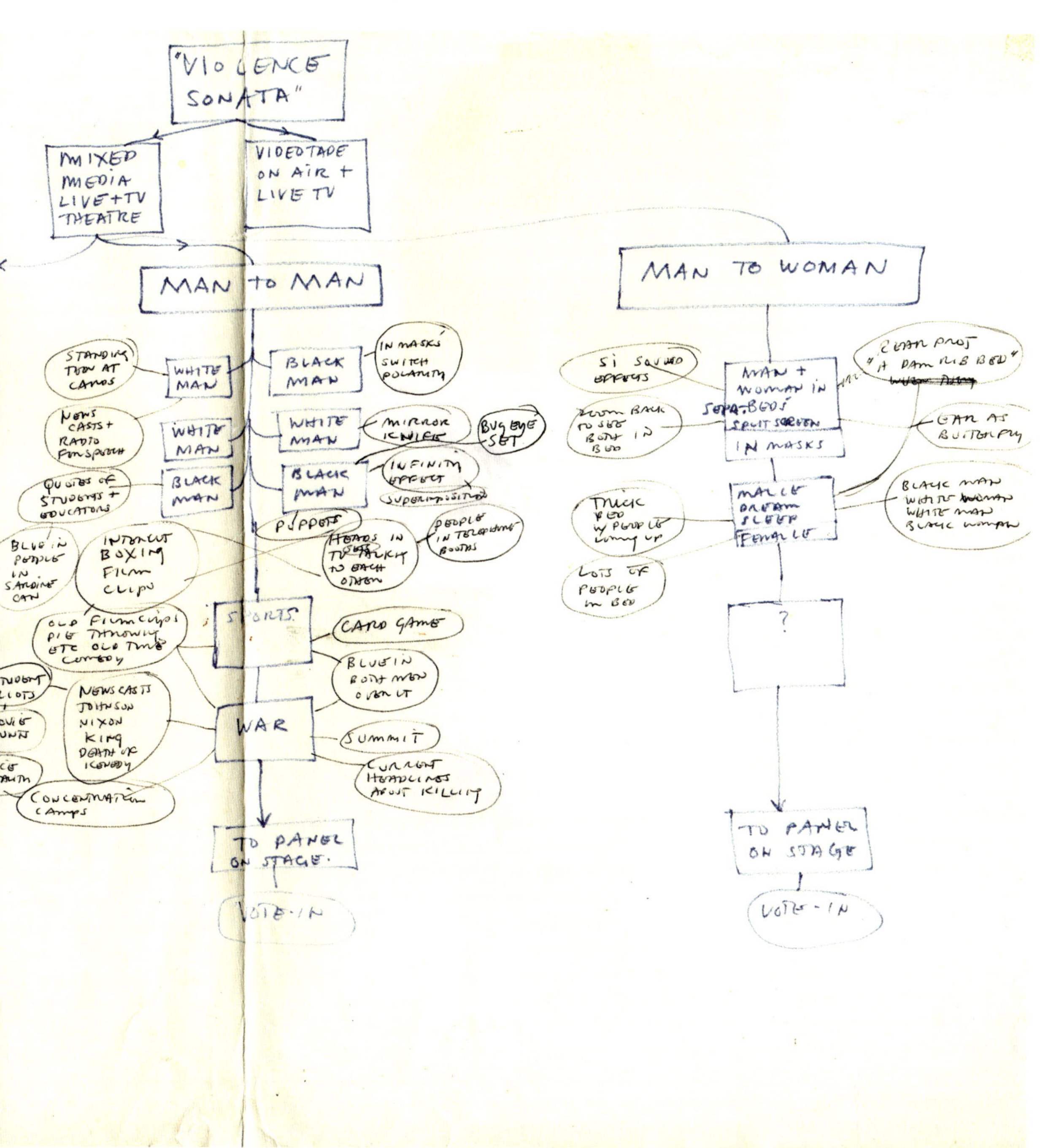

"VIOLENCE SONATA"
MIXED MEDIA LIVE + TV THEATRE
VIDEOTAPE ON AIR + LIVE TV
MAN TO MAN
MAN TO WOMAN
STANDING THEM AT CAMERAS
WHITE MAN
BLACK MAN
IN MASKS SWITCH POLARITY
NEWS CASTS + RADIO FM SPEECH
WHITE MAN
WHITE MAN
MIRROR ICNIFE
BUG EYE SET
QUOTES OF STUDENTS + EDUCATORS
BLACK MAN
BLACK MAN
INFINITY EFFECT SUPERIMPOSITION
BLUE IN PEOPLE IN SARDINE CAN
INTERCUT BOXING FILM CLIPS
PUPPETS
HEADS IN TVS TV TALKING TO EACH OTHER
PEOPLE IN TELEPHONE BOOTHS
OLD FILM CLIPS PIE THROWING ETC OLD TIME COMEDY
SPORTS
CARD GAME
RIOTS
MOVIE UNIT
CE TRUTH
NEWSCASTS JOHNSON NIXON KING DEATH OF KENNEDY
WAR
BLUE IN BOTH MEN OVER LIT
SUMMIT
CURRENT HEADLINES ABOUT KILLING
CONCENTRATION CAMPS
TO PANEL ON STAGE
VOTE-IN
SI SQUAD EFFECTS
MAN + WOMAN IN SEPARATE BEDS SPLIT SCREEN IN MASKS
SCRN PROJ "A DAM RIB BED"
ZOOM BACK TO SEE BOTH IN BED
CAR AS BUTTERFLY
TRUCK BED W/ PEOPLE COMING UP
MALE DREAM SLEEP FEMALE
BLACK MAN WHITE WOMAN WHITE MAN BLACK WOMAN
LOTS OF PEOPLE IN BED
?
TO PANEL ON STAGE
VOTE-IN

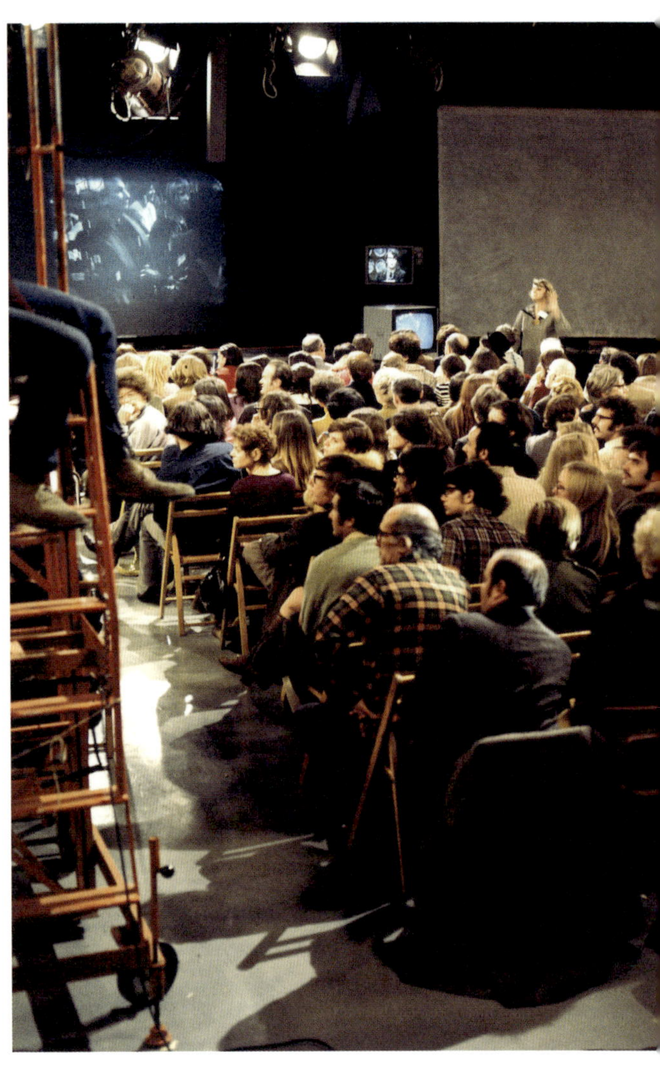

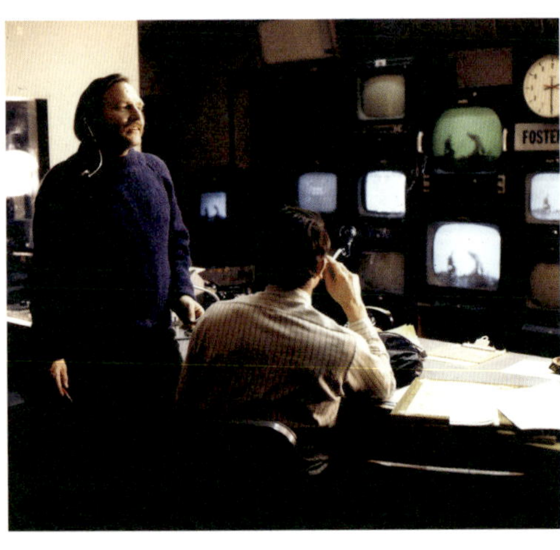

[Above] *Violence Sonata*. WGBH TV studio,
Boston, MA, 1970.

[Left] Stan VanDerBeek in WGBH TV studio,
Boston, MA, 1970.

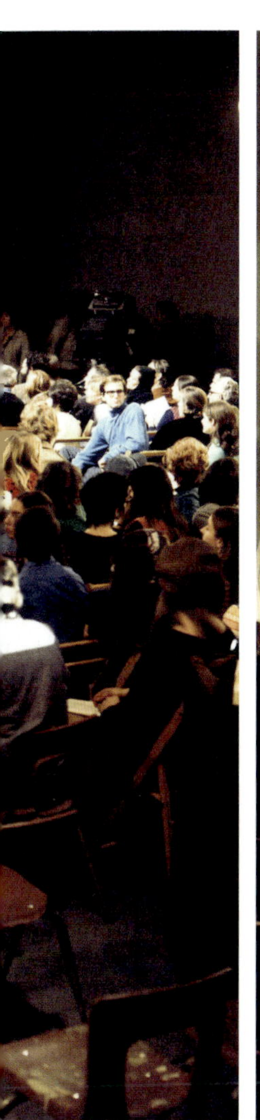

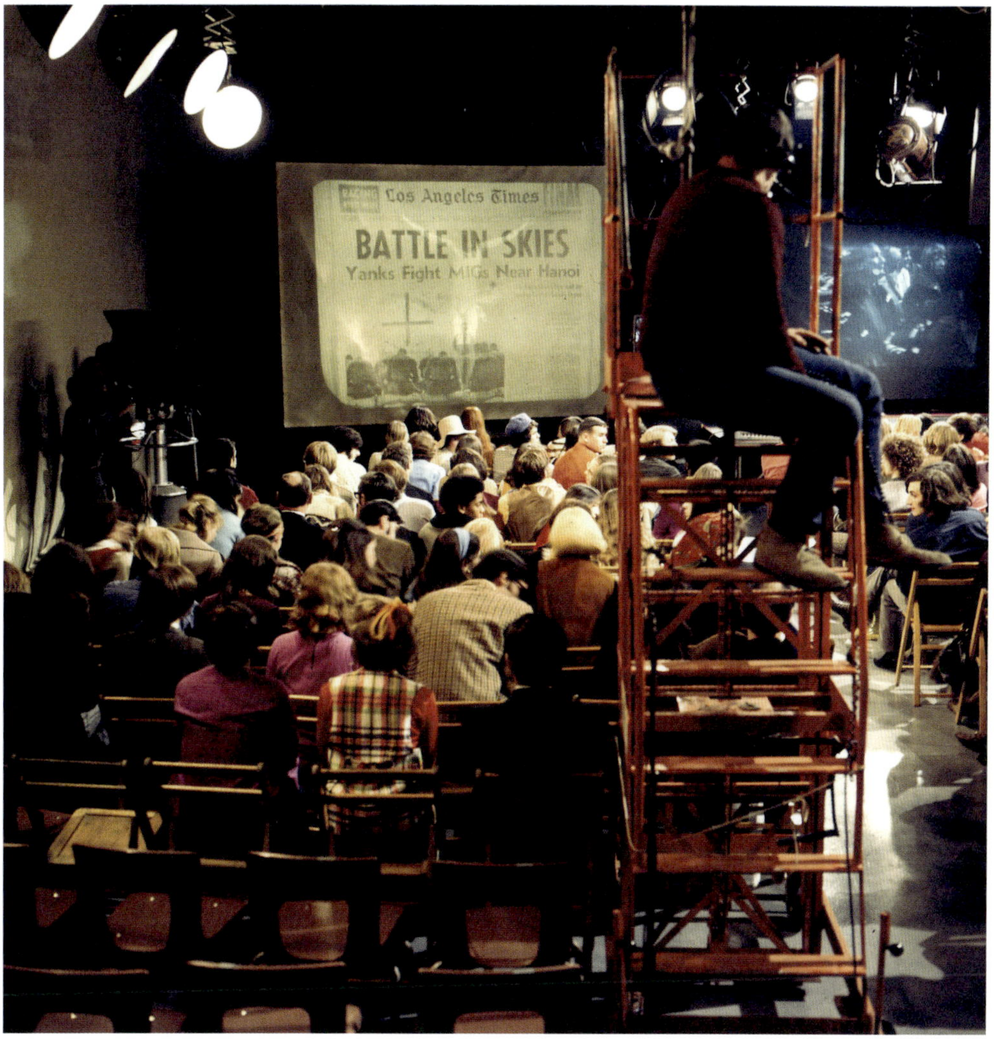

Los Angeles Times
BATTLE IN SKIES
Yanks Fight MIGs Near Hanoi

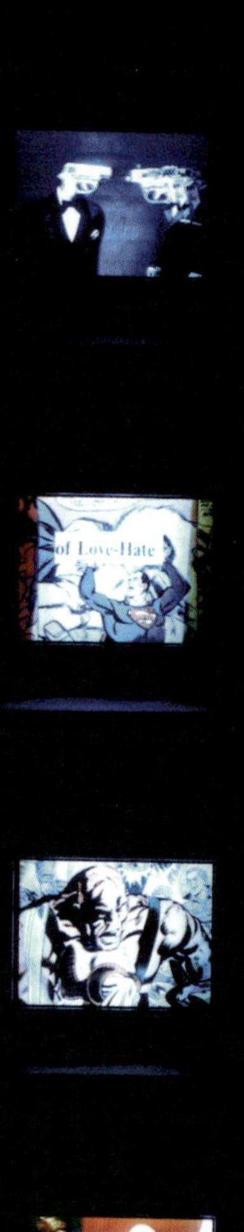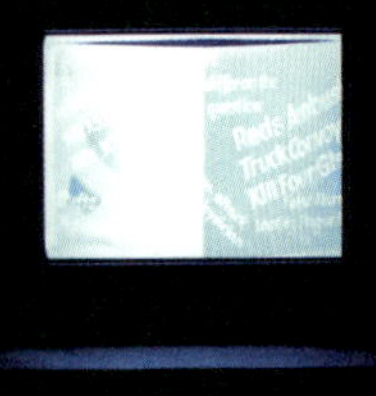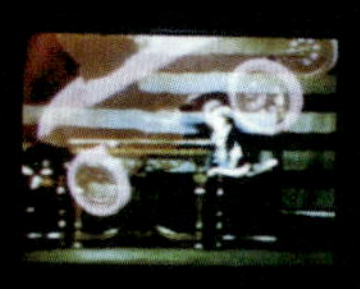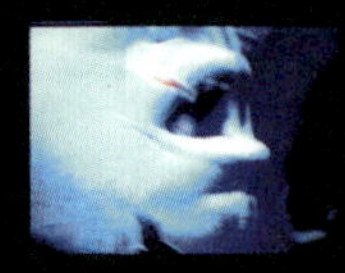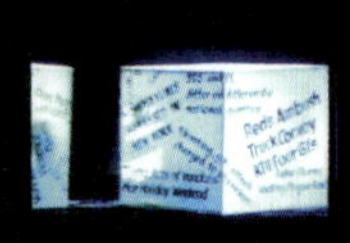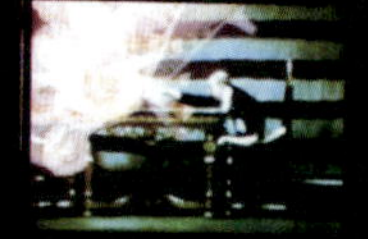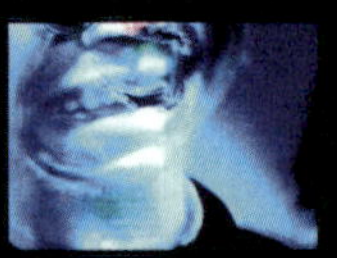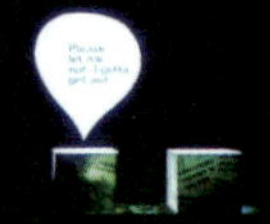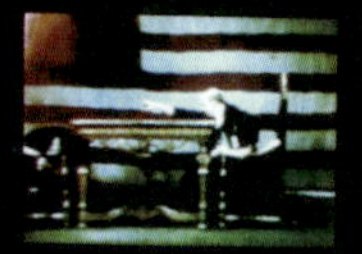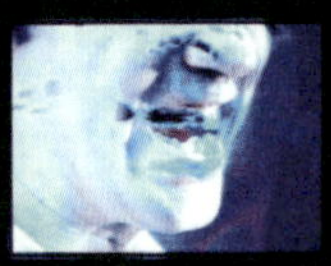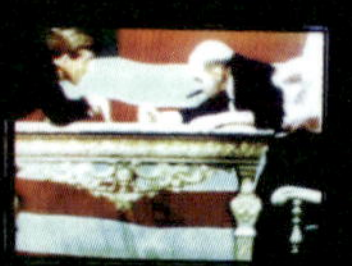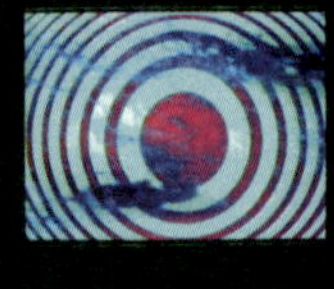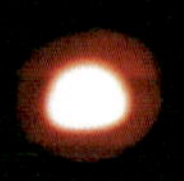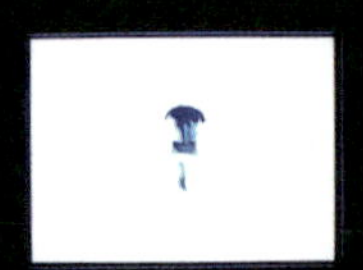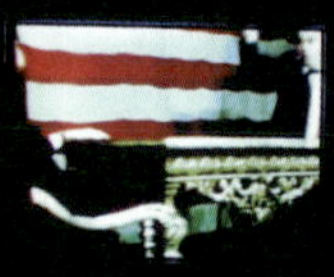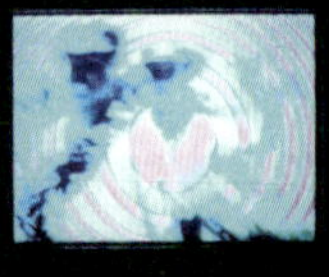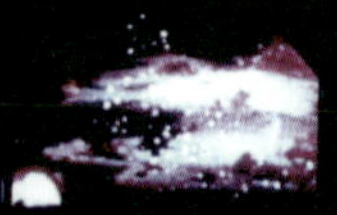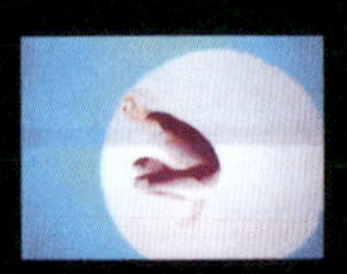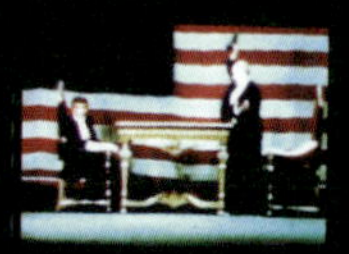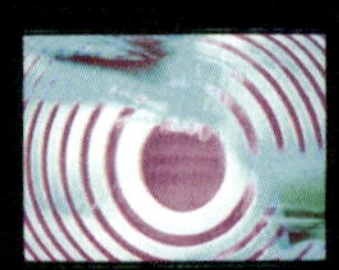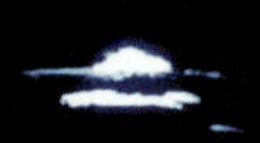

Violence Sonata. Installation view,
Guild & Greyshkul, New York, NY, 2008.

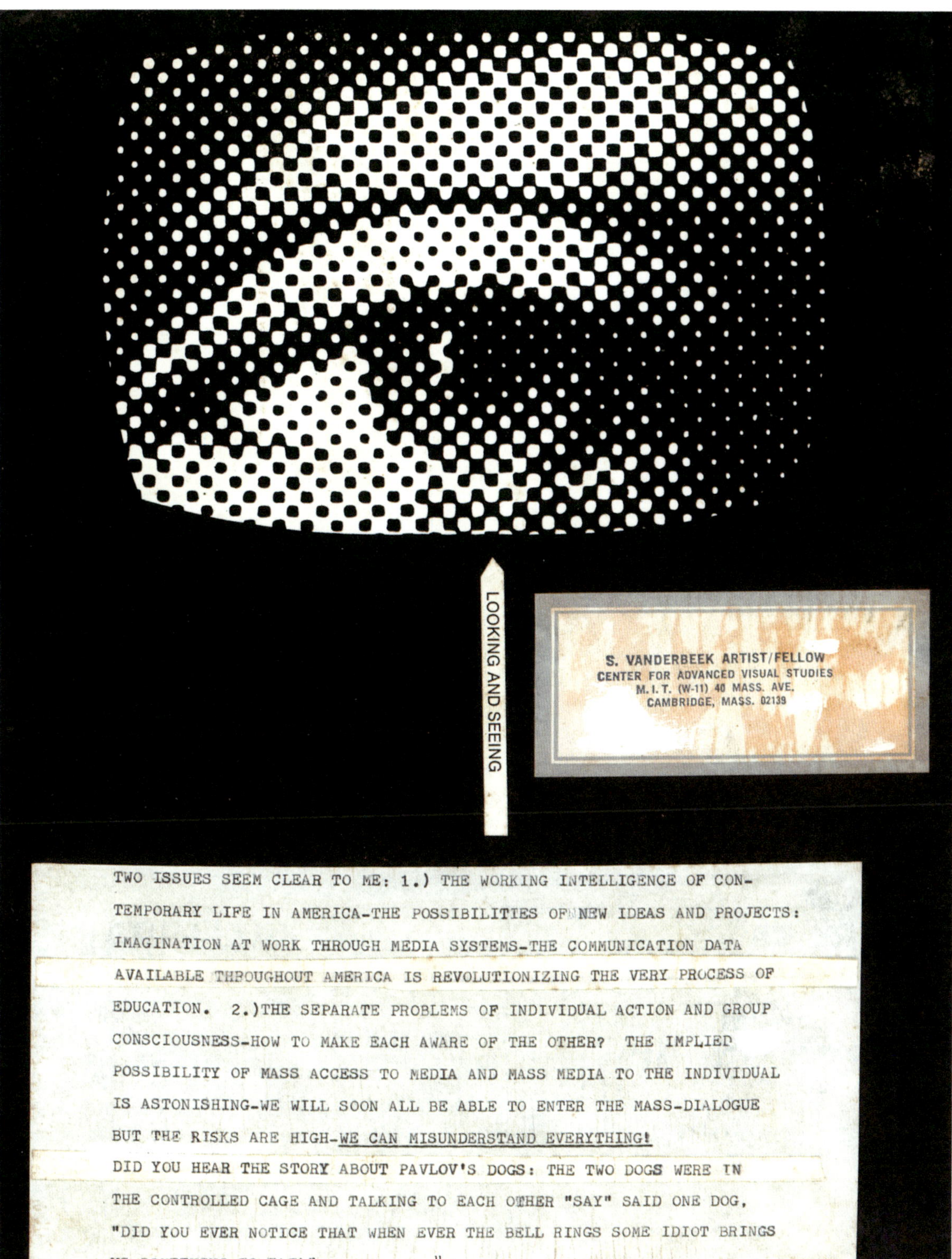

History of Violence in America, ca. 1970.
Collage on paper, 11 x 14 in.

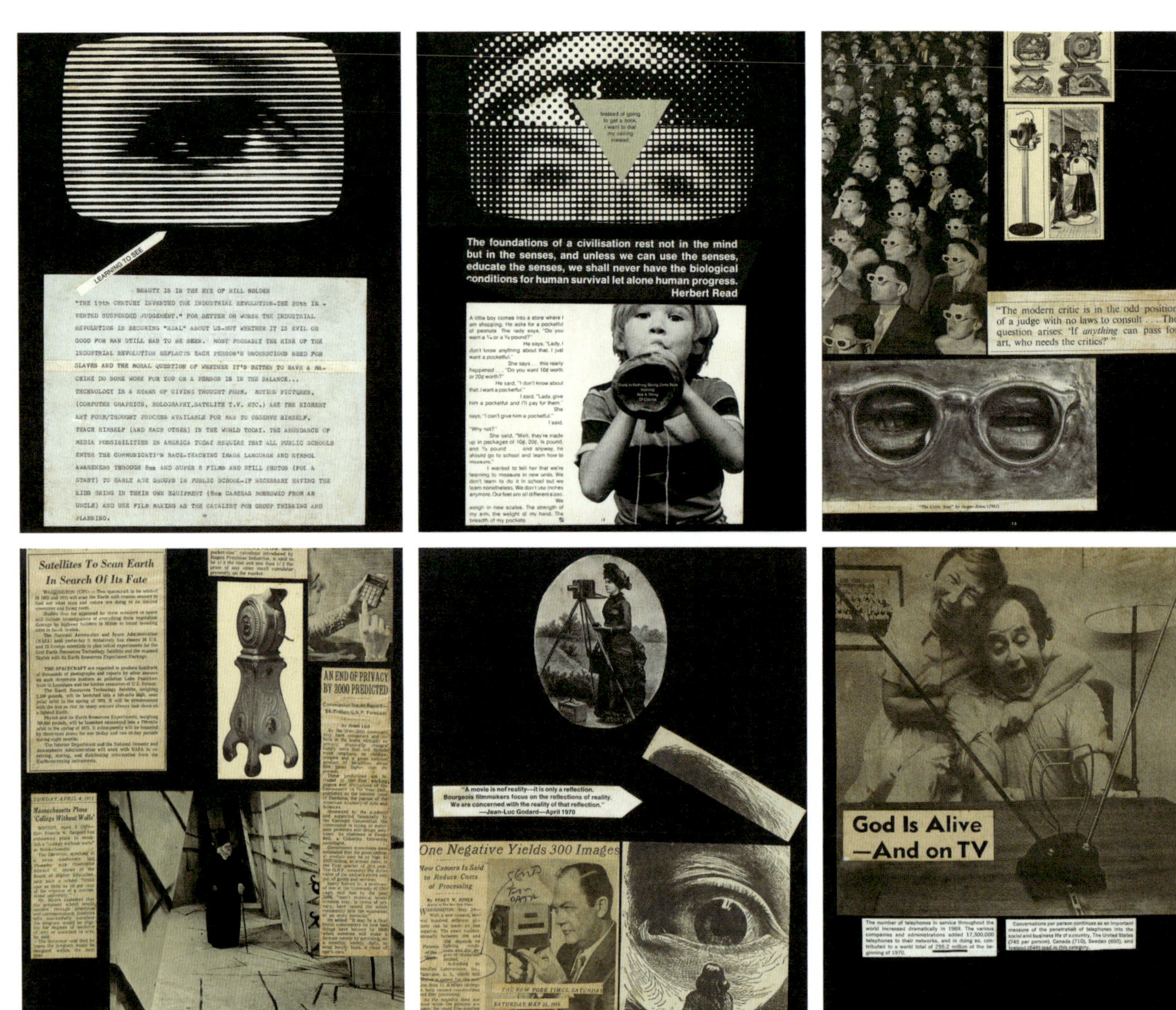

All: *History of Violence in America*, ca. 1970.
Collage on paper, 11 x 14 in.

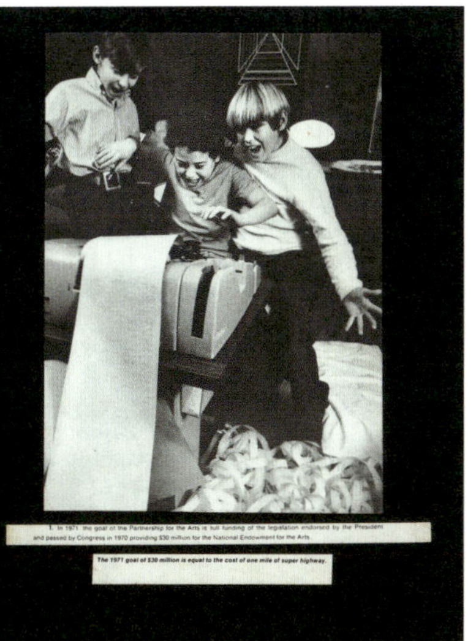
In 1971 the goal of the Partnership for the Arts is full funding of the legislation endorsed by the President and passed by Congress in 1970 providing $30 million for the National Endowment for the Arts.
The 1971 goal of $30 million is equal to the cost of one mile of super highway.

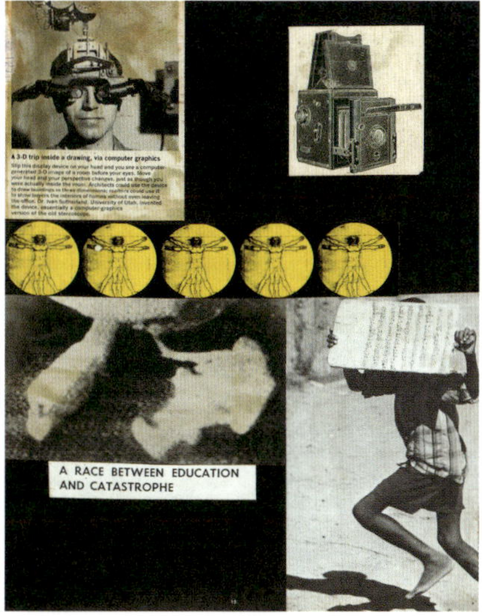
A 3-D trip inside a drawing, via computer graphics
A RACE BETWEEN EDUCATION AND CATASTROPHE

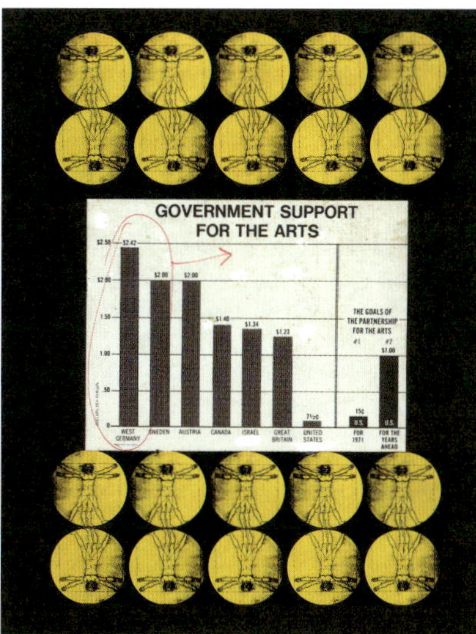
GOVERNMENT SUPPORT FOR THE ARTS
THE GOALS OF THE PARTNERSHIP FOR THE ARTS
WEST GERMANY
SWEDEN
AUSTRIA
CANADA
ISRAEL
GREAT BRITAIN
UNITED STATES
U.S. FOR 1971
FOR THE YEARS AHEAD

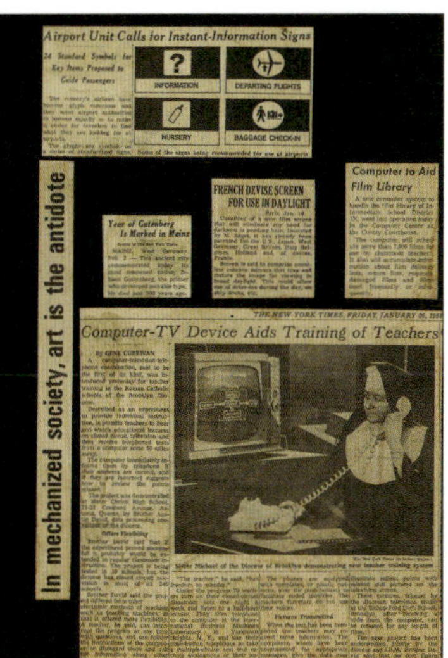
In mechanized society, art is the antidote
Airport Unit Calls for Instant-Information Signs
FRENCH DEVISE SCREEN FOR USE IN DAYLIGHT
Computer to Aid Film Library
Text of Gutenberg Is Marked in Mainz
Computer-TV Device Aids Training of Teachers

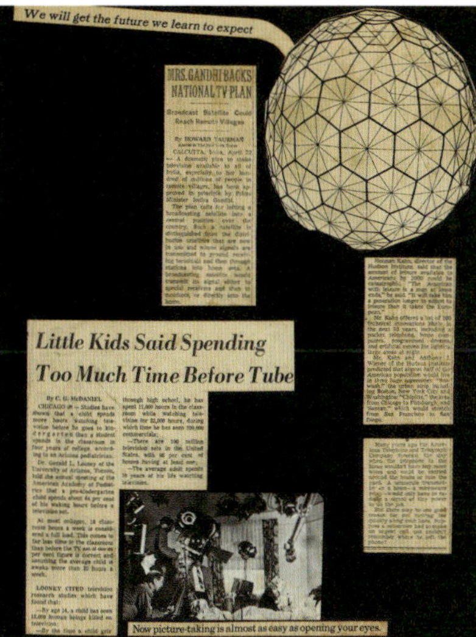
We will get the future we learn to expect
MRS. GANDHI BACKS NATIONAL TV PLAN
Little Kids Said Spending Too Much Time Before Tube
Now picture-taking is almost as easy as opening your eyes.

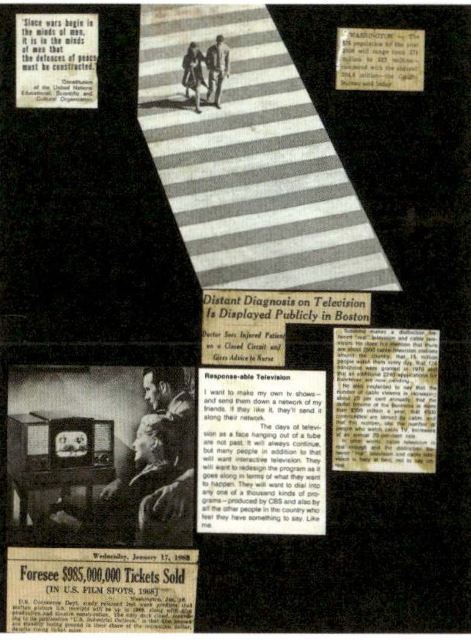
Since wars begin in the minds of men, it is in the minds of men that the defences of peace must be constructed.
Distant Diagnosis on Television Is Displayed Publicly in Boston
Response-able Television
Foresee $985,000,000 Tickets Sold
IN U.S. FILM SPOTS, 1968

Cine Dreams, 1972

Stan VanDerBeek staged multimedia screenings during which the audience was encouraged
to fall sleep and collectively dream. An eight-
hour event of sounds and projected films,
Cine Dreams was organized at the 240-seat
Star Theater at the Strasenburgh Planetarium
in Rochester, New York, and subsequently
presented at the University of South Florida's
planetarium. VanDerBeek envisioned the work
as a "group dream" in which projected imagery
could affect the dream state of each individual. Projected on the theater's ceiling were
computer-generated films, documentaries, and
slides, as well as animations, in a program
divided into 90-minute intervals, mimicking
both the natural sleep cycle and the length of
feature films. The performance was part of a
larger body of dream research in which he catalogued dreams mailed to him from around the
world, per his request at the conclusion of his
film *Newsreel of Dreams* (1963–64).

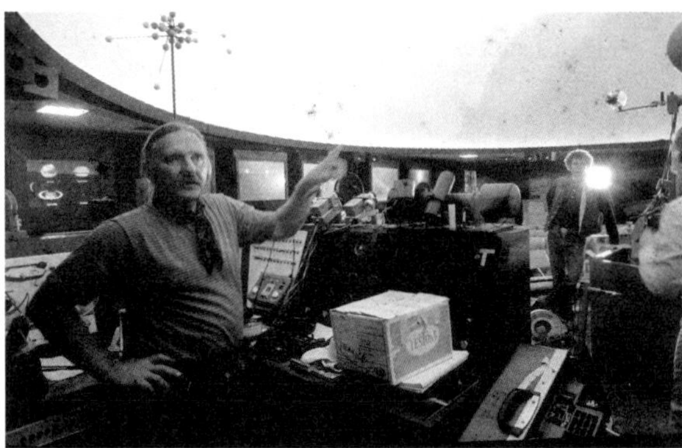

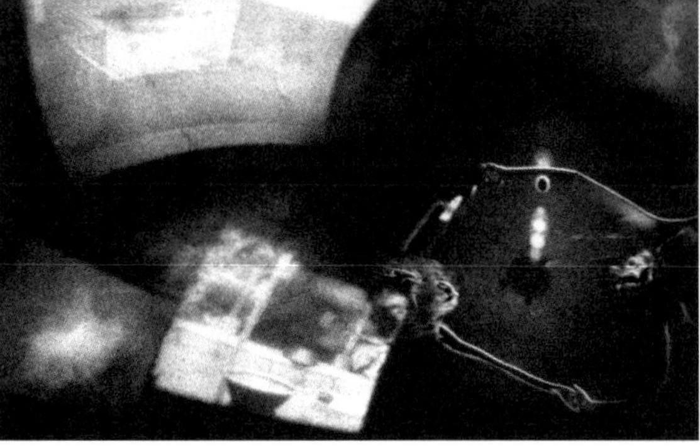

All: *Cine Naps*, USF Planetarium,
Tampa, FL, February 16–23, 1973.

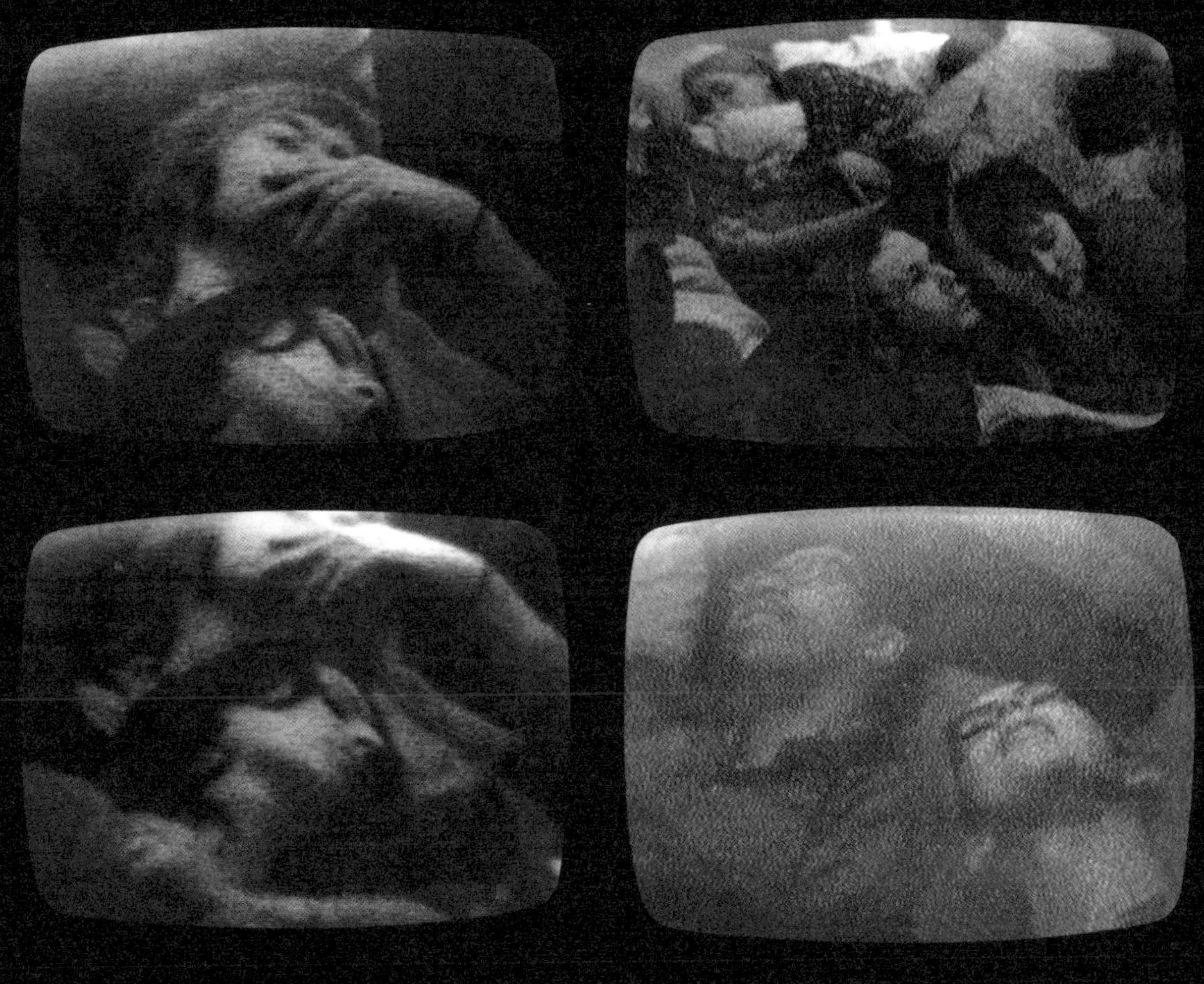

Cine Dreams: Future Cinema of The Mind.
Audience view, Strasenburgh Planetarium,
Rochester, New York, February 25–27, 1972.

[Below] *Cine Naps*, USF Planetarium,
Tampa, FL, February 16–23, 1973.

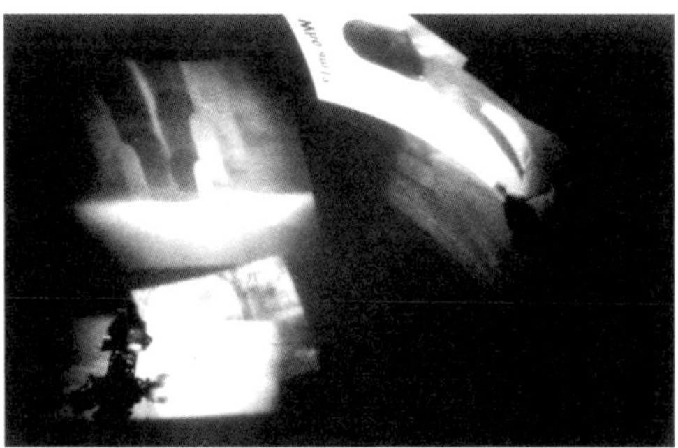

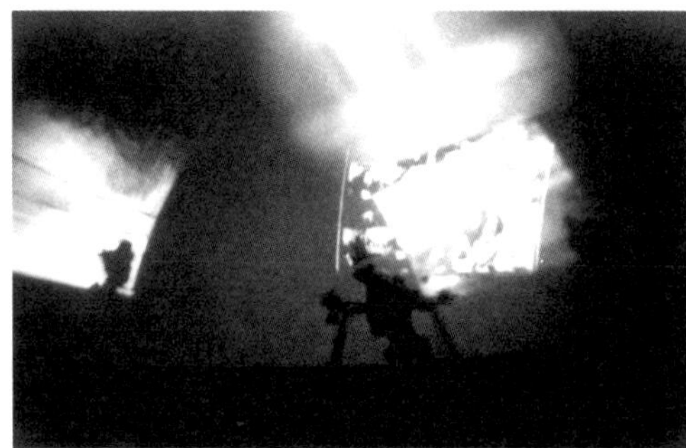

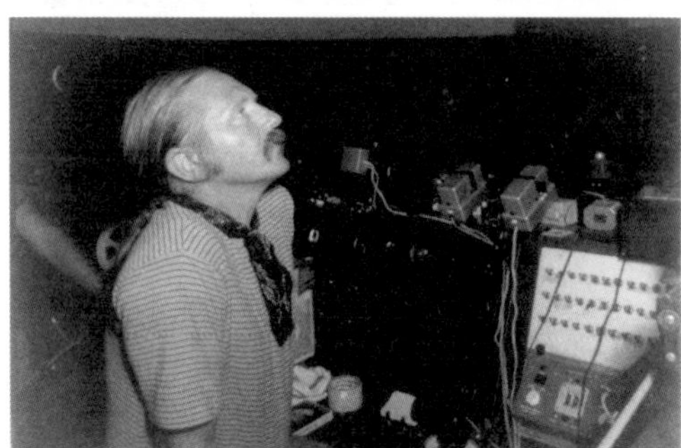

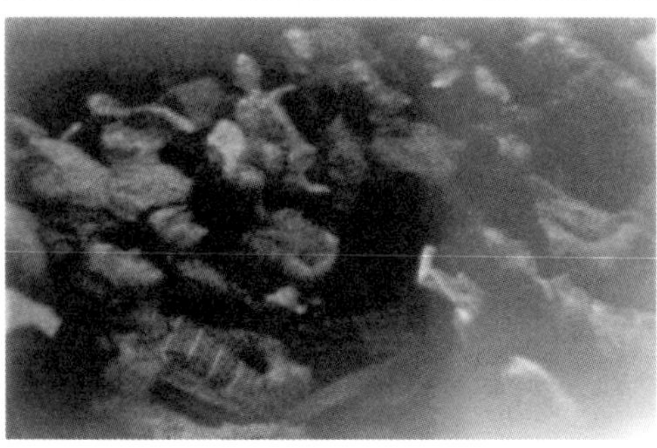

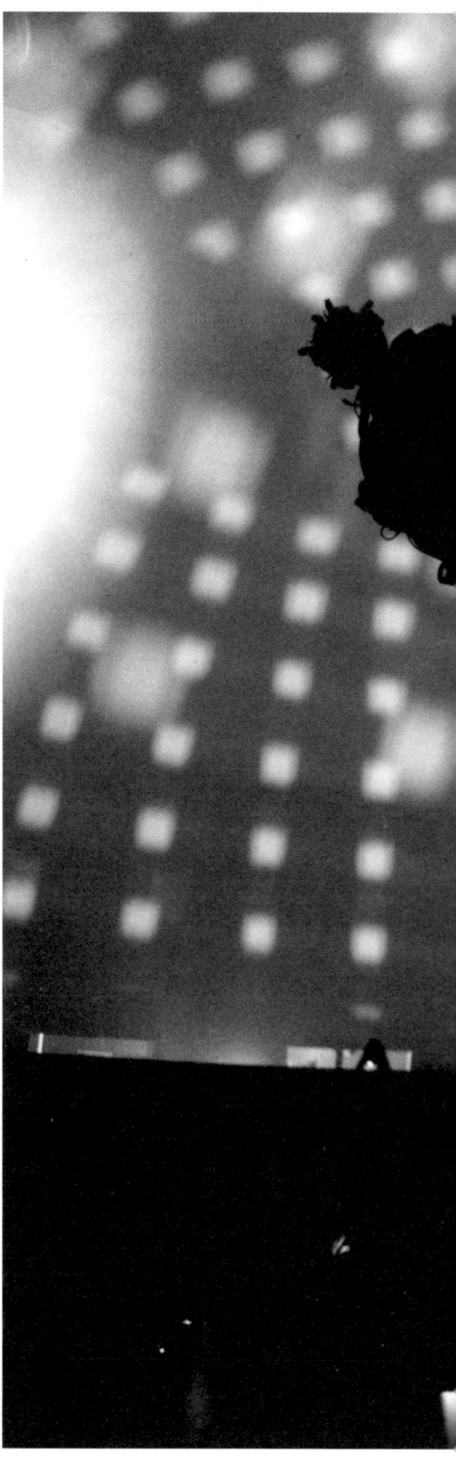

[Above] *Cine Dreams: Future Cinema of
The Mind*. Audience view, Strasenburgh
Planetarium, Rochester, NY, February 25–27,
1972.

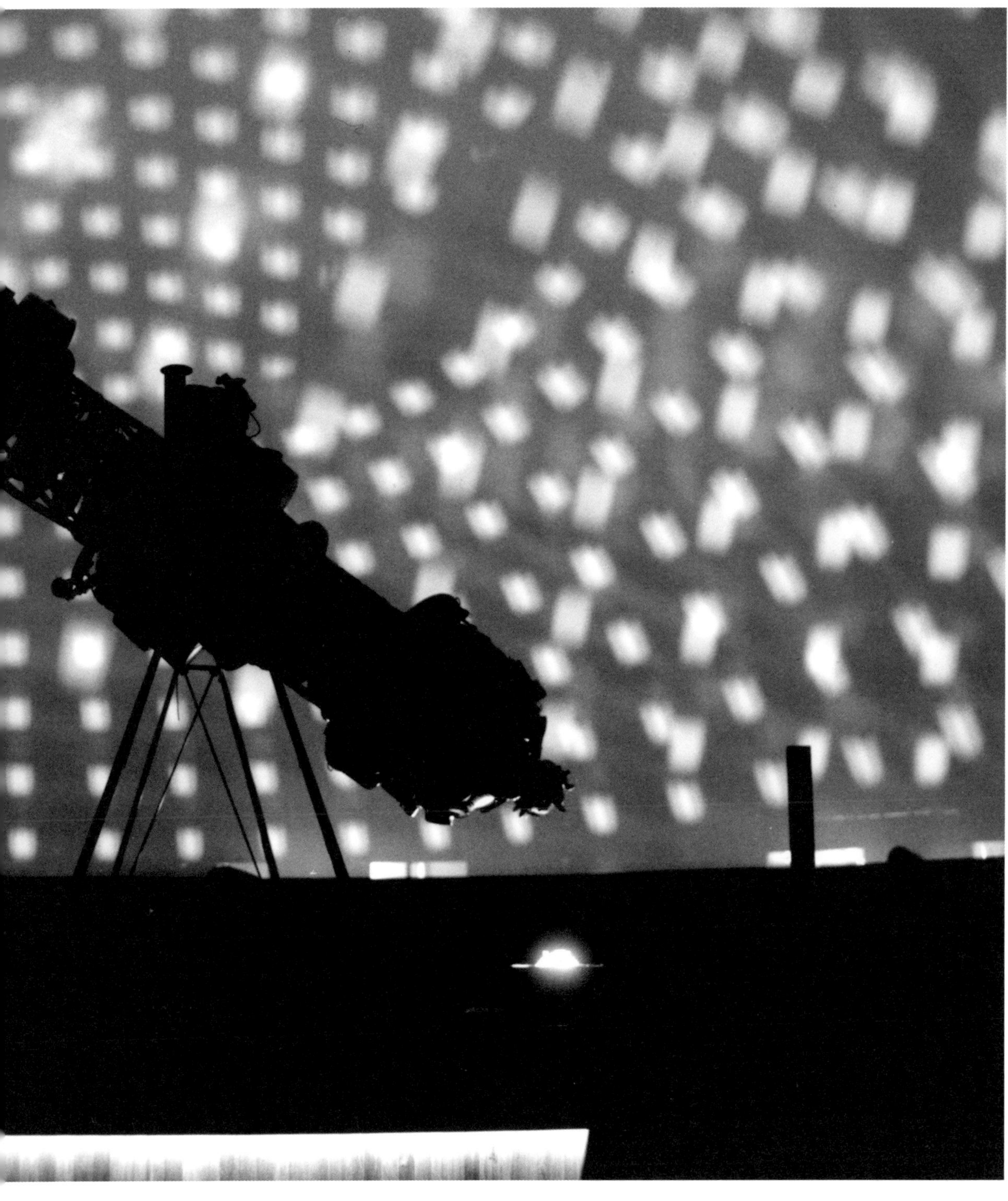

[Below] Equipment detail of *Cine Dreams: Future Cinema of The Mind.* Strasenburgh Planetarium, Rochester, NY, February 25–27, 1972.

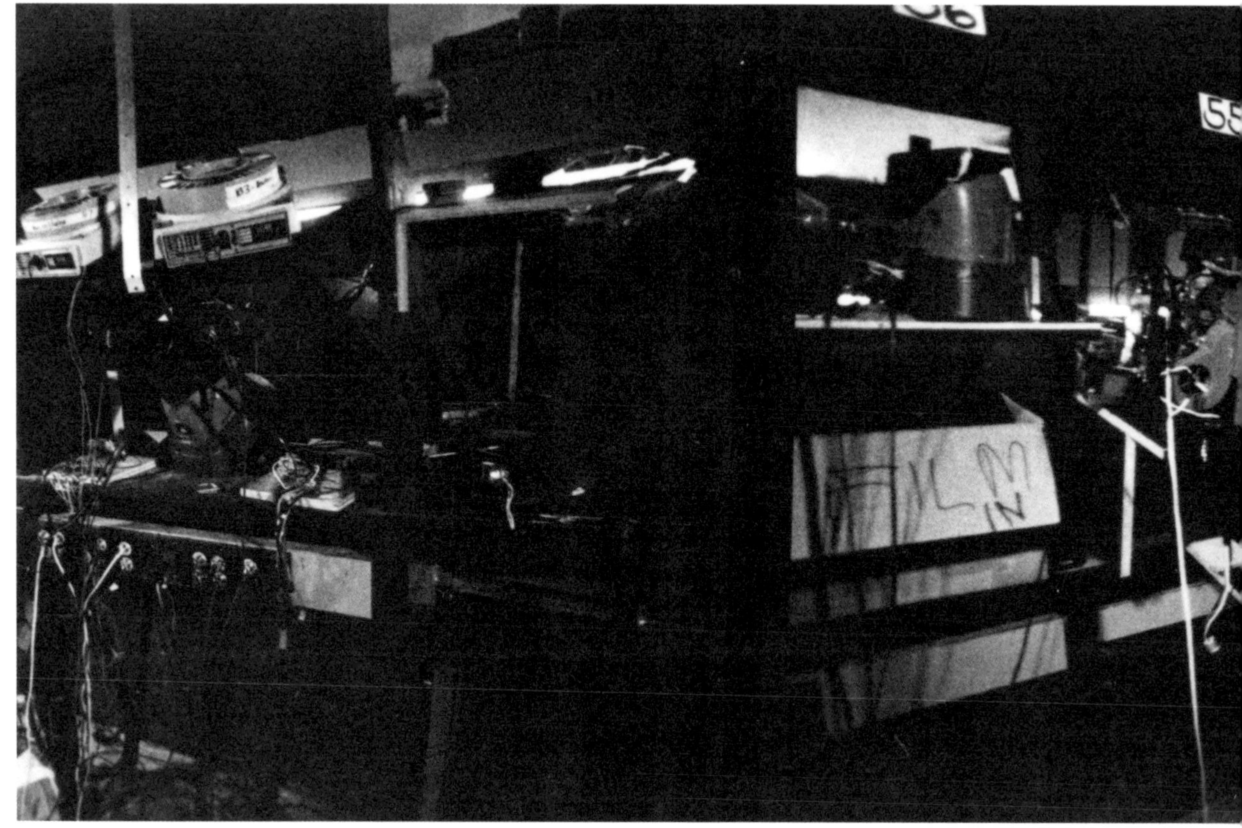

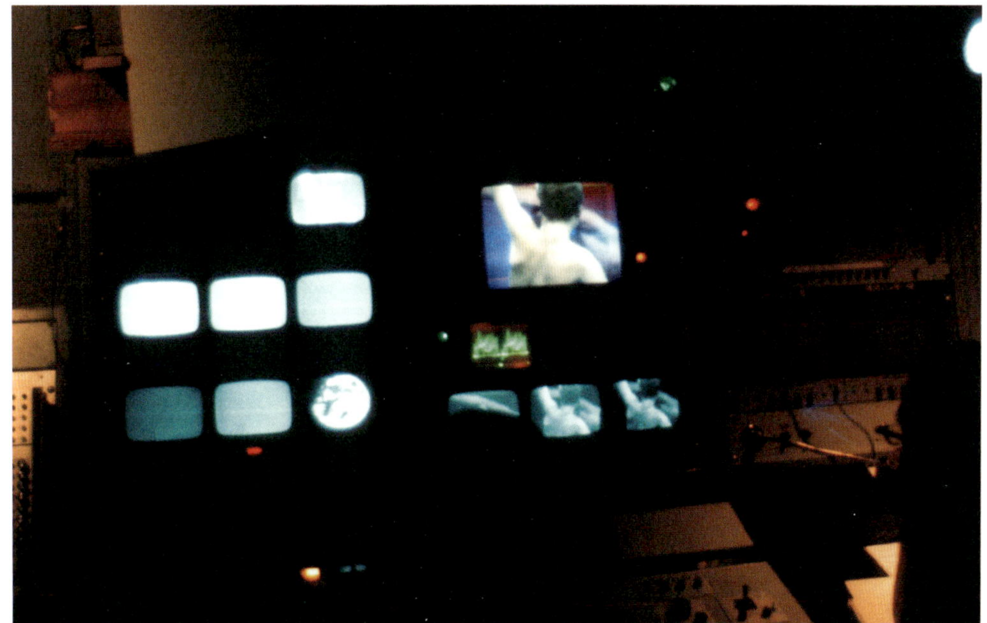

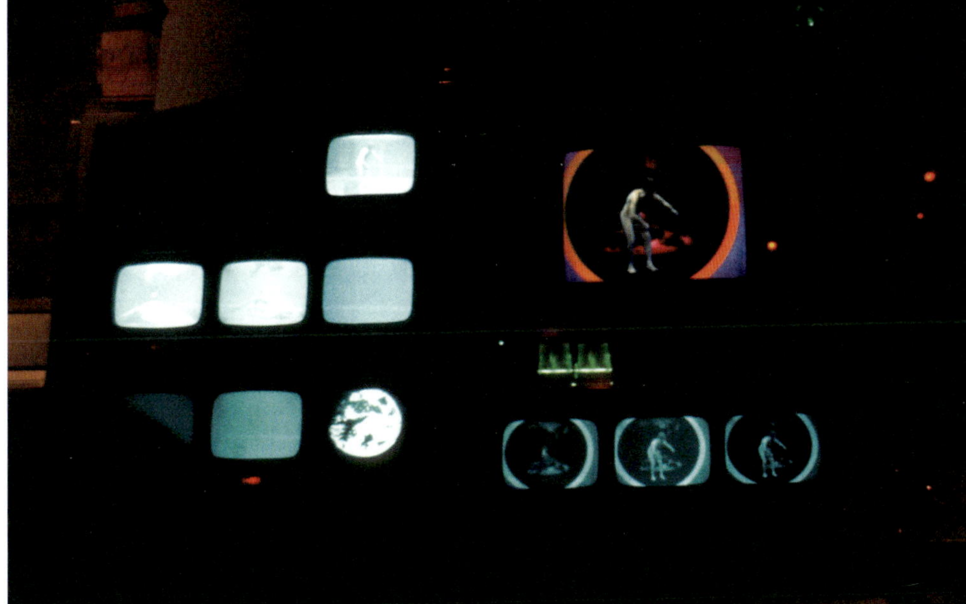

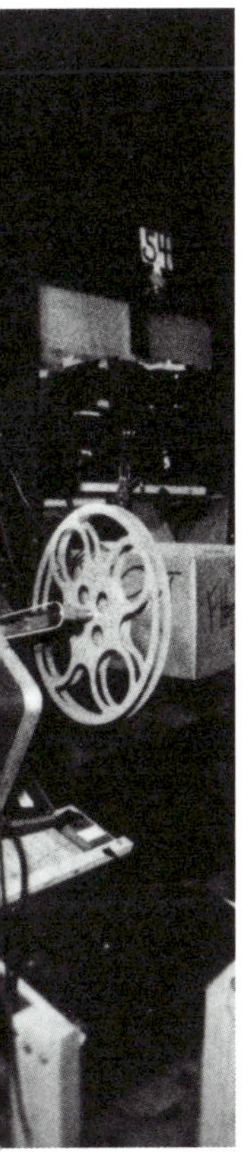

[Above] All: *Newsreel of Dreams:
Part I*. Production view, WNET studio,
New York, 1976.

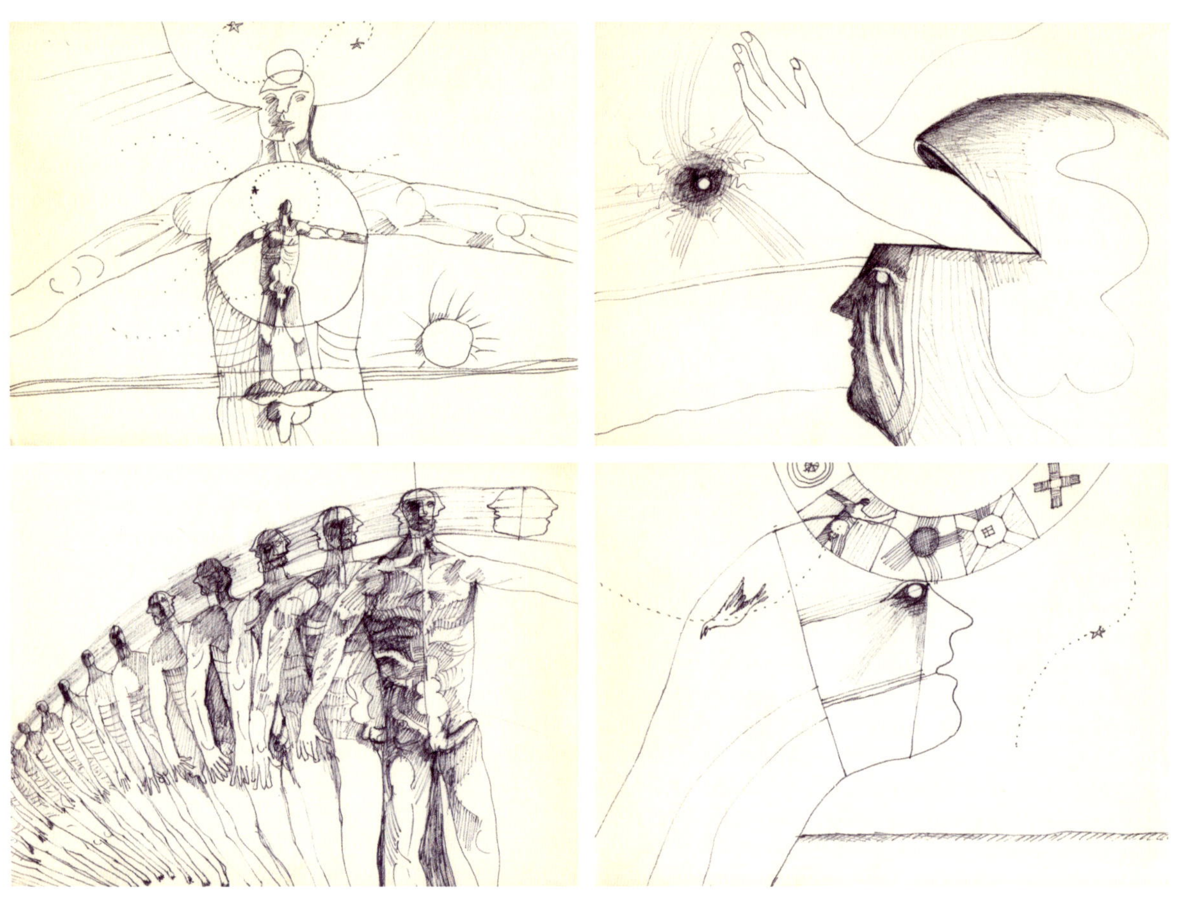

[Above] *Untitled (drawing)*, n.d.
Ink on paper, 8 1/2 x 11 in.

[Right] *Disappearing Man*, 1981.
Ink on paper, 19 x 9 in.

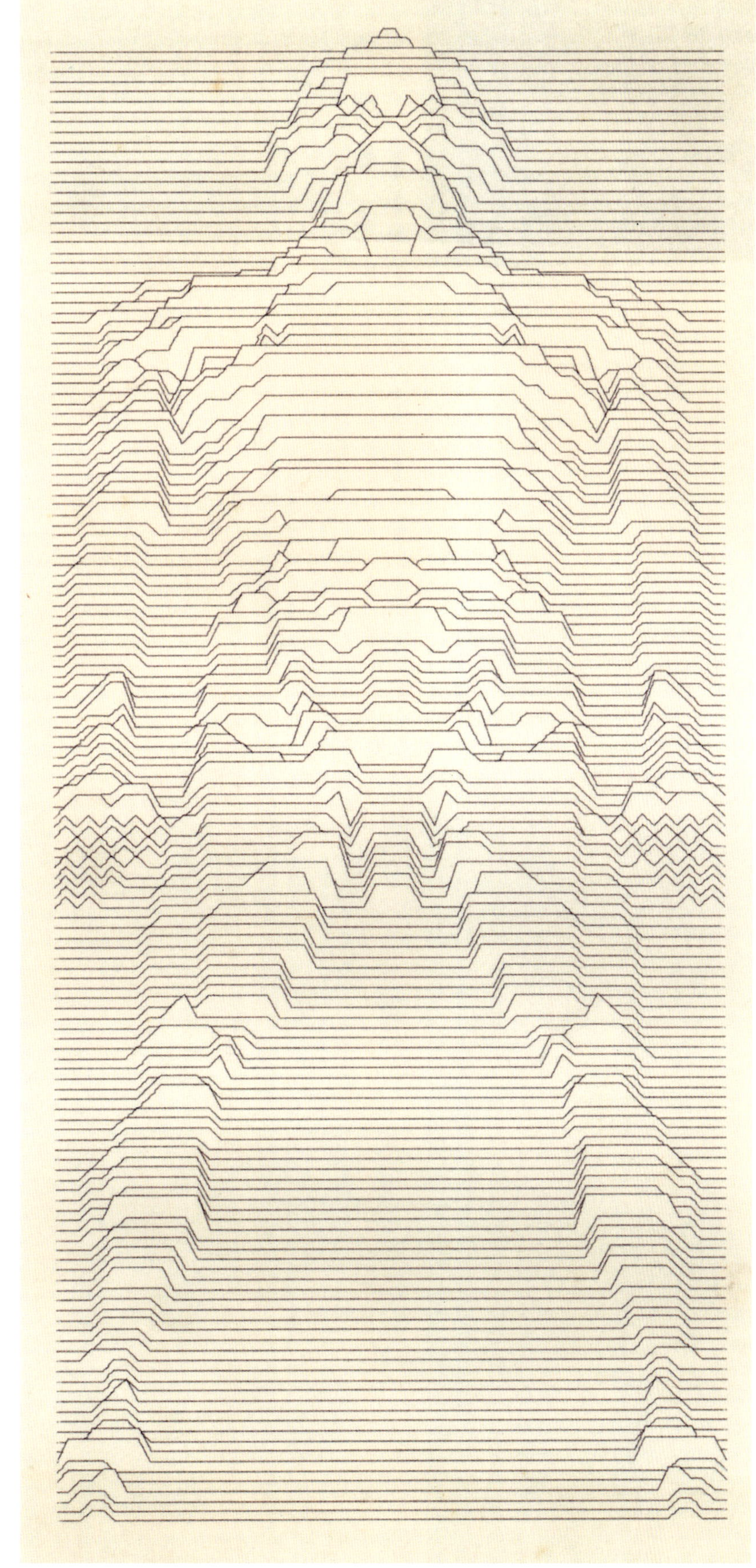

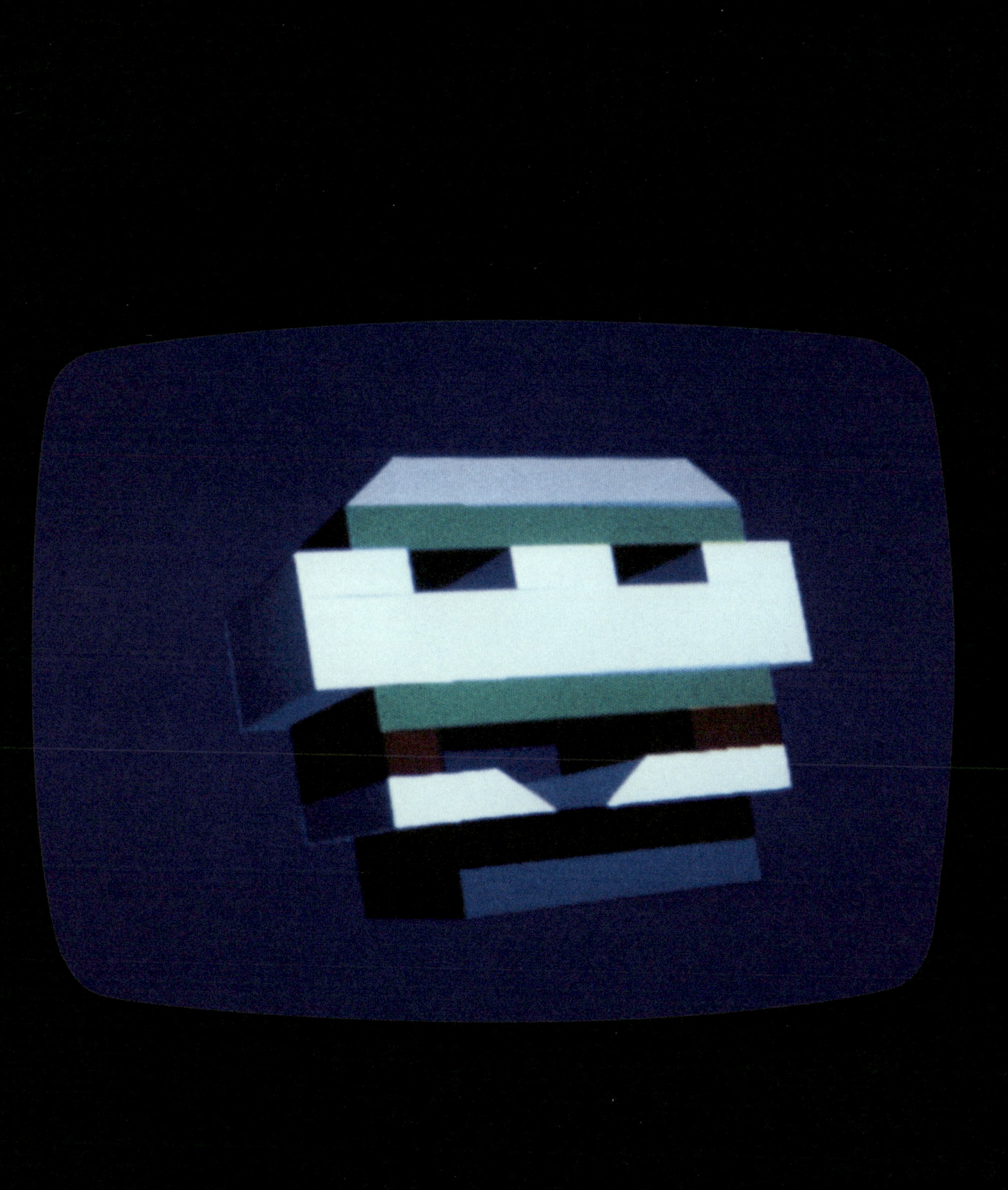

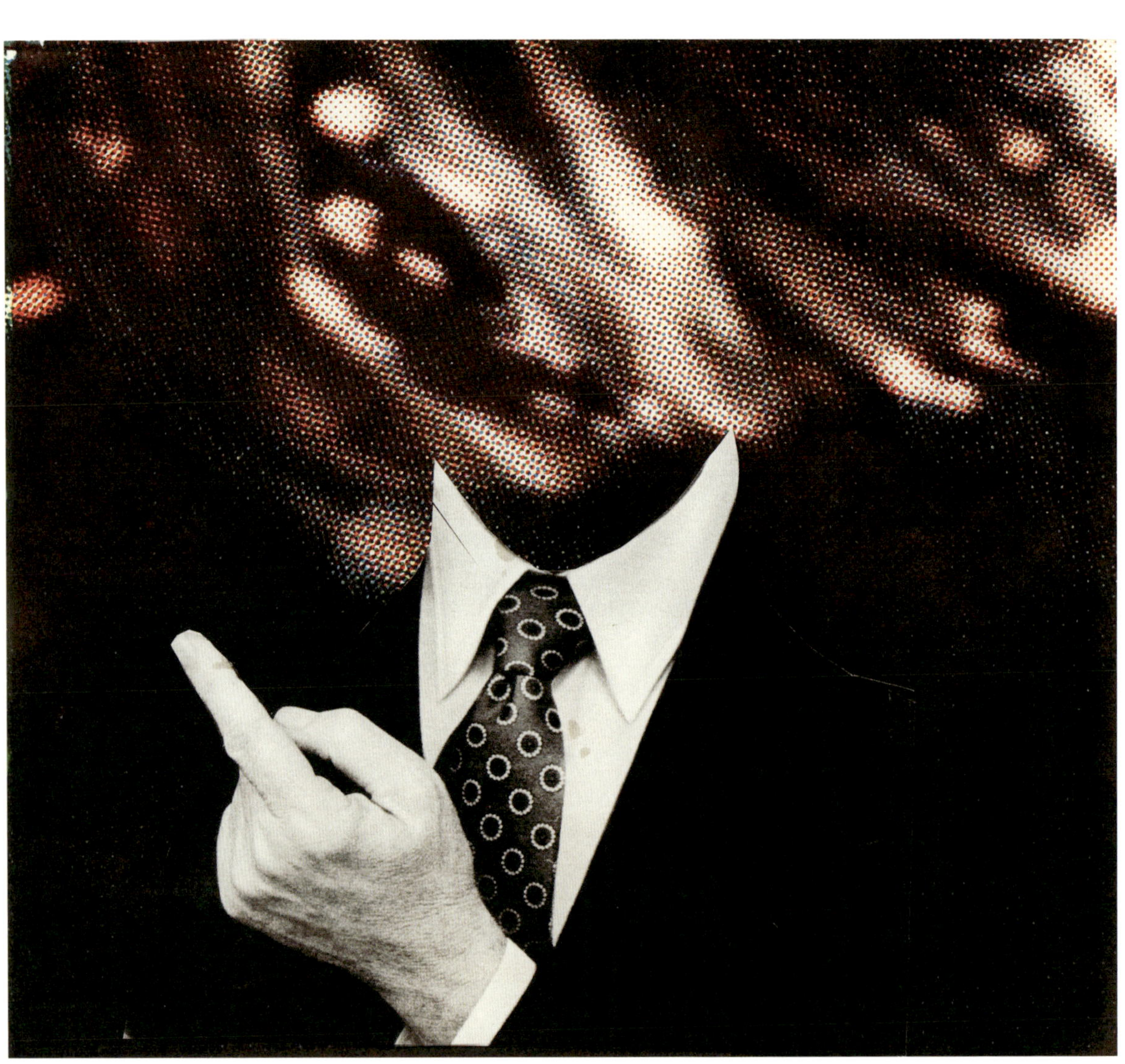

Untitled, ca. 1978–83. Collage
on billboard paper, 12 x 12 in.

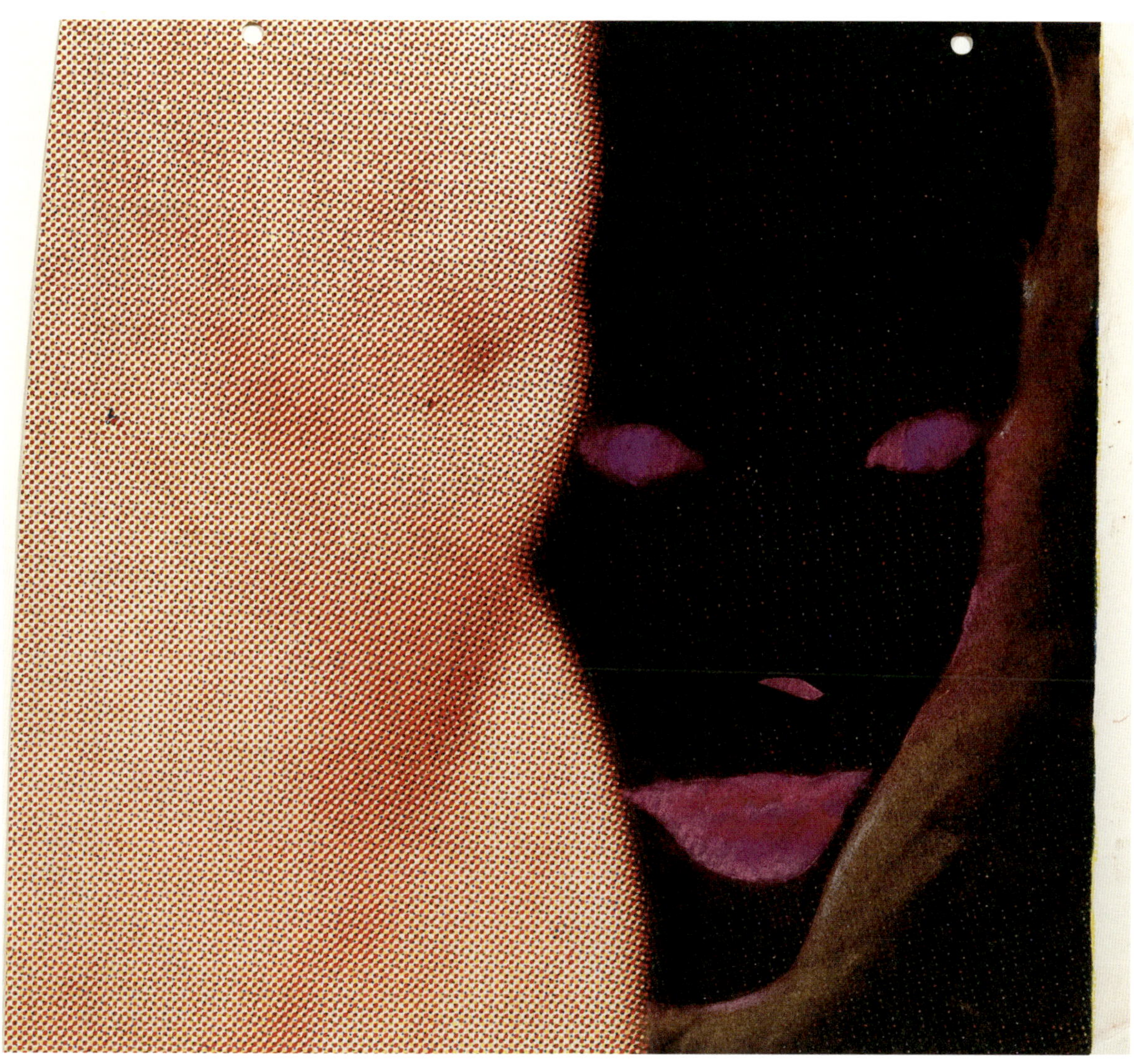

Untitled, ca. 1978–83. Pastel on
billboard paper, 12 1/2 x 12 1/2 in.

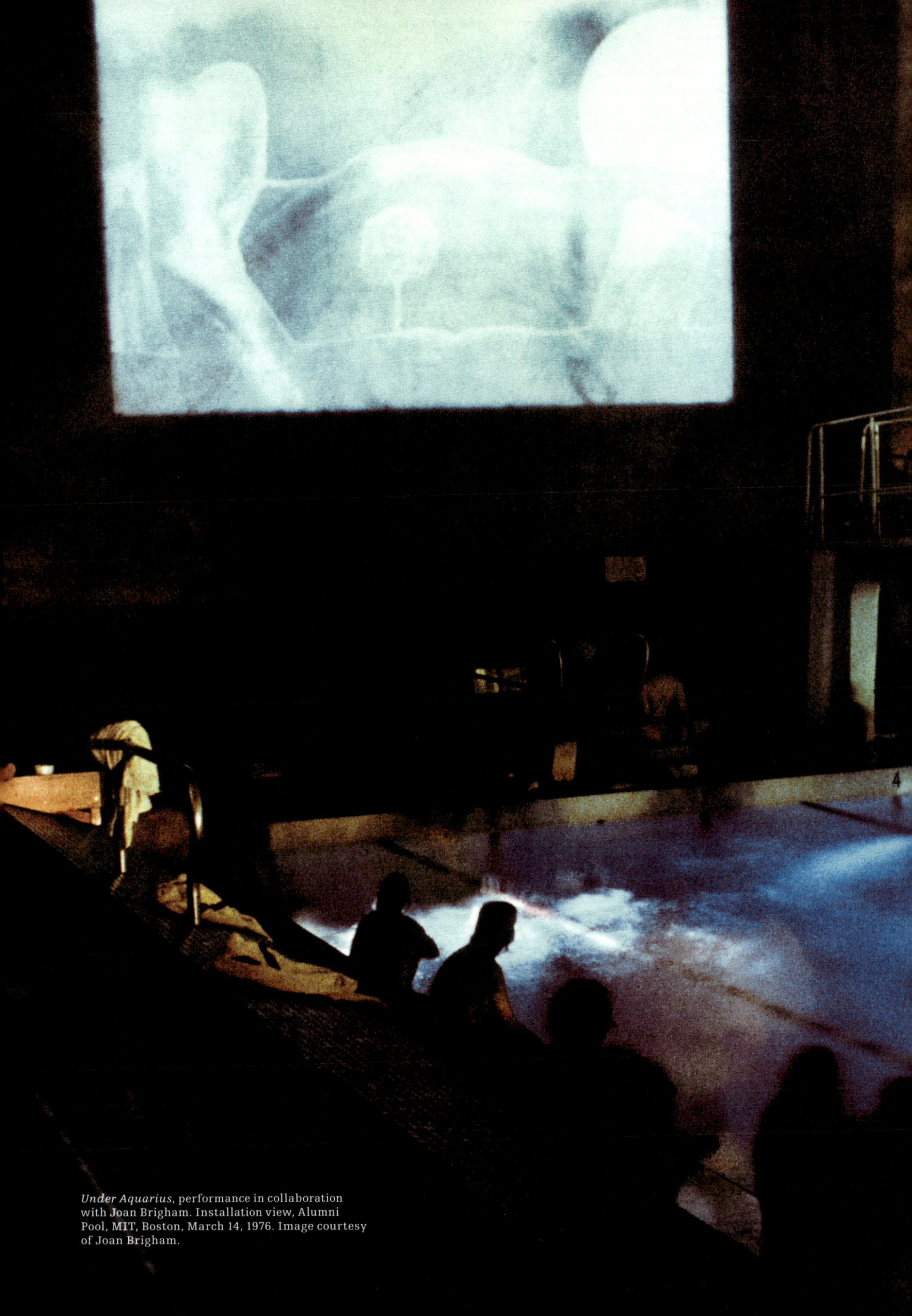

Under Aquarius, performance in collaboration
with Joan Brigham. Installation view, Alumni
Pool, MIT, Boston, March 14, 1976. Image courtesy
of Joan Brigham.

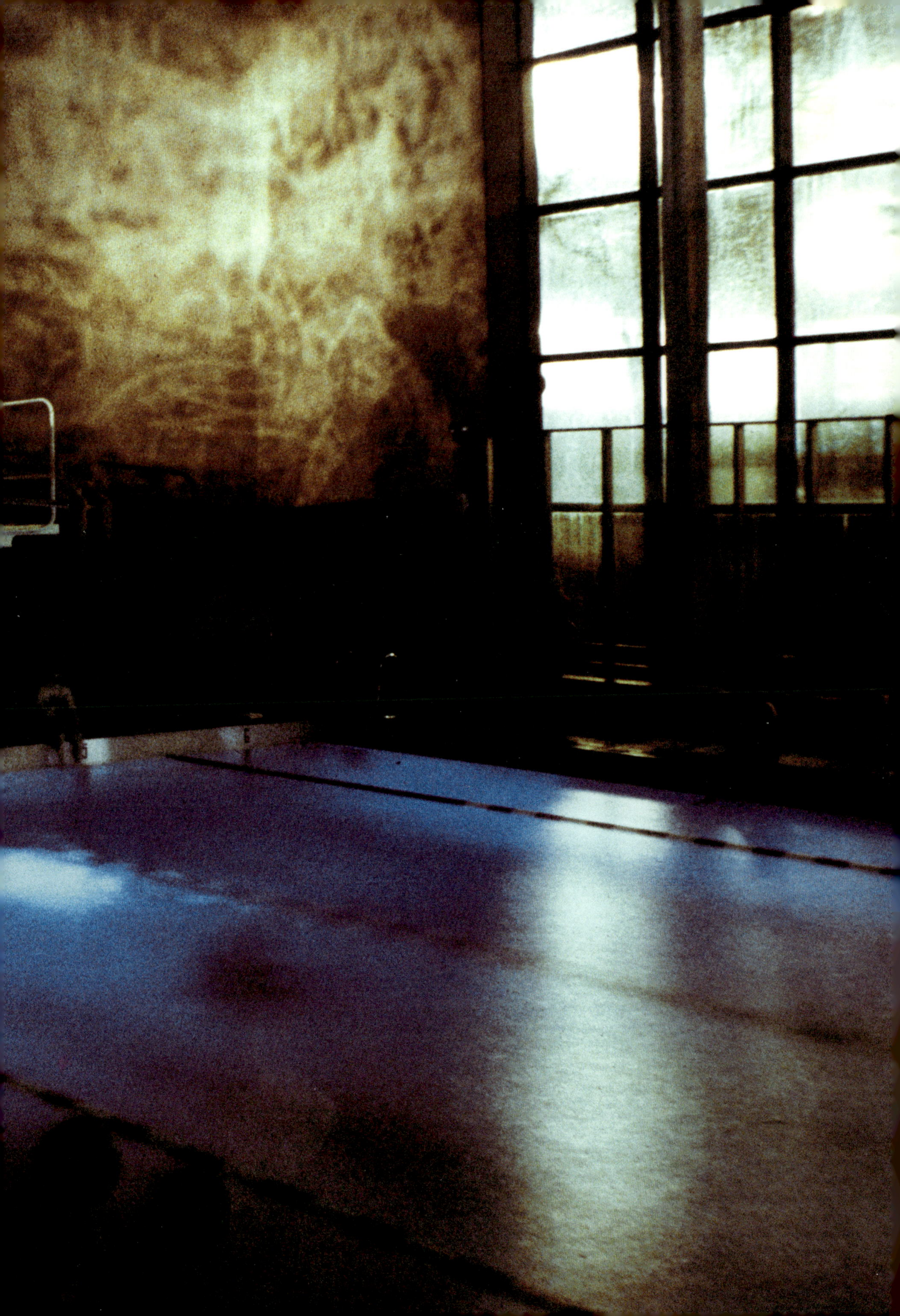

Under Aquarius, 1976
Steam Screens, 1979–81

From 1975 to 1981, VanDerBeek experimented with projecting multiple images
and computer generated films onto clouds
of steam in collaboration with Cambridge-
based artist Joan Brigham, who was a
research fellow at the Center for Advanced
Visual Studies at MIT from 1974–99. An
extension of VanDerBeek's immersive environments of the late 1960s and early '70s,
Under Aquarius was conceived as a "multimedia, above-and-below-water theater," and
was comprised of light displays and underwater projections. The piece was performed
in MIT's Bauhaus-inspired Alumni Pool
building and the following year the piece
was modified and presented in Hampshire
College's swimming pool, with performances
by the American Underwater Band of Miami
and synchronized swimmers choreographed
by VanDerBeek's daughter August. *Steam
Screens* was performed in the sculpture
garden at the Whitney Museum of American
Art, New York, and later at the Walker Art
Center, Minneapolis, in 1981. During the
performance, moving steam waves refracted
projected films and computer-generated
animations, such as *Euclidean Illusions* by
VanDerBeek and Richard Weinberg, allowing
the viewer to walk through the images. These
projects extended VanDerBeek's focus on
freeing cinema from the limits of the theater
and the white cube, and fulfilling its utopian
potential to bring people together through
shared media experiences.

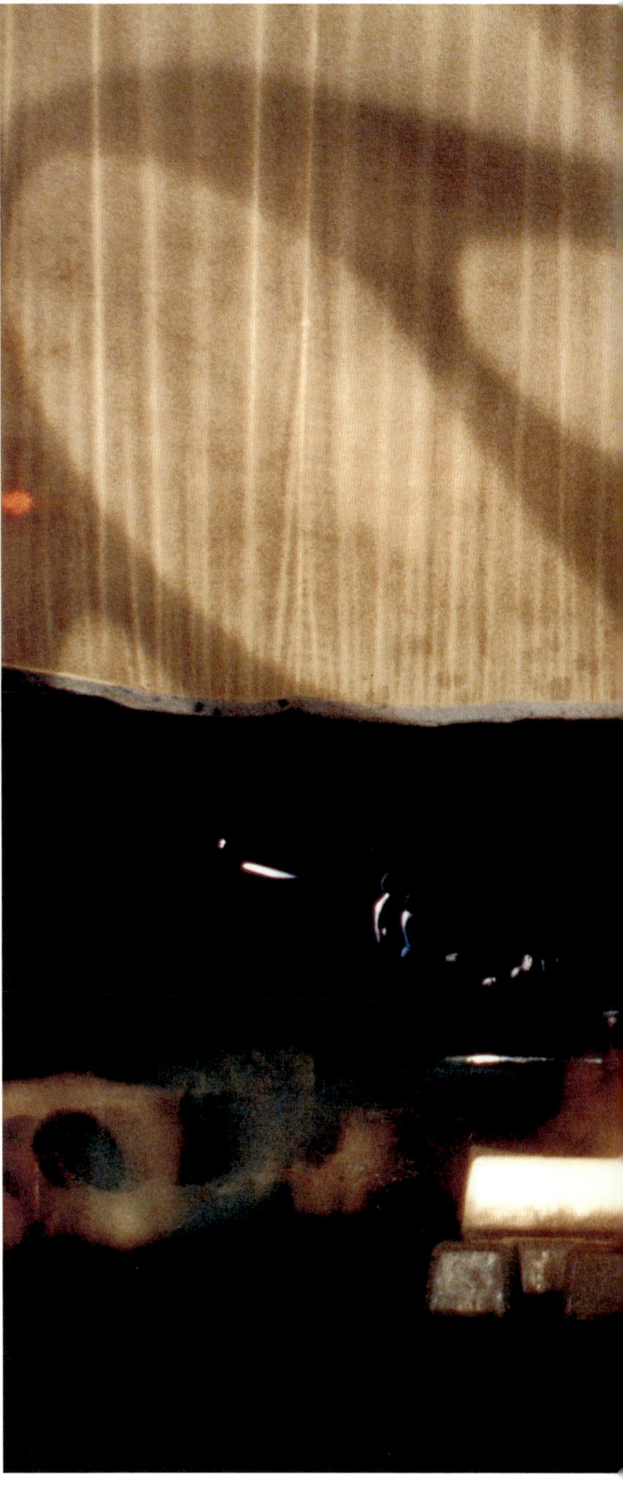

Under Aquarius, performance in collaboration
with Joan Brigham. Installation view,
Alumni Pool, MIT, Cambridge, MA, March 14,
1976. Image courtesy of Joan Brigham.

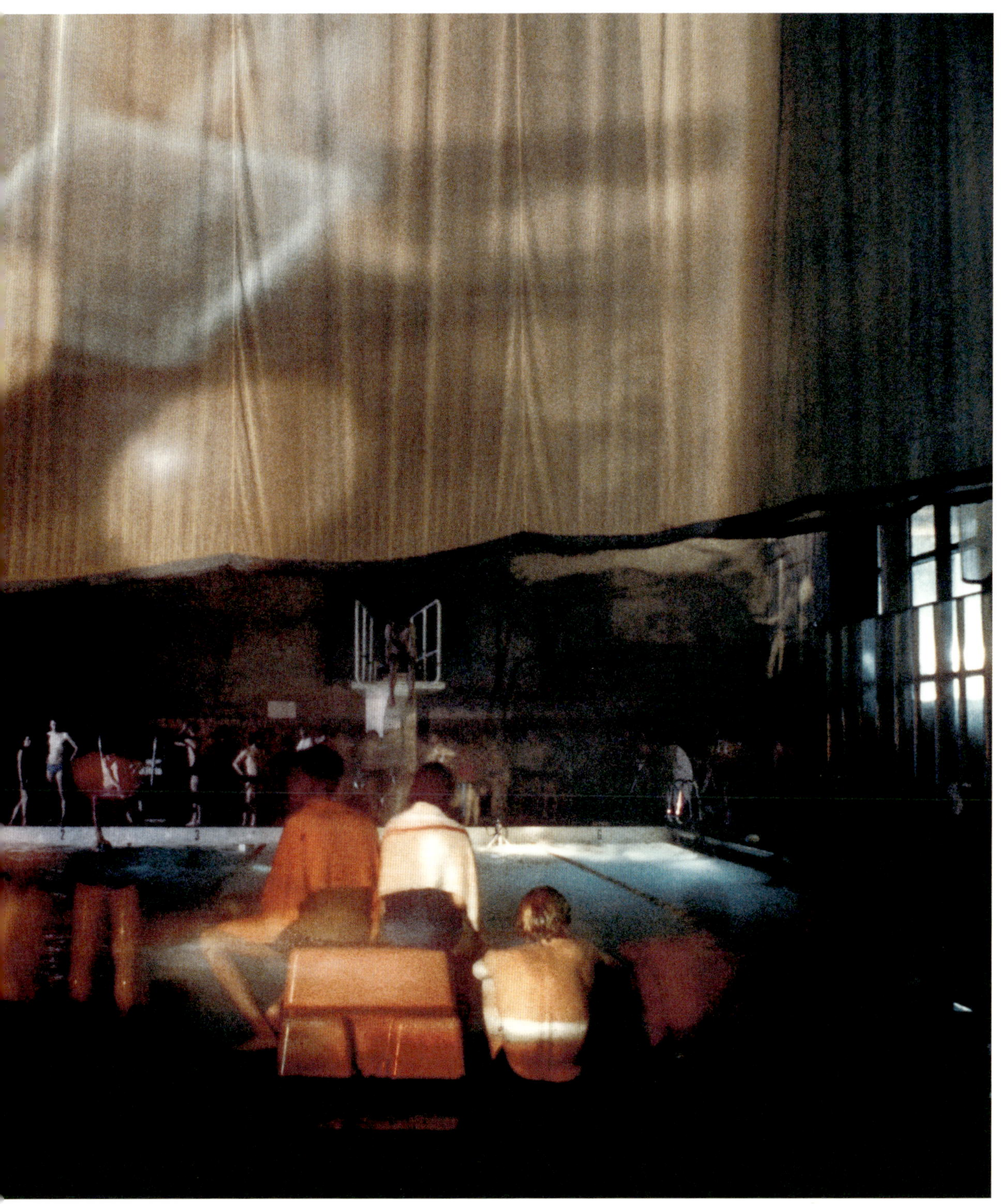

[Below] All: *Under Aquarius*, performance
in collaboration with Joan Brigham.
Installation view, Alumni Pool, MIT,
Cambridge, MA, March 14, 1976.
Image courtesy of Joan Brigham.

[Right] *Fog, Mist, and Dreams*,
performance in collaboration with
Joan Brigham. Installation view,
MIT, Cambridge, MA, 1975. Image
courtesy of Joan Brigham.

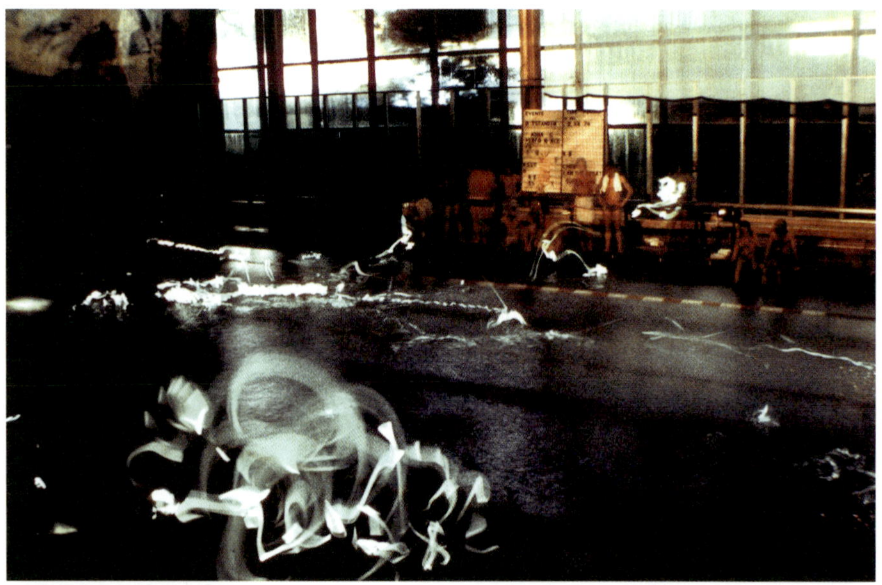

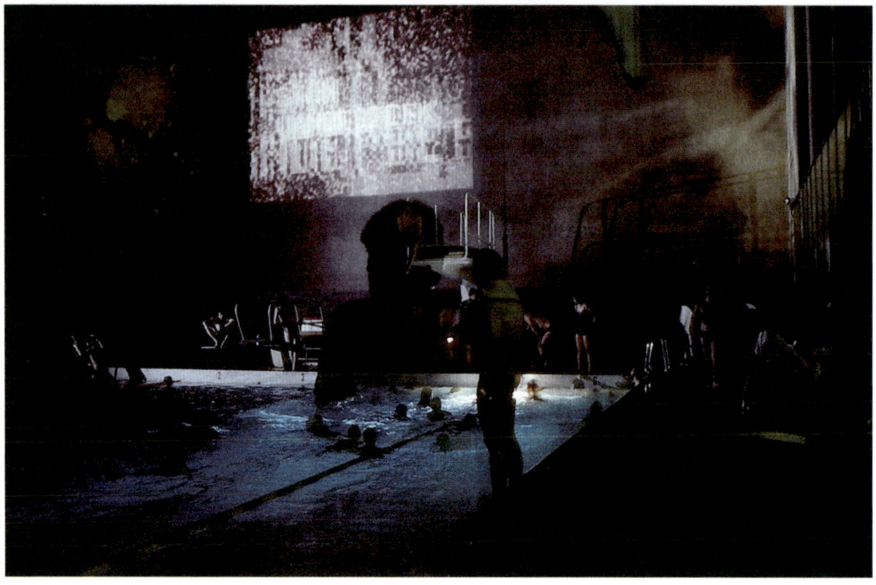

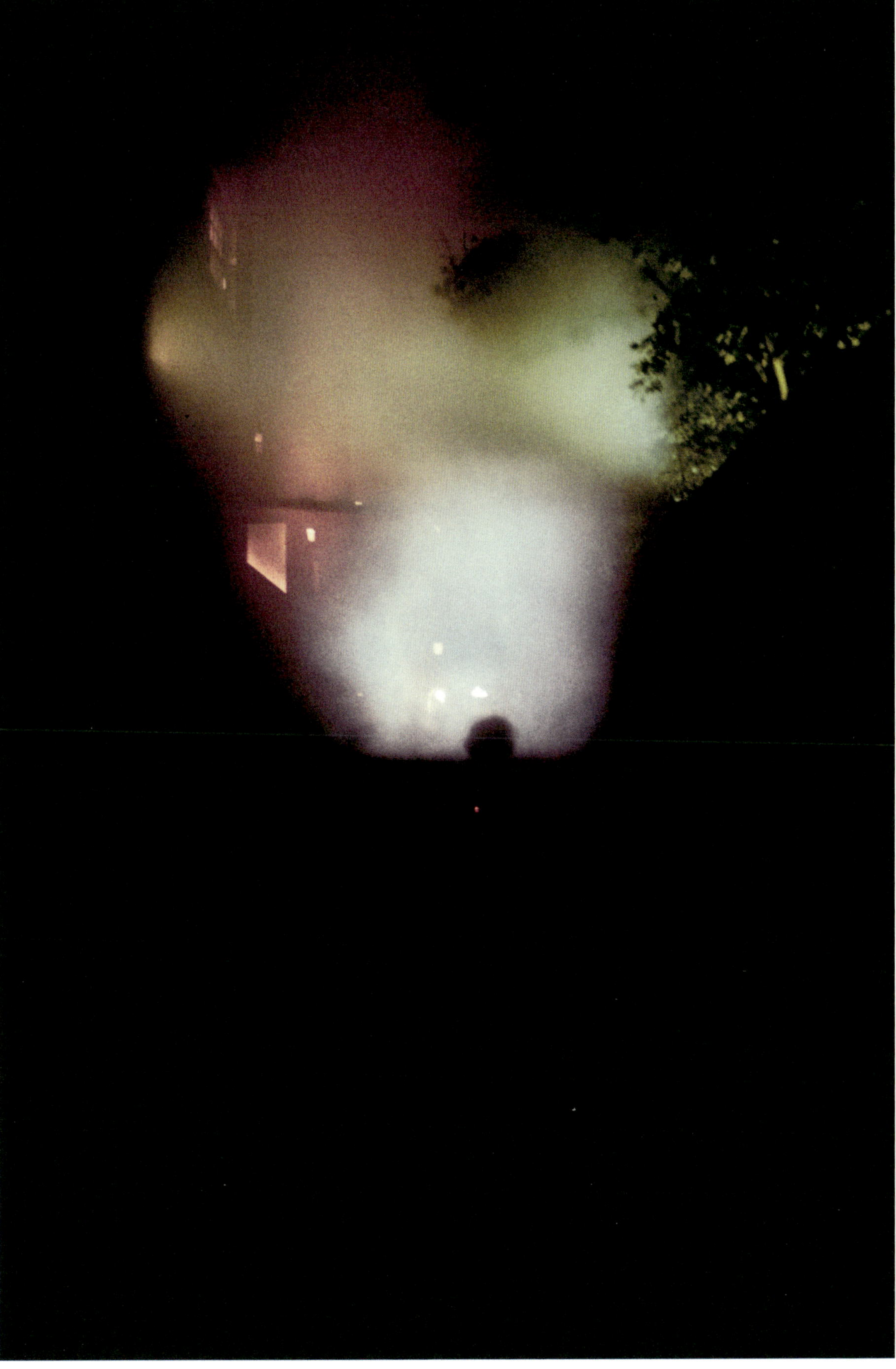

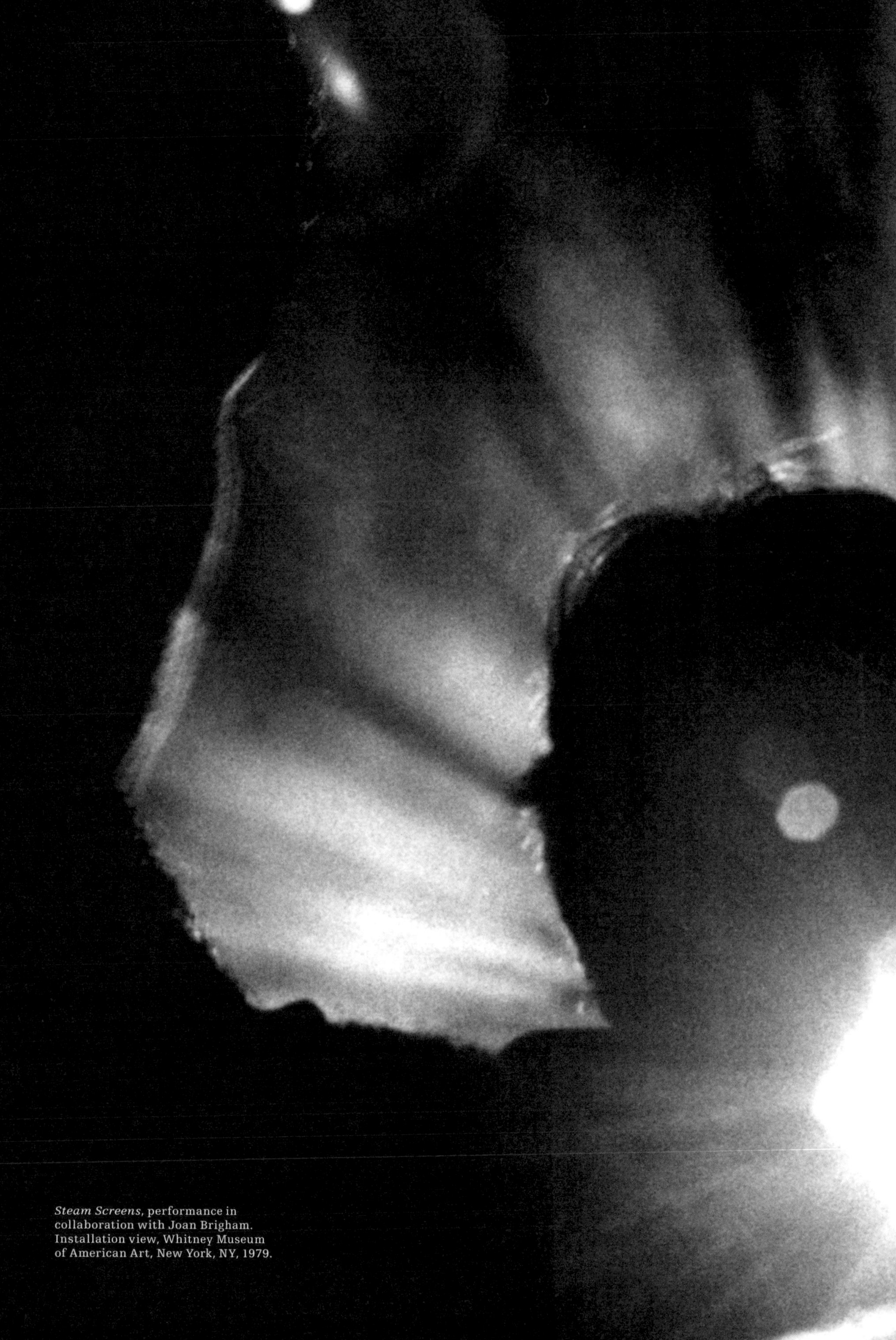

Steam Screens, performance in
collaboration with Joan Brigham.
Installation view, Whitney Museum
of American Art, New York, NY, 1979.

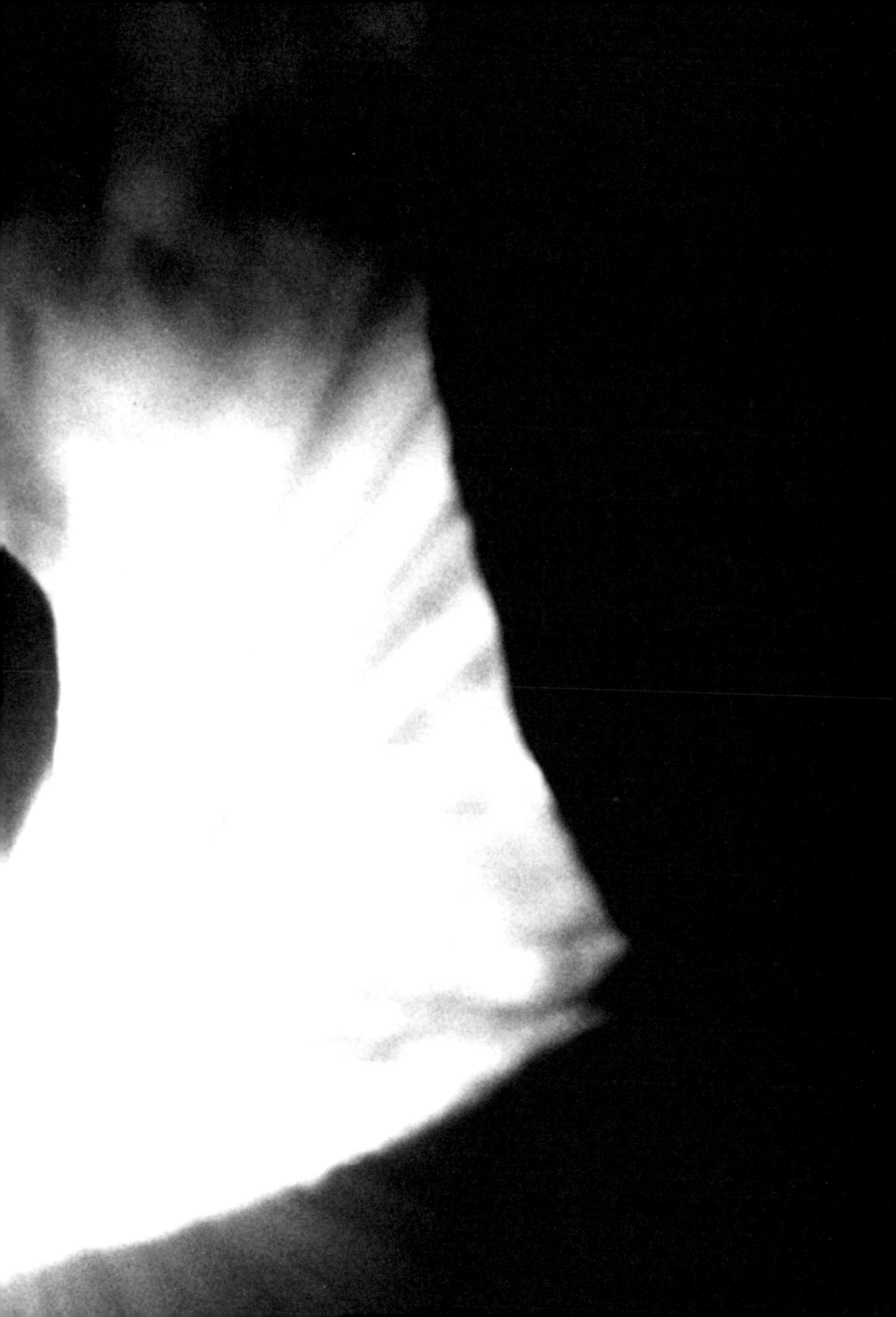

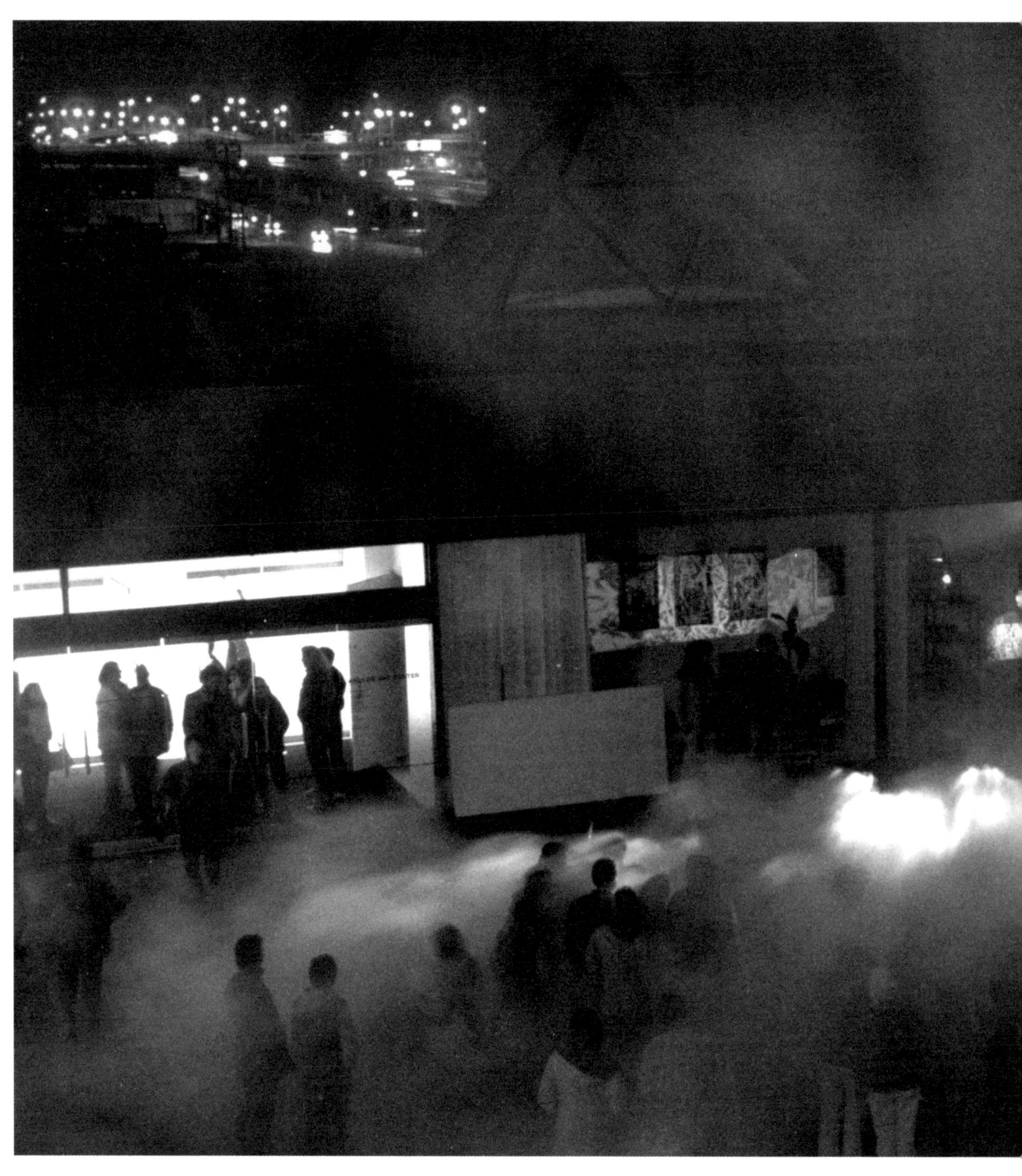

All: *Steam Screens*, performance
in collaboration with Joan Brigham.
Installation view, Walker Art
Center, Minneapolis, MN, 1981.

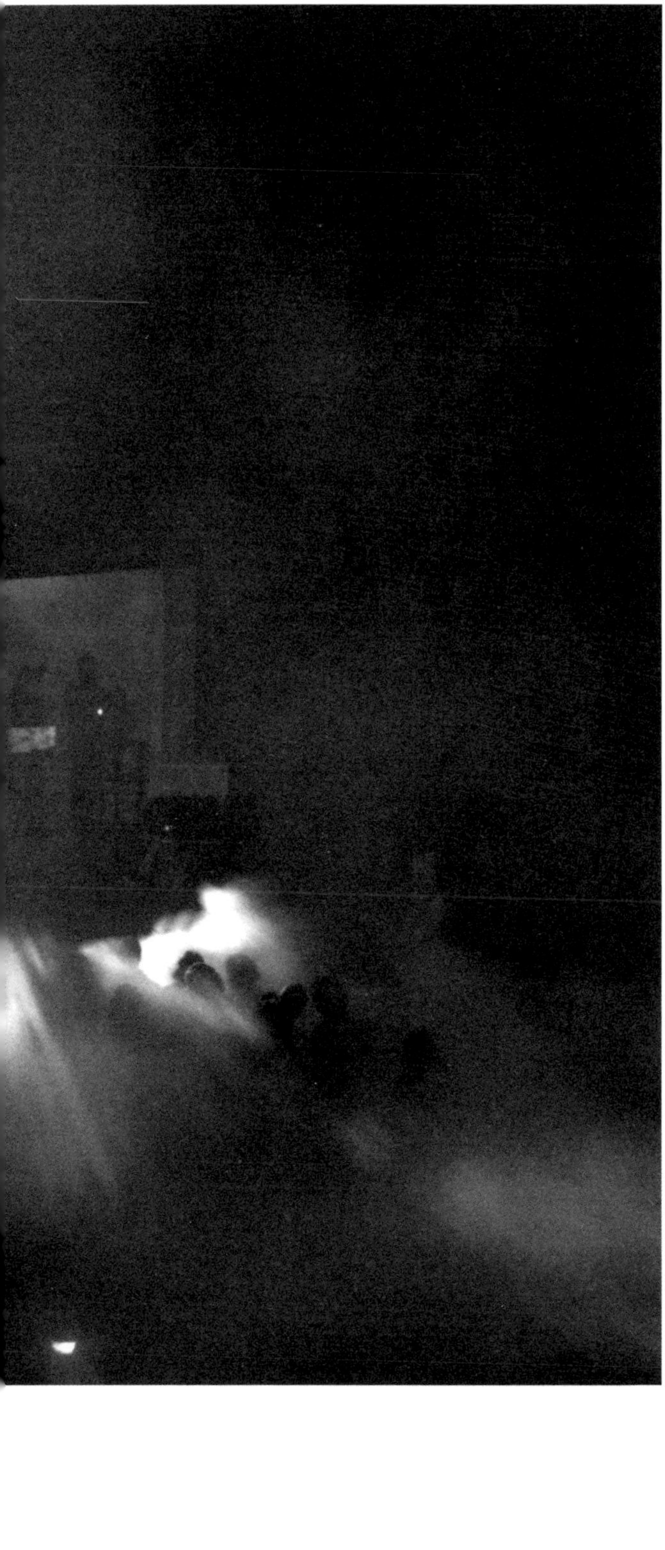

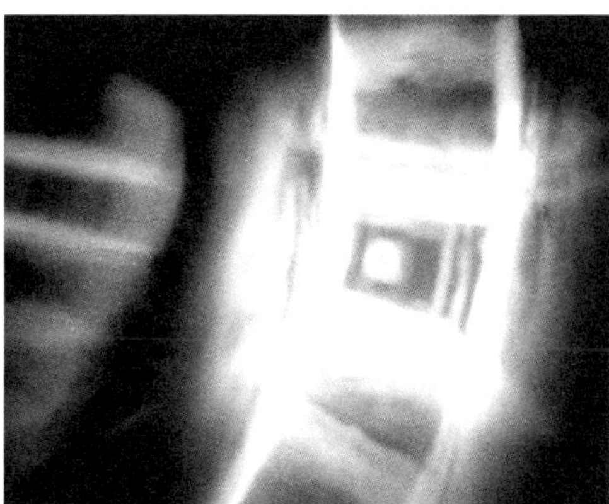

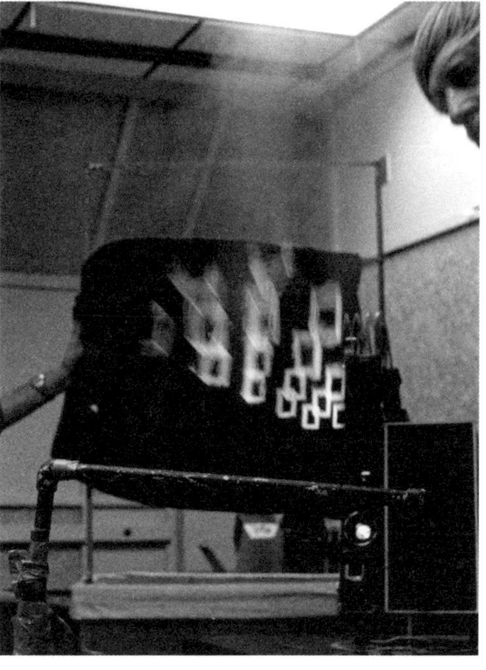

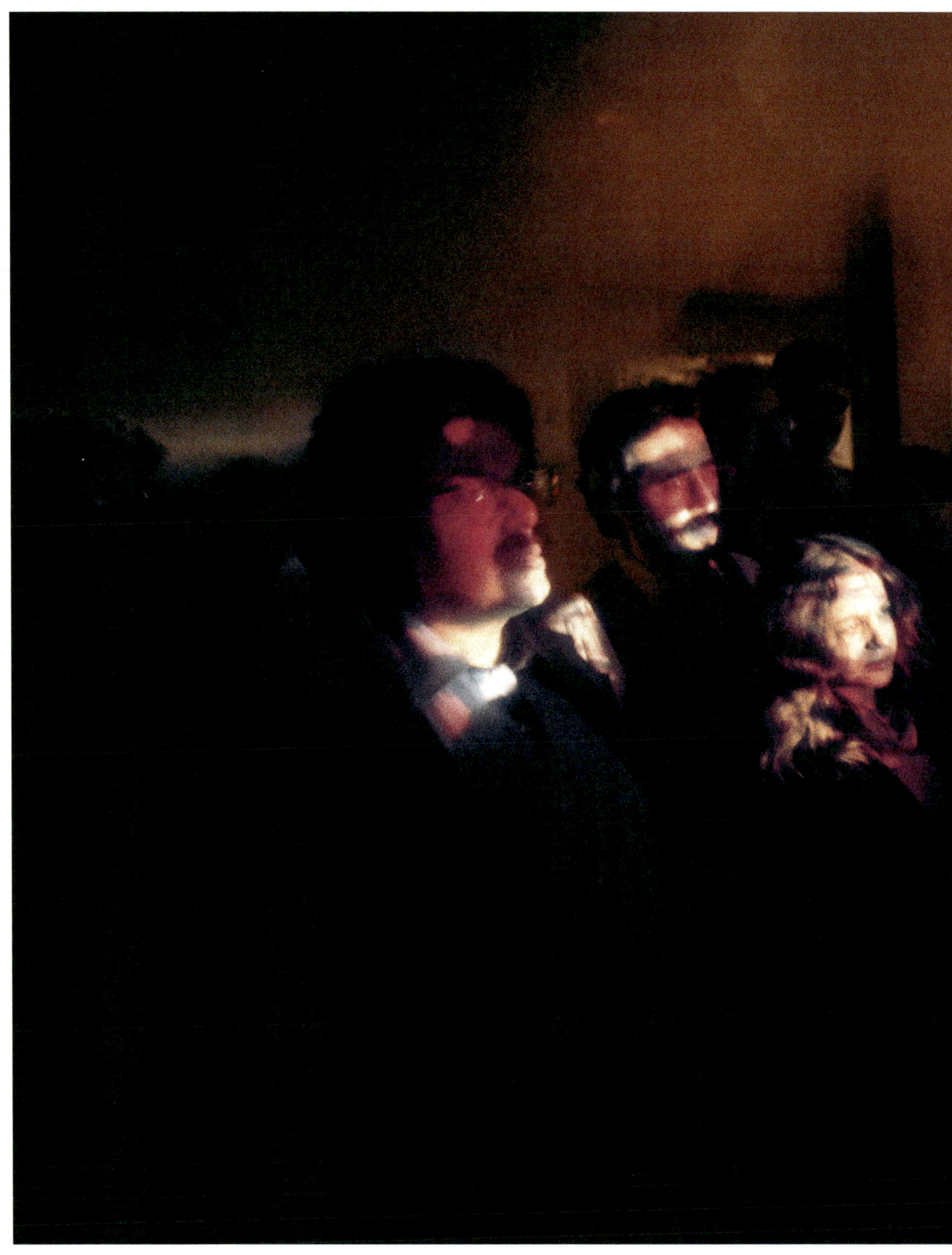

Steam Screens, performance in
collaboration with Joan Brigham.
Installation view, Whitney Museum
of American Art, New York, NY, 1979.

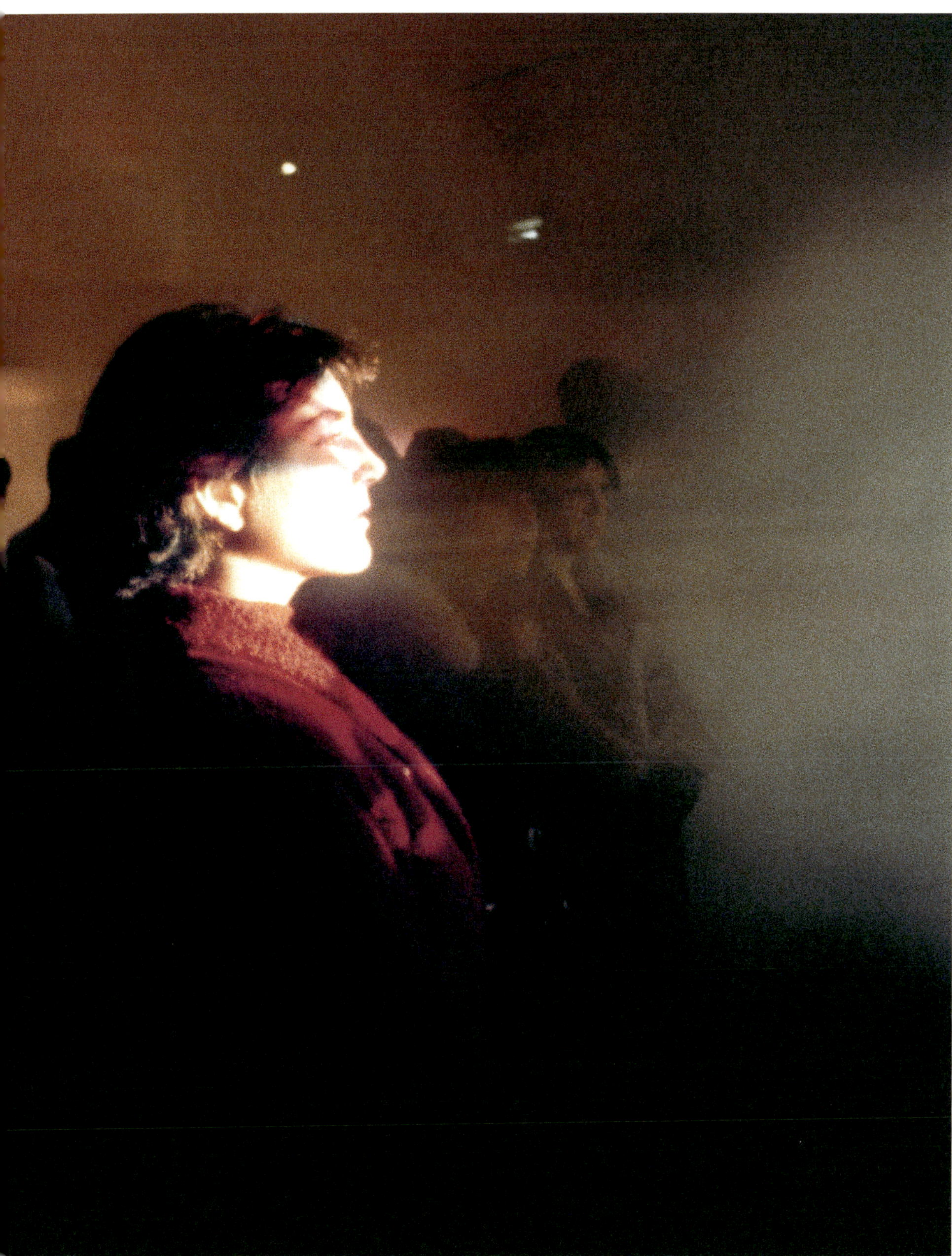

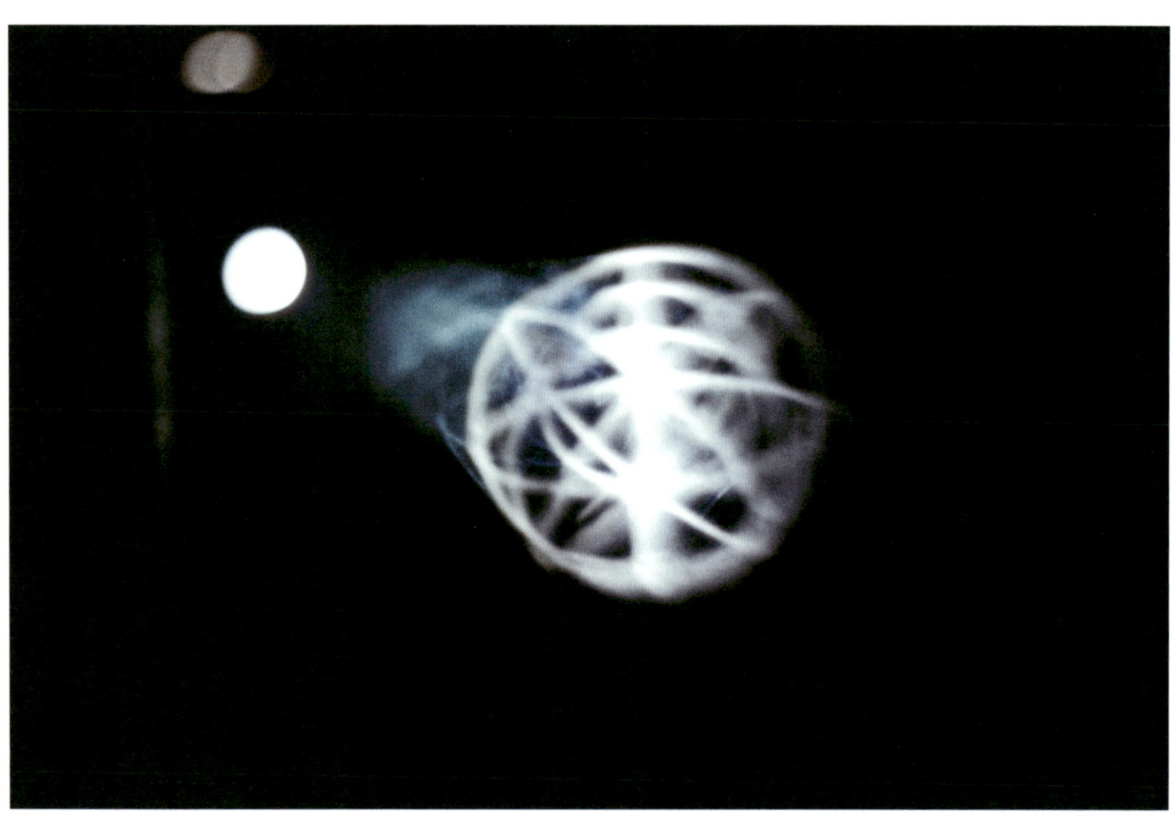

All: *Steam Screens*, performance in
collaboration with Joan Brigham.
Installation view, Whitney Museum
of American Art, New York, 1979.

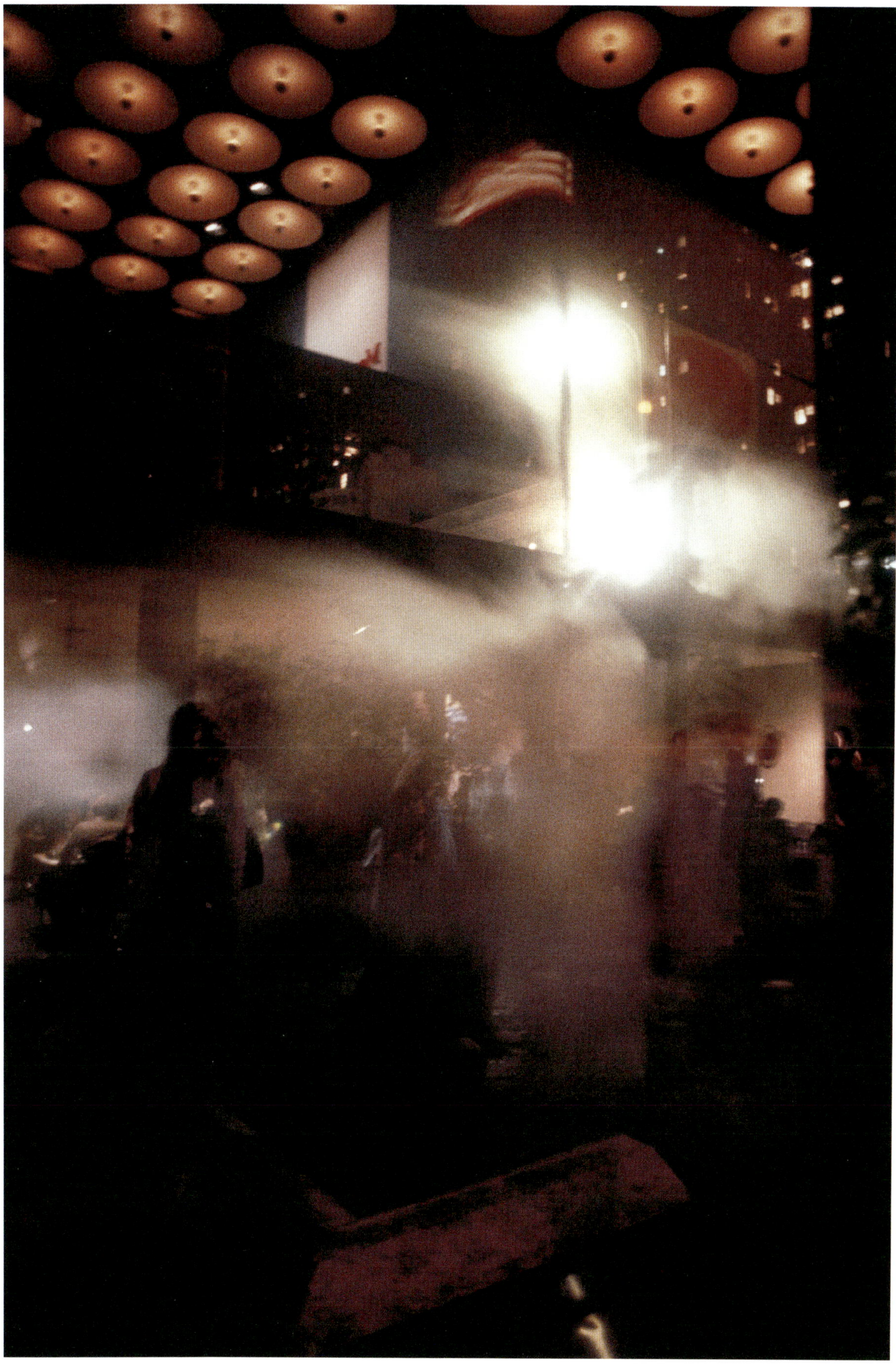

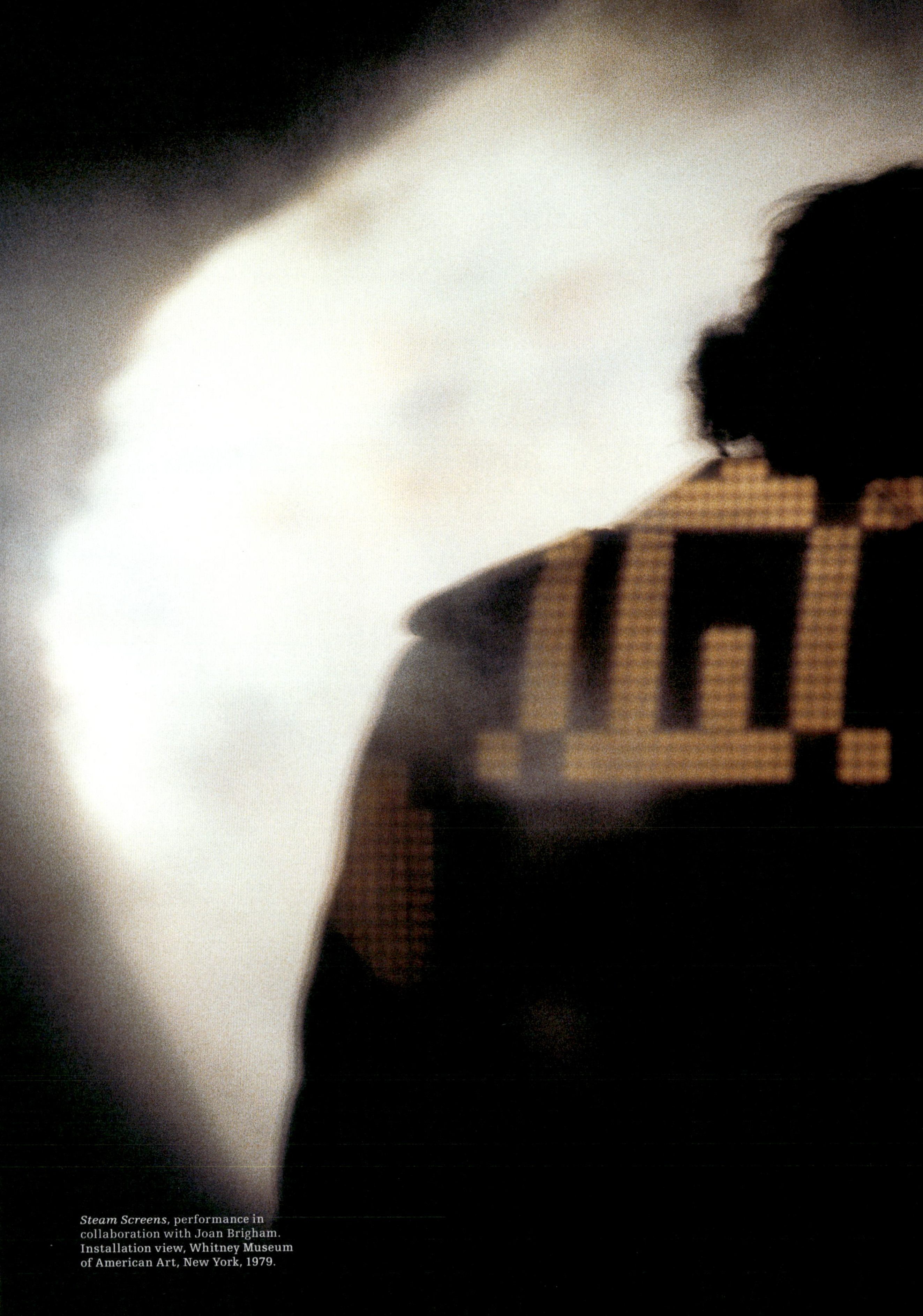

Steam Screens, performance in
collaboration with Joan Brigham.
Installation view, Whitney Museum
of American Art, New York, 1979.

1 See Gloria Sutton's essay in this volume, 79.

2 Ibid, 80.

3 See Gloria Sutton's essay in this volume, 85.

4 Media Art Net, http://www.medienkunstnetz.de/works/variations-v/

5 John Cage Database, http://www.johncage.info/workscage/variations5.html

6 Gloria Sutton, "Stan VanDerBeek's Poemfields: the Interstice of Cinema and Computing" in *Mainframe Experimentalism: Early Computing and the Foundation of the Digital Arts*, Hannah Higgins and Douglas Kahn, eds., (Berkeley: University of California Press, 2011).

7 WGBH, http://openvault.wgbh.org/catalog/org.wgbh.mla:MLA000126

8 Ibid.

ISBN: 9781933619330   52495